The State and Land Records Modernisation

Pradeep Nayak

FOUNDATION
BOOKS

FOUNDATION
BOOKS

Foundation Books is an imprint of Cambridge University Press, India

4843/24, 2nd Floor, Ansari Road, Daryaganj, Delhi 110002, India

www.cambridgeindia.org

First published 2015

Printed in India at Thomson Press India Ltd., New Delhi 110001

ISBN 978-9-382-99346-9 Hardback

To my parents,
wife Swayamprava and
daughter Swati

Contents

List of Figures and Tables

Figures

Tables

Foreword

This book is a pioneering work in an extremely important area that has received little scholarly attention so far, except in the laudatory genre of 'best practices in e-governance.' Social scientists are only just beginning to seriously engage with the land question in contemporary India, and this book provides a critical governance perspective on this emerging area of scholarship.

In times past, the modernisation of land records was viewed as crucial for implementation of land reform programmes. It was widely acknowledged that the objectives of land reform, ranging from the abolition of intermediaries to the securing of tenancy rights and the application of land ceilings, could not be accomplished without proper records of land ownership. Despite this acknowledgement, land records remained for the most part a complex tangle of disputes and presumptive ownership. It is only in recent years that the modernisation of land records has once again acquired policy importance, and the inauguration of the National Land Records Modernisation Programme (NLRMP) in 2008 provides the impetus for this comparative study of its implementation in two states: Karnataka and Odisha.

These two states stand at opposite ends of the success–failure continuum. Official data show that Karnataka completed updating the Record of Rights for all its villages in January 2012. However, in Odisha, by contrast, this work is pending in all its villages. In several states, the implementation of the NLRMP has been partially accomplished, while in others – including Madhya Pradesh, Rajasthan, Punjab and Bihar – it appears to have not been attempted at all. This is probably the explanation for the news report, in 2012, that the utilisation of financial allocations for the NLRMP was a mere 14 per cent.

Even as ministerial statements have attributed Maoist insurgency to the insufficient progress made in recovering and securing to adivasi people their lands, Nayak's study shows that the current renewal of interest in the modernisation of land records is aligned to a techno-managerial approach to public sector management in a neo-liberal context. He boldly situates the NLRMP in the context of the hegemony enjoyed by the principles of the New Public Management, as also the World Bank's advocacy of promoting land markets through digitisation. Nayak demonstrates the subtle policy shift that has occurred from the earlier emphasis on land records modernisation as an instrument of progressive land reform, to the current justification for modernisation, in digital form, for the market-linked objective of generating clear and undisputed rights to private property.

The interrogation of the NLRMP in this work occurs at two levels. The first is an internalist perspective in which the book asks whether the NLRMP has accomplished its own stated goals. Here, the study shows that even Karnataka is not the unmitigated success in service delivery that it is commonly assumed to be. Through detailed field-work, Nayak demonstrates that, far from eliminating corruption, the computerisation programme has expanded the network of rent-seeking activity and kept intact the power of intermediaries. Transparency and accountability remain uncertain outcomes despite this initiative in e-governance. At the second level, the author adopts an externalist perspective and connects the design of the project itself to the larger policy framework of economic reform with the principles of the New Public Management, such as Public-Private Partnerships and outsourcing to private vendors, holding sway. He outlines the implications of these mechanisms for state capacity and especially for a bureaucracy that is expected to be responsive to citizens' interests.

Pradeep Nayak is to be commended for providing a critical governance perspective that is simultaneously attentive to the ground reality of the computerisation of land records and to the larger policy framework within which the slogan of e-governance makes its often hollow claims.

Niraja Gopal Jayal
Centre for the Study of Law and Governance
Jawaharlal Nehru University

Preface

In 1973, Herbert Simon, a much celebrated scholar in social sciences, observed that the major problem the governmental, corporate and educational organisations face is not the departmentalisation or coordination among the departments or operating units but that of organising information storage and information processing. He had opined that rapid development of information and communication technologies had made the public and corporate organisations more 'sophisticated and rational' than in the past.

The new technology as a 'symptom of progress' would be used as an 'analytic tool' for understanding human problems and helping their solution (H. Simon, 1973). Much before Herbert Simon's observation, Anthony Downs' perceptive piece asks us to rethink the very rationale and purpose of applying information systems, given the uncertainty of technical payoff. The future of management of the information system, to him, depends upon the ways in which such data system increases the power and positions of the persons who apply such a system. 'We must focus from the dazzling computer systems to the way in which the computers are applied by the men who use it' (Downs, 1967). On the other hand, P. H. A. Frissen has also cautiously observed that the relationship between politics, administration and technology appears ambiguous notwithstanding the rationalising and modernising role of technology over the politico-administrative system (Frissen, 1999).

Therefore, given the scenario of difficulties and wider implications of the subject matter, pursuing a multidimensional and an interdisciplinary research on the role of state, ICTs and governance with reference to land records modernisation, at the Centre for the Study of Law and Governance,

JNU, is somewhat a challenging task. The paucity of research materials and the demand for regular field visits have made it more difficult. By studying the computerisation of land records in India, one is required to straddle many aspects of the subject matter such as historical background of the land records management; role of the state and its policy shifts; impact of computerisation on the taluk/tahsil and its bureaucracy; the capacity of the government officials to handle cutting-edge ICTs and work in partnership with IT professionals and vendors; role of the political and administrative leadership; and role of ICTs in contributing governance reforms and its impact on democratic governance, citizenship, federalism and the development process.

At the outset, I express and record my sincere gratitude to Professor Niraja Gopal Jayal for her help and guidance. Her useful advice and comments helped me all the way in writing this book. Above all, her professionalism and academic rigour always goaded me to work on my research to the best of my ability.

I owe a great deal to Professor Kuldeep Mathur, the Founder Director of the Centre, Pratiksha Baxi, Jaivir Singh, Navroz Dubash and Professor Amit Prakash, the learned faculty members at the Centre for the Study of Law Governance, for their invaluable suggestions that helped me grapple with the subject matter with ease and confidence.

I am grateful to Professor Pradipta Chaudhury, CESP, JNU and Pushpanjali Swain, NIHFW, New Delhi for extending their warm hospitality to me. They remain a source of encouragement to me. I sincerely acknowledge Bibhu Prasad Nayak, Assistant Professor, ISEC, Bengaluru, for extending help in my frequent field visits to Karnataka for data collection. I owe my gratitude to Rita Sinha, formerly Secretary, Department of Land Resources, (DOLR), Ministry of Rural Development, and Chinmay Basu, Additional Secretary, DOLR, A. K. Singh, formerly Director, DOLR, Ministry of Rural Development, Government of India for extending their cooperation and allowing me access to official records and permitting me to attend important review meetings and workshops on the implementation of the National Land Records Modernisation Programme. I owe immense gratitude to G. B. Upadhyay, Under Secretary, DOLR, for his cooperation in collecting official documents related to my research.

I take this opportunity to thank Rajeev Chawla, Special Secretary, Bhoomi and K. S. Prabhakar, Secretary, Revenue Department, Anil Kumar; KAS, G. Gurumurthy, KAS of the Bhoomi Monitoring Cell Bengaluru; C. N. Sreedhara and Rudresh of the Survey and Settlement Directorate, Bengaluru and other officials at the Revenue Department like Kathyani Devi, KAS for extending full assistance to my research works. I thank N. Gatty Narayan, Bhavani Nayak, Anjan Sahoo, Susanta Mallick, Smruti Dhal, Sujit Pruseth, Arindam Dakua, Bharat Tarai and Purna Parida, for their help in collecting research materials.

I am also grateful to G. V. V. Sharma, the then Secretary, Revenue Department for sympathetically considering my request for study leave that enabled me complete the research. Thanks are due to K. P. Das, Additional Secretary, Revenue Department; R. K. Sahoo, Assistant Director; Bijay Nayak, OSCS; Hemanta Nayak, Dealing Assistant; Basudev Mallick, Section Officer at the Land Records and Survey Section, Board of Revenue, Odisha, Cuttack for extending their support in collection of data and sparing their valuable time in engaging in frequent discussions with me.

My sincere thanks to Vinay Thakur, Director, Land Records, NIC, New Delhi; S. K. Mohapatra, Senior Scientist, NIC, Bhubaneswar; Dipak Das, Senior Technical Director, NIC at the Land Record Information Centre Cuttack and Samartharam, Senior Technical Director, NIC, Bengaluru and the District Informatics Officers and *tahsildars* of both Karnataka and Odisha for sharing useful information during my interviews with them. I am also thankful to Rudra Narayan Mohanty, OAS; Harapriya Dash, OSCS, and Sameekshya Nayak, OSCS for sharing information pertaining to my research.

I am thankful to R. K. Mohapatra, Librarian NCDS, and R. K. Routray, Librarian, Gopabandhu Academy of Administration, Bhubaneswar and library staff of the Central EXIM Bank and CSLG libraries of JNU for extending their help in collecting research materials. My sincere thanks are also due to Qudsiya Ahmed, Suvadip Bhattacharjee and Ranjini Majumdar of Cambridge University Press for their sincere interest in the book, and to the external reviewers for their helpful comments.

I am indebted to my parents, my wife Swayamprava and daughter Swati for their constant support in all my endeavours.

Last but not the least, I would like to add here that this book is the outcome of a study leave granted by the Government of Odisha, India. The views expressed here are personal and in my capacity as a researcher and not necessarily attributed to my role of a civil servant under the Government of Odisha.

Pradeep Nayak

List of Abbreviations

BMC	Bhoomi Monitoring Cell
C&AG	Comptroller and Auditor General of India
CLR	Computerisation of Land Records
D&LRS	Director of Land Records and Survey
DIT	Department of Information Technology
DOLR	Department of Land Resources
ETS	Electronic Total Station
FIFO	First -In -First -Out
GPS	Global Positioning System
IAS	Indian Administrative Service
IT	Information Technology
ICT	Information and Communication Technology
IMP	Integrated Mutation Phodi
KAS	Karnataka Administrative Services
LRC	Land Record Centre
MIT	Ministry of Information Technology
MORD	Ministry of Rural Development
NeGP	National eGovernance Plan
NIC	National Informatics Centre
NICSI	National Informatics Centre Services Inc
NKC	National Knowledge Commission
NLRMP	National Land Records Modernisation Programme
NPM	New Public Management
OAS	Odisha Administrative Service

OCAC	Odisha Computer Application Centre
ORSAC	Odisha Remote Sensing Application Centre
OSCS	Odisha Settlement and Consolidation Service
RI	Revenue Inspector
RoRs	Record of Rights
RTC	Record of Rights, Tenancy and Crops
SDC	State Data Centre
SMART	Simple, Moral, Accountable, Responsive and Transparent
SLSC	State Level Steering Committee
SRA&ULR	Strengthening Revenue Administration and Updating of Land Records
UNDP	United Nations Development Programme
UTs	Union Territories
WAN	Wide Area Net Work

1

The State, ICTs and Governance

A Theoretical Exploration

Introduction

The study of the role of the state in promoting ICTs adoption and governance reforms is now being recognised world over as central to any discussion on administrative reforms or modernisation of the public sector. The state in India, as in other parts of the world, is no longer impervious to the challenges of Information and Communication Technologies (ICTs). Rather, new and interesting terminologies like virtual state, automated state, network state, information polity, informatisation of public administration, digital era governance, e-governance and smart governance have been repeatedly used in research works and public policy documents.

Neoliberal economic reforms and the IT revolution have influenced the role of the state in society and economy, as well as its relationship with citizens. All over the world, governments have made elaborate policy and institutional changes for the early adoption of cutting-edge technologies like ICTs in their governance structures as well as processes. International financial institutions like the World Bank, IMF and ADB and international organisations such as UNDP and UNCTAD have been prominent votaries for the adoption of ICTs in public administration. The rapid use of ICTs by the governments and the popularity of web pages of government departments led some scholars to describe ICTs as the 'new face of government' and 'a new vehicle for citizen initiated contacts'.[1]

[1] John Clayton Thomas and Gregory Streib. 2003. 'The New Face of the Government: Citizen Initiated Contacts in the Era of E-Government,' *Journal of Public Administration Research and Theory*, 13(1), 83–102.

The role of the Indian state has been crucial in the phenomenal growth of informatics development. The Indian state has been actively promoting the informatics sector and such promotional and infrastructural activities of the Indian state, coupled with its success in building public and private networks, has been crucial to India's emergence as a global player in the IT sector. Such a perspective is important to understand the contemporary Indian state's integral role in determining and promoting, on a massive scale, the application of ICTs and IT industry in its governance structures for better service delivery, ushering transparency, empowering people, improving efficiency and furthering the interface of the state with IT business and industry.[2] According to Peter B. Evans, the role of the Indian state through its regulatory agencies and state-owned ICT industries during the 1980s revealed tentative attempts to increase state action aimed at complementing and promoting private entrepreneurship. The economic liberalisation in India since the 1980s changed the import substitution model to one in which the state plays supporting and auxiliary role to private entrepreneurial development, and by the way promoting infrastructural activities that enabled Indian software companies to emerge as world leaders in software development.[3]

It is now declared, in the report of the Second Administrative Reforms Commission,[4] that the application of ICTs to government functioning will create 'SMART government' (Simple, Moral, Accountable, Responsive and Transparent) and will bring out 'revolutionary changes in our institutional structures, procedures and practices.'[5] The emphasis on ICT intervention in governance and functioning of government needs to be seen in the context of the restructuring and reorientation of the role of the state in India and its conscious attempt to incorporate market rationality in the functioning of the state.

---

[2] See C. Ramachandriah. 2003. 'Information Technology and Social Development,' *Economic and Political Weekly*, March 22–29, 1192–1195. Also see Jyoti Saraswati. 2008. 'The Indian IT Industry and Neoliberalism: The Irony of Mythology,' *Third World Quarterly*, 29(6), 1139–1152.

[3] Peter B. Evans. 1992. 'Indian Informatics in the 1980s: The Changing Character of State Involvement,' *World Development*, 20(1), 1–18.

[4] Government of India. 2008. Preface to the *Second Administrative Reforms Commission – Eleventh Report on 'Promoting e-Governance: The Smart Way Forward,'* New Delhi, December.

[5] Ibid.

The main motivating factor or reason for the adoption of ICT initiatives by governments across the world is to refocus, improve and strengthen public service delivery in the era of neoliberalism. Therefore, e-government initiatives pose challenging questions of adoption, management, coordination among government offices, the design of service delivery and its relation to the citizens. ICT policy initiatives also raise other questions like how to manage change in the application of ICTs, investment and development of knowledge, skills and assumption of responsibility to sustain a desired change or transformation of public sector agencies.[6] From a Foucauldian perspective, the present drive of the Indian state towards a national land records modernisation programme and national smart cards system for all Indians will make India better 'governable' as it will enable a correspondence between governmentality and the knowability of the population by the state, along with massive computerisation of land records, survey maps and allotment of unique identity cards (UID).

The central issue

The widespread use of computers and other ICTs by government is viewed by both practitioners and academics as having democratising implications. The contemporary state and modes of governance are not only in the process of redefinition but 'multiple visions of the state'[7] find their place in the discourse of Indian politics that now requires reinterpretation and a relook, thanks to the ICT revolution which has deeply influenced various spheres of industry, business, commerce and governance in India.

It is believed that ICTs could not only help better implementation of the policy but also facilitate new citizen-state interactions. At the same time, there are skeptics who are apprehensive of the government's hold over the technological reins, the influence of private ICT companies, and of adding complexity and cost to the administration. It is therefore argued by the cyber skeptics that only historical experience with adoption and management of ICT applications in the

---

[6] Nada Korac Kakadbase and Alexander Kahzmin. 1996. 'Innovation Strategies for Adoption of New Information Technology in Government: An Australian Experience,' *Public Administration and Development*, 16(3), 17–30.

[7] Niraja Gopal Jayal. 2001. 'Reinventing the State: The Emergence of the Alternate Models of Governance in India in 1990s' in Niraja Gopal Jayal and Sudha Pai (Eds.) *Democratic Governance in India: Challenges of Poverty, Development and Identity,'* New Delhi: Sage Publications, 133; 149.

public sector rather than a future perspective of computerisation in government organisations, would promote an understanding of the effect of ICTs-enabled public service delivery on the state-citizen relationship, as the trend towards web-enabled service has been around since the 1990s.

The earlier process of manual land records management and the present programme of computerisation of land records by the Indian state through techno-managerial policy instruments can be understood from a Foucauldian perspective as micro-governmental rationalities with prescriptive implication for the citizens or the subjects. The analysis of specific problems like the management and maintenance of land records detailing some information about the individual citizen as a land holder, conditions and nature of ownership, soil type and nature of produce and other rights and liabilities over the land are critical aspects of understanding the activity of governing. The land records, both textual (RoRs/RTC) and spatial (cadastral map), can be described as vital techniques and technologies of the government to control and manage its population or 'mechanisms and instruments through which governing is accomplished.'[8] Thus we could argue that land records as technologies of government 'emphasise the practical features of government' which include the way of collecting, collating, storing and processing the quantitative and qualitative data on land and its related attributes like ownership and nature of soil condition.[9] Viewed from this perspective the land records prepared and maintained by British India served multiple purposes of the empire. The studies on the contemporary aspects of Record of Rights prepared by the British Imperial rulers show us how the land records, village records and the district reports served as 'instruments' and a linkage to a wider 'discourse between knowledge and administrative control' as well as 'photographs of the ruled for the use of the ruler'.[10]

A study of government records and various public policy documents leads one to believe that the Computerisation of Land Records (CLR) now redesigned

[8] Richard F. Huff. 2007. 'Governmentality' In Mark Bevir (Ed) *Encyclopedia of Governance*, London, Sage Publications, 389.

[9] Jon Simons. 1995. *Foucault and The Political*, London: Routledge, 37. , Dean Mitchell. 2006. *Governmentality: Power and Rule in Modern Society*, London: Sage Publications, 27; 212.

[10] Richard Saumarez Smith. 1985. 'Rule by Records and Rule by Reports: Contemporary Aspects of the British Imperial Rule of Law,' *Contributions to Indian Sociology*, 19(1), 154.

as the National Land Records Modernisation Programme (NLRMP) is one of the biggest National e-governance Plans (NEGP) initiated by the Indian state since the 1990s. It is interesting to note that though the subject of land is listed under the State List in the Indian constitution, it is the central government which has been the real driver of the change. Behind the massive computerisation and web-enabled updating and maintenance of land records, modern survey and electronic integration of revenue offices lies the objective of effecting a radical change from the existing land tenure system based on presumptive title to a conclusive one guaranteed by the state.

The problem of land records management, maintenance and updating continues through manual methods which is time-consuming and prone to errors and manipulation. The present system of land records management in India is a legacy of land records management introduced by Raja Todarmal during the Mughal rule and later on much modification by the British Government was carried out. The dearth of up-to-date and correct land records is now believed to be one of the main reasons for the failure in agrarian reforms, growing land disputes and the frequently fraudulent nature of land transactions. Land records contain vital statistics relating to agriculture, cropping patterns, land holding, nature of tenancy, land revenue and irrigation, forest and mines resources that are useful in planning and development. The central government's first policy document on computerisation (1988–1989) reads as follows:

> To remove the problems inherent in the manual systems of maintenance and updating of land records and to meet the requirements of various groups of users, it was decided that efforts should be made to computerise CORE DATA contained in land records, so as to assist development planning and to make records accessible to peoples/ planners and administrators.[11]

The pertinent questions that arise are: what has been the role of the Indian state in land records management and what factors and forces have shaped the formulation of public policy on the computerisation of land records in recent years? What are the impacts of computerisation on the revenue administration? What has been the progress in the land records computerisation started since

---

[11] http://www.dolr.nic.in/land_reforms.html (accessed on June 12, 2008). The said objective is however changed to attending the conclusive land title as the sole objective of the CLR programme subsequently with the launch of the NLRMP scheme in 2008.

1988–89 to this date? What factors are responsible for a strategic shift in the objective of land records computerisation? Will the state be able to modernise its land records system given its failure to implement land reforms? What are the governance issues and legal matters that are thrown up in the current land records modernisation programme? What has been the governance implication of land records computerisation with the help of private IT vendors? Interestingly, very little scholarly literature is available on this multidimensional subject which merits attention.

Hence, it becomes imperative to study the role of the Indian state in promoting land records modernisation by way of computerisation of land records, updating land records management and making them available to the citizens online as well as the impact of adoption of ICTs on the bureaucracy and governance process.

This subject may best understood by studying the role of three variables–the state, ICTs and governance with reference to a specific policy reform area—land records computerisation—where 'high modernist ideologies' are being applied to modernise the land records and their management. The importance of political factors such as the shifting role of the state and emergence of the governance discourse cannot be overlooked in this context. The current neoliberal land records modernisation programme, or computerisation of land records, as has been analysed in succeeding chapters, does not help the state-led land or agrarian reforms. This rather becomes a piecemeal and incremental strategy, which switches over from the presumptive nature of land records to a conclusive land title system.

A critical survey of literature

The authors who write on e-governance and informatisation of the public sector and public administration may be categorised into two groups: ICT optimists and ICT skeptics. The former group includes all those who perceive and advocate a techno-managerial-determinist approach to solve the complex question of governance, and who regard ICTs are value neutral. The latter group includes the critics of ICT-enabled governance reforms as well as those who express their reservations about the democratic prospects of e-government and its capacity to address the challenges of governance apolitically.

Helen Margetts's *The Automated State* elaborates on the challenges posed by the increasing adoption and innovation of ICTs. The state has to rely on big IT corporates for its policy design, development and deployment of the information systems due to the necessity. Hence the challenge before the state is how to 'control these new players in policy relevant decision making.' Such radical outsourcing policy will pave the way for a 'commodification dynamic in public services' where the large multinational IT corporations will be able to exercise a 'proprietorial authority' and such policies would be difficult to reverse in the contemporary neoliberal reform regime.[12]

Subash Bhatnagar's study analyses e-government as basically 'an enabling tool to increase efficiency, transparency and strengthening public sector' rather than as a panacea for performance improvement. He cites three factors such as political willingness to reform, availability of ICT infrastructure and institutional capacity to absorb and manage change as being crucial to successful change in e-government.[13] His arguement that ICTs can play a valuable role in advancing the good governance agenda of the World Bank is important in the context of growing emphasis laid by the World Bank on developing countries to adopt ICTs in their development discourse and practice. The role played by the private IT firms in pushing the e-governance agenda and the suitability of the techno-managerial approach of governance reforms, the capacity of the bureaucracy and role of political commitment to ICT adoption in public sector reforms have not been critically examined by him.

Richard Heek's widely cited book *Implementing and Managing eGovernment: An International Text* focuses on some of the operational issues related to policy, politics and organisational problems in implementing e-government from a techno-managerial perspective. For Heeks, most of the e-government programmes fail and there is a huge gap between its hype and actual performance as politics is more important than ICT applications, and political support combined with cooperation and involvement of all levels of bureaucracy in e-government programmes, is the key to success.

Chrisanthi Avgerou's work, *Information Systems and Global Diversity* is an attempt to understand the relationship between the institutional nature of ICTs and management and the challenge of ICT adoption in the institution. Stating that contemporary research and development in the information system is

---

12 Helen Margetts. 1995. 'The Automated State,' *Public Policy and Administration*, 10(2), Summer, 88–98.

13 Subash Bhatnagar. 2004. *E-Government: From Vision to Implementation: A Practical Guide to with Case Studies*, New Delhi: Sage Publications, 11–13.

heavily influenced by market forces, she argues that the private sector's emphasis on the role of ICTs in enhancing productivity is only a partial one and other social dynamics also contribute to productivity. From an institutional point of view, ICT may not be seen as a technical artifact functioning according to technical rules and embedded in their physical components but it is 'a product of social networks embedded in social institutions.'[14]

Despite the failure of many e-government programmes in the developing countries and its demoralising effect on public officials for their inability to handle the first changes in technologies, the craze for application and adoption of ICTs in public administration by the developing countries (DLCs) is on the rise. Chrisanthi Avgerou says that the emergence of management and ICTs as institutions in their own right cannot be denied as ICTs find strong support in management, and their alliance is a formidable force in the context of globalisation. New ideas of management such as Business Process Reengineering, Change Management and e-commerce have centred on ICT. Further ICT management and innovation are concerned and shaped by international development discourse (e.g., NPM) by MNC IT firms and international financial business. ICT has acquired a role as a means for any organisational rationalisation and as an instrument for enacting change. It has largely been fostered in formal organisations like bureaucracy to strengthen its central coordination mechanism and efficiency.[15]

In one way, e-government also fulfils the NPM principles of techno-managerial reforms of outsourcing and privatisation of public service delivery. Christopher Hood has aptly observed that the transformative potentiality of ICT has been made popular and acceptable with the reinvention movement and the ideas of Osborne and Gaebler across the world. 'Every self-respecting government today has to have a relentlessly upbeat version of the future that involves information and communication technology decisively improving the way it interacts with the citizens.' [16]

On the other hand, scholars like Benjamin Barber and Robert Wade have charged IT consultants and uncritical scholars for spinning the IT success

---

[14] Chrisanthi Avgerou. 2002. *The Institutional Nature of ICT and Organisational Change*, Oxford: Oxford University Press, 30.

[15] Ibid, pp. 37; 44; 42.

[16] Christopher Hood. 2006. 'The Tools of Government in the Information Age' in Michael Moran et al *The Oxford Handbook of Public Policy*, Oxford University Press, 472.

stories from one or two pilot projects without scaling up such achievements. Barber points out that though ICTs, especially the internet, can spread democratic values and awareness, its use is determined by access, portal, software platform and the monopolistic nature of the content. It tends to serve as a 'mirror' in reflecting the culture that produces them. [17] The ICTs are being promoted as a tool for increasing governmental effectiveness and responsiveness. The poor developing countries are being pressurised by the multilateral funding agencies to adopt e-governance for 'leap frogging' their institutional and infrastructural barriers. Massive infusion of computers and cyber kiosks, it is assumed, would remove the problem of digital divide.

The rural poor people could access the World Wide Web through cyber kiosks and get governmental information. The e-government agenda implemented with the help of private IT firms carry a typical political agenda of 'government by the market' in which public administration can run on the market principle of customer-business relations. In this process, the IT consultants, multinationals and national firms are emerging as the greatest beneficiaries. The growing failures in e-government initiatives in developing countries are ascribed to cultural barriers, lack of political will and ineffective bureaucracy by scholars who spoke in favour of revolutionary and transformative potential of ICTs in creating a digital state. [18]

Nevertheless, the phenomenal increase in ICT-related industries and trade and the massive employment opportunities created in the process of the production and information of knowledge and distribution has led some to use 'the ICT paradigm' as a manifestation of the general structural change in the economy, and are driven by 'irrational exuberance' that the spread of ICTs will pave the way for radical social-political consequences like the decline of the state, bureaucracy and deterritorialisation of the nation state.[19]

Manual Castells has observed that 'a new society' is being developed, thanks to revolutionary advances in the field of ICTs as these technologies are

---

[17] Benjamin Barber. 2001. 'The Uncertainty of Digital Politics: Democracy's Unease Relationship with Information Technology,' *Harvard International Review*, Spring, 43.

[18] Robert H. Wade. 2002. 'Bridging the Digital Divide: New Route to Development or New Forms of Dependency?,' *Global Governance*, 8, 443–466.

[19] Chris Freeman. 2007. 'The ICT Paradigm' in Robin Mansell et al. *The Oxford Handbook of Information and Communication Technology*, New Delhi: Oxford University Press, 37; 45–49.

embedded in society as a material culture. New social contact and new forms of social organisations are being formed by the enabling tools of ICTs. Internet has appeared as the 'back bone of new culture, the culture of real virtuality in which the virtuality becomes a fundamental component of our symbolic environment and thus our experience as a communicative being.'[20] There is a widespread claim that the web-enabled ICT has heralded a third industrial revolution and can 'leap-frog' the economies of the countries like India, China and other East European countries and in the process enable these countries to bypass the traditional stages of economic development.

There is even talk of replacing the industrial age of government by information age government, thanks to the 'information revolution' and even prediction of dramatically altering the lifestyle of the common people through access to the World Wide Web. Globalisation, liberalisation and deregulation of economic activities across the world have stimulated the popularisation of the wide spread use of internet.[21] The talk of the reinvented state found in the writings of NPM advocates who argued that the historical entity of the state can be made more flexible by making public agencies focus on results rather than procedures and more responsive to 'customers' through application of information and communication technology. [22]

Needless to say, such an approach to the state is based on an ahistorical perspective as one should not forget that the internet is still a novel phenomenon and governance institutions have been in existence even before the invention of the typewriter, radio and telephone. Therefore, writing about the importance of ICTs in governance and application in public administration 'ignoring the prior existence of government institutions is to exogenise many factors that determine how and whether e-governance succeeds.'[23]

The ICT-based service delivery at public offices creates an impersonal relationship between the citizens and the public servant and it is argued by

---

[20] Manual Castells. 2000. 'Towards a Sociology of the Network Society,' *Contemporary Sociology*, 29(5), September, 694.

[21] E. Giovanneti, M. Kagami and M. Tsuji (Eds) *The Internet Revolution: A Global Perspective*, Cambridge University Press, 1; 262.

[22] Paul Starr. 2010. 'The Liberal State in a Digital World,' *Governance: An International Journal of Policy, Administration and Institutions*, 23(1), 4.

[23] Richard Rose. 2005. 'The Internet and Governance in a Global Context,' *Journal of Public Policy*, 25(1), 1.

the proponents of the e-governments that the lessening of contact between the public and public servant will reduce the rent-seeking behaviour of officials and promote transparency. However, in practice, as Victor Bekkers and Vincent Homburg in their studies of e-government policies of some European countries show the idea that citizens as empowered and intelligent customers can avail public services from cyber kiosks on their own is harboured by e-government advocates guided by rational choice theory. Such an idea, of treating the citizen as a rational consumer of public services, it is argued, ignores or undervalues the political and public character of service delivery, narrows the multidimensionality of citizenship and public administration and diminishes its legitimacy. The dominant myth that has been created around the notion is that ICT-enabled service delivery mechanisms will enable a change from bureaucratic silos to citizen-oriented service organisations. Bekkers and Homburg advise us to bear in mind the rhetoric and myths that exist in the ICT policy objectives and muddy practice of e-government implementation strategies by politician-bureaucracy and IT vendor networks which are an important arena of research and discussion.[24]

The internet's role in the policy-making process studied by R. Karl Rethemeyer revealed that it is being used by well-educated, wealthy, highly influential and well-positioned brokers or public authorities for their communication purposes. Internet may facilitate the growth of 'networked corporatised regime' and even a decline of representative democracy. Debunking the assumptions of the cyber optimists that ICTs, particularly, the internet have given an opportunity for reinventing democratic governance in western democracies by enhancing direct participation, access and communication of citizens with administration, he views, '...Internet will not fix what ails representative democracy. Indeed, the internet may reinforce the much resented organisational dominance of politics. Reconnecting politics with society is still primarily the work of organisational and institutional reformers, not hardware and software engineers.'[25]

---

[24] Victor Bekkers and Vincent Homburg. 2007. 'The Myths of E-Government: Looking Beyond the Assumptions of a New and Better Government,' *The Information Society*, 23, pp. 373–380. The European countries referred by them are the USA, the UK, the Netherlands, Canada and Denmark.

[25] R. Karl Rethemeyer. 2007. 'The Empire Strike Back: Is the Internet Corporatising Rather than Democratising Policy Process?,' *Public Administration Review*, March–April, 199; pp. 205–209.

Reinventing governance through ICTs

Some scholars have perceived the growth of the ICT industry to its linkage with the growth of e-governance agenda and the clamour for reinventing government through ICTs. It would be naive to presume that the world wide trend in adopting e-government strategies and preferring to deliver services electronically on business principles has been due to the success of e-commerce. The present study shows that the policy of computerisation of land records has opened a vast market for the private IT firms in India for which e-government policy is a *sine qua non* for their business growth. A network of 'cyber-libertarian' civil society groups, IT professionals, corporate funded NGOs and retired bureaucrats have been vigorously clamouring for complete digitisation of government offices for promoting a techno-managerial notion of transparency and accountability in governance.

The World Bank has led donor agencies in applying ICTs as a strategic tool of its governance reforms agenda. The phenomenal development of ICTs have come as handy for the Bank and other multilateral funding agencies to press for application and adoption of ICTs in the administrative reform policies as it views ICTs as a neutral tool which can be pushed to promote its "technocratic discourse of development."[26] The World Bank advocates the adoption and application of ICTs for enhancing transparency, efficiency and accountability of government [27] and "transforming the relationship with citizen and business and between the arms of government."[28] It also stresses that the e-government programme be part of broader public sector reforms in developing countries for advancing its agenda of 'good governance.'

The government officials, in implementing costly e-government projects through lucrative outsourcing, have also developed a network for their personal benefits. It is rightly observed by a functionary in the union ministry of information and communication technology, that the e-government is 'ordinarily understood' as the application of e-commerce techniques and

---

[26] Mark Thompson. 2004. 'Discourse, Development & the 'Digital Divide: ICT &the World Bank,' *Review of African Political Economy*, 31(99), March, pp. 103–123.

[27] World Bank. 2000. *Reforming Public Institutions and Strengthening Governance: A World Bank Strategy*, Washington: World Bank, p. 28.

[28] World Bank. 2004. '*Building Blocks of e-Government: Lessons from Developing Countries*,' August, Number-91, The World Bank PREM notes.

tools to public services and to improve services to businesses and citizens in India. A survey of web services in twenty countries revealed that government websites provide information on public service delivery and information on business transactions to citizens as well. [29] It is not surprising to see that the regular holding of national level e-governance summits in India are being sponsored and conducted at different cities by corporate houses and national and multinational IT firms with the help of state and central government departments, highlighting the imperative of partnerships in applying and adopting ICTs in public sector organisations and, in the process, the private IT firms foresee a windfall for business growth on a sustainable basis.

Public private partnership has been the most preferred and dominant policy strategy for the Indian government and private IT vendors. Similarly, electronic-government in the UK is not only viewed as a means to join up government but also an intricate and integral strategy to promote the business of multinational IT firms as well as making the country as a leading player in global electronic commerce. As a result, the policy of e-government or e-governance is as Christine Bellamy aptly observes, 'being regarded, in some quarters at least, as no more or less than an important branch of e-commerce.'[30] Such trends in the UK are not specific to that country. A detailed and exhaustive survey of literature shows that the increasing application of ICTs has led to a blurring of the distinction between e-government and e-commerce, and has been a crucial factor in the growth of network governance. It is even claimed that reinventing government, which was a fashionable idea in the 1990s has become a reality now, thanks to the internet. Governments across the world are relying on the infrastructure and business processes and market logic of e-commerce. Further, government offices are now willing to outsourcing, contracting and partnerships with the IT firms. There is a risk of e-government eroding the distinctiveness of public service as perceived by the citizens as well as the IT vendors. The universality of public service shows rapid decline after it began charging user fees. This interesting development has been studied in detail in land records management in India where unequal land relations, access and growing landlessness are prominent features.

---

[29] C. Satpathy. 2000. 'Role of the State in E-World,' *Economic and Political Weekly*, September 23, pp. 3494–3497.

[30] Christine Bellamy. 2000. 'Implementing Information-Age Government: Principles, Progress and Paradox,' *Public Policy and Administration*, 15(1), p. 29.

It may be mentioned here that governance in this study is understood from two dominant perspectives—both as network governance (based on the notion of inter-jurisdictional cooperation between the public and private agencies and network management) as well as the new public management approach of running government bureaucracy on market principles.[31]

Networks and partnerships in governance

The public sector reforms no doubt has put more emphasis on NPM in the beginning, but the second wave of reforms which have gained ground supplement NPM ideas as it stressed on building, promoting and strengthening networks and partnerships between the public, private and civil society actors in public sector reforms. Some have used the terms such as 'joined-up governance.'[32] Joined up governance actively promotes horizontal and vertical coordination between the organisations involved in any given aspect of public policy.'[33]

R. A. W. Rhodes observed that the network governance can be viewed as a policy shift from hierarchies in welfare state to privatisation and 'emphasis on partnership and joined up governance.'[34] The network governance approach supplemented the NPM approach to public sector reforms by emphasising on the networks and partnerships in dealing with the societal problems.

New public management and ICTs

The New Public Management (NPM), in the context of neoliberal reforms worldwide, is basically 'a liberation and market-driven management' and is influenced by what Larry D. Terry calls 'neo-managerialism.' He has based

---

[31] Nikolas Rose. 1999. 'Governing' in *Powers of Freedom*, Cambridge University Press, pp. 16–17 and also Tom Christensen and Per Laegreid. 2012. 'Governance and Administrative Reforms,' in David Levy-Faur (Ed) *The Oxford Handbook of Governance*, Oxford University Press, p. 256.

[32] Mark Bevir. (Ed). 2007. See Introduction to *Public Governance*, London, Sage Publications, p. xxx.

[33] Ibid.

[34] R.A.W. Rhodes. 2006. 'Policy Networks Analysis', in Michael Moran et al. (Eds). 2006. *The Oxford Handbook of Public Policy*, Oxford University Press, p. 430.

his analysis upon Christopher Pollit's works on managerialism and its five core beliefs, of which the application of modern cutting edge technologies like information technology is one of the prominent and relevant factors in increasing productivity.[35]

Patrick Dunleavy and Helen Margetts estimate that in the internet age, government organisations face four alternative pathways or options: a continuation of NPM trends in the public sector strengthened through web-based developments; increasing state marginalisation where government organisations lag behind the rest of the society especially the large IT firms in developing the web presence with consequent loss of nodality of position by the state for its inability to command information from societal actors freely; possibility of radical web-enabled change inside the government or digital state to replace NPM and finally, apprehension of a policy mess where conflicting NPM and e-government initiatives produce no coherent direction of development. In such uncertain scenario, governments across the world have to steer a delicate path between utopian and dystopian pathways to maximize the benefits of the internet age as influence of ICTs on the functioning of the governments will be more than NPM and other practices and ideas.

The emphasis on electronic delivery of public services and customer-oriented information flows at the expense of citizen participation and interaction with government in the contemporary e-government initiative is leading to 'reification of New Public Management ideology in e-government technology' and one may conclude that NPM is now made possible as a reform strategy through e-government.[36]

Contemporary public administration, already under the influence of NPM and the reinventing government movement, is responding by informatising and networked computing which enables it to be economic, efficient and responsive in a more or less competitive environment. The adoption of ICTs now appears as fundamental to the innovation process in public administration.[37]

---

[35] Larry D. Terry. 1998. 'Administrative Leadership, Neo-Managerialism, and the Public Management Movement,' p. 196.

[36] Vincent M. F. Homburg. 2008. 'Red –Tape and Reforms: Trajectories of Technological and Managerial Reforms in Public Administration,' *International Journal of Public Administration*, 31, p. 766.

[37] John A. Taylor and Howard Williams. 1991. 'Public Administration and Information Polity,' *Public Administration,* 69, Summer, pp. 172; 185.

From public administration to information polity

The application of ICTs in public administration is viewed as a challenging opportunity by some scholars like Ignace Snellen as public administration is based on information relating to policy decisions, policy design, policy implementation and its outcome. In other words, every activity of public administration has an informational and communicative effect. Hence, it is argued that ICT adoption will have a 'fundamental effect' on the way the administration of the government functions though this view is a contested one.'[38]

Paul H.A. Frissen emphasises the integral relationships between ICTs and public administration and writes, 'Information is at the core of public administration, information technologies affect this core.'[39] Paul Frissen has gone ahead in putting all his hope on the transformational and transcending nature of ICTs and even predicted that ICTs will herald the post-modern fragmented and decentred nature of public administration.[40]

As the state goes for informatisation process with the help of private IT firms, the concept of information networking and redistribution of informational resource of the state around the network will inevitably raise important and profound constitutional, legal and political issues.[41]The significance of new kinds of informational resources and flows in government and their interaction with broad directions of reform in contemporary public administration and New Public Management led Christine Bellamy and John A. Taylor to formulate the concept of 'information polity.'[42] Viewed from that perspective, ICTs have been identified as the key to 'reinvention and

[38] Ignace Snellen. 2005. 'E-Government: A Challenge for Public Administration' in Ewan Ferlie et al., *The Oxford Handbook of Public Management,* Oxford University Press, pp. 399; 417–418.

[39] Paul H. A. Frissen. 1992. 'Informatisation In Public Administration: Introduction,' *International Review of Administrative Sciences,* 58, pp. 307–310.

[40] Paul H. Frissen. 1997. 'The Virtual State: Post modernisation, Informatisation and Public Administration', In Brian Loader (Ed) *The Governance of Cyberspace: Politics, Technology and Global Restructuring*, London: Routledge, pp. 112–115.

[41] John A. Taylor. 1992. 'Information Networking in Public Administration,' *International Review of Administrative Sciences,* 58, pp. 385–386.

[42] Christine Bellamy and John A. Taylor. 1994. 'Exploiting IT in Public Administration-Towards an Information Polity,' *Public Administration*, 72, Spring, pp. 1–2.

reinvigoration of public administration' as it offers an opportunity to reduce cost and increase efficiency.[43]

Mainstream public administration has generally ignored or remained impervious to this trend till recently, as they regard ICTs as a merely neutral administrative tool. The widespread use and applications of ICTs and huge budgets by governments for the development of e-governance challenges such beliefs. The impact of adoption of ICTs remains 'a continual source of uncertainty within public administration' in future.[44]

Neoliberal techno-managerial governance

This study on computerisation of land records undertakes a critical view of neoliberal techno-managerial view. Through an intensive study of the policy documents, research works and reports by various organisations and field work involving interviews with key functionaries and focus group discussions, it has sought to analyse the issue of land records modernisation drive of the Indian state initiated since the late 1980s from a broader perspective. The framework is based on the assumption that the land records modernisation programme or computerisation of land records policy initiated by the Indian government is formulated from a perspective of neoliberal techno-managerial ideology.

The features of the policy suggest—(i) the neutrality of ICTs to promote transparency and accountability in land records management and maintenance; (ii) the conviction that land records problems can be handled through realistic approaches like installation of systems with necessary software and hardware, and other electronic instruments; (iii) an apolitical approach to the problem of land records management; (iv) the imperative of minimising bureaucratic discretion and monopoly through ICTs; (v) the delivery of services like land records and their correction on business principles like charging user fees from the users; (vi) incremental nature of changes in the institutional and legal structures for promoting or facilitating market; (vii) top-down policy design formulated by the policy elites and the influence of the multilateral agencies like the World Bank in policy reforms; (viii) a policy implementation

[43] Ibid, pp. 2–3; 11.

[44] Helen Margetts. 2003. 'Electronic Government: A Revolution in Public Administration,' in B. Guy Peters and Jon Pierre. (Eds.) *Handbook of Public Administration*, London, Sage Publications, pp. 366–375.

strategy based on outsourcing, contracting and partnership drawn from NPM and network governance models; and (ix) importance of project leaders for ownership and steering.

The central government recently formulated its strategy called 'change management for e-governance projects' and 'government business process reengineering for e-governance projects' for reorganising the bureaucratic structure to use ICTs in public service delivery and manage the probability of success of e-governance projects. The former seeks to manage the human side of organisational change like training, manpower planning, performance management, communication and creating incentive structures for smoothening the path for adoption of ICTs, and the latter addresses the redesigning of the bureaucratic process, structures and institutional arrangements in a piecemeal approach to make the system 'adaptable to e-governance' for realisation of its benefits.[45] These apolitical techno-managerial strategies deliberately avoid coming to terms with the political, economic and socio-cultural factors of bureaucratic malfeasance in India, placing their faith on techno-managerial strategies.

It is necessary to understand that the objectives of the e-governance policy of the Indian state are essentially techno-managerial in nature. Similarly, the National Land Records Modernisation Programme (NLRMP) as 'a high-tech and complex project'[46] seeks to computerise the land records, digitise maps, integrate registry with tahsil /taluka/ mandal (an administrative unit at local level or sub-district level within a district that consists of a specified area of land with a city or a village that serves its headquarters, and usually a number of revenue villages and hamlets) and undertake modern land survey and mapping for providing citizen services like issue of Record of Rights (RoRs), online correction, maintenance and updating of land records and 'modernising and bringing efficiency to the land revenue administration as well as offering a comprehensive tool for planning various land based developmental, regulatory and disaster management activities needing location-specific information'

[45] Government of India. 2010. *Change Management for e-Governance Projects & Report on Business Process Reengineering for e-Governance Projects*, Department of Administrative Reforms and Public Governance, Ministry of Personnel, Public Grievances and Pensions, November, New Delhi.

[46] Government of India. 2011. *Annual Report, 2010–2011*, Ministry of Rural Development, New Delhi, p. 177.

and ultimately to switch over from the present historic and colonial nature of presumptive land titles to a conclusive title system.[47]

The Indian government claims that the National Land Records Modernisation Programme (NLRMP) is the biggest e-governance programme in the world and the first successful e-governance initiative for the 'common man.'

> The NLRMP is one of the largest land records modernisation and titling reforms initiative in the world. Each aspect of the NLRMP involves use of high end sophisticated technology for survey, such as aerial photogrammetry, high resolution satellite imagery (HRSI), total stations (TS) and the global positioning system (GPS), and updating and computerisation of land records, digitisation of maps and integration of textual and spatial data, and inter-connectivity between the revenue and registry system...The Cabinet...while approving ...the NLRMP had allowed scope for private sector participation in the programme in the public-private partnership (PPP) mode.[48]

The language of the above quotation is reminiscent of James C. Scott's popular work, *Seeing Like A State: How Certain Schemes to Improve the Human Conditions Have Failed (1998).* It is important to understand the great social and administrative engineering and reordering programme, in the shape of the NLRMP, in the backdrop of the neoliberal economic reforms in India. The socially, regionally and locally complex, diverse and dynamic nature of land records and maps in India is being sought to be simplified and codified through a state-initiated computerisation programme. It can be aptly described as a 'high modernist ideology' which according to Scott is a 'version of the self-confidence about the scientific and technical progress.'

The Indian context

Since the 1990s, the steady growth of the IT sector in India facilitated by the liberalised economic policies pursued by the central government led to the growth of the 'new economy' propelled by the massive growth of exports of IT products and their increasing application in the financial and banking

---

[47] Government of India. 2009. *Annual Report, 2009–2010*, Ministry of Rural Development, New Delhi, pp. 151–152.

[48] Ibid, p. 155.

sectors, and the private and public sectors.[49] The Indian state has formulated an e-governance policy, enacted IT Act, and launched a massive exercise in the computerisation of government offices on a mission mode. The private IT vendors and IT firms have seised the opportunity in expanding their market as the work of computerisation and digitisation are outsourced to private companies.[50]

The study of state becomes central given the importance of land and land records in the everyday lives of Indians, and its political and economic value and the role of the state in initiating the revolutionary policy shift in the land title regime. Further, it becomes imperative to question the role of the state in undertaking such policy changes and shifts, viewed as reforms, and specifically about the computerisation and digitisation of land records maintained at the level of tahsildar and revenue inspectors. The Indian state is viewed here as an idea and system, internalised widely by ordinary Indians, lower government officials, local politicians.

The *patwari* (revenue inspector/ village accountant), tahsildar and sub-registrars and land surveyors play a critical role in the lives of ordinary as well as powerful citizen by virtue of being the officials of the state dealing with the management of land records, hitherto the monopoly function of the state. The role of the *patwari* as the lowest grassroots authority of the state in dealing with maintenance of land records and varied other revenue and administrative nature of duties is highlighted in many studies.[51] The boundary between the state and society at the level of these so-called street level officials is not totally blurred but unclear, fluid and negotiable.

---

[49] Jati Sengupta and Chiranjib Neogi. 2009. *India's New Economy: Industry, Efficiency and Growth*, Houndsmills: UK: Palgrave-Macmillan, p. xii.

[50] For example, various pressure groups and lobbies such as NASSCOM and ASSOCHAM have been sponsoring e-governance conferences, workshops and research projects to highlight the 'transformational' potential of ICTs and their contribution in governance reforms. NASSCOM, an industry association for IT-BPO sector in India, claims that its objective is to 'Transform Business and Transform India' and its mission is to 'is to deepen the IT-BPO industry's footprint in its core markets and expand beyond, building a strategic partnership with its customers.' (see http://www.nasscom.org/vision-and-mission accessed on February 20, 2012).

[51] See for example Paramjit S. Judge. 1989. 'Role of Patwaris in Land Reforms,' *Mainstream*, October, 14, pp. 11–14.

The anthropological understanding of the everyday state by these scholars forms the conceptual understanding of the state in this study:

> Our collective gaze shows how banal, mundane and routinised-how unexotic-so much of the state now is in contemporary India. The idea of the state and the myth of its sublime qualities are still extant, as we have seen, but the everyday structures and institutions of the nation state, in most political and administrative contexts, are now very prosaically at the centre of modern India's imagination.[52]

Such a perspective on understanding the Indian state marks a newer focus on practices of the state, and governmentalities that supplement earlier studies on 'the state and high politics.'[53]

The state in India, notes Neera Chandhoke, is 'pluralised in the collective political imagination'[54] due to the involvement of civil society organisations, private and market organisations, self-help groups and resident welfare organisations, which seek to empower the citizens from being passive recipients of public services to the active participants by mobilising them to secure and assert their rights. Nonetheless, the common citizen and the poor in India look to the state with high expectations and continue to fix responsibility on the state, with the little hope or faith in the civil society or market-based organisation's ability to negotiate their problems. 'It is the state that is central to the collective and individual life—despite all the changes that have been affected through the practices of governance.'[55]

The changing role of the state

The nature of the state in India before the 1990s and after economic liberalisation has undergone a radical change. Now a virtual political consensus exists among political parties about facilitating rapid private investment and economic growth. The nature of the capitalist class since the 1990s has also

---

52 Ibid. p. 26.

53 Niraja Gopal Jayal and Pratap Bhanu Mehta. 2010. *The Oxford Companion to Politics in India*, New Delhi: Oxford University Press, p. xvii.

54 Neera Chandhoke. 2005. 'Seeing' the State in India,' *Economic and Political Weekly*, March 12, p. 1034.

55 Ibid. p. 1036.

changed. With the dismantling of the license regime, there has been 'distinct ascendancy' of the corporate capitalist class, side by side with the weakening of the developmental state. The urban middle class that was earlier associated with the autonomous and developmental state appears to have been disenchanted with the public sector and bureaucracy equating it with corruption and inefficiency. There is now greater social acceptance for managerialism and professionalism as the middle class has come under the strong influence of moral and political values of big capital.[56] The new-found attraction of the middle classes for the computerisation of government offices has been discussed as a neoliberal orientation for the public service delivery and administration.

Land continues to be the critical factor in India's growth and the economic reforms and growing pressure on land have influenced the reorientation of policies for land records management. The *Committee on State Agrarian Relations and the Unfinished Tasks in Land Reform* (2009), in its report claimed that land issues had made their forceful 'reappearance as a matter of national discourse after a significant gap.'[57] From the 1950s to the launch of the Eighth Five Year Plan in 1988, land reforms had carried symbolic political and economic importance for the planners though state agencies admitted their failure in implementing the radical land redistributive measures. Since the 1990s, the issue of land management, coupled with land records maintenance, has come to occupy a prominent place on the public policy agenda as 'the land issue of the marginalised was overwhelmed by the shift in the development paradigm towards neoliberalisation.'[58]

A 'vital mistake' made by the state in India is its continuous neglect of revenue administration and land record management. The revenue department was kept as non-revenue earning and non-plan department and, thus, treated as a burden on the state exchequer despite the growing nature of agrarian unrest and Naxal violence in the country side. The declining share of land revenue to state governments' revenue earning, abolition of land revenue from agricultural land and the almost total neglect of survey and settlement

[56] Partha Chatterjee. 2008. 'Democracy and Economic Transformation in India,' *Artha Vijnana*, L (1), pp. 9–10.

[57] Government of India. 2009. *Report of the Committee on State Agrarian Relations and the Unfinished Task in Land Reform*, Department of Land Relations, MORD, GOI, New Delhi: pp. 144–146; 150–151, 154.

[58] Ibid.

operation and updation of land records and maps by the states are now cited as harming the interest of the poor. The existence of multiple institutions like tahsil, sub-registrar, survey and settlement, urban land holding and survey have made coordination among the agencies very difficult in the maintenance and updating of land records as lands are very dynamic in nature.

A change in the entries in the land records effected in an institution like the tahsil make the same records outdated in other departments like survey and settlement. The committee on *State Agrarian Relations and the Unfinished Task in Land Reform* (2009) has arrived at the conclusion that the present system of land management has lacked transparency, perpetuated a system of rent-seeking relationships with the public and this trend has become more visible since the 1990s, thanks to economic liberalisation and massive demand for land for industrial, commercial, residential purposes and expansion of services and leisure industries. A vicious circle has arisen from lack of accessibility to land records to lack of proper maintenance of land records, to a growing number of outdated and inaccurate land records and rent-seeking behaviour and fraudulent land transactions arising out of the process.

The central government has launched the National Land Records Modernisation Programme (NLRMP) after merging its earlier two centrally sponsored schemes of Computerisation of Land Records (CLR) and Strengthening Revenue Administration and Updating Land Records (SRA&ULR) with the objective of computerising and digitising the land records, maps, integrating tahsils with registry and survey and settlement organisations for achieving the objective of conclusive titling. The Second Administrative Reforms Commission in its report on e-governance in India has also recommended adopting a similar approach to the implementation of the e-governance initiative. It observed that, 'the focus has to be on governance reforms with the technological tools provided by ICT being utilised to bring about fundamental changes in the governmental processes.'[59]

It is also interesting to note that, the World Bank is the main ideological force behind the conscious policy shift from the present presumptive land titles to conclusive land titles which would open up the land market and has recommended 'policy options' and 'priority areas' to be undertaken by

[59] Government of India. 2008. *Second Administrative Commission – Eleventh Report on 'Promoting e-Governance: The Smart Way Forward,'* December, New Delhi, p. 176.

the central government for achieving the objective.[60] The Bank has been consistently associated with all stages of policy formulation and implementation of NLRMP, and has shown its eagerness to finance and provide technical-managerial assistance in the implementation of the land records modernisation programme by the state governments.

The programme of land records computerisation, now redesigned as NLRMP, can thus be seen as part of a larger set of structural and legal changes to liberalise land management in India and a conscious policy design to shift away from the present state-led agrarian reforms to a market-led agrarian regime. A study of the strategies for land reforms during the Tenth and Eleventh Five Year Plans makes it clear that the state in India has already made slow but strategic moves or in Rob Jenkins's word 'reform by stealth' to achieve the objective of a liberal land governance regime.

It may be submitted here that the process of land records modernisation or the computerisation and digitisation of land records is a long term strategy of change in the entire spectrum of institutional-legal and agrarian relationship. The need for correct and up-to-date land records has been reemphasised by the central government when it put forth the draft Land Title Bill in June 2010, that seeks to move away from the present presumptive nature of land title system to a conclusive system of land title with an objective to promote the growth of the land market and land transaction. Hence the need for correct and up-to-date land records being the prerequisite for the success of a title guarantee regime, and the renewed thrust of the government for land record updation and computerisation.

Examining the role of the state, ICTs and governance in the computerisation or modernisation of the land records programme in India is challenging as one has to look at these concepts as both dependent and independent variables. The study cannot be confined to public policy assessment or analysis of the land records modernisation programme alone, which started during 1988–1989 and acquired momentum in each passing year. Comprehensive understanding of neoliberal governance reforms, the reorientation of the state to land records, the role of multilateral funding agency like World Bank and the application, adoption and management of ICTs as a tool of government in the information age helps us to understand the political economy of the land

[60] World Bank. 2007. *India: Land Policies for Growth and Poverty Reduction*, Report No. 38298-In, July 9, pp. xiii–xiv;61–62.

records modernisation in the light of the failure of land reforms, and the shifting priorities of the state with regard to the management of land in tune with neoliberal reforms. Through its primary focus on land records modernisation, the study also unravels the important trends and emerging issues like network governance, consumer citizenship and its impact on democratic governance, bureaucracy, institutionalism, the role of central and state governments in implementation of the land records modernisation, which have not yet been studied from an inter-disciplinary perspective. The computerisation of land records programme of the Indian state can never be understood in isolation from the specific political and economic context of the reform process. It is only by studying the role of the state, ICTs and governance together, as these are invariably interlinked, one may acquire a comprehensive understanding of the subject.

Critical observations/e-governance and its limitations

The governance discourse has been able to forge a network of relationship with the state, civil society and market. Contrary to the cyber optimists' beliefs, e-governance practices have not led to accountability and transparency and increased productivity; yet, states across the world have not forsaken their belief that e-governance would be a panacea for bad governance.

1. There is lack of integration and cohesion with the contemporary public administration theories and research with the growing 'theories', and 'models' of e-government, or e-governance.
2. Much of the research on e-government lacks any theoretical framework and research methods. Neither in theory building nor in applications of theory has e-government research helped to significantly improve e-government in practice. In the absence of methodological rigour, many research works on e-government carry a note of over-optimism and hype, and lack of balance on the impact of e-government.[61]
3. Most of the literature on e-government (produced by public managers or cyber-utopians) on the impact of e-government has been normative, prescriptive and predictive in nature. We find very few writings which have attempted an interdisciplinary and critical study of ICT

[61] Richard Heeks. 2007. 'Analyzing e-Government Research: Perspectives, Philosophies, Theories, Methods and Practice,' *Government Information Quarterly*, 24, pp. 243–265.

application, adoption and management in the public sector and government departments, and its impact on institutional changes, democratic governance and the rights of citizens.

4. We are yet to come across e-governance literature which provides an in-depth and systematic study of the impact that ICT interventions have on the internal workflow or rationalisation of workload in public sector organisations from an institutional perspective. Institution here refers to 'authoritative, established, rule like procedures in society with self sustaining character' and from an institutional perspective, ICT is not simply a technical artifact, but an institution in its own right, taking shape in relationship with other institutions of contemporary society.
5. The most important limitation of the various studies on e-governance is the absence of any research on the role of the state or the study of public policy or policy support that plays a critical role by making a conscious policy shift in promoting e-governance. The state has been the real mover in the adoption of ICTs across the world. The shift to a neo-liberal economy, exposure to forces and ideas such as reinventing government, NPM, network governance, minimalist state and success of ICTs in e-commerce have been the ideological factors behind the acceptance of e-government for reshaping and reforming the functioning of the public sector. The e-governance initiatives in India cannot be understood in isolation from these larger changes in the policy domain of the country.
6. A number of e-government programmes use and adopt ICTs that are applied in the private sector or are managerial and entrepreneurial in nature. None of these studies, however, highlight the question whether the IT strategies and practices employed in the private sector should be adopted to the public sector or to what extent the public sector informatisation process should outsource its ICT requirements. Such issues are crucial in studying the role of the state in e-government.[62]
7. The e-government initiatives by the state with the help of private IT firms has not eclipsed the state's role of steering as well as rowing

[62] Bruce Rocheleau. 2007. 'Whither E-Government?,' *Public Administration Review*, 67(3), p. 584.

(policy execution). The state, despite outsourcing the e-government works to private vendors, still retains its role in designing, adopting and overseeing the implementation of all policies and policy instruments. The government and governance are both complementary in the process without merging themselves. In the information age, the state still plays a crucial role in the implementation of its ICT policy, growth, facilitation and adoption of ICTs and legal framework for enabling e-government and e-commerce transactions.[63]

8. The ascendance of neoliberal governance constitutes a specific political rationality that is focused and centred on certain widely accepted nostrums and theoretical assumptions that currently informs policy making. According to Mark Beeson and Ann Firth, political rationalities are particular and history-specific instances similar to Foucault's concept of governmentality which 'refer to a particular way of thinking about government' and 'which has its object the economic security and prosperity of the state itself.'[64]

The emergence of neoliberal political rationality since the 1980s is a manifestation of new ways of thinking about national economy and their possible management. Government is itself a problem and a complex activity that cannot be viewed simply from the implementation of a particular political or economic policy. Therefore the incorporation of normative economic and political ideas into governmental practice is always partial and requires administrative techniques and forms of political calculation which alter the normative ideas and their purposes.

Thus it can be argued that in the neoliberal economic regime, reorganisation of the public service delivery mechanism in line with market principles has affected deeply the structure, role and logic of the state. Foucauldian ideas of political power beyond the state, analysed by Nikolas Rose and Peter Miller, are relevant here to understand the problem of the contemporary neoliberal government. According to Rose and Miller, the concept of governmentality

---

[63] See Andrew Jordan et al. 2005. 'The Rise of New Policy Instruments in Comparative Perspective: Has Governance Eclipsed Government?,' *Political Studies*, 35, pp. 477–496. Christopher May. 2002. *The Information Society: A Sceptical View*, Malden, MA (USA), Blackwell Publishers, pp. 127–145.

[64] Mark Beeson and Ann Firth. 1998. 'Neo-Liberalism as a Political Rationality: Australian Public Policy Since the 1980s,' *Journal of Sociology*, 34(3), pp. 216–217.

drew our attention to a certain way of thinking and acting embodied in all attempts to know and govern the population with the objective of maximising the wealth, health and happiness of the population.

> Knowledge is thus central to these activities of government... for government is the domain of cognition, calculation, experimentation and evaluation. And we argue government is intrinsically linked to the activities of expertise, whose role is ... of enacting assorted attempts at the calculated administration of diverse aspects of conduct through countless, often competing, local tactics of education, persuasion, inducement, management, incitement, motivation and encouragement.[65]

According to Foucault, 'the state can only be understood in its survival and its limits on the basis of the general tactics of governmentality', i.e. way of thinking how to control or regulate populations in the societies.[66] One needs to look into the practices of the government in order to understand the problem of the state. There are two dimensions of governmentality: political rationality and set of technologies of government. The relationship between the political rationality and technologies of government are close. This understanding leads us to explain the problem of government in terms of political rationalities and governmental technologies. By political rationality, it implies the discursive field of exercise of power by diverse authorities and their moral justifications (e.g., plans, policies, projects and practices). Secondly, the governmental technologies refers as the humble and mundane mechanisms by which authorities seek to 'instantiate government', i.e., techniques of notation, computation, calculation, procedures of examination, assessments, surveys and standardisation systems, building and architectural forms, land records, statistics and so on.[67]

---

[65] Nikolas Rose and Peter Miller. 1992. 'Political Power Beyond the State: The Problematics of the Government,' *The British Journal of Sociology*, 43 (2), p. 175.

[66] Thomas Lemke. 2002. 'Foucault, Governmentality, and Critique,' *Rethinking Marxism*, 14(3), Fall, p. 58.

[67] Dorte Salskov-Iversen et al. 2008. 'The Governmentality of Globalizing Managerial Discourse: The Case of New Public Management in Local Government Practices,' in Bidyut Chakravorty and M Bhattacharya (Eds) *The Governance Discourse: A Reader*, New Delhi: Oxford University Press, pp. 188–189.

Conceptual framework

The impact of computerisation of land records and the role of the state in driving such e-government initiatives, and of the application of information technology for public service delivery and its impact is the focus of this study.

Information and Communication Technologies (ICTs) in the proposed research is understood from a layman's perspective as basically information handling tools that comprise a set of goods, applications and services that are used to store, process, retrieve, distribute, communicate and exchange information. This includes the 'old' ICTs of radio, television, telephone, fax and scanner and the 'new' ICTs of computers, satellite and the wireless technology, mobile phones and internet. Convergence of technologies now enables these to work together and combine to form a 'networked world.' The revolutionary potential of the ICTs lies in its capacity to connect organisations and individuals across the world instantaneously at a very low cost. We have conceptualised ICTs not merely as a tool or enabler but rather as an ensemble that contextualises ICTs application to activities and interactions performed in specific social, political, economic and cultural contexts.[68]

Most of the definitions of e-government or e-governance are loaded with strategies and motivations to achieve excellence in service delivery based on the use of internet technology. The term e-government gained currency only in the 1990s when internet became popular in the public domain, though the history of ICTs use goes back to the beginning of computer history. There exists a divergent perspective on the very concept of e-government. Some view it as a transactional mechanism to deliver services to citizens only, while others perceive it as a means to achieve continuous rationalisation of public service and some others look for comprehensive adoption of ICTs in government and public sector offices. Many of the definitions of e-government range from a perspective of technological determinism to a cautious approach to ICT's ability to make government better with three explicit goals viz., more efficient government, better services to citizens and improved democratic process. E-government is understood here as the use of ICTs in communicative processes involved in government activities. This concept addresses the broader

[68] Maung K. Sein and G. Harindranath. 2004. 'Conceptualising the ICT Artifact: Toward Understanding the Role of ICT in National Development,' *The Information Society*, 20(1), pp. 18–19.

issues of application of ICTs for better results and requirements of process engineering or organisational changes for a successful adoption of ICTs.[69]

Most e-governance and e-government research tend to use the two terms interchangeably as most of the literature on ICT-driven reform projects, such as public service delivery improvement, bringing better efficiency and transparency, is produced by government agencies. Most of the definitions on ICT applications for government highlight e-governance rather than e-government as they focus on the outcomes for society. While *e-government* is concerned with how to optimise the function of traditional government processes by the application of ICTs, *e-governance* is concerned with the transformative impact of ICTs on state in dealing with the collective problems of society. If governance is construed as the growing involvement of non-state actors in managing collective problems, then e-governance could be understood as the active usage of ICTs for such collective problem solving. E-governance is therefore described here as a vision as well process by which the ICTs are increasingly adopted to support governance mechanisms at all levels, involving all types of actors and governance functions.[70]

Sharon S. Dawes has listed five interrelated objectives which are basically seen from the perspective of linear development from e-government to e-governance. She suggests e-governance as policy framework based on statutes and policies, and which could be used for enhanced public service, high-quality and cost-effective government operation, citizen engagement in democratic process, for administrative and institutional reform of process and structures as well as culture of the government business with emphasis on accountability, transparency and trust.[71]

Seen from these broad objectives, e-governance can be understood as not merely an adoption of ICTs and organisational change but also facilitating citizen participation and interaction. Both the concept of e-government

---

[69] Ake Gronlund. 2007. 'Electronic Government' in Ari-Veikko Antiroiko and Matti Malkia (Eds.) *Encyclopedia of Digital Government*, Hershey: Idea Group Reference, pp. 634–639.

[70] Mathias Finger and Thomas Langenberg. 2007. 'Electronic Governance' in Ari-Veikko Antiroiko and Matti Malkia (Eds.) *Encyclopedia of Digital Government*, Hershey: Idea Group Reference, pp. 629–632.

[71] Sharon S. Dawes. 2008. 'The Evolution and Continuing Challenges of E-governance,' *Public Administration Review, 68 (Spl Issue)*, p. 87.

and e-governance are supportive of each other's objectives and missions and satisfy diverse administrative and political missions. While e-government 'provides governmental services electronically, usually over the web, to reduce physical character of customer transactions,' e-governance on the other hand, 'envisions employing the web and internet to overhaul how the state conducts its democratic dealings by networked interactions with citizens to foster transparency and participation.'[72] In all these conceptual analyses, the role of the citizen is reduced to that of a consumer of services and the objectives and the means to attend e-government and e-governance are grounded in a techno-managerial notion. The ultimate objective is to reinvent or reform or strengthen the existing governance system with the help of ICTs.

State here is understood as 'a set of institutions and structures' and 'stateness or saliency of the state.'[73] Thus it 'encompasses not only state institutions but also and indeed substantially state projects, practices and discourses.'[74] The concept of the state is broad and inclusive and includes 'apparatus and its relation to society, in terms of what it is and what it does.'[75] When one studies the role of the state in land records modernisation, one looks into 'the state as an effect' on the process.[76] The Indian state is conceptualised as a neoliberal state that plays a facilitator role in the market-driven information economy, but at the same time, remains a dirigiste state. It not only is a key player in policy implementation in accordance with a pre-determined set of objectives, but also a consumer and owner, regulator, arbiter and leader of the information world in its domain.[77] Such a perspective is justified on the ground that the government as an agent of the state consciously chooses ICTs as new instrumentalities of

[72] Donald J. Calista and James Melitski. 2007. 'E-Government and E-Governance: Converging Constructs of Public Sector Information and Communication Technologies,' *Public Administration Quarterly*, Spring, p. 101–102.

[73] J.P. Nettl. 1968. 'The State as a Conceptual Variable,' *World Politics*, 20(4), pp. 562; 579; Philip Abrams. 1988. 'Notes on the Difficulty of Studying the State,' *Journal of Historical Sociology*, 1(1), March, pp. 58–89.

[74] Niraja Gopal Jayal. 1999. *Democracy and the State: Welfare, Secularism, and Development in Contemporary India*, New Delhi: Oxford University Press, pp. 9–12.

[75] Ibid.

[76] Timothy Mitchell. 1991. 'The Limits of the State; Beyond Statist Approaches and Their Critics,' *The American Political Science Review*, 85(1), pp. 94–95.

[77] Nick Moore. 1997. 'Neo-Liberal or Dirigiste? Policies for an Information Society,' *Political Quarterly*, 68(3), pp. 278–279.

governing and undertakes policy measures for their comprehensive application in its acts of governing.

The computerisation of the land records programme or the National Land Records Modernisation Programme (NLRMP) has important implications for governance. Here it is argued that both government plays a steering as well as rowing role in land records computerisation or modernisation in partnership with non state agencies and adopts various policy instruments for implementation of the policy objectives. Nevertheless, several concerns of governance such as participation, accountability, transparency, fairness, access to information, regulation, structural and legal reforms and rule of law are intricately involved in the current land records modernisation programme. Role of ICTs in enhancing the quality of public service, the participation of civil society and private sectors in the land records modernisation programme inexorably draws the government into the detailed process of designing, adopting and overseeing the implementation of the policy.

Computerisation of land records here means both the computerisation of Record of Rights (RoRs) and cadastral maps. The term land records is a generic term which covers the varieties of land records and registers including the map and RoRs prepared by the settlement authorities, registered sale deeds available at the sub-registrar office, the records and registers maintained by tahsildar and revenue inspectors at their respective offices and the registered sale deeds executed and preserved at the sub-registrar's office. Among these, the RoRs and the cadastral maps corresponding to the plot numbers and their boundaries are of most significance and computerisations of these records are central to the land records modernisation programme.

There are other components in National Land Records Modernisation Programme like construction of modern record rooms, electronic integration of registry with tahsil/taluk and modern survey but the computerisation of land records remain the central focus of the programme. Computerisation or modernisation of land records are therefore sometimes used interchangeably in the book.

The impact of the computerisation of land records (CLR) on the quality of democracy in governance needs to be looked at from the context of the state's efforts in strengthening the administrative mechanism by facilitating greater accessibility and transparency in maintaining and updating land records. Given the unequal nature of land holding and prevalence of a varied nature of land tenures, the CLR may have a serious impact on the landlord (state) and tenant relationships.

The poor and illiterate tenants may find it difficult to access their land records online owing to their socio-economic deprivation. Therefore, the concept of democratic governance is here understood as a legal-administrative arrangement and the processes which enable the common citizen to easily access their land records or avail of public service delivery in a transparent, smooth, efficient and equitable manner. The notion of democratic governance would imply the creation of fair and inclusive legal-institutional arrangements with particular concern for the poor farmers/tenants. The prospects of CLR and online delivery of public services furthering democratic governance are contingent upon the public official's role in the creation and application of ICTs. The nature of legal-institutional reform is also an important factor in the prospects of democratic governance in the modernisation of land records management.

The scope of the book

This book offers a comparative study of policies concerning public service delivery and impact of the computerisation of land records on tahsils/taluks of Karnataka and Odisha as also the role of the state in the process. The field studies were conducted during 2009 to 2011. Suffice to say here that, such a study of the computerisation of land records programme helps us to understand the implementation of the public policies in its broader as well as specific context. Karnataka is projected by the central government as the role model for the other states for implementing the centrally sponsored scheme of the computerisation of land records and making them available online through its e-governance project called Bhoomi.

Odisha has taken up a number of initiatives in the computerisation of land records. Both the states had started computerisation of land records simultaneously but whereas Karnataka has emerged as a role model through its Bhoomi project, Odisha has lagged behind. That apart, selection of Odisha as a unit of study is because of the fact that it is the poorest state in India and an agriculturally backward state in which nearly 40% of its total population belong to SCs and STs groups.

There exists a wide variety of land tenure systems since the British period in Odisha as well as Karnataka. In such a context, modernisation of land records management through computerisation process calls for an in-depth study. The study of the public policies, institutional arrangements and role of public officials, user satisfaction and participation of stakeholders is focused upon random selection of tahsils/taluks and districts in the two states and field studies are carried out. The recently released *India: E-governance Readiness Report, 2005* indicates that Karnataka occupies the first place in terms of its e-preparedness while Odisha occupies the bottom position. Further a comparative study made by Public Affairs Centre, Bengaluru shows that Karnataka is one of leading states in India for providing minimum public service delivery whereas Odisha occupies the bottom place in achieving the progress in public service delivery.

Methodological approach

The study has extensive reference to primary as well as secondary sources. Both exploratory and descriptive methods of research are adopted as we focus on the role of the state in promoting ICT intervention by computerisation of land-records and facilitating e-governance process as well as its impact. Primary sources such as Planning Commission reports, various government reports and other secondary sources like assessment/impact studies and findings conducted by UNDP, World Bank, and NGOs have been examined in our research. For the collection of data from primary sources, interviews with the revenue officials have been conducted and non-participant observation technique adopted to observe the present process of the computerisation of land records and their delivery. Some tahsils /taluks in Karnataka and Odisha are selected through random sampling. Data have been collected firsthand from the tahsils/taluks offices where people file applications for getting online land records and updating of the same through mutation process.

Random interviews were conducted with the farmers and land holders who obtain online RoRs (Record of Rights) at these offices in order to find out their views and opinions on the whole process of computerisation of land records. A comparative analysis is made with regard to the collected data from both sources, and afterwards findings from the field are analysed and presented. Out of 171 tahsils in Odisha and 141 taluks in Karnataka, random sample of some tahsils were taken up and the computerisation of land-records were studied by way of observation and interviews. In addition to this, group discussions were conducted among the villagers who had obtained the copy of computerised land records from the tahsil/taluk counters and got their land records corrected through mutation process.

A comparative study of the computerisation of land records in Odisha and Karnataka becomes useful from the point of view of gaining better knowledge about the governance system and processes of the two states. The role of the state in land records computerisation and its impact on bureaucracy, citizen and organisational structure of the tahsil administration has been examined in detail through comparative case studies of Odisha and Karnataka.

The problems in the implementation of computerisation of land records, the challenges of applying, adopting and managing Information and Communication Technologies (ICTs) in the above-mentioned states, the role of bureaucracy and the long term and short term impacts on democratic governance and citizenship has also been taken into account. The study critiques the prevalence of an apolitical and ahistorical approach to land records modernisation by the Indian state which does not take into account the complex historical evolution and diversity of land records management and the importance of political factors that determine the nature and context of land records modernisation and management.

It has also examined the study of the process of governance reforms and the agencies involved in it such as the bureaucracy, private IT firms, central government agencies, and the World Bank. Focusing on the effectiveness of ICTs in bringing about an efficient management of land records and better service delivery, it explores the shifts in public policy objectives on the comprehensive computerisation of the land records process in the context of neoliberal governance reforms in India, and the impact of ICTs on democratic governance as well as on citizens.

2

E-Governance in Public Policy Discourse in India

The discourse of e-governance has struck its root in India as a consequence of her achievement in IT sector and the English educated middle class population. Thanks to the liberal economic reforms, the rise of IT professionals and software export earnings has led some observers to propose that ICTs will enable India to leapfrog industrial age economies to information age.[1]Undoubtedly, such developments have also strong significance for governance reforms and citizenship. There is growing influence of the IT entrepreneurs and NGOs who advocate the adoption of IT corporate governance model to the public bureaucracy.[2] Ideologically, e-governance discourse in India promises to bring political transparency and techno-managerial notion of governance. In India, the whole discourse of e-governance is anchored on using ICTs to prevent corruption. Mazzarella observes:

> The Indian incorporation of the information society did not just invoke both a new commodity fetish (sleek consumer computing) and a new human right (the right to information). Computers networked by means of the Internet…offer a new weapon against the most ingrained of official infirmities: corruption…

---

[1] C. J. Fuller and Haripriya Narsimhan. 2007. 'Information Technology Professional and the New-Rich Middle Class in Chennai,' *Modern Asian Studies*, 41(1), p. 123.

[2] Shimanthi Dasgupta. 2008. 'Success, Market and Ethics: Information Technology and the Shifting Politics of Governance and Citizenship in the Indian Silicon Plateau,' *Cultural Dynamics*, 20(3), pp. 213–244.

> the attraction was rooted in a naïve notion of the inherent incorruptibility of the digitised information, as opposed to the surreptitious modifications to which handwritten ledger entries were so manifestly subject.[3]

In understanding the current e-governance discourse in India, it is necessary to understand the contemporary ideological trends and practices in public policy sphere. Govindan Parayil locates the euphoria of IT led development beliefs in the context of contemporary neoliberal developmental discourses advocated by donor agencies and many civil society organisations in the context of failure of the modernisation and dependency theories of development. India is not immune from such intellectual trends. 'ICT fetishism and cyber libertarian development thinking has enveloped the discourse on information revolution and socio-economic development in the world.'[4]

Scholars in India have been confronted with two types of issues with regard to neoliberal reform agenda in India viz., the kind of governance institutions or arrangements or specifically political institutions that are required by an economically liberalising, multireligious and multicultural society, and the capability of the neoliberal governance agenda to retain an emphasis on redistributive and welfare goals and address the rights, claims and demands for justice of disadvantaged groups.[5]

The ongoing policy reform of the state and governance structure has given the necessary back up to the neoliberal economic reforms. It is important to remember that administrative reforms and change are not value-neutral terms rather guided by prevalent socio-economic and political forces and interests as well as history specific. The administrative reforms that gained momentum since the 1990s with implementation of the New Economic Policy (NEP) and acceptance of external aid conditionalities of IMF and World Bank by India had ideological imprints than mere techno-bureaucratic content.[6] The restructuring of the state in India has some significance in so far as it is an

---

[3] William Mazzarella. 2006. 'Internet X-Ray: E-Governance, Transparency and the Politics of Immediation in India,' *Public Culture*, 18 (3), p. 477.

[4] Govindan Parayil (Ed). 2006. *Political Economy and Information Capitalism in India: Digital Divide, Development and Equity*, Houndsmill: Palgrave-Macmillan, p. 2.

[5] 3. Gurpreet Mahajan, Sudha Pai and Niraja Gopal Jayal. 1994. 'State and New Liberal Agenda in India,' *Economic and Political Weekly*, 29(19), 7 May, pp. 1112–1116.

[6] Kuldeep Mathur. 2008. 'Administrative Reforms and Demand for Good Governance,' in Bidyut Chakravarty and Mohit Bhattacharya (Eds.) *The Governance Discourse: A Reader*, New Delhi, pp. 113–114.

attempt to incorporate market rationality in it. The Eighth Five Year Plan has clearly stressed the need for reorientation of the role of the state e.g., from centrally planned economy to market led economy and has advocated shedding the prevalent developmental practices and precepts which have outlived its utility.[7] The reasons for such an ideological shift, which would be subsequently discussed, are due to the crisis of the welfare state, failure to sustain high growth rate, corruption and bureaucracy and their poor performance.[8]

On the other hand, scholars taking an institutionalist stance, give importance to the functioning of the public institutions as these are the sites of the exercise of state power and go into the making of the state. The functioning of the public institutions in India is a matter of concern for democratic governance and mostly a modest quality could be attributed to them. The poor performance or lack of effectiveness in attaining the stated goals by the public institutions in India is not due to its capture by elites but lack of the capability of the personnel to govern the system and deliver the goods.[9]

ICTs for good governance: a public policy perspective

The role of the state in India is very important in understanding public policies for promoting e-government and Information and Communication Technologies (ICTs). The case of Andhra Pradesh is an example of state support, through promotional public policies for the growth of the IT industries. The state government in the 1990s provided infrastructure like land, buildings, exemptions from sales tax and concession on import duties and amendment to labour laws etc that created a favourable atmosphere for the growth of IT industries there.[10] India's success in software exports and growth in ITES has created a favourable atmosphere in furthering the growth of IT industries by promoting the e-governance agenda through the involvement of the state machineries.

---

[7] Government of India. 1992. See 'Preface and Objectives and Orientation' in to *Eighth Five Year Plan,* Planning Commission of India, Yoyana Bhawan,New Delhi, pp. 1–19.

[8] Sara Joseph. 2007. 'Neoliberal Reforms and the Democratic Agenda in India,' *Economic and Political Weekly,* 4 August 2007, pp. 3213–16.

[9] Devesh Kapur and Pratap Bhanu Mehta, (Eds.) 2005. Introduction to *Public Institutions in India: Performance and Design*, New Delhi: Oxford University Press, pp. 1–22.

[10] T. H. Chowdhury. 2002. 'Information Technology and Development: Necessary Conditions,' *Economic and Political Weekly,* September 21, pp. 3886–3887.

Systematic computerisation in a phased manner of all government offices and computerisation of land records, development of appropriate management of information systems as an integral part of administrative reforms and easy access to the government information to the public on the services and activities of government were accepted as one of the agendas for effective and responsive government in the conference of chief secretaries held under the chairmanship of Prime Minister in November 1996.[11] At the third national conference on e-governance, at Bengaluru (1999) the IT secretaries of the states and UTs committed themselves 'to providing one-stop nonstop, efficient, effective, responsive, transparent citizen governance through use of information technology' without however specifying the time schedule for such overambitious objectives.[12]

In 2002, the *Report of the Committee on India Vision, 2020* declared that India's economy would be substantially increased if it uses ICTs in its governance, social sectors like education, health, employment etc as IT is a revolutionary force in bridging the digital divide between the rich and poor and can 'increase government accountability and stimulate democratic participation.'[13] Thus, one can easily get an impression that the current thrust of application of ICTs in public sector reforms in India has integrated the objective of serving the public, as well helping to the growth of indigenous industries.

The Ninth Five Year Plan provided clear support to the IT policy. The Plan promised to establish in somewhat rhetorical sense the position of the Indian state. The Plan document asserted that, 'Government of India has resolved to make India a global IT superpower and front runner in the Information revolution.' To achieve this ambitious objective, the central government had set up a National Task Force on Information Technology and Software Development under the chairmanship of Jaswant Singh in May 1998. In its second report, the Task Force suggested making conscious efforts to spread 'IT culture to all walks of life' and also recommended earmarking one to three per cent of the budget of all ministries/departments for expenditure on IT applications as it would help to increase productivity, timeliness of project

[11] Government of India. 1996. 'Action Plan for Effective and Responsive Government', DARPG, Ministry of Personnel and Public Grievances, New Delhi reprinted in *Indian Journal of Public Administration*, XLIV(2), April–June,1998, pp. 646–647.

[12] Anupama Katakam. 1999. 'Towards e-Governance' *Frontline*, December 10, p. 78.

[13] Government of India. *Report of the Committee on India Vision 2020*", Planning Commission of India, Yoyana Bhawan, December, pp. 57–61.

implementation and minimisation of cost overrun as well as pave the way for the growth of domestic IT industry and e-commerce. The recommendation was thus a clear reflection of sustaining high growth rate in the IT sector and opening up the domestic market base.[14] One could thus well understand how e-commerce on ICTs has direct linkages on the promotional role of government in the e-governance sector.

The application of ICTs in public administration limited to improving the public service delivery was thus adopted as a strategy to promote growth of e-commerce in India. Government of India in the current Eleventh Five Year Plan has continued its earlier approach of combining the growth of IT industry and promoting e-governance policy. The National e-Governance Policy (NeGP) launched by the central government has calibrated its policy of playing a proactive role in such a manner that use of ICTs in all development programmes for increasing transparency will simultaneously create demand for massive and sustained growth of domestic IT market. The central government's plans to promote ICTs through e-panchayati raj, e-post office, e-education, e-judiciary through village cyber kiosks as it has expected that such policy measures will automatically spur domestic IT market and industry.[15]

The National Task Force on Information Technology and Software Development (1999) in its report also recommended the creation government wide electronic information infrastructure for e-delivery of services which will be beneficial to government and businesses, reengineering the government services to improve efficiency, transparency and economy in single window or point service delivery. It further outlined development of public private partnerships and a business model for setting up of Service Delivery points (SDP) or cyber kiosks for electronic delivery of services on payment of transaction fees, recommended setting up the National Institute of Smart Government (NISG), reengineering the state administrative institutes and development of unique identity cards or smart cards for citizens which will have a multifunction card that will enable them to receive public services.[16]

---

[14] Government of India. 1999. 'Information Technology' in *Ninth Five Year Plan, Volume-II,* Planning Commission of India, Yoyana Bhawan, New Delhi, para. 7.5.1.

[15] Government of India. *Report of the Working Group on Information Technology, Eleventh Five Year Plan,2007–2012,* Department of Information Technology, Ministry of Communication and Information Technology, New Delhi, p, pp. 63;93–99.

[16] Government of India. 1999. *Report of National Task Force on Information Technology and Software Development, IT Action Plan-III,* Chapter–IV, New Delhi.

The central government set up National Institute of Smart Government (NISG), a not for profit company, under U/S 25 of the Companies Act, 1956 with 49 percent of equity by the government at Hyderabad. The objective of the Institute would be 'to raise social awareness of and capability in smart governance by promoting policies and practices which reinforce the hassle free environment for the citizens' and 'to develop high-impact e-governance applications in delivery of citizen services for central and state governments.'[17]

In the Tenth Five Year Plan, the central government went ahead in adopting e-governance as an end as well as means of administrative reforms and 'good governance.' Government of India even expected that the whole approach to governance in public service delivery would undergo a 'fundamental shift' through e-governance. The cumbersome bureaucratic procedures and lack of transparency in administration-oriented public services delivery would be changed by the application, adoption and management of ICTs which 'can have immense impact on the quality of services that the government delivers to its citizens and can, also demystify the government procedures making them citizen friendly.' E-governance was conceptualised as electronic interaction with citizens transforming them from passive recipients of government services to active citizens involved beyond the electronic government confined to mere delivery of government services. The advantages of e-governance included increasing transparency and accountability, impacting corruption, greater convenience for workers as well as citizens, revenue growth and cost reduction.[18]

Legal basis of e-governance

The enactment of the Information Technology Act, 2000 (w. e. f. 09/06/2000) is an important milestone in legalising the application of ICTs in trade and commerce and 'to promote efficient delivery of government services by means of reliable electronic records.'

By enacting and implementing the IT Act, India became one of the earlier countries to enact cyber laws and create the basic legal infrastructure for the promotion and growth of e-commerce as it enabled companies and

[17] http://www.darpg.nic.in/arpgwebsite/Reforminitiatives/eGovernance/nationalinstituteofsmartgovernance/nisg.asp.(accessed 16 September 2009)

[18] Government of India. 2001. *Report of the Working Group on Convergence and E-governance for the Tenth Five Year Plan, 2002–2007*, planning Commission of India, Yoyana Bhawan, November, New Delhi, pp. 33–35.

individuals to interact with different government departments thereby save cost and manpower.[19] Section 4 to 10 of the said Act lays the foundations of e-governance in India by giving legal recognition to electronic records and digital signatures, permitting the use of electronic records and digital signatures in government and its agencies, retention of electronic records, publication of rule, regulation, etc. in electronic Gazette. The statue however shall not to confer any right on the citizens to insist documents should be accepted in electronic form by government agencies. The last provision in the Act thus clearly avoids fixing a timeframe for e-governance and ushering in of the so called paperless office as predicted by cyber optimists. The act has avoided defining e-governance or e-government, mechanism for parliamentary control, and coordination between the government organisations of central and state government, role of government organisations in promoting the e-governance initiatives, process reengineering and financial arrangements etc.[20]

The Act has created deep apprehension in the minds of academics, human rights activists, civil rights groups for giving unbridled power to the authorities to prevent any form of cyber crimes, threat to computer security and situations arising from cyber attacks. The statute betrays the legislature's scepticism of the internet and at the same time requires an act to grapple with challenges posed by cyberspace and dynamics of ICTs.[21] The discretionary power given by the state to police in the Act is a cause of worry. It is also said that the IT Act, 2000 straddles the known and the unknown as evidenced by the substantial nature of amendments that the Act has undergone recently by enactment of the IT (Amendment) Act, 2008. Arguably, it can be said that the Act is basically technical in nature and addresses the needs of technical opacity rather than transparency and not much debate or discussion had taken place in Parliament or at the level of civil society about the pitfalls of the law.[22] Recently, the Act

---

[19] Pavan Duggal. 2005. 'Cyber Laws and Its Implementation in India' in R. K. Bagga, Kenneth Kenniston and Rohit Raj Mathur (Eds.) *The State, IT and Development*, New Delhi: Sage Publications, pp. 136–148.

[20] Government of India. 2008. *Eleventh Report of the Second Administrative Commission, Promoting e-Governance: The Smart Way Forward, New Delhi*, p. 169.

[21] Subhajit Basu. 2005. 'Indian Information Technology Act, 2000: Review of the Regulative Powers under the Act,' *International Review of Law, Computers and Technology*, 19(2), p. 225.

[22] Sruti Chaganti. 2003. 'Information Technology Act: Danger of Violation of Civil Rights,' *Economic and Political Weelky*, 23 August 2003, pp. 3587–3595 and also Shiv

underwent drastic amendments that reveal the dynamic nature of the ICTs makes the regulative power of the state obsolete day by day, the wide ranging criticism of its provisions and the difficulties in implementing the same. [23]

In India, ICT driven development and institutional reforms have gained importance under the current neoliberal economic policies. Governments both at the centre and states seek to overcome the bureaucratic problems that stymie the proper implementation of developmental programmes as well as reform measures. The role of social, cultural and structural factors of state backwardness has been set aside and technological solutions by way of policy implementation have found growing acceptance in policy making circles. The current thinking for effecting techno-managerial reforms in administration under the rubric of governance reforms for promoting transparency, accountability and access to information is also spearheaded by several donor agencies and multilateral institutions and cyber utopians basing their arguments on the hypothesised benefits from e-government. [24]

The Tenth Five Year Plan laid emphasis on governance standards and the proper implementation and targeting of beneficiaries which depended upon efficient institutions and delivery mechanisms and a supportive framework of rules and procedures. The government was expected to play an important role in improving personal capability and community capacity building and improving the efficiency of the public sector. E-governance was defined by the Indian state as 'the application of IT to the processes of government functioning in order to bring about Simple, Moral, Accountable, Responsive and Transparent (SMART) governance' with an emphasis on reengineering of rules and procedures, selective application of ICT solutions in public service delivery, developing the formalities for Government to Citizen (G2C), Government to Business (G2B) and Government to Government (G2G) domains, sustainability, standardisation of e-governance programme, emphasis

---

Visvanathan. 2000. 'An Invitation to Quarrel: Case of IT Bill,' *Economic and Political Weekly*, 7 May 2000, pp. 1789–1793.

[23] Government of India. 2009. *The Information Technology (Amendment), 2000* published in the *Gazette of India (Extraordinary) Part-II, Section -1, February 5, 2000, Ministry* of Law and Justice, New Delhi.

[24] Aswani Saith and M. Vijayabaskar. 2008. 'Introduction: ICTs and Indian Social Change-An Agenda for Change' in Aswani Saith and M Vijayabaskar (Eds.) *ICTs and Indian Social Change: Diffusion, Poverty and Governance,* New Delhi: Sage Publications, pp. 14–17.

on PPP model in view of resource crunch and developing suitable softwares in local languages for enabling people to interact and use computers in local languages. [25] The Plan advocated that 'e-governance and IT will have to be given a big push to increase transparency, fair play and make systems faster and user-friendly.'[26]

Further, the Tenth Five Year Plan outlined that IT exports and outsourcing have enabled India to maintain her global lead in the software sector. Information and Communication Technology has not only spawned a new knowledge economy but has helped some sections of people in terms of the creation of wealth and gaining high quality employment. The Indian state has responded by taking up a slew of supportive policy measures that are aimed at maintaining a competitive edge for the domestic software industry; expanding the domestic market and greater use of IT in governance; like setting up a ministry of IT in 1999, rechristened it in 2001 as Ministry of Communication and Information Technology; setting up a National Task Force on IT in July 2000; and enacting IT Act, 2000 for giving legal sanctity to e-commerce and e-governance; creation of websites of central government and state government departments; launching of some e-government initiatives and giving a big push to computerisation of government by earmarking three percent of the budget on application of ICTs; and initiating moves to set up 487 Community Information Centres at the Block headquarters in the North-Eastern states for bridging the digital divide.[27]

It was noted in the Tenth Five Year Plan that e-governance would be promoted both by central and state governments in a major way for improving efficiency and transparency in delivery of public services and to reduce the monopoly power with discretion. To achieve the objective, the master plan of e-governance in the Tenth Five Year Plan outlined some guiding principles such as : a clearly focused vision on e-governance, defining of a range and standards of delivery of information and services to people, sustainability of e-governance programme instead of a passing fad, standardisation of technology, spelling out public–private participation and funding, state and region specific drawing

[25] Government of India. 2002. See 'Governance and Implementation' in *Tenth Five Year Plan, Vol.*-1, Planning Commission of India, Yoyana Bhawan,New Delhi, pp. 177–187.

[26] Ibid, p. 188.

[27] Government of India. 2002. See 'Information Technology' in *Tenth Five Year Plan, Vol.*-11, Planning Commission of India, Yoyana Bhawan, New Delhi, pp. 801–802.

of e-governance plans, emphasis on interactive schemes and development of government to business (G2B), government to citizen (G2C), and government to government (G2G) modalities and inclusion of local and private corporate bodies. Setting up of the National Institute of Smart Governance (NISG), creating a citizen data base through ID and smart cards and development of local language tools and content were also given a thrust for ushering e-governance in India.[28] The foregoing description brings home the point that the wider use of computers to promote efficiency and transparency in public service delivery and develop and use software in Indian languages may be the policy objective but the other integral aspect of the policy is to expand the domestic market for the IT industry. Therefore, it would not be wrong to say that the policy objective of ensuring sustained growth in software and hardware manufacturing sector has been dovetailed with the thrust on e-governance.

The Eleventh Five Year Plan went one step further in outlining the neo-liberal reforms agenda of government and here we find a techno-managerial approach to the so-called 'good governance' in clear formulation. The Plan document even went to the extent of linking the objective of enhancing transparency, accountability and efficiency in administration by adopting its strategies for achieving e-governance. The Eleventh Five Year Plan laid down that inclusive growth and bridging the divide is contingent upon 'good governance' and at the same time based its perspective of 'good governance' on neoliberal ideas by defining broadly to cover all aspects of the interface between individuals and businesses on the one hand and the government on the other. To achieve the objective of promoting the quality of governance, the central government enacted the RTI Act, 2005, launched National e-Governance Plan (NeGP), set up Second Administrative Reforms Commission and brought out a Code of Governance which includes among other things, the improvement of public service delivery by applying ICTs.[29]

Accordingly, e-governance in India aims at the use of ICTs and reengineering the government process for more efficient and effective service delivery to both citizens and business, and delivery of various programmes, projects and schemes. It talks about 'any time anywhere' service provision and disintermediation through the use of ICTs to minimize corruption by setting

---

[28] Ibid, p. 805–811.

[29] Government of India. See in 'Governance' in *Eleventh Five Year Plan*, 2007–2012, Planning Commission of India, Yoyana Bhawan, New Delhi, pp. 223–224.

up citizen service centres on e-Seva model in Hyderabad. 'If attributes of good governance are transparency, efficiency, responsiveness, cost effectiveness, and accountability, e-governance is the means to attain these attributes through the application of technology.'[30] For achieving this policy objective, the government has concentrated on bringing out a business process reengineering by reviewing and redesigning the existing procedures and rules of various departments as its foremost concern so that e-governance strategy with the help of private sector participation would be easier.[31]

The citizen satisfaction in service delivery has been recognised as the basis for governance and public service delivery reforms and the recording the identity of the citizens for developmental and regulatory administration and to create a common platform for service delivery and programme, a database called Unique Identity (UID) in government to citizen domains (G2C) and corporate identity number (CIN) in government to business domains (G2B) would be developed. The UID would be regularly updated and could be used by all departments for better targeting of the beneficiaries.[32] The central government has set up Unique Identification Authority of India (UIDAI) in June 2009.The government claims that the UIDAI programme when fully operational will provide financial inclusion of the poor and marginalised people by better targeting the beneficiaries and smoother delivery of direct services to them. Some of the main features of the UIDAI programme launched in India are: The UID number will provide identity; the UID will prove Identity, not citizenship; a pro-poor approach; enrolment of residents with proper verification; a partnership model of implementation; enrolment will not be mandated; the UIDAI will issue a number, not a card; process to ensure no duplicates and timeliness of completion.[33]

While the UID will create the core data base on citizens as consumers of various service provision, the government has also gone ahead with allocating huge funds for ICT enabled service delivery infrastructure across the country for achieving the e-enabling of various departments for 'any time anywhere' service delivery. To achieve the ambition of providing service delivery at the

[30] Ibid, p. 231.

[31] Ibid , p. 231.

[32] Ibid, pp. 231–232.

[33] Government of India. 2010. *Economic Survey, 2009–2010*. New Delhi: Oxford University Press, pp. 279–280.

doorstep of the citizen, a common service delivery platform is being created. Three important elements of the service delivery framework are:

1. State Wide Area Network (SWAN): This will involve to create an intra governmental network across the state that will provide connectivity from state head quarters to block level offices via district headquarters and will facilitate rolling out of various citizen centric services under Mission Mode Projects (MMPs) under the National e-Governance Plan (NeGP) in all the states and Union Territories.
2. Common Service Centres (CSCs): Also known as cyber kiosks, these are front-end outlets for the service delivery envisaged for delivery of government and private services at the doorsteps of every citizens through the setting up of one lakh CSCs across the country. Such outlets will be implemented in an entrepreneur driven PPP mode.
3. State Data Centre (SDC): Government of India has taken initiatives to set up State Data Centres for all the states and UTs along with disaster recovery system to provide shared, secured and managed infrastructure for consolidating and securely hosting state level data and applications. It would provide management and operation of data and a central repository of data and consolidation of line departments /ministries, internet and internet portal, state messaging infrastructure, remote management and business continuity sites needed for their G2C, G2B, G2G services. Further various Mission Mode Projects (MMPs) unveiled under central, state government control and integrated services are to use the services of SDCs for delivering of their services.[34]

Interestingly, the Mid-term appraisal of the Eleventh Five Year Plan and Twelfth Five Year Plan take note of constraints and changes in adoption and implementation of e-governance mechanisms instead of harping on the cyber optimists' position. The Indian state has admitted that several limiting factors like inefficient service delivery mechanism, inadequate emphasis on portability and scalability of e-governance initiatives, and overemphasis on some 'showpiece projects' that failed to replicate elsewhere due to their success in a 'small, controlled environments' are some of the factors that are responsible

[34] Ibid, pp. 232–233.

for partial results.[35] The current Twelfth Five Year Plan outlines the vision of enacting Electronic Delivery of Services Act enabling the delivery of all government services in electronic mode, acceleration of e-governance adoption and innovation, business process reengineering for creating 'an enterprise architecture framework,' ethical use of ICTs and strengthening data safety and security and capacity building of the staff.[36]

National e-Governance Plan (NeGP)

The most important e-governance policy of the Indian State is the National e-Governance Plan (NeGP) launched in May, 2006. Its proclaimed objective is to benefit the common man and change the functioning of government service delivery by making 'all government services accessible to the common man in his locality, through common service delivery outlets and ensure efficiency, transparency and reliability of such services at affordable costs to realize the basic needs of the common man.'[37] The NeGP seeks to lay emphasis on the need for political ownership of the programme at the national level, a dedicated team for providing leadership, new areas of public private partnership, policies addressing issues of privacy, need to develop the basic support infrastructure, need for pilot projects before scaling up and issues of effecting process reengineering and management of change.[38]

The NeGP aims to 'leverage e-governance optimally and radically change the way the government delivers services to citizens,' addresses the developmental challenges in key areas like education, health, agriculture, implements major programmes, including to change the way the government conducts its own business. 'In fact, key governance like citizen centricity, transparency and efficiency cannot be achieved without the extensive and pervasive use of

[35] Government of India. 2011. *Mid-Term Appraisal of Eleventh Five Year Plan, 2007–2012*, planning Commission of India, Yoyana Bhawan, New Delhi: Oxford University Press, pp. 53–54.

[36] Government of India. 2013. *Twelfth Five Year Plan, 2012–2017, Volume-II*, Planning Commission of India, Yoyana Bhawan, New Delhi: Sage Publications, p. 271 and Government of India. *Report of the Working Group on Information Technology Sector, Twelfth Five Year Plan(2012–2017)*,DIT, Ministry of Information and Communication &Information Technology, New Delhi, p. 2.

[37] Ibid, pp. 233–234.

[38] http://www.mit.nic.in(accessed on November 15, 2009)

technology.'[39] The NeGP at present consists of 27 Mission Mode Projects (MMPs) and eight support components being implemented at the central, state and local levels. Computerisation of land records and e-registration at sub-registrar offices are one of the prominent NeGP programmes. The Department of Information Technology (DIT) has initiated steps for creating Common and Support Infrastructure like State Wide Area Network (SWAN), National/State Data Centres, Common Service Centres, and Electronic Service Delivery Gateways and monitoring and coordinating the implementation of NeGP.[40]

Thus the NeGP claims to lay the foundation for long term growth of e-governance in India and also seeks to lay the governance and institutional mechanisms and appropriate policies and core infrastructure support for the programme.[41] The ambitious programme is sought to be implemented at multiple government, multiple departments, and an involvement of multiple state and corporate agencies as there is a plan for a massive expenditure of 23,000 crores of rupees and in partnership with private enterprises.[42] The problem with such an overambitious informatisation of public sector and public service delivery by massive process reengineering is that the bureaucratic capacity to undertake implementation of such programmes through a network of inter-governmental and inter departmental public and private partnerships is not taken into account or at best overlooked.

The ambitious NeGP policy suffers from severe limitations. The policy does not have a fixed time schedule for implementing the programmes and no monitoring agency is constituted to oversee the implementation of the policy. The Twenty Second Report of the Parliamentary Standing Committee on Information Technology (2005–2006) has summed up the constraints and limitation of NeGP which in fact put a question mark on the viability of the programme and attaining of its objectives. Some of these constraints are lack of capacity of the bureaucracy to conceptualise and implement the scheme and lack of technological infrastructure; lack of resources; leadership and ownership of the project; lack of continuity of the project team and its lack of autonomy to take decision; lack of standards to secure inter operability; poor affordability by the masses; need for multiple language interface; no

---

[39] Ibid.

[40] Government of India. 2007. *Eleventh Five* Year *Plan*, p. 234.

[41] Ibid, p. 234.

[42] http://www.mit.gov.in (accessed on November 28, 2009)

institutional mechanism for replication on mass scale of successful e-governance practices; inadequate project implementation strategy including appropriate PPP/procurement models; inadequate internal capacity of the bureaucracy to conceptualise and implement change; poor data connectivity and poor literacy rate; poor affordability by the masses; lack of standards for interoperability and integration of different applications and the need for data security and privacy and lack on necessary high level political support.[43] The Committee has also observed that no concrete plan for implementation of the programme by the Union and state governments and assessments of their e-readiness to take up such e-governance programmes not taken into account.

Working group report on IT for the masses

The report of the Working Group on Information Technology for the masses was constituted by Government of India on 10 May 2001 and the Committee submitted its report with a number of unrealistic and impractical recommendations for taking ICTs to the masses. Interestingly, the report was considered by the Government of India and a National Mission for Information Technology was constituted. The report had sought the opening up of the domestic market for IT industries in India and had pleaded for intensive back office and front office computerisation as a means to promote e-governance in India. The report observed:

> Government is well aware that substance of such a high growth rate in the long run requires an equally strong and vibrant domestic IT market. Government has therefore decided to use Information Technology as a major vehicle for all round socio-economic development in the country and thus as a byproduct, facilitate creation of strong domestic IT market. [44]

The problem of the digital divide was perceived in a very simplistic fashion as the poor citizens in the country, constituting around 40 percent of the total populace, do not have access to IT based services. The report sought to remove the problem of digital divide by application of IT in creating new opportunities

---

[43] Parliament of India. 2005. *Twenty Second Report of Standing Committee on Information Technology (2005–2006), Ministry of Communication and Information Technology*, December, New Delhi, Lok Sabha Secretariat, p. 79.

[44] http://www.itformasses.nic.in (accessed on November 20, 2009)

for these people to move above the poverty line by setting up millions of cyber kiosks or common service centres across the country. Given the resource constraints, the only option available before the government is to ensure that selective and intensive application of IT on certain public service delivery of central or state government so that some 'visible impact of the benefit of IT on people' could be made. The IT sector, the report says, will bring economic opportunity for all sections of people by way of providing employment opportunities and would create solutions to the age old problems in the social sectors like health, education, poverty alleviation and rural development and thereby promote 'good governance.'

The report further outlined that massive and sustained investment in front-end and back-end computerisations of all central and state government offices and compulsory IT education for all government officials would ensure sufficient pressure of public to sustain the quality of service using IT and even predicted that common man would not be required to visit government offices by 2005 if all day to day government functions were e-enabled and internet facility for common man was provided by setting up one million cyber kiosks in rural India with the help of private sector. The state should play only a facilitator and enabler role and free the IT sector from rules and regulations. It would effect process reengineering in government offices on priority that would pave the way for extensive use of e-governance which would be beneficial to the domestic IT vendors as well companies.[45]

The National Knowledge Commission report on e-governance

The National Knowledge Commission (NKC) under the chairmanship of Sam Pitroda was appointed by Government of India in June 2005 to study and recommend on the creation of 'institution building and of excellence in the fields of education, research and capacity building' and one of the terms of reference of the Commission was 'to promote the use of knowledge capabilities in making government an effective, transparent, and accountable service provider to the citizen and promote wide spread sharing of knowledge to maximize public benefits.'[46] The NKC in its report suggested the reengineering of government

45 See the web site. http://www.itformasses.nic.in(accessed on November 20, 2009)

46 http://www.knowledgecommission.gov.in/downloads/recommendations/eGovernanceLetterPM.pdf (accessed on November 15, 2009)

services and change in the basic governance pattern for simplicity, transparency, productivity and efficiency, development of common standards and deployment of common infrastructures for e-governance, simplifying and offering at least 10–20 important and critical public services programmes and offering them as web based services and monitoring and implementing new flagship programmes like MGNREGA and NRHMS and Bharat Nirman through the web. Its observation on the drive for computerisation in government offices and its advocacy for reengineering the government offices are significant as the idea of reengineering in some ways reflects the ideas of reinventing government movement through a techno-managerial perspective.

The second administrative reforms commission on e-governance

The report of the Second Administrative Reforms Commission has carried forward the contemporary neoliberal reform agenda of governance reforms. The Commission, constituted in August 2005 under the Chairmanship of Veerappa Moily, submitted its eleventh report on promoting e-governance in December 2008. One of the terms of reference of the Commission was to suggest measures to promote e-governance and in particular to the following aspects of this subject:

1. To reduce red tape, delay and inconvenience through technology interventions including the use of modern tools, techniques and instruments of e-Governance.
2. Promote knowledge sharing to realise continuous improvements in the quality of governance.[47]

The Commission took a purely technological determinist position on the capability of ICTs in promoting 'good governance' and it pinned high hopes on adoption ICTs as a tool for promoting transparency, accountability, responsiveness in bureaucracy and reducing the cost of administrative machineries. '...the tools of modern technology such as Information and Communication Technology (ICT) should be used to transform the

[47] Government of India. 2008. Introduction: *Eleventh Report of the Second Administrative Commission*, p. 1.

relationship of the government with its constituents, citizens and businesses, and also between its agencies.' [48]

E-governance in India is understood by it as 'the application of information and communication technology to government functioning in order to create 'simple, moral, accountable, responsive and transparent (SMART)' governance.'[49] The commission has viewed it as 'the core issue in improving the governance as a whole.'[50] The reason for the growing adoption of e-governance, according to the Commission, is due to growing complexity in managing 'governance per se' and rising expectations of citizens which could be addressed by adopting ICTs.[51]

The Second Administrative Refroms Commission has viewed ICTs as a panacea and value neutral tool for all the problems inherent in the present governance structures in India like lack of accountability, cumbersome official procedures, and prevalence of corruption which can be redressed 'through adopting e-governance as an inextricable part of government functioning, be they in routine matters or major projects.'[52] The observations of the Commission on the 'islands of e-governance initiatives' in different parts of India which have been described as successful by Government of India are very relevant here. The Commission emphasises that political support for e-governance initiatives; the need for process reengineering of bureaucracy; the need for administrative leaderships; provision for connectivity and electricity in rural areas and launching of e-governance initiatives that will focus the pressing need or the demand side of the local population are some of the lessons that the scattered e-governance initiatives have brought out for the policy makers.[53] The plethora of e-governance initiatives in India, mostly in pilot project stage, are not scaled up or widely replicated. The slew of failures of e-governance initiatives mostly related to public service delivery which moved the Commission to observe that e-governance is an integral part of governance reforms.

---

[48] Ibid, p. 7.

[49] Ibid, p. 8.

[50] Ibid, p. 5.

[51] Ibid, p. 1.

[52] Ibid, p. vi.

[53] Ibid, p54.

The Report of the Commission is undoubtedly very ambitious and very difficult to implement as even in the post-liberalisation era, the character of the Indian state remains elitist, and the bureaucracy is entrenched in its narrow interests. There is also a question mark on the capability of poor Indians to access the cyber kiosks and utilize the information without the help of intermediaries.[54] The Commission points e-governance as a means to achieve 'good governance' by overlooking the capacity and motivation of the vast bureaucratic structure both at the central and state administrative structure. The political and administrative leadership in India lacks initiative and will power to reform the functioning of the bureaucracy including the police administration, and so long as the political leadership is unable to enforce reform measures, the transformative agenda proposed by the Commission will remain in backburner.

Further the prohibitive costs involved in application, adoption and management in the public sector, and the client-oriented architecture that overlooks the rights of the citizens rendering them consumers, and the IT industry lobbying for massive diffusion of computers to promote the domestic market base, are either sidelined or overlooked by the Commission. Surprisingly the Commission has shown its ignorance or lack of awareness on the impact of client oriented delivery of services by IT vendors on the citizenship and democratic values in India. It also avoided in laying down guidelines or mechanisms of managing the networks of IT vendors and public bureaucracy in PPP model of electronic service delivery.

ICTs for good governance: A cyber optimist view

It is important to study and analyse the views and opinions of the cyber optimists known for their technological determinist position, as they take for granted the benefits from ICTs application.[55] The cyber optimists belong to various persuasions like the top civil servants, World Bank policy advocates and consultants, political leaders and some non serious academics in their writings

---

[54] Samit Kar. 2006. 'Ideals vs. Realities: Limitations of Governance,' *Economic and Political Weekly*, 14, October, pp. 4322–4324.

[55] Sam Pitroda. 1993. 'Development, Democracy and the Village Telephone,' *Harvard Business Review*, November–December. He argues that 'as a great social leveler, IT ranks second only to death' as it has the potentiality to remove socio-cultural barriers and democratise society.

have portrayed adoption of ICTs in the Indian bureaucratic system as means to solve all the problems related to its performance. Most notable among the cyber optimists are the officers belonging to Indian Administrative Services some of whom are associated with the launching of some scattered e-governance programmes, have brought out some changes in the performance of the public service delivery organisations, and now want the same to be replicated in other departments. Their writings, which form an important part in the emerging discourse on application of ICTs for good governance will be discussed in depth. Such an approach to the adoption of ICTs in government betrays a sense of cynicism of the senior administrative executives to the present nature of the administrative system and poor quality of service delivery and efficiency. They wanted to effect a change by relying ICTs as tool as they are under the sway of New Public Management ideas and eager to transplant some of the techno-managerialist ideas from the advanced western countries unmindful of their limitations and implications on the democratic governance in India.

The World Bank has been instrumental in shaping the adoption of ICTs in public sector reforms for what it believes can 'have profound impact' on increasing efficiency, responsiveness and accountability of government and removal of poverty in India. [56] However, its policy advocacy of ICT application in public sector remains at best predictive. According to World Bank thinking, ICTs can empower the poor people in rural India only if policies and projects are designed to exploit its potential in helping the poor to gain access to markets, health and enable them to use government services in a cheaper and easier manner.[57] Subash Bhatnagar, an ardent advocate of e-government practices on the lines of World Bank thinking, makes a strong case for online service delivery as it would be convenient and also promote transparency on the ground that the standardisation of rules and procedures and computer coding may reduce the scope for discretion of public officials and possibility of corruption and promote accessibility by which the decisions and actions can be tracked. He is however cautious to admit that reduction of corruption is

---

[56] Michael Carter. 2004. '*E-Governance-Transforming India*', The World Bank, February, 17. (http://go.worldbank.org/10BBYV9M90 (accessed on July 17,2010)

[57] World Bank. 2002. 'Using Information and Communication Technology to Reduce Poverty in Rural India', PREM NETWORK Notes, Report No 24856, and June. http://www-wds.worldbank.org/external (accessed on September13, 2009)

an 'incidental benefit' of e-government rather than an explicit objective.[58] He further argues, taking the World Bank approach, that in India public services suffer from lack of quality and complexity, effectiveness and reliability. So the need of the hour is adoption of ICTs which can 'partially solve' some of the problems like high costs in service delivery, corruption, lack of access to information, lack of citizen participation and supervision as the ICTs has the benefit of delivering faster processing, more accurate and improved access to information. This simplistic approach is based on some isolated or scattered initiatives of ICTs adoption in some public service deliveries.[59]

In a similar perception, Nandan Nilekani, one of the founders of Infosys, India's leading software company, and presently the chairman of Unique Identity Authority of India (UIDAI) project of Government of India has argued that ICTs would strengthen India's advantage as it has an open democratic society and would ensure the flow of information, knowledge and services. India's open society is an ideal condition for the ICTs to grow and IT led transformations of public policy should be the centre piece of our development and reform strategy as the masses in India have accepted it. What is required is a positive attitude to IT that would transform India.[60] To substantiate his argument, he cites the case of the land records management system where there exists massive potential for IT application to modernise the existing system. As 90 percent of land records in India are under disputed category and 30 percent pending court cases are related to land, what is required are 'reforms in land titling and property rights and linking such titles into national ID system, would be a big step for our national market' and he goes on to saying that computerisation of land records 'would have a dramatic, cleansing effect on land productivity, equity and litigation'.[61]

---

[58] Subash Bhatnagar. 'E-Government and the Access to Information'. http:// www.unpan1.un.org/intradoc/groups/public documents/unpan008435.pdf(accessed on December 4, 2008)

[59] Subash Bhatnagar. 2004. 'Public Service Delivery: Does E-Government Help?' in Sadiq Ahmed and Suman Berry (Eds.) *Annual Bank Conference on Development Economics, 2003.* New Delhi: The World Bank and National Council for Applied Economic Research (NCAER), pp. 11–15.

[60] Nandan Nilekani. 2008. *Imagining India: Ideas for the New Century*, New Delhi: Penguin p. 382.

[61] Ibid, pp. 377–378.

Some cyber utopians though admit that poor countries like India are unable to cope with the pressure of providing basic amenities like primary education, health, drinking water, road and electricity, but the idea of digitally oriented development still appears seductive in India. Despite her phenomenal success from export earnings of ITES and massive employment opportunities created for high-technology jobs, India has not been able to raise the living standards and capabilities of her people. Since there is no immediate panacea for the present socio-economic malaise 'digital development affords a new perspective from which to imagine the future directions of India's political economy. Rather than remaining locked in the paradigm of the developing society, it is now possible to aspire for a knowledge society.[62]

Taking a cyber utopian position and apologetic about India's state-backed rise of IT industry and its integration to world economy, Anna Greenspan writes that India's economic progress is IT driven and e-governance initiatives will be able to revolutionise Indians' lives. 'Though e-government is spreading throughout the world, nowhere is it more important than in a place like India, where people spend an inordinate turnaround of time and money dealing with even the simplest government service.'[63] There has been growth of a number of uncritical studies mostly by cyber utopians rushing to declare that India's communication 'revolution' and informatisation strategy of development that took shape since the 1990s has dramatised the lives of Indians by the rapid use of internet, satellite TV and cell phones, though many of them in the countryside keep still rely on bullock carts for transportation.

The e-government initiatives taken up by Chandrababu Naidu, the then Chief Minister of Andhra Pradesh has been showcased as 'monumental' capacity of ICTs to streamline the government and create a responsible, accountable and transparent system of governance.[64] Hypothesised and presumed benefits from early adoption of ICTs have been presented as the ground for adopting e-government which would pave the way for downsising the bureaucratic structure, establish the legitimacy and credibility of

---

[62] Aditya Sood. 2001. 'How to Wire Rural India: Problems and Possibilities of Digital Development,' *Economic and Political Weekly*, 27 October, pp. 4134–4135.

[63] Anna Greenspan. 2004. *India and the IT Revolution: Networks of Global Culture*, Hampshire: Palgrave-Macmillan, p. 52.

[64] Arvind Singhal and Everett M. Rogers. 2001. *India's Communication Revolution: From Bullock Carts to Cyber Marts*, New Delhi: Sage Publications, pp. 19; 108.

institutions, demystify procedures, improve the citizen government interface, eradicate corruption and improve the quality of life.[65] Since citizens are having 'harrowing experience' in encountering government officials, thanks to complicated official procedures and indifferent officials, the need is to have a single window system of integrated services in such a manner that the government to citizen interface would become seamless, faceless, nameless and the flow of information would be made possible cutting across all boundaries. [66] Such views of a public servant and the reports of the *Second Administrative Reforms Commission (2008)* described earlier, represent a line of thinking among the policy makers that ICT is a panacea for the present architecture of the bureaucratic system. The popularity of cyber kiosks rendering common services to the urban citizens such as deposits of various public utility service bills like water, electricity and building taxes in Hyderabad and Secunderabad (e-Seva model) is being projected as stepping stone to revolutionise the public service delivery and other business of government and will 'dismantle' the existing bureaucratic structure.[67]

The vision of the former President of India A. P. J. Abdul Kalam for 'a transparent smart e-governance with seamless access, secure and authentic view of information crossing the interdepartmental barrier and providing a fair and unbiased service to the citizen'[68] appears too ambitious to achieve. A big country like India with billion plus growing population, providing seamless flow of information and its access by her citizens are challenging task. He has stressed the need to have a national citizen database as the foundation of e-governance; need for the standards for the exchange of secure information with non-repudiation across states and central government departments seamlessly; need for empowered and reformed administrative systems to accelerate the decision

---

[65] Jagadish C. Kapur. 2000. 'IT and Good Governance,' *Indian Journal of Public Administration*, July–August, pp. 386–395.

[66] Anita Karwal. 2007. 'Effective Public Service Delivery and e-Governance: Who Drives Whom?' in Anil Aggarwall (Ed.) *e-Governance: Case Studies*, Hyderabad, University Press, pp. 58–61.

[67] M. Phani Kumar. 2005. 'E-Seva: Transforming Service Delivery to Citizens in Andhra Pradesh,' in R K Bagga, Kenneth Kenniston and Rohit Raj Mathur (Eds) *The State, IT and Development*, New Delhi: Sage Publications, pp. 207–210.

[68] A. P. J. Abdul Kalam. 2005. 'A Vision of Citizen Centric Governance in India' in R. K. Bagga, Kenneth Kenniston and Rohit Raj Mathur (Eds) *The State, IT and Development*, p. 39.

making for faster implementation of e-government process and outsourcing the e-governance work and government to retain only management data centres for online applications are simply difficult to execute without a firm political and administrative will power and commitment.

The former President of India's emphasis on adopting ICTs as a tool for promoting transparency and efficiency in administration and 'good governance' in the country is an optimistic vision than the reality.[69] Similar is the assertion of former Chief Vigilance Commissioner N. Vittal who pointed out that the ICTs would not only achieve transparency, speed and access to information systems of governance but could minimize corruption. When government transactions would be completely net based there would be scope for complete eradication of corruption.[70] But others however do not take such an optimistic position on the scope of ICTs to deliver the so-called 'good governance'. E. A. S. Sarma, a bureaucrat, has noted that in India, e-government constitutes an 'elitist discourse' being goaded by political leadership though the country lacks providing basic infrastructure to primary schools. Unless we address effectively the basic elements of good governance such as empowering the citizen especially the poor, empower and strengthen local bodies, promote decentralised decision making, transparency in government services and inter-agency coordination and convergence, the adoption of ICTs in public administration with involvement of huge cost will not be successful. Further the sustainability of e-government programmes is dependent upon how it affects the lives of the poor and the underprivileged as was the case of green revolution in India.[71]

Jayaprakash Narayan, who was one of the members of the Second Administrative Commission, has observed that though adoption of ICTs in government practices may deliver some 'expected benefits' like promoting efficient and effective administration, cost minimisation and convenience to the citizen services, enhancing services and accessibility to government information, it cannot insulate administrative system from corruption or

---

[69] Ibid, pp. 38–42.

[70] N. Vittal. 2005. 'Role of ICTs in Minimizing Corruption in India,' in R. K. Bagga, Kenneth Kenniston and Rohit Raj Mathur (Eds) *The State, IT and Development*, p. 151–152.

[71] E .A. S. Sarma. 2005. 'ICT and Good Governance', in R. K. Bagga, Kenneth Kenniston and Rohit Raj Mathur (Eds) *The State, IT and Development*, pp. 68–75.

safeguard against corruption. There is need for data safety and privacy as the involvement of private sectors through PPP model may lead to misuse of government information.[72]

Such perspectives are based on flawed assumptions that ICTs are autonomous artifacts, not embedded in any prevalent socio-economic and political practices or systems, and are therefore inherently value-neutral and can serve to checkmate bureaucratic malpractices. This leads them to conclude that massive computerisation of government establishment and public service agencies through the help of IT vendors will inevitably promote the techno-managerial notion of transparency, accountability and 'good governance.'

ICTs for good governance in India: a critical analysis

In India, the spread of information technology particularly the personal computer is very limited. The latest World Bank data revealed that only 1.08 percent of population in India have the access to internet connectivity.[73] Similarly Confederation of Indian Industry (CII) study revealed that in India only one broadband connectivity is available for 100 inhabitants in 2009 and India occupies 118th position out of 158 countries in terms of ICT parameters..[74] Starting from a low base of around one computer per 800 persons in the population in 1995, the figure indeed has been climbed up to 1.6 computers per 100 people in 2006. This average conceals the concentration of computer use in corporate, trade, and urban concentration. What is significant is that there has been a steady roll out of hardware components of computers system and their installation at the government offices than the diffusion at the lower level like in the areas of direct provision of service delivery for the disadvantaged and common people. The success of diffusion of ICTs depends upon the creation of necessary environments and circumstances like quality schooling and universal primary education.[75]

---

[72] Jayaprakash Narayan. 2005. 'Governance: Virtual to Real', in R. K. Bagga, Kenneth Kenniston and Rohit Raj Mathur (Eds) *The State, IT and Development*, pp. 44–61.

[73] http://data.worldbank.org/indicator/IT.NET.BBND (accessed on June 18, 2013).

[74] Confederation of Indian Industry and IMRB International. 2009. *India: 2009–2014: Broadband Roadmap for Inclusive Growth*, September, New Delhi, p. 3.

[75] C. P. Chandrasekhar. 'Aspects of India's Traverse to an Information Society', pp. 49–51. http//www.itforchange.net/poleco_is.html (accessed on September 23, 2008)

There is a need for a prolonged strategy for spread of computer education through quality primary education along with improvement of basic human resources not the vendor driven excessive hardware roll out in the name of computerisation. The challenge and opportunities offered by ICTs in India calls for partnerships between the state-private, private-civil society organisations and government organisations. The role of the state is not only central to promoting and regulating such partnership but also to investing scarce resources in development of human resources like education, health and nutrition. The state also needs to promote communication infrastructure for faster diffusion of the ICTs. But it is observed that the excessive concern for software services export and business process outsourcing activities have resulted in India's public policy for e-governance being biased towards costly proprietary software where e-governance applications are being viewed as profit as opposed to facilitating and encouraging free software which stands for development.

The state also needs to reduce growing income inequalities and take effective steps for reduction of poverty by pursuing an egalitarian path of development, effective implementation of anti-poverty schemes, increase in agricultural productivity and expansion of non-agricultural employment for improvement of the standard of living of the vast masses so that they can take the opportunities in diffusion of ICTs otherwise their growth and use will be confined to elites and may worsen the problem of the digital divide.[76]

The cyber optimists in India have hailed some of the scattered 'islands of e-governance initiatives' like Gyandoot programme, e-Seva programme, online delivery of land records in Karnataka, and the CARD system in Andhra Pradesh as the harbinger for a new transparent delivery of service at the doorstep of the people without critically studying the user's perspective in detail or the viability of such supply side e-governance programmes. It is argued that corruption in India persists because of lack of transparency, monopoly and discretionary power of the public authority which could be redressed by adoption of ICTs in government offices. The introduction of Computer Aided Registration of Deeds and Stamp Duties (CARD) in Andhra Pradesh was expected to remove the antiquated property registration process and corruption by the middlemen and officials.

---

[76] UNDP and NASSCOM. 2004. *ICTs for Human Development in Asia: India*, New Delhi, pp. 89–91.

The government introduced ICT enabled computerised registration process, delivery of certified copy and encumbrance certificate by digitisation of deed documents in all the sub-registrar offices (SROs). But the actual implementation of the CARD system failed to prevent or reduce corrupt practices in the sub-registrar offices (SROs) as the traditional actors like deed writers involved in the land registration were retained in the new system of computerisation. In Andhra Pradesh, corruption in SROs is systemic and embedded. The informal actors such as deed writers (DWs) play middlemen in the whole process of obtaining a certified copy, encumbrance certificate and executing a registration of deed.

The CARD system failed to remove the informal linkage of the deed writers with the registry officials in execution of registered deeds and payment of bribes to the latter. Without payment of a bribe to the officials in SROs, they will either delay or put up objections on flimsy grounds thereby harass the people. The CARD system has in no way reduced the discretionary power of the sub-registrars. Therefore, the technological rhetoric of controlling or minimising corruption by application ICTs in public service delivery only depoliticises it. The ICTs thus has the limited role in restricting the factors that generate the rent seeking behavior among the officials at the sub-registrar offices.[77]

The top down approach of ICT based reform is only a facade and it only helped to sustain institutionalised corruption as the users were not effectively involved in the tailor-made ICTs programme. The failure of the CARD system draws a lesson that sustained administrative and political support or commitment, involvement of stakeholders, organisation wide fixing of the responsibility, changing the work culture, participation of media and civil society organisations are essential conditions for any ICTs based reform success.[78]

The role of the Indian state

The role of the Indian state in the development and promotion of ICTs has been categorised into four aspects. First, the Indian state is carefully nurturing its growing ICT industry or informatics sector especially the software exports.

---

[77] Paven Malhotra. 2005. 'Technology and the Politics of Corruption: Andhra Pradesh's CARD Experience' in R. K. Bagga, Kenneth Kenniston and Rohit Raj Mathur (Eds.) *The State, IT and Development*, pp. 159–178.

[78] Jonathan Caseley. 2004. 'Public Sector Reform and Corruption: CARD Facade in Andhra Pradesh', *Economic and Political Weekly*, 13 March, pp. 1151–1156.

Secondly, in public policy arena, the state has been playing a proactive role by way of effecting liberalisation of telecom policy, formulation of New Telecom Policy, 1999, Telecom Regulatory Authority Act, 2000, and Internet Service Provision Policy in 1998. Such substantial policy changes provided legal environment for private participation of telecom companies. Thirdly thrust has been given to the research and development activities in the ICTs sector by setting up institutes like C-DAC, C-DOT, NIC and DOEAC. Fourth, the state is pursuing a vigorous policy of applying the ICTs especially the web enabled computer network in running its business to achieve 'good governance' through application of ICTs or what is now called as Simple, Moral, Accountable, Responsive and Transparent (SMART) government.

But despite such ambitious policies, several difficult problems have cropped up in India's path towards SMART government. The growing issue of digital divide or digital poverty, India's e-readiness and poor human development index, costly nature of investment in ICTs, the complicated problem of bringing out process reengineering in the bureaucratic structure, problem of regional language content development and to provide low cost and affordable ICT access to the rural poor in cyber kiosks on a sustainable basis are some of the insurmountable challenges before the Indian state.[79] Therefore some observers have rightly argued that 'ICT for the masses and the movement for bridging the digital divide still pose larger doses of exaggeration and wishful thinking.'[80] The failure of the state to provide common minimum needs to vast millions of people has put a question mark on the viability of e-governance which at present benefits only the few educated, urban and mobile Indian middle classes. The government in India tends to portray e-governance as the panacea for a variety of problems of governing and it has emerged as one of the leading developing countries in adopting e-governance. Yet no promising results or positive outcome have been detected. The problem is how the poor and illiterate in India would get access to the internet in rural areas as most of them are unable to meet their basic needs. The growing digital divide in India is 'reinforcing' social-economic disparities.[81]

---

[79] R. K. Bagga, Kenneth Kenniston and Rohit Raj Mathur (Eds). 2005. Introduction: *The State, IT and Development,* New Delhi: Sage Publications, pp. 29–32.

[80] Ibid, p. 33.

[81] M. Shamsul Haque. 2002. 'E-Governance in India: Its Impact on Relations among Citizens, Politicians and Public Servants,' *International Review of Administrative Sciences,* 68(2), pp. 240–250.

Cyber kiosks and the capability approach

Some scholars have taken a skeptical view of India's journey to an information society.[82] The capability approach of Amartya Sen has been relied on by Thomas and Parayil in their study to give importance to social and institutional factors rather than simply going for assessment of e-governance performance quantitatively. To them, capability here refers to the various combinations of functionings (being and doing) that a person can achieve and a set of achievements reflecting the person's freedom to lead to one type of life or another. For Example, two persons availing cyber kiosks facility in a village locality can have vastly differing potentials or opportunities for life owing to their different social, educational, physical and economic positions. Therefore access to ICTs facilities will not automatically lead to empowerment or upliftment as the capability to use ICTs and capability to use the information content depend upon social position and context. IIlteracy and various forms of social exclusion prevailing in large parts of India act as a handicap for accessing to IT skills in rural India as well her dismal performance in provisioning basic education, health and connectivity are other impediments for improving capabilities.[83]

Jayan Jose Thomas and Govindan Parayil also in another study (2004) on impact of computer literacy on villagers in two districts, one in Kuppam area of Chittoor district in Andhra Pradesh and another in Malappuram district in Kerala, have applied the capability approach of Amartya Sen. In Kuppam area of Chittoor district, a joint venture of computer company Hewlett Packard (HP) and Andhra Pradesh government called as i-community centres (inclusive community) and in Malappuram district the Akshaya computer literacy training programme were surveyed. These are cyber kiosks that impart computer literacy on nominal fees to the villagers. The study revealed that access to computers does not lead to an increase in the capability to use computers and only the educated and richer villagers got the maximum benefits.[84] They found that the digital divide is not about access but also social

[82] See for example Geoff Walsham. 2010. 'ICTS for the Broader Development in India: An Analysis of the Literature,' *EJISDC*, 41(4), pp. 1–20.

[83] Jayan Jose Thomas and Govindan Parayil. 2008. 'Bringing the Social and Digital Divides in Andhra Pradesh and Kerala: A Capabilities Approach,' *Development and Change*, 39(3), pp. 409–413.

[84] Ibid, p. 425.

context as personal ability and social environment are determining factors of capability to use and access ICTs and utilize the same for one's benefits. The capability to use ICTs and harness its benefits is higher among the villagers of Malappuram district than the villagers of Kuppam area in Chittoor district thanks to higher ranking in Human Development Index of Kerala and its progress in educational achievements, redistributive reforms, past and present achievements in high standard of living, gender equality etc. Therefore to bridge the digital divide complementary social intervention has to be made as 'social divisions are mirrored in the digital divide.'[85] The Akshaya model of cyber kiosks itself face contradiction in its operation as it cater to social development by spreading computer education at an affordable price and the need for its financial sustainability. Many kiosks have been shut down as these were financially not sustainable. Even providing computer education and training to rural population no way directly helps in social development.

The studies on the functioning of the Akshaya model of cyber kiosks revealed that running private owned kiosks on business principles and providing services to the rural people through high technologies at affordable prices is problematic and creates tension in meeting the twin goals of commercial viability and social development and as a result both the goals are not achieved. The assumptions that 'market based solutions and private enterprises, and advanced technologies can increase the well being of the poor and concurrently increase the profits of the private sector- is in tension in Kerala's Akshaya model.'[86] The ICTs can bring about positive administrative, social and economic changes in rural areas provided basic socio-economic amenities like primary education, health, roads and electricity are met.[87] The impact of ICTs depends on the structure of society in which the technologies are applied. In the prevailing social condition in India, ICTs can aggravate inequality as fundamental constraints to development and empowerment like unequal access to literacy and assets ownerships persist and the craze and optimism

---

[85] Ibid, p. 432.

[86] Rene Kurian et al. 2008. 'Information and Communication Technologies for Development: The Bottom of the Pyramid Model in Practice', *The Information Society*, 24(2), pp. 93–104.

[87] Jayan Jose Thomas. 2006. 'Informational Development In Rural Areas: Some Evidence from Andhra Pradesh and Kerala' in *Political Economy of Informational Capitalism in India: Digital Divide, Development and Equity*, Houndsmill: Palgrave-Macmillan, p. 109.

for supply side informational development in rural areas may detract attention towards critical intervention in income growth, education and land reforms.[88] The social and institutional issues and factors are important as vehicle for capability creation since people's knowledge, beliefs, values of the society in which they live shape their capability. The abilities, needs and motivations of people in electronics service delivery need to be taken into account. The inherent distrust of common people to the public service delivery mechanism and pervasive corruption in administration invariably shape people's attitude towards e-governance measures for revamping public service mechanisms by government. [89]

Amartya Sen's capability approach to development is a useful analytical framework to examine the claims of the cyber optimists about the beneficial impacts of the cyber kiosks run by private entrepreneurs in rural areas. To Sen, the Indian state needs to secure 'constituent elements of our basic capabilities' like quality primary education, primary health, social security cover and sweeping land reforms and such other 'social opportunities' for the poor and under privileged sections of society to raise their economic productivity and standard of living. In such enabling condition, the poor and weaker sections can avail of the advantages of knowledge society and economy.[90]

The Gyandoot experience

The participation of people in designing and implementing ICTs related projects like Gyandoot (means the purveyor of knowledge) is recognised as the reason for its success. It is an intranet in Dhar district in Madhya Pradesh 'connecting rural cybercafés catering to the everyday needs of the masses.' The Gyandoot project was launched in 1999 by the initiative of the district collector of Dhar district. The objective was to provide the local people relevant information as well as acting as an interface between the district administration and the people by setting up cyber kiosks or Community Information Centres

---

[88] Ibid. pp. 113; 130.

[89] Shirin Madon. 2008. 'Evaluating the Developmental Impact of the E-Governance Initiatives: An Exploratory Framework', in Aswani Saith and M. Vijayabaskar (Eds.) *ICTs and Indian Social Change: Diffusion, Poverty and Governance,* New Delhi: Sage Publications, pp. 270–272.

[90] Amartya Sen and Jean Dreze (Eds). 1997. *Indian Development: Selected Regional Perspectives*, United Nations University, pp. 3; 6; 22; 25–26.

(*soochanalayas*) both by government and private initiative in which rural people could obtain information on market price of agricultural commodities and delivery of miscellaneous certificates like caste and residence, copy of land records, BPL family lists etc. The problem of supporting infrastructure like electricity, tele-connectivity, and charging of higher user fees are some of the bottlenecks that put question marks on the sustainability of the initiatives. The Second Administrative Reforms Commission has observed that the Gyandoot initiatives that took e-governance to rural areas confront with problems related to supporting infrastructure, affordable user charges for the poor, citizen friendly and simple interface with the users and demand side emphasis of ICTs applications to make such initiatives successful and sustainable.[91]

However, this project has generated a lot of interest among academics working on e-governance projects in India. Some of them are of the view that the Gyandoot experiment in a poverty stricken and backward district like Dhar shows that given the administrative support, ICT for development project could be viable provided people participated and were involved in designing, planning and implementing the projects as demand for information exists in rural areas.[92] Meera Tiwari's study on user's perspective of the Gyandoot project shows that villagers with higher education and income have availed of services more than the poor and illiterate persons. The human capital and skill enhancing services listed in the Gyandoot intranet such as e-education and healthcare advice/information modules were found to have negligible acceptance. Lack of information on the Gyandoot services and of understanding and awareness among the villagers about the e-governance initiative may not lead to benefit the socially and economically disadvantaged groups[93] T. T. Sreekumar's empirical study of the rural cyber kiosks like TARA kendras and Gyandoot set up by the ICT based NGOs in collaboration with government in some states revealed that contrary to the claim that cyber kiosks in rural areas will provide digital inclusion and reduce gender and caste divide, the study found that information technology has a limited role in removing gender and social

---

[91] Government of India. 2008. See *Eleventh Report of the Second Report Administrative Reforms Commission on Promoting e-Governance*, p. 36.

[92] Satish K. Puri and Sandeep Sahay. 2007. 'Role of ICTs in Participatory Development: An Indian Experience,' *Information Technology for Development*, 13(2), pp. 150–156.

[93] Meera Tiwari. 2009. 'ICTs and Poverty Reduction: User Perspective Study of Rural Madhya Pradesh,' *The European Journal of Development Research*, 20(3), pp. 448–461.

divide. The existing social divides are rather reinforced in such ICT based community centres. The ICTs alone cannot further the participation of the socially deprived sections of populations in rural areas. The NGOs perceive ICTs as a medium of socio-economic development with loosely defined idea of developmentalism. They also mediate in their activities within the caste-class dynamics in the rural and backward area and have therefore inherent social limitations to promote cyber inclusion. The participation of dalits, tribals and women in rural cyber kiosks is found to be limited.[94]

Such simplistic findings on the transformative potential of rural cyber kiosks are challenged by others who have questioned the assumption of neutrality of ICT initiatives. Such initiatives are embedded within specific political and social processes and structures of power relations. The Gyandoot project is basically an administered programme with no involvement of civil society groups and some common problems about the cyber kiosks are infrastructural problems, the failure to redress the grievances filed by the local people in time, delay in delivering the services, lethargy and unresponsiveness of the kiosk operators, and indifference among the poor and landless to such kiosks put the question marks on the transformative impacts of ICTs and assumed neutrality of technological processes.[95]

Thus, we can argue that application of ICTs in rural areas without addressing the socio-economic inequalities and deprivation cannot serve as a socio-economic equalizer, rather they actually reinforce social divides and more importantly create digital divides. The multilateral agencies and NGOs advocate for application and adoption of ICTs for development by overlooking the overarching social barriers and fail how to surmount the challenges. The rural cyber kiosks may be beneficial for the big and wealthy farmers or dominant castes in finding appropriate market price for their product than the poor and small farmers whose capability to take such opportunities may be limited due to his indebtness or lack of resources. So the unidirectional relationship between the ICTs and development discourse necessitates a critical

---

[94] T.T. Sreekumar. 2007. 'Cyber Kiosks and Dilemmas of Social Inclusion in Rural India,' *Media Culture and Society*, 29(6), pp. 869–889.

[95] T.T. Sreekumar. 2007. 'Decrypting E-Governance: Narratives, Powerplay and Participation in the Gyanadoot Intranet,' The *Electronic Journal of Information Systems in Developing Countries*, 32(4), pp. 1–24. http:www.ejisdc.org (accessed on September 20,2009)

understanding as their advocates overestimates the potential benefits of ICT application in rural areas and at the same time overlook or avoid to address the question of capabilities of the rural poor and their entitlements. [96] Recent studies on function of cyber kiosks in two Indian states like Uttar Pradesh and Meghalaya brings out the unviability of running cyber kiosks despite charging of high user fees. The usages of such kiosk are obviously limited to better off and literate people and more personal in nature than serving any common developmental purposes of the local community.[97] The sustainability failure of cyber kiosks in Melur taluk of Madurai District in Tamil Nadu brigs out some interesting facts which can be generalised as the reasons for failure of common service centres across India. The Madurai district collector took initiative in launching SARI-E-Gov project (Sustainable Access in Rural India) in 39 villages in that taluk for delivery of various computer and web based services of government but the programme was collapsed due to the transfer of the project champion. Lack of trained personnel to man the cyber kiosks, lack of supervision and commitment by the government officials, lack of involvement of the stakeholders (the villagers) and lack of partnership and coordination with private vendors and government officials concerned have resulted in failure of the project to attend its envisaged objectives.[98]

As analysed previously, the challenge of providing costly ICT based development in India could be met through partnerships with private entrepreneurs. It is now widely advocated that only way to ensure that ICTs to reach the poor and promote broad based economic development is to promote private development of cyber kiosks in partnership or collaboration with the government. P. D. Kaushik and Nirvikar Singh's study in 2001 on the privately operated cyber kiosks such as the TARAhaat started in Bhatinda district, Punjab and the Drishtee in Sirsa district, Haryana has shown that the objective of setting up these kiosks was to bring IT services to the rural population and provide market accessibility to rural population. The most significant impact

[96] T. T. Sreekumar and Milagros Riveria-Sanchez. 2008. 'ICTs and Development: Revisiting the Asian Experience,' *Science, Technology and Society*, 13(2), pp. 159–174.

[97] Rohit Prasad and Rupamanjari Sinha Ray. 2006. 'Critique of the Common Service Centre Scheme', *Economic and Political Weekly*, 11 February, pp. 18–23.

[98] Rajendra Kumar and Michael C. Best. 2006. 'Impact of Sustainability of E-Government Services in Developing Countries: Lessons Learned from Tamil Nadu,' *Information Society*, 22(1), pp. 1–12.

according to the authors is innovation of an institution based on hybrids of commercial and non-profit organisations as the initiating institution and a more standard entrepreneurial franchise model for public service delivery at the local level due to the partnership with the state government agencies. Thus private institutional innovation can play important role in ICTs diffusion than the government mechanism and 'some economic and social changes can be effected through entrepreneurial innovation'.[99]

The role of such cyber kiosks has been highlighted in the Eleventh Five Year Plan as well as in the ongoing National e-governance Plan (NeGP) on recognition of the fact that given the size and spread of the country and extent of socio-economic deprivation, the provision of teleconnectivity to each household is not a realistic solution through the so-called universal service obligation rather locating low cost PCOs and Cyber Kiosks in all villages in partnerships with private entrepreneurs is the viable policy option. The low cost ICTs facilities is not the necessary and sufficient condition for the participation of the rural poor as they invariably depend on the help of cyber kiosks owner for operating and getting access to the cyber world. So the kiosk operators play the role of intermediaries and should be given proper incentives to work in rural areas.[100]

The IT experience all over the world has raised the issue of digital divide and access before the state. In India, only a sizeable number of populations who can speak English have the advantage of information age and as there is no market for Indian language and development of regional language fonts in India have been slow.[101] Overall, the developmental goals achieved by application of ICTs in India are limited and e-government services like filing tax return, rail and air ticket booking and banking transaction have been benefited by the relatively better off and educated sections of the society.[102]

---

[99] P. D. Kaushik and Nirvikar Singh. 2004. 'Information Technology and Broadbased Development: Preliminary Lessons from North India', *World Development,* 32(4), pp. 591–607.

[100] Simone Cecchini and Christopher Scott. 2003. 'Can Information and Communication Technology Applications Contribute to Poverty Reduction?' *Information Technology for Development*, 10, pp. 73–80.

[101] Kenneth Kenniston and Deepak Kumar. 2004. *IT Experience in India: Bridging the Digital Divide*, New Delhi, Sage Publications, pp. 12–15.

[102] Geoff Walsham. 2010. 'ICTs for Broader Development of India: An Analysis of the Literature,' *EJISDC, 41*(4), pp. 1–20.

Conclusions

The uncritical approach towards e-governance of the political and administrative leaderships in India has given rise to ICT fetishism. The applications of ICTs in governance arena are being spearheaded by multilateral financial institutions, UNDP, NGOs, civil society organisations in India as well in other developing countries as it is argued that it would enable these countries to transcend their poor governance and backwardness. The Indian government is of the view that e-governance will lead to a fundamental transformation of citizen-state relations based on a client oriented public service delivery. It has now put a thrust on massive frontend and backend computerisation.

The euphoria over the prospects of ICTs application in the bureaucratic set up is more intense in India than other developed countries as traced in our analysis of policy documents. What is interesting that while the current literature on e-governance in the developed countries reflects critical, sombre and realistic perspectives, but in India whether in policy documents or other writings-one can see an unthinking approbation for e-governance without taking into account its effects on democratic governance and citizenship given the dominance of IT corporates in shaping the e-governance policy. The deep influence of the techno-managerial and apolitical approaches to the problem of governance are clearly evident in the policies of the government in use of ICTs in public administration. The linkage between the growth of the domestic IT market and IT professionals and growing thrust for vendor driven approach to application of ICTs in governance and a false presumption that ICTs offer solution to bureaucratic inefficiencies need be to seen as integral to the approach to e-governance of the Indian state.

E-governance as an aspect of the neoliberal agenda of 'good governance' may be viewed from a political perspective. Two major incentives that may motivate the political leadership to go for such techno-managerial governance reforms in the context of land records computerisation or modernisation are: the incentive to maintain the existing support base or political alliances and incentive to generate the new support base as governance reforms involve considerable strain or risk on the support base and patronage of the political leadership and may affect the interest of vested groups. The incentives to political leadership for reforms and administrative innovation are those that will not put an end to rent seeking or old style of political deals or threaten the established procedure of functioning that may invite resistance from bureaucrats or create new political groups.[103]

The earmarking funds for computerisation of government offices and launching of the National eGovernance Plan (NeGP) by the Indian state for making 'all government services available to common man in his locality' has raised the challenge of providing universal access to the public services especially to the poor who must be the ultimate beneficiary of e-service deliveries as the rich and powerful get their work done by engaging intermediaries or leveraging their position. Now e-governance has become a new mantra for achieving 'good governance' in the public policy discourses as well the advocacy by the cyber utopian bureaucrats and cyber-libertarian civil society groups as they take a patently technologically determinist position and have gone ahead in making policy design of process reengineering of Indian bureaucracy. The complex issue is how the apolitical approach to ICT for development and governance reforms would work in the existing social structure in India that determines the digital access and impacts.

The availability of cyber kiosks in rural areas do not mean that all sections of rural people will get access as poverty, social and educational barriers and gender factors play their limiting role. The low penetration of computers and internet is itself a reflection of the digital divide in India.[104] There is a lurking apprehension that the present drive for e-governance in India may reinforce or mirror the socio-economic inequalities as the capabilities of the common people have not been enhanced. The broad view has been that ICTs being an enabler cannot produce results on its own. Much depends upon the political and administrative will and leadership of the government on allowing the space and freedom of operation and functioning of e-government systems that would ultimately raise the quality of public service.

The experience of production, export, diffusion and adoption of ICTs in India is a complex and intriguing matter. India is home to one of the largest set of civil society experiments using the ICTs to empower the rural people and promote 'good governance.' The possibilities ICTs may offer in ushering good governance practices may begin with the understanding of their limitations in effecting organisational change as ICTs do not have any

---

[103] Mark Robinson. (Ed.) 2009. See 'Introduction' to *The Politics of Successful Governance Reforms*, London: Routledge.

[104] D.N.Ghosh 2001. 'ICTs in Rural Poverty Alleviation', *Economic and Political Weekly*, 17 March, pp. 917–920.

intrinsic leverage to undermine the existing rent seeking bureaucratic procedure unless the political and administrative leadership so desires or committed to such system.[105] Otherwise, the experience of computerisation of government offices and government programmes in India has been a vendor driven exercise lacking ownership and initiative. It has become an addition to the existing layers of bureaucratic structure rather than a replacement of it. Richard Heeks observes such process as 'electronic development that place ICTs centre-stage.' For him, the approach to ICTs needs to be integral, intelligible and indegenised to the development objectives and it must be 'i-development, not e-development.'[106]The various discourse on e-governance lead us to raise some issues such as whether the common people and their pressing needs and demands are going to be addressed effectively and in an affordable manner in the community information centres run in partnership with private entrepreneurs as outlined in the National eGovernance Plan (NeGP).

Secondly, the efficacy, motivation, incentive structure and skill of the bureaucracy which will execute the e-governance programmes in partnership with the private enterprises or IT vendors and their capacity to defend and secure public interest while working in networks or partnership arrangement with private players have not been critically studied given its poor record in delivering public services, its involvement in corrupt practices, and its unholy nexus with politicians and brokers/middlemen. As a result, a sense of pervasive uncertainty looms large on the prospects of e-governance that would seek to change the dynamics of closed system of bureaucracy to an open network for promoting governance agenda like openness, accountability and transparency which is not an easy thing to happen. Dependence on computers and associated apolitical reform strategies like change management and government business process reengineering to change the entrenched culture of bureaucracy and corruption would not succeed. It is rightly observed that, 'handing over the responsibility of initiating administrative reforms to the very people who stand to lose by it jeopardises the search for innovative solutions.'[107]

---

105 M. Vijayabaskar and V. Gayathri. 2003. 'ICT and Indian Development: Processes, Prognoses and Policies,' *Economic and Political Weekly*, 14 June, pp. 2360–2364.

106 Richard Heeks. 2002. 'I-Development Not e-Development,' *Journal of International Development*, 14(1), p. 10.

107 Kuldeep Mathur. 2008. 'Administrative Reforms and the Demand for Good Governance,' p. 221.

Thirdly, the long term impact of such massive informatisation of public sector to primarily serve the government to citizen (G2C) and government to business (G2B) and business to government (B2G) domains with the participation of private players, simultaneously to effect the process reengineering of bureaucracy that would be predisposed to techno-managerial governance and its impact on the democratic governance and ideals of Indian democratic state has not been critically deliberated upon either at the policy making level or at informal or civil society level. The reason is, as rightly commented by Kuldeep Mathur that in India administrative reforms do not give importance to improving public service delivery but to changing ownership.[108]

[108] Ibid, p. 228.

3

The State and the Policy of Land Records Management

The study of policy of land records management and the role of the Indian state cannot be completely understood without taking into account the history of the land records system along with its bewildering regional diversities, and its management particularly since the British period. British rule laid the foundation of property rights on land and took elaborate measures for survey and settlement.

The land records system: a historical perspective

The land records and revenue system and its tenurial relations have been intricately related to its social conditions since long, and to a large extent sustained by the agrarian nature of India's society and economy. For centuries, there have been layer upon layer of landholders and revenue collections interrelated among themselves. '... what we see is a spectral view of socially structured land control relationships with gradations...' on the one extreme lord over land and labour and on the other end labourer on land. Between the two extreme positions there exist innumerable strata of lesser lords and larger labourers.

The land tenure systems and land relations in India is very complex due to the existence of a 'veritable jungle of overlapping terminologies.'[1] Dharma

[1] Robert Eric Frykenberg. (Ed.). 1969. *Land Control and Social Structure in Indian History*, Madison, London: The University of Wisconsin Press, p. xv.

Kumar, a historian, writes that the period prior to British occupation and rule was marked by chaos as the Mughal reign was in decline. The Britishers were 'confused about the rights they had to confirm and administer' as very scanty information on land records was available to them. They had to choose between various claimants to rights in a tenure system largely unknown to them, and used in a multiplicity of local languages, as well as Persian/Arabic terms coined by Muslim rulers. The British added further confusion 'in their natural tendency to look everything from an English Law or Lord-of-the-manor point of view.'[2] Therefore the linguistic overlapping of land holdings and tenures has been prone to errors and misinterpretations.

Despite the variegated nature of terminologies one could observe that all kinds of holdings and rights were intricately linked to definite socio-ceremonial, communal, economic and political roles. Neither hereditary ownerships nor customary authority constituted a legal claim to ownership of the land—this complicates the process of defining and classifying the many interrelated positions of social status and landed interests. The classical threefold classification of landlords, tenant-farmers and laborers does not encompass the social and structural complexity of India's agrarian scene. Thorners observes, 'no where in the world are agrarian relationships more complex than in India. We have here state ownership as well as proprietary ownership. There are tenants, below tenants and a wide variety of types of crop sharers.'[3]

The importance of detailed land records was repeatedly felt in British India but nothing concrete was done or achieved. Daniel and Alice Thorner have noted that though the Famine Inquiry Commission, 1945 sought to look into the relationships between the land tenure systems and the efficiency of agricultural production, the Commission could neither ascertain precisely how the land in India was owned (i.e., pattern of ownership of land holding) or how land was operated (operational holding). The data about ownership of land were generally incomplete and data about farms or land actually cultivated by given persons were practically not available.[4]

---

[2] Dharma Kumar. 1965.*Land and Caste in South India,* Cambridge: Cambridge University Press, p. 9.

[3] Daniel and Alice Thorner. 1962. *Land and Labour in India*, Bombay: Asia Publishing House, p. 151.

[4] Ibid, pp. 166–167.

Baden Powell in his three volumes of work titled, *The Land Systems of British India* (1974) outlined in a most authoritative manner the evolution of the land and tenure system, its conditions and the different nature of administration in India from a historical perspective. To him the land records system in India reveals that all land must have some landlord with tenants attached to him and in such a complex manner that the Indian land tenures have become 'unintelligibles'.[5] Moreover, as the colonial state derived its main revenue from land, the collection and assessment of land was organised and fixed for a term of years instead of relying on an extortionist approach. The adjustment of payment of land revenue to each class of cultivated land gave rise to the necessity of thoroughly understanding each class of people, their modes of landholding, subsistence of interest and the extent of such revenue burden to be carried by them.

Such an approach to land relations demands systematic maintenance of land records, and understanding of agricultural situation in the country along with the determination of landed rights and the record of everything which related to the agricultural and social habits of the people. '...consequently a knowledge of the land administration and the records it requires and the procedure it employs, is, in fact, a knowledge of the largest class of population and the conditions under which it lives.'[6] For example, the village records of the early British period in Punjab enabled the construction of the official version of India. It provided the core information on which the settlement reports of the districts were based and further the entry of the caste or status in the official village records indicated the rights of land holders in terms of caste.

Classification of village records by caste 'was the mortar that linked local administrative practice to both law and general knowledge.'[7] The village land records with the patwari (revenue inspector) still constitute the standard source material to study the socio-economic history and life of rural India as India continues to be an agrarian society and land has been a significant economic resource and the most important determinant of socio-political status in the community. Further, statistical materials on *jamabandi* (rent schedule), size of plots, rents, area cultivated by the tenants, homestead lands can be used

[5] B.H. Baden Powell. 1974.*The Land Systems of British India*, Volume-l, Oxford: Clarendon University Press, pp. 2–3.

[6] Ibid, p. 25–26.

[7] Richard Saumarez Smith. 2008. 'From Village to Community' In Ishita Banerjee Dube (Ed) *Caste In History*, Delhi: Oxford University Press, p. 68.

'for examining some straight questions of agricultural economics' as well as changing social structure and social relations of a village.[8]

Baden Powell has observed that the land records are basically 'preservation of the information as to rights and as to agricultural conditions gained in the process of settlement.' The land records documents are partly 'statistical' bearing information on agricultural conditions, soil products and other particulars of the estate or land and partly contain the 'reference to rights' in the soil, the revenue shares and rent payable and village customs bearing on the land. In general, land records being a very generic term contains the following documents.

- The village map with different local names and terminologies.
- The fields index (*khasra*), which is a descriptive register showing the serial number, who owns, who cultivates and what crop, if any, each field bears
- *Khatian* (record of rights) of the tenants/rayaits.
- Village-statements showing concisely all the statistical facts, population, and other details, about the village.
- The *khewat*, which is a record of the shares and revenue responsibility of each member of the proprietary body.
- Jamabandi or the list of tenants, and their rents.
- The *wajib-ul-arz* or record of village customs.[9]

The land records or the entries made in thereof has, when properly attested, are legally presumed to be correct until the contrary is proved, which may be either by a law suit or changes made in the records made either due to sale, inheritance or otherwise. The common elements of survey and settlement in British India were: a complete survey of the land involving a preliminary 'demarcation' of the necessary boundary lines in each village, valuation of land assessment, the revenue assessment for each estate or holding in a village. Baden Powell interestingly notes that even after preparation of settlements of land gradually the records 'cease to correspond with the existing state of things' and the land records and registers outlived their utilities after thirty

[8] Tom G. Kessinger. 1970. 'Historical Materials on Rural India', *The Indian Economic and Social History Review,* 7(4), December, p. 495–495.

[9] B. H. Baden Powell. 1894. *A Short Account of the Land Revenue and its Administration in British India; With a Sketch of the Land Tenures*, Oxford: The Clarendon Press, pp. 147; 193–194.

years when the next settlement operation was to be taken up again[10] but these settlement operations were never carried out in time in many districts. Under all systems of land revenue administration in British India, 'great care is taken to record all changes in proprietary rights'. This process is called *Dakkhal-khariji* (i.e. putting in and taking out) or mutation of names which prevents the land records prepared by the last settlement operations being outdated. The mutation process initiated whenever there is sale, mortgage, gift, and inheritance of the land in question. Baden Powell's findings on maintenance of records appear quite relevant to the contemporary problem of land records.

> The whole object of land records system is to obviate future re-survey and re-record by seeing that the initial maps and records of Settlement are kept correct and in conformity with facts at the time. Good records mean, the security of titles, the impossibility of encroachment on subordinate rights, and the facility of decision in case a dispute occurs, and especially in all kinds of cases between the landlord and tenant.[11]

Contrary to the popular belief that the land records maintained by the British in India are crucial and reliable means to understand the agrarian relations in India, Dietmar Rothermund argues that such reliable records were conspicuous by their absence. Rather, the Record of Rights (RoRs) never fully recorded and existed only in the minds of men and suited to the wealthy and powerful sections in Indian society.[12]

Historical accounts reveal that India had a long tradition of assessment and collection of land revenue since it was the mainstay of state finances, and the Britishers maintained the continuity with some changes with the objective of facilitating revenue collection. Land rights were recorded only for collection of land revenue and the security of land titles as purely incidental in nature. The revenue records were not treated as records of title. In northern India, the Record of Rights (RoRs) of the village communities was maintained for revenue assessment whereas in ryotwari (cultivator-based system) areas of South India no such records of rights existed at all.[13]

---

[10] Ibid, p. 195–196.

[11] Ibid, p. 248–249.

[12] Dietmar Rothermund. 1969. 'Government, Landlord and the Tenant in India, 1875–1900,' *The Indian Economic and Social History Review*, 6(4), pp. 364–365.

[13] Dietmar Rothermund. 1971. 'The Record of Rights in British India,' *The Indian Economic and Social History Review*, 8(3), September, p. 443.

Rothermund has argued that in British India, neither the money lender nor the cultivator was interested to keep their name recorded. In Madras Presidency, the actual possession of the land was the unit of settlement but the changes of ownerships were not reflected. In Bombay Presidency, a cultivator was allotted one name for every survey number. The indifference on the pattern of ownerships in Bombay and Madras Presidencies were in contrast to Northern India where rights on land were recorded by village *patwari* (revenue inspector).[14] These Presidencies were however maintaining survey of land not ownership and unable to appreciate the importance of RoRs. The repeated pleas by Government of India to these Presidencies to maintain the Record of Rights (RoRs) for dealing with the problems of land alienation and of tenancy protection 'were considered quite irrelevant to the Ryotwari provinces.'[15]

The Government of India later on asked these presidencies and other areas of its jurisdiction to update the agricultural statistics for the whole country as that could serve as the basis for revision of revenue assessments and towards formulating a policy for the prevention of famines and land alienation. However, such direction according to Dietmar Rothermund created confusion in the minds of the officers regarding what they were supposed to do— a RoRs, or agricultural statistics, or information on land alienation, or rainfall statistics or crop reports, or all these. Thus the maintenance of land records did not take up in these provinces earnestly.[16]

The British India government was not genuinely interested to update the Record of Rights (RoRs) as the settlement operation was a long duration work, and did not seek updating of records due to change in ownership, inheritance and alienation which they perceived as burdensome. Baden Powell wrote that Survey and Settlement officials had upset all the regular works of the tahsils and the entire area where survey or resurvey works were undertaken was put into a state of political unrest for several years to the detriment of agricultural, social well-being and administrative function.[17]

Even the government's attempt to check land alienation and protection of tenants against landlord by maintaining a Record of Rights (RoRs) were opposed and did not progress as both landlords and tenants perceived obscurity

[14] Ibid, p. 444.

[15] Ibid, pp. 445–446.

[16] Ibid, p. 457.

[17] B. H. Baden Powell. 1974. *The Land Systems of British India*, Volume-1, pp. 356–357.

in such matters an advantage. This was natural owing to the introduction of rent credit squeeze system by the British rule and dwindling customary rights on land for which neither the tenant nor the landlord were eager to put all the facts on the record. Rather in its place a *benami* transaction was preferred.[18]

The wisdom to have the Record of Rights (RoRs) to keep as presumptive value rather conclusive one was apparent to the British authorities. The courts established by them relied on oral evidence not on records of presumptive value. Moreover, presumptive records were flexible, adapted themselves to facts, and could be useful in dealing with exceptional cases. The presumptive value of records could also be left to the courts to decide when it came to conclusive proofs through other evidence.[19] Rothermund interestingly puts that the British authorities were not clear whether to treat land records in India as mere Record of Rights (RoRs) or records of title as there were strong views of officials involved in survey and settlement works to giving state guarantee or finality to land title given the very difficult and cumbersome process of survey and settlement works and dynamic quality of land records.

Towards the last quarter of the colonial period, the law relating to land holdings gave more importance to the role of courts in deciding titles and the revenue official's role was confined to the collection of revenue, its assessment and maintenance of records. After Independence, the government gave less importance to land revenue, and so contributing to the decline of records maintenance. The necessity for correct and up-to-date land records for the abolition of the zamindari and other intermediary tenures were felt during the implementation of the First Five Year Plan itself.[20] The inadequacy of land records drove the Government of India to launch a census of land holdings which could not produce the desired results. Here again in the matters of detection of tenancy the land records were proved to be unreliable as most of the tenancy transactions remained unrecorded to evade tenancy legislation.[21] In summing up, it will be pertinent to quote Rothermund for his in-depth observation on the nature of land records management in India:

---

[18] Dietmar Rothermund. 1969. 'Government, Land-lord and the Tenant in India, 1875–1900', p. 365.

[19] Dietmar Rothermund. 1971. 'The Record of Rights in British India,' p. 452.

[20] Ibid, pp. 459–460.

[21] H. Laxminarayan and S. S. Tyagi. 1977. 'Tenancy: Extent and Inter-State Variations,' *Economic and Political Weekly*, 12 (22) May 28, p. 880.

A realistic agrarian policy in India is almost impossible in view of this lack of an accurate record of rights not to speak of a record which would distinguish between ownership and tenure so as to provide information about the actual units of cultivation.

The land reform measures of independent India were undertaken without any reference to the land revenue system which was allowed to decay further until some states actually abolished land revenue. In this way ironically enough the administrative machinery for the maintenance of land records disappeared where these records should have been improved.[22]

Land records management under five year plans: shifting priorities

The Five Year Plans give a broad outline of the public policies towards land records and the intention of the state in pursuing the policy agenda of land records management and the contemporary policy shifts towards neoliberal agrarian reforms.

The First Five Year Plan formulated in 1951 emphasised in clear terms the need for immediate abolition of intermediaries, giving security to tenants by conferring occupancy rights on them and advocated for putting reasonable restriction on retention of land for personal cultivation and ownerships. Land records management thus occupied a pre-requisite need for agrarian reform.

> A revenue administration depends, in the last resort, upon a good system of village records. In states like West Bengal, Bihar, Odisha, Rajasthan and Ajmer there are scarcely any village records. In Hyderabad and certain other areas, over large tracts, there existed a system of village records maintained by Zamindars and Jagirdars through their own pretty employees. These records were seldom of adequate quality and could not be relied upon. Records of rights and other land records become even more important at a time when rapid changes affecting land have become a normal feature of legislative activity. It would not in fact be too much to say that in some states because of the defective records the implementation of the reforms already enacted will remain incomplete and may even raise new problems which will come in the way of good administration.[23]

---

[22] Dietmar Rothermund. 1971. 'The Record of Rights in British India,' pp. 460–461.

[23] Government of India. 1951. *First Five Year Plan, 1951–1956*, Planning Commission of India, Yoyana Bhawan, New Delhi. See www.planningcommissionofindia.nic.in (accessed on May,15 2009)

The Second Five Year Plan (1956) similarly took into account the defective and inadequate nature of land records in 'as much as they do not provide information in respect of the holdings of tenants and crop sharers' and no regular updating of cadastral maps in large areas. It stressed the urgency of correct and up-to-date land records in the light of the abolition of intermediaries and a pre-requisite for land reforms and efficient revenue administration. The reason for poor maintenance of land records, according to the Plan document was lack of adequate supervisory staff in most states for which annual updating of land records were not carried out.[24] The Third Five Year Plan (1961) admitted that the problem of non-implementation of land reforms was due to non-availability of land records. It laid particular stress on the preparation of correct and up-to-date record of rights and the need to strengthen revenue administration.[25]

The Fourth Five Year Plan (1969–1974) acknowledged the lack of correct and up-to-date land records including the record of tenancies as a 'serious constraint' on the expeditious implementation of land reforms and also on the availability of credit and other inputs to the cultivating tenants. The Plan advocated a revision of the Record of Rights in the next five years in the areas where resurvey and settlement was going on. Interestingly, the Plan document advocated the preparation of land records that would have presumptive value and would reflect the rights of the tenant on the land cultivated and rent payable by him so that the land records so prepared could be used by him to enforce the legal provisions concerning the abolition of tenancy. It talked about the launching of a central sponsored scheme to help the states to in creating an up-to date land records in the Fourth Five Year Plan.[26]

The Fifth Five Year Plan (1974–1979) observed that 'unless up-to-date records are prepared, it will be not possible to ensure the effective implementation of any measure of land reforms or to consolidate agricultural holdings.'[27] The Sixth Five Year Plan (1980–1985)[28] recognised that updating

[24] Government of India. 1956. *Second Five Year Plan*, Planning Commission of India, Yoyana Bhawan, New Delhi, p. 208.

[25] Government of India. 1961. *Third Five Tear Plan*, Planning Commission of India, Yoyana Bhawan, New Delhi.

[26] Government of India. 1969. *Fourth Five Year Plan*, Planning Commission of India, Yoyana Bhawan, New Delhi, pp. 128;182.

[27] Government of India. 1974. *Fifth Five Year Plan*, Planning Commission of India, Yoyana Bhawan, New Delhi, p. 115.

[28] Government of India. 1980. *Sixth Five Year Plan*, Planning Commission of India, Yoyana Bhawan, New Delhi.

of land records is essential for implementation of land reforms and also access for agricultural credit. It noted that where the zamindari system was prevalent some relationship existed between the entries in the Record of Rights and ground realities. It also outlined a plan to launch a systematic programme for the compilation of land records within a period of five years and issuance of land pass book for each cultivator indicating his status and title to land, description of land schedules like areas, class of land etc along with a copy of *khasara* (map) and such other details as are considered necessary and statutory change may be made to confer the legal status on such land pass book.

The Seventh Five Year Plan (1985–1990) talked about the necessity of updating of land records for improving the farmer's demands to credits and inputs. It emphasised that the land records formed the base for all land reform measures and therefore regular and periodic updating of land records was essential for all states. It stressed the need for scientific surveys of unmeasured lands and recording of rights of tenants and share croppers which still remained unrecorded. The Seventh Plan proposed to launch a centrally sponsored scheme on the basis of matching contributions by the centre and the states for updating of land records. The Plan also proposed to assist the states in revamping their revenue administration and imparting training to the revenue functionaries in improving their efficiency and effecting their attitudinal changes. The Plan also referred to the efforts made by the central government in setting up a *One Man Committee on Status of Record of Rights in Land* by the Planning Commission of India under the chairmanship of Professor D. C. Wadhwa. It was during the Seventh Plan, two ambitious schemes called Computerisation of Land Records (CLR) and Strengthening of Revenue Administration and Updating of Land Records (SRA&ULR) were launched by the central government.[29]

Launching of computerisation of land records (CLR)

Initially, the Centrally Sponsored Scheme (CSS) on Computerisation of Land Records (CLR) was launched by the central government[30] as a pilot project

[29] Government of India. 1985. *Seventh Five Year Plan*, Planning Commission of India, New Delhi: Yoyana Bhawan, pp. 34; 63.

[30] A decision to computerise land- and crop-based statitics on pilot basis sponsored by the central government was taken at the coference of state Revenue Ministers held on 18 May, 1985 at New Delhi

in 1988–89 with 100 per cent financial assistance in the eight districts viz., Gandhinagar (Gujarat), Rangareddy (AP), Sonitpur (Assam), Singhbhum (Bihar), Morena (MP), Wardha (Maharashtra), Mayurbhanj (Odisha), and Dungarpur (Rajasthan) of the states 'to remove the problems inherent in the manual system of maintenance and updating of records and to meet the requirements of various groups of users.' It was decided to 'computerise only the CORE DATA' of the land records which could be used by development planners and administrators but the broad objectives that were originally envisaged and later on modified in 1994, 1999 and 2002 are as follows:

1. Computerisation of ownership and plot wise details for delivery of timely and accurate copy of the Record of Rights (RoRs) to the land owners;
2. to achieve low cost and easily reproducible storage media for reliable preservation for a long time;
3. to provide fast and efficient retrieval of information, both graphical and textual;
4. creation of land information system (LIS) and data base for agricultural census; (web source)
5. to provide legal sanctity to computer-generated certificates of land records after authentication by authorised revenue officials;
6. to provide a comprehensive land information system for better land-based planning and utilisation of land resources;
7. to focus on citizen-centric services related to land and revenue information;
8. to ensure accuracy, transparency and speedy dispute resolution; and
9. On demand distribution of computerised copies of Record of Rights to the land owner at the reasonable charges with a provision of online mutation module for ownership changes, seasonal crop updation etc at the tahsil level.[31]

[31] S. D. Meena et al. 2005. 'Computerisation of Land Records: National Perspective' In Wajhat Habibullah and Manoj Ahuja (Eds) *Computerisation of Land Records: Land Reforms in India, Volume-10*, New Delhi: Sage Publications, p. 23. Also see the Revised Guidelines for the Implementation of the Centrally Sponsored Scheme on Modernisation of Revenue and Land Administration issued by Department of Land Resources, Ministry of Rural Development, Government of India, New Delhi dated 3rd December 2002; *Annual Report, 2004–2005*, Ministry of Rural Development, Government of India, New Delhi, p. 114.

Under the scheme, the central government provided financial assistance to the states for completing data entry works, digitisation of spatial maps, setting up computer centres at the tahsil/taluk, block or circle level, subdivisional level, district level and a monitoring cell at the state level. Funds also provided for imparting computer training and awareness of software application to the revenue officials for regular updating of Record of Rights (RoRs) and smooth operation of the computerisation programme.[32] During the Seventh Plan, 24 districts were approved for computerisation of land records. In the Eighth Five Year Plan, funds were released for taking up the programme in 299 districts. The Tenth Five Year Plan sanctioned funds for the CLR project in additional 259 projects. In 1997, it was decided to extend the programme of computerisation to the tahsil/taluk level to facilitate distribution of computerised land records on demand and during the Ninth Five Year Plan, the central government released funds for setting up of computer centres for 2787 tahsil/taluk offices. The Tenth Five Year Plan extended the programme further to 1615 tahsils /taluks and setting up of computer centres in 1019 subdivisions, land records data centres in 365 districts and monitoring cell in 16 state headquarters.[33] Since its inception the scheme is under implementation in 582 districts, 4423 tahsils/taluks and 1021 subdivisions. Computerised copy of RoRs is being delivered in 2902 tahsils/taluks and computers have been set up in 3356 tahsils/taluks throughout the country.[34]

The scheme was reviewed in 1993–94 and it was observed that some states were facing technical problems like non-availability of skilled software personnel and hardware maintenance. The National Informatics Centre (NIC) conducted its system study in seventeen states and prepared the ICT system requirement specifications and flow. The system design developed by the National Informatics Centre was standardised and implemented in all the states with local variations. It also designed the biometric scanner and smart card for adding an extra layer of security of data and its storage.[35]

---

[32] Government of India. *Annual Report, 2006–2007*, Ministry of Rural Development, New Delhi: pp. 140–141.

[33] Government of India. *Annual Report, 2007–2008,* Ministry of Rural Development, New Delhi: p. 173.

[34] Ibid, p. 173.

[35] S. D. Meena et al. 2005. 'Computerisation of Land Records: National Perspective,' p. 22–23.

Government of India conducted evaluation studies on the pilot programmes in eight districts in different states in 1998 through LBSNAA, Mussorie. The findings have shown the need for strengthening the monitoring mechanism, training of officials and creating public awareness for the programme. Further, the pilot programme also made it imperative for digitisation of cadastral map for developing Land Information System (LIS) and the need for networking of the scheme at different levels through the NICNET (National Informatics Centre Network).[36]

In September 1999, the central government in giving further importance to computerisation of land records, declared that the CLR programme would be implemented on complementary basis by both rural development ministry and NIC of India. NIC was asked to provide all the necessary technical and infrastructural support to the programme.[37]

Strengthening of revenue administration and updating of land records

Prior to the Computerisation of Land Records (CLR) scheme, the Ministry of Rural Development had launched a Centrally Sponsored Scheme (CSS) for Strengthening of Revenue Administration and Updating of Land Records (SRA &ULR) in 1987 in Bihar and Odisha initially. Later on it covered all states and UTs during 1989–1990. Until its merger with the CLR programme and launching of National Land Records Modernisation Programme (NLRMP), the scheme was being implemented by the state governments through their revenue and land reforms departments. It is funded by the centre and the state on 50:50 sharing basis and Union Territories are fully assisted by the central government. The rationale for launching of the scheme was recognition of the importance of maintaining correct and up-to-date land records in rural areas. Poor land records are attributed to the cause of failure of land reforms and growing agrarian violence in the countryside. The reason for poor maintenance and management of land records are cited by the government as inadequate revenue administration, poor infrastructure, use of outdated technologies, and absence of training and resource constraints in the states.

---

36 Ibid, p. 31.

37 See Supplementary Guideline on implementation of CLR issued by Ministry of Rural Development, GOI, New Delhi, LN.18014/15/90-LRD dated 22 September 1999.

Further, the scheme also provided funds for modern survey equipments like Global Positioning System (GPS), Total Stations, office equipment like photocopiers and basic office infrastructural facilities like construction of state training institutes and construction of office-cum-residence of revenue inspectors. To improve the efficiency of lower functionaries of revenue departments, the central government has so far released ₹ 417.20 crores towards the central share under the scheme since its inception to all the states and UTs of which ₹ 283.13 crores have been utlilsed and the percentage of expenditure comes to 68 per cent.[38]

The Eighth Five Year Plan (1992–1997) reaffirmed the old emphasis of updating land records as one of the important objectives of land reforms and unlike previous plans it had laid stress on imparting training for enhancing the skills and capabilities of the lower level revenue functionaries for management of land records so that they would help rather hinder the evolution of an 'equitable agrarian order.' Significantly, the Eighth Plan advocated reorientation of the role of state and planned economy and facilitating the growth of market economy. It also admitted that the scope for redistributive policies in land reforms are now limited. Instead it laid stress on 'recording the rights of tenants and sharecroppers with the objective of giving them security of tenure' [39] The conference of the state revenue ministers held in December 1995 at New Delhi, reiterated its resolve to carry forward the two centrally sponsored scheme on computerisation of land records, modernisation of revenue administration and updating land records and decided to implement Kissan passbooks to land owners as suggested in the Appu Committee report. The conference considered that 'computerisation of land records will be a definite step forward for modern land management and it will substantially improve the implementation and monitoring of land reform programmes...'[40] Such holding of the periodic revenue ministers conference, it may be suggested, is the long-term political strategy of the central government to lend a political

[38] Government of India. *Annual Report, 2007–2008*, Ministry of Rural Development, New Delhi: p. 175.

[39] Government of India. *Eighth Five Year Plan,1992–1997, Volume-I,* Planning Commission of India, Yoyana Bhawan, New Delhi, p. 33;40.See also the 'Objectives and Reorientations' of Eighth Five Year Plan.

[40] Government of India. 1995. Recommendations of the Conference of Revenue Ministers held on 27 December 1995 at New Delhi, MORD, New Delhi.

legitimacy to its techno-managerial and top down policy design and to make a strategic shift to a more market-friendly policy reorientation of land records management.

The Ninth Five Year Plan (1997–2002) once again emphasised the need for recording and updating the land records management system 'as the pre-requisite for any land reform measure' but shifted the responsibility on to the states on the ground that the land reform is a state subject. 'It cannot be gainsaid that the essential pre-requisite of any land reform measure is the recording of land rights and their updating.' [41] The important observation of the Planning Commission in the context of neo-liberal reforms was that some states have liberalised their land laws like ceiling of land holdings to facilitate corporate farming on a large scale and also there is a move from the state governments to reconsider the tenancy laws by amending its provisions to make more attractive for corporate investment in agriculture. 'Hence it is necessary to reconsider the issue of land reforms, particularly from the point of view of poor, as access to land is still a major source of livelihood in rural India.'[42]

The revised guidelines for Strengthening Revenue Administration and Updating Land Records and Computerisation of Land Records (SRA &ULR) and Computerisation of Land Records (CLR) were issued in 2002. The previous guidelines were issued in 1993–94 and subsequently modified in 1999. The guidelines issued after nearly fourteen years argued that 'in this electronic age, as the country embarks on e-governance initiatives, it is necessary to revamp the land administration system to keep pace with the times to provide a fair, efficient and transparent service to the citizens of the country.' It was admitted that though evaluative studies on the two centrally sponsored schemes (CSS) have not taken place yet certain problems have cropped up such as poor infrastructure at the village level revenue administration, untrained and unskilled settlement staff and their inability to integrate modern survey technologies provided under the scheme, no correct updating of land records, non-utilisation of the IT potential and no steps taken for restructuring and reviewing the existing land laws and procedures.

Further non-existence of land records and cadastral maps in some areas in the north-eastern states and the demand of these states to bear expenses of

[41] Ibid.

[42] Government of India. *Ninth Five Year Plan, 1997–2002*. Planning Commission of India, Yoyana Bhawan, New Delhi, pp. 25–26.

SRA & ULR scheme on 90:10 sharing basis due to their resource constraints, and the resolution of state revenue minister's conference to expedite the implementation of the schemes have led the central government to revise the guidelines on CLR and SRA&ULR programmes. It was also claimed that the revised guidelines were formulated from the feedback of the experiences gained by the states in the implementation of the programmes, addressed the problem of human resource management in handling cutting edge ICTs and introduced online monitoring mechanism and setting up of state level data centres for the creation of land records data base for planning and developmental purposes.

The two composite schemes were called Modernisation of Revenue and Land Administration (MORALA). The revised guidelines did not however highlight the progress and difficulties experienced by the states and UTs in implementation of the scheme. The revised guideline in effect sought to further broaden the scope of activities without critically examining the capacity of the state governments to undertake such works and the concrete achievements made so far in implementing the complex computerisation works.

The Tenth Five Year Plan (2002–2007) formulated in the context of India's neoliberal economic reforms acknowledged that 'land reforms seem to have been relegated to the background in the 1990s' and many Indian state governments have liberalised land laws to promote corporate farming in sharp contrast to the earlier policy frameworks on land reforms that were meant to provide ownership rights to the small and marginal farmers on redistributive considerations. The Plan document explained that due to ban on tenancy in certain states like Odisha and Bihar, land leases are impossible resulting in concealed tenancies to the extent of over 34 per cent of land under operation in the latter state. It stressed that a 'land records management system is a pre-condition for an effective land reform programme.' The problem of concealment of land in India is due to the lack of a comprehensive land rights database. So the Tenth Plan provided thrust on detection of the concealment of land, increasing access to land, computerisation of land records and updating the Record of Rights of land owners.[43]

The report of the *Committee on Computerisation of Land Records* (2005) by Department of Rural Development, New Delhi is an important document which helps us understand the progress made by computerisation of land records

[43] Government of India. *Tenth Five Year Plan, 2002–2007*, Volume-II, Planning Commission of India, New Delhi, pp. 301–302; 311; 313.

by following a techno-managerial and apolitical approach. The report says that many technological changes and new requirements like data security, process reengineering and change management, interoperability and sustainability have cropped up that necessitate revision of the last guidelines issued in 1999, in particular the need to 'devise practical and implementable solutions and suggest modalities to integrate the process of digitisation of cadastral maps and registration process with computerisation of land records for early completion of the scheme in all the states.' Interestingly, the committee claimed that Computerisation of Land Records (CLR) is 'the first successful e-governance initiative in India, at the grass-root level' and the focus of the 'entire operation has been to employ the state of art Information Technology (IT) to galvanise and transform the existing land records system of the country.'[44]

The Committee also set time bound targets for the states for completion of various activities under Computerisation of Land Records (CLR). In fact, the Committee's report expanded further various activities such as computerisation and integration of sub-registrar's office with tahsil, prescribed necessary legal changes and laid a special thrust on data security and privacy. The report clearly highlights the growing complexity and scope of activities under the CLR scheme and the role of central government in shaping the policy. Strangely the report did not look critically and went deeper in the problems in application, adoption and management of ICTs in tahsil administration through the private vendors and various policy issues that have raised before the revenue administration in outsourcing the computerisation works and the capacity of the lower level tahsil officials to handle the high-end technology. The Committee report was rather based on the intrinsic belief that problems of land records in India are technological in nature and massive computerisation and integration of the existing land records and automation of the land records administration with the help of IT vendors would address the inefficiencies of the land records management apolitically.

The above report may be viewed as a precursor to the policy outline and shifts to the land title guarantee regime. The Report of *the Working Group on Land Relations for Formulation of Eleventh Five Year Plan, 2006* was appointed under the chairmanship of D. Bandyopadhyay to consider modernisation

[44] Government of India. 2005. Excutive Summary to *Report of Committee on Computerisation of Land Records,* Department of Land Resources, Ministry of Rural Development, New Delhi.

of land management with reference to updating of land records and use of modern technological developments for online maintenance of the records and demarcation and digitisation of land boundaries. The Committee observed that the land records in India lack credibility and the one way out is to guarantee title or conclusive title which would 'make our records closer to ground reality' and would thus 'become catalyst in the overall development of the nation.' As conclusive titling system is 'prohibitively costly' there is need for incremental progress and strengthening the registration process for future transactions.

The Committee recommended that the registration and mutation process be combined to form registration of deeds after effecting legal changes, by an authority called land officer substituting tahsildar and sub-registrar who shall check all the legalities of land records such as the right and title vested on the transferor or the legality of the transaction and the competence of the parties to take part in the transaction before registering the deed. Production of parcel maps or the sketch of the land intended to be transacted clearly demarcating the transacted extent at the time of registration should be made compulsory. The village maps and parcels maps need to be updated and digitised with the help of modern survey equipments. Registration of title will require for computerisation and scanning of mutations over 50 years and creation of such an archive. The Report, therefore, enabled the Planning Commission to go for adoption of conclusive titling system in the National Land Records Modernisation Programme (NLRMP) in its Eleventh Plan.[45]

The current Eleventh Five Year Plan (2007–2012) makes a clear policy departure to the land reforms policies hitherto pursued by the Indian state. Earlier land reforms policies advocated better and more efficient enforcement of tenancy laws and ceiling of land holding but the current Plan made a radical break from the past. Instead it prescribes reforming and liberalising ceiling and tenancy laws and a modernisation of the management of land records. The Plan document that clearly outlined the policy orientations of the government in the context of neoliberal economic reforms says:

> Correct and updated land records are crucial for the security of the land rights and to encourage investment. These result in fewer disputes and conflicts,

[45] Government of India. 2006. *Report of the Working Group on Land Relations for Formulations of Eleventh Five Year Plan*, 31 July, New Delhi, pp. 34–37.

> allow land to be used as collateral, lower transaction costs and corruption, ensure efficient land markets, and help in implementation of land reforms and planning for various developmental programmes. [46]

The Eleventh Fivc Year Plan also hinted at going beyond the present system of computerisation and digitisation of spatial and textual land records and suggested the integration of mutation and registration of deeds. The registration of the deeds will be preceded by verification of land records to be transacted. The land records of the previous fifty years will be computerised or as may be prescribed in the relevant state laws for conferring title guarantee of the land to be registered.[47]

The Plan document further suggested the delivery of citizen services at cyber kiosks based on land data such as providing residence certificate, caste certificate, income certificate, Record of Rights with maps to scale and land pass books with relevant information for agricultural credit etc. The Plan underlined the need for integrating three layers of data viz. forest survey maps, cadastral maps and revenue records to harmonise them on a Geographic Information System (GIS) which would serve as a comprehensive tool for pro-business planning and projects such as corporate farming, mining and industrial activities apart from regulatory and disaster management and other location-specific purposes. The Eleventh Plan has also proposed for integration of registration and mutation works as a part of 'modernisation of land administration' for switching over from the present registration of deed based on presumptive land records to the 'Torrens' system based on title guarantee by the state after setting up a few pilot projects. It also prescribed for the merger of the two centrally sponsored schemes on computerisation of land records and strengthening revenue administration into National Land Records Modernisation Programme (NLRMP) and launching of the programme as a pilot projects in each state. Taking an ahistorical and apolitical approach to the problem of the land records system the ambitious and unrealistic Plan further states:

> After the validation of the proof of concept (*in the pilot projects*) within the next two years, the scheme would be extended to the entire country. It is expected

[46] Government of India. *Eleventh Five Year Plan. 2007–2012,* Planning Commission of India, Volume-III, Yoyana Bhawan, New Delhi, p. 29.

[47] Ibid.

> that the digitisation of land records after under taking comprehensive land survey would be completed by the end of twelfth five year plan. It is expected that after availability of the basic record, the country would move towards the Torrens system in the Thirteenth Five Year Plan.[48]

Finally, the Twelfth Five Year Plan (2012–2017) clearly delinked the expediency of updating land records with land reforms and set the path forward for formalisation of property rights in land and instead declared that 'unambiguously recorded land rights, firm in law, are the foundation for investments in higher farm productivity.' It talked about launching of NLRMP 'to move decisively' towards the land title regime from the existing presumptive nature of land records.[49]

This description of the policy perspective on land records management and policy shifts and reorientations of the Indian state could be better understood if we supplement our understanding with a consideration of some other policy measures taken in land records management.

The present status of record of rights in land

Land in India is not merely an economic resource; it is rather embedded in a social, customary and political context. One has to take into account the historical facts for a broader understanding of the problem as the land relations, agrarian structure and land records in the contemporary period are merely a legacy of the past. The argument is further buttressed if we look into the recent steps to confer right to inheritance of the parental property on the daughters under Hindu Succession Act (Amendment), 2005, Forest Rights Act, 2006 and the attempt to ease the tenancy laws to facilitate renting and tenancy. Robert Frykenberg rightly comments that:

> Whatever the terminology, attempts to classify and differentiate between myriad varieties of zamindars, Jagirdars, and ryots, whether great or small, become meaningful only if the observer recognises that all kinds of holdings and rights were intricately linked to definite socio-ceremonial and communal as well as economic and political roles. When seen in this perspective, the

[48] Ibid, p. 29.

[49] Government of India. *Twelfth Five Year Plan. 2007–2012,* Planning Commission of India, Volume-I, Yoyana Bhawan, New Delhi: Sage Publications, p. 199.

> tenant and landholder look very much the same, no matter how large and superior the holding and or how small and subordinate the tenancy...Land control and land bondage were mutually shaded and overlapping conditions.[50]

Viewed from this perspective we could observe that the rights of an Indian with respect to land, his or her rights as well as the rights of his family and community over the government land or public land now referred as common property resources, the superior or the paramount right as of the government as the landlord or (the state) are found to have been arranged against one another in order of preference in a body of documents maintained by the state is called Record of Rights comprising textual record and cadastral map.

These records are dynamic in the sense that the proprietary rights accrued through inheritance, purchase, gift, mortgage, lease, resumption, surrender, acquisition and alienation require constant correction or updating. The sub-registrar deals with transfer of property under the Transfer of Property Act, 1882 and Registration Act, 1908. The Record of Rights (RoRs) are prepared by survey and settlement organisations after taking a decade or more time, its maintenance and constant correction and updatation are done by tahsildar/taluqdar and revenue inspector/patwari. Settlement reports as a whole consists of the village maps and indexes, the records of the revenue engagements and the Record of Rights (RoRs). The entries in the RoRs made and attested shall be *presumed to be true till the contrary is proved.*[51] The recent report of the *Committee on State Agrarian Relations and the Unfinished Task in Land Reforms (2009)* has tried to explain the intricate web of land relations and wide local and regional variations that are reflected in the Record of Rights.

One of the reasons for poor land records management in India is due to neglect of land revenue administration in the post-independence period. The declining share of land revenue to the state exchequer, deployment of revenue officials in miscellaneous administrative works, preoccupation with implementation of land reforms laws and the general deterioration of governance standards in all departments of government contributed to the neglect of land records management. It is argued that lack of monitoring,

---

50 Robert E. Frykenberg. 1969. (Ed*) Land Control and Social Structure in Indian History*, p. xv.

51 B.H. Baden Powell. 1974. *The Land Systems of British India*, Volume-ll, Oxford: Clarendon University Press, pp. 87; 91.

accountability and supervision, poor governance and distortion of priorities rather than technical capacity are the reasons for the deteriorating standard of revenue administration as well as contributing factors to poor land records management.

In many north-eastern states, no land records or cadastral map exists and these areas continue to remain unsurveyed till today. In many parts of the schedule areas of southern and western Odisha, no land records exist for the tribal population living on the hilly slopes and practicing shifting cultivation. In Jharkhand, the revision settlement started in 1958 is still continuing in many districts and the local people are resisting such settlement operations that record the common property land as government land. [52] The problem is acute in urban and metropolitan areas and urban fringes experiencing rapid urbanisation and leading to conversion of agricultural land to non-agricultural purposes. It is very difficult to establish ownership rights in respect of urban properties.[53]

Poor governance has also affected the survey and settlements organisations. In almost all states and UTs revision settlements have not been conducted for long owing to administrative and political reasons and it has become 'one of the unpleasant duties of the state to declare new survey operations in an area' and in some states revision survey and settlements are going for more than decades. In Rajasthan, the state government has decided to abolish the settlement department altogether and transform it into a much leaner department of land records with no system for periodic revision of land records. In Madhya Pradesh, revision survey and settlement ordered in 26 districts were suspended due to persistent complaints and protests from the people. In Odisha, the survey and settlement office have been merged with tahsil office to facilitate single window delivery and in some coastal districts like Puri, where the settlement operations are continuing since 1964 to this date and the draft but not final RoRs yet to be declared as final after disposal of public objections. It is argued now that in view of its political implications, the political leadership is unwilling to allow the present deficient nature of land records continue and update it after undertaking survey and settlement operations that would reflect

---

[52] Carol Upadhya. 2005. 'Community Rights in Land in Jharkhand,' *Economic and Political Weekly*, October 8, p. 4435–4436.

[53] N. C. Saxena. 2005. 'Updating Land Records: Is Computerisation Sufficient,' *Economic and Political Weekly*, 22 January, p. 313–315.

ground situations. The other alternative is to improve the transaction based maintenance through computerisation.[54]

Some of the states where survey and settlements works remain neglected in the post independence period are given below that will amply explain the state of land records.

Table 3.1

Years of Original and Years of Revision Settlement

State	*Year of Settlement*	*Year of Last Revision Settlement*
Andhra Pradesh	1861–1888	1892–1911
Assam	1900–1927	1991, still continuing
Karnataka	1806–1904	1966–1978
Kerala	1866–1934	Not attempted
Madhya Pradesh	1901–1950	1990–2000, but stopped without completion
Maharashtra	1840–1880	1917–1920
Odisha	1922–1932	Done in a few districts in the last three decades
Punjab	1889–1912	Survey is merged with consolidation
Uttar Pradesh	1938–	NA
West Bengal	1889–1942	1956–1961, Second revision began still continuing

Source: *Report of the Committee on Revitalisation of Land Revenue Administration*, Government of India, Ministry of Rural Development, New Delhi, 1995: p.77.

Apart from the failure to carry out the periodic updation of land records, the management system of land records in the state is as diverse as the nature and status of tenants of the land. It has been rightly observed by the *Committee on State Agrarian Relations and the Unfinished Task in Land Relations (2009)* that, 'the land management in each state has evolved through a historicity of thousands of years and is rooted to the soil, climatic conditions, agronomical, social relations, ownership relations, the nature of administration and that of the economy.'[55] Such great regional diversities, knowledge and experience in managing the land records system is a significant fact to keep in mind in view of the attempt to develop UNICODE database for all records in India by the central government.

[54] Ibid, pp. 316–317.

[55] Government of India. 2009. *Report of the Committee on State Agrarian Relations and the Unfinished Task in Land Relations*, p. 150.

According to the *One-Man Committee on Record of Rights in Land,* (1989) the problems of land records in the country is in very bad shape as in many parts of the country the land records exist in the name of a person(s) who is no more or the land has been transferred without quick consequential mutation in the record. The names of public, and the private persons under whose name land records exist no longer possess the land or those who possess the land for long are not able to get their land recorded in their names. Millions of mutation cases are pending for disposal. The entries in the land records do not have correlation with reality on the ground and such disharmony gives rise to various legal and administrative complicacies and overburdening the judicial machinery in the country. The record of rights in India continue to be presumptive and fiscal in nature as long as the owner of the piece of land continues to pay land revenue he or she is presumed to be the proprietor or *prima facie* title holder of the land until the contrary is proved. It means the entries made in the record of rights are not final. Entries in the Record of Rights are open to challenge in the court of law and the state or government or its officials are not liable against any claim for an entry made in any record or register that is maintained by government or to have any entry omitted or amended or added due to presumptive nature of land records.[56]

Two possible solutions for the problems were identified by the Committee. The first is to usher in the title guarantee regime known as the Torrens System and the second is the practice of arranging title insurance. The Torrens system involves a change from registration of deeds to a system of registration of title to land. 'The system regards registration of title to land under the authority of government as necessary whereby the official certificate of title will always show the state of title to land and the person in whom the title is vested.'[57] The insurance system on the other hand 'offers a guarantee for title, is normally issued by title companies which maintain elaborate records to keep current information of all properties under their surveyance'[58]

The need for registration of title to land according to the Committee has assumed significance in the context for growing demand for land and

---

[56] D. C. Wadhwa. 2002. 'Guaranteeing Title to Land,' *Economic and Political Weekly,* 23 November, p. 4702.

[57] D. C. Wadhwa. 1989. 'Guaranteeing Title to Land: A Preliminary Study, *Economic and Political Weekly*, 14 October, p. 2324.

[58] Ibid, P. 2324.

its consequent scarcity due to changing socio-economic conditions, need for proprietary rights on land for investment and credit and imperatives for maintaining a well defined boundaries of parcels of land. The Report observed as '... land changing hands more frequently than before, with more and more land passing into the hands of companies and corporations, and with more and more securities being created on land, the desirability of good title in land must grow in importance.'[59]

With the introduction of the title guarantee system, it is argued that the Record of Rights will always remain up-to-date and will reflect the ground position correctly because there will be no registration without mutation and both will be done simultaneously and at the same time.[60] According to D. C. Wadhwa, the land records under the title guarantee regime are maintained by the state as an authoritative record and the state accepts the responsibility for providing validity of land records which was not possible under the presumptive nature of land records. The system therefore does away with the need for pre-checking of the validity of the land records by the prospective buyers. A continuous finality to the land title increases its market value.[61] The Wadhwa Committee therefore recommended that since switching over to conclusive titling 'will put a heavy administrative burden on the state and in the present set up the existing administrative machinery will not be able to cope with the task,' the revenue functionaries must not be assigned diverse nature of non revenue works and be suitably trained to handle the work. A 'Land Title Assurance or Guarantee Corporation' or 'Land Title Corporation' on the pattern of the USA may be formed to undertake the responsibility on account of 'fear of financial liability or on account of administrative reasons.'[62] Revision survey and settlement operation may be carried in most part of the country barring a few areas where revision surveys have been completed, under central assistance first to update and prepare cadastral maps and *Khatian* (textual record) which could be used as a basis to adopt conclusive title system. However the *One-Man Committee* suggested for implementation of a pilot project in one district or two

---

[59] Ibid, p. 2329.

[60] Ibid, p. 2333.

[61] D. C. Wadhwa. 2002. 'Guaranteeing Title to Land,' *Economic and Political Weekly*, 23 November, p. 4705.

[62] D. C. Wadhwa. 1989. 'Guaranteeing Title to Land: A Preliminary Study,' *Economic and Political Weekly*, 14 October, p. 2331.

in each state where revision surveys have undertaken so that the conversion of the present presumptive title to conclusive title may be introduced.

In the north-eastern states where customary laws govern land records and relations, revision survey may be conducted first to determine presumptive title and after a period of thirty years, switch over to a conclusive title may be made. The operation of the conclusive title system is to progress gradually from village by village and district by district and general public have to be made well aware of the process in advance. The decision about the conclusiveness of the land title will have to be left to the civil court.[63] Clearly, the implementation of the reports and recommendations of the Committee will bring a radical transformation in the existing administrative and legal machineries.

The reports of *One–Man Committee on Record of Rights* (1989) found favor among the judges, lawyers and policy makers and even enthusiastically among the World Bank policy advocates. However, it can be argued that the reports of the Committee and its recommendations bear similarities of the World Bank's policy notes on promoting market led agrarian reforms. The Wadhwa Committee approached the land as an economic resource and overlooked its social, cultural and political underpinnings while strongly advocating for adoption of the title guarantee system.

The Wadhwa Committee report also found acceptance by the *National Commission to Review the Working of the Constitutio*n. The Commission was formed to review the working of Indian Constitution in the past fifty years and to suggest the ways the Constitution can respond to the changing socio-economic conditions. Its report (2002) noted that nearly 1.3 per cent economic growth in India is lost due to disputed titles which also affect capital investment and credit supply. It recommended for bringing out 'a fundamental change' in the way the land records are maintained. The ideas of New Public Management appear to have influenced the Commission's prescription.

> The Commission recommends that we move to a system where the state guarantees the title to land after carrying out extensive land surveys and computerising the land records. It will take some time but the results would be beneficial for investment in land. This will be a major step forward in revitalising land administration in the country as it would enable Right to Access, Right to use, Right to enforce decisions regarding land. Similar

[63] Ibid, pp. 2330–2331.

rationalisations of records relating to individual rights in properties other than privately held lands (which are held in common) would improve operational efficiency which left unattended foment unrest. The Commission is of the view that a coherent public policy addressed to the modern methods of management would contribute to better use of assets and raise dynamic forces of individual creativity. Run away expansion of bureaucratic apparatus of the state would also get curtailed by new management system.[64]

Parliamentary standing committees on computerisation of land records

The Parliamentary Standing Committee on rural development has often examined the two interrelated schemes on computerisation of land records and strengthening of revenue administration especially its overall performance and utilisation of funds and demand for grants. The Standing Committees have given some useful recommendations which are related to policy aspects of the scheme but most of the recommendations have not been accepted by the Government of India. The study of such reports is relevant for our research on land records management policies like the role of the legislature in shaping the policy and their understanding of the matter and the response of the executive to policy examination by the legislative body. Interestingly, the Standing Committee has brought out some issues that have not been addressed by the Department of Land Resources. The Standing Committee in its Forty Seventh Report (2003) had recommended the opening of computerised land records data centres at the sub-division level for redressal of public grievance, proper supervision of the tahsils and its functioning as land records data centre for all tahsils under its jurisdiction. The committee recommended the merging of the two schemes as they were closely interrelated and increasing the funding arrangements for strengthening of revenue administration and updating land records to 100 per cent as they states were unable to provide the matching contributions. Its observation on poor performance in computerisation of land records and updating of land records among the states has been sought to be explained by central government by shifting the responsibility on states for their failure to spend the funds allotted by it. The spending of approximately

[64] Government of India. 2002. *Report of the National Commission to Review the Working of the Constitution, Volume-II,* New Delhi: Para 6.4.2.

60 per cent of the total outlay till 31st March 2003 since the inception of the schemes as attributed by the centre to delay in development of software, delay in transfer of funds from states to implementing authority, non-availability of data entry agencies, delay in porting data from UNIX-FOX base to window base, lack of trained staff to handle computers and delay in procurement in hardware by the state governments as some of the reasons for poor performances by the states. The Committee noted that the monitoring of the schemes was not being done by the states, legal sanctity not accorded to computerised copies of land rectors in most states, underfunding to the schemes occurred as many states were unable to contribute to their matching share of 50:50 basis owing to their financial constraints thereby resulting in delayed proposals from states to release the central share for the ongoing schemes.[65] One could get the notion of 'transparency' as one of the objectives of ICT applications in land records management as well as promoting e-governance from the stand taken by government before the committee. The central government has claimed that computerisation of land records and uploading on the web would bring transparency in the following techno-managerial ways:

- Easy access by the landowner in getting computerised copy of RoRs on payment of reasonable charges which would empower the landowner at the grassroots level;
- Use of the computerised copy of RoRs for availing loan from banks and
- Setting up of cyber kiosks will promote transparency.[66]

Computerisation of Land Records and Strengthening Revenue Administration and Updating of Land Records were merged as National Programme for Comprehensive Land Records Modernisation Programme (NPCLRM) in 2007–2008 and Eleventh Five Year Plan has proposed an outlay of ₹ 3,104 crores for the implementation of the programme.

The restructured programme demonstrates an urgency to complete the programme of 'computerisation of whatever land records are available with professional input on a mission mode within three years.' It was observed by

[65] Parliament of India. 2003. *Forty Seventh Report of the Standing Committee on Rural and Urban Development*, The Thirteenth Lok Sabha, 2003–2004, Lok Sabha Secretariat, New Delhi.

[66] Ibid, para. 3.94.

the committee that strengthening revenue administration and updating land records has been reduced to a construction of building programme by the state governments and an unspent amount of ₹ 219 crores under CLR and ₹ 94 crores under SRA &ULR remain unspent till 2006. The central government's response was that, there was a serious technological problem in computerisation of vast quantity of land records at the outset which has been dealt with later on with the advancement of information technology. Too much focus on computerisation of textual land records (*khatian*) has led to total neglect of digitisation of spatial record (map). The bad shape of revenue maps, and no regular correction and updation of the maps has created difficulties for the delay in digitisation of maps. Alternatively the digitisation of revenue maps have been going on through the process of vectorisation by creating analogous data basing upon the existing error-prone revenue maps.

The Standing Committee has observed that, some state governments even after spending a good amount of public money on computerisation of land records are yet to accord legal sanctity to computerised copy of land records or stop the issue of manual land records as they lack political and administrative will and absence of public awareness. The Committee apprehended that the restructured programme (i.e., NLRMP) would be beneficial to the well performing states that have started issuing computerised land records (RoRs) and would punish the poor performing states. It therefore suggested the continuance of the programme for Strengthening Revenue Administration and Updating the Land Records (SRA &ULR) for the North-Eastern states where no land records exists and the land ownership and tenurial conditions are vested with the community. The Committee apprehended that the restructuring of the land records management programme would worsen the disparity among states due to the differential nature of achievements in land records modernisation. The central government has sought to allay the apprehension by clarifying that in the newly restructured scheme, district will be the focal point of implementation and 'handholding support would be provided' to the states so that no state would lag behind.[67] The Standing Committee took exception of the reports about total utilisation of funds in the year 2006–2007 and 2007–2008 but in terms of physical achievements there was serious shortfall. Throughout the country, the physical target for

---

[67] Parliament of India. 2007. *Standing Committee on Rural Development, Twenty Seventh Report,2006–2007*, Fourteenth Lok Sabha, New Delhi, pp. 53–61.

installation of computers in sub-divisional offices were seventy-five in 2007 but only in two sub-divisions computer centres could be established. The Committee opined that 'it is really very difficult to comprehend the status of the various land records schemes/programmes of the scheme.'[68] In its Thirty Third Report (2011–2012), the Parliamentary Committee exclusively devoted in studying the working of CLR and NLRMP and made a harsh observation on the performance of the land records modernisation programme.

> The Committee are at a loss to understand as to why the Department went into slumber for more than two decades after initiating CLR and SLA & ULR schemes and failed to identify the shortcomings of these schemes despite spending more than one thousand crore rupees .The Committee are of the view that Government was not sincere in implementing these schemes as specific directions were not spelt out before initiation of the schemes.[69]

Thus the observations and recommendations of the Parliamentary Standing Committee on land records computerisation and strengthening revenue administration brings to light some governance issues like the capacity of the states especially its bureaucratic machinery in policy implementation, relationship between the centre-states in carrying forward the land records modernisation which is a State List under Seventh Schedule of the Constitution, growing interstate disparity in implementation, impact of the two technology-driven centrally sponsored scheme (CSS) in promoting transparency in land records management and strengthening revenue administration. Interestingly, examination of the Committee reports and the response of the central government thus revealed that both the executive and the legislature wing of the state have reposed their faith on the techno-managerial and expenditure-driven programme approach.

The Committee has not evinced any interest to understand the long-term and short-term impact of vendor-driven approach to computerisation and delivery through cyber kiosks and its impact on the public. The Committee members belonging to both the Lower and Upper houses have tended to believe on the ability of the lower level bureaucracy to handle such modern

[68] Parliament of India. 2008. *Standing Committee on Rural Development, Forty Second Report,2008–2009*, Fourteenth Lok Sabha, New Delhi, pp. 34–40.

[69] Parliament of India. 2012. *Standing Committee on Rural Development, Thirty Third Report, 2011–2012*, Fifteenth Lok Sabha, New Delhi, p. 65.

survey equipment in land records modernisation overlooking the motivation of the bureaucracy and their rent-seeking interest in the present system. The Committee reports are mechanical in nature as like the central government it tended to believe the problems of land records management are techno-managerial ones. By merely pulling up the central government machineries for poor implementation, the Committee members interestingly avoided in making a critical examination of the land title system and guaranteeing property rights on land as envisaged in NLRM Programme and its implication on India's state-led land reform policy. A critical look into the draft land title bill, 2010 by the House Committee members could have generated a public debate on feasibility of adopting the land title system by replacing the present conclusive land title system. The Committee reports and recommendations are basically based on the information supplied by central government. Therefore, it failed to reflect ground realities on slow progress of implementation and critically appreciate the apolitical nature of the programme and the strategic policy shifts by the executive from land reforms to securing property rights through computerisation of land records. The Standing Committee reports also revealed that the Committee believes the computerisation of land records from the context of improving service delivery only not for attending the egalitarian objective of land reforms.

Second administrative reforms commission on mission mode project on the computerisation of land records

The Second Administrative Reforms Commission in its eleventh report, *Promoting e-Governance: The Smart Way Forward (2008)* has dealt with some of the issues of land records computerisation as one of the select e-governance initiatives. The Commission has observed that nearly 410 crores of rupees have been released by the centre for implementation of CLR and SRA & ULR schemes but only 67.85 per cent of the funding was utilised.[70] The weaknesses of the two schemes that have delayed implementation are explained by the government to the commission as: computerisation and scanning of outdated records, neglect of survey and settlement by most states, both the scheme excluded inter connectivity between GIS mapping and registration

[70] Government of India. 2008. *Second Administrative Reforms Commission-Eleventh Report on 'Promoting e-Governance: The Smart Way Forward'*, p. 138.

of documents, the choice of activities were left to states and UTs who gave importance on construction activities, funds were thinly spread, absence of time frame of completion and the absence of a specific system of monitoring.[71]

The Commission observed that the lessons drawn from the twenty years long operationalisation of the schemes are that the scheme failed to address the main defect of the land records in India, i.e., the land records do not reflect the factual ground reality and it computerised existing outdated land records thereby perpetuated existing loopholes and errors. Further, land records computerisation, updating and strengthening of revenue administration are complex e-governance projects that demand holistic approach in implementation.[72] Although the Commission did not go into the mechanisms, rationalities of the schemes and their impact on governance process and centre-state relationships, it has given some recommendations which are broadly in accordance with the techno-managerial approach of the Government of India to the issue of land records management particularly evolving a land title system with help of modern technology. The recommendations of the Commission are as under:

- Surveys and measurements need to be carried out in a mission mode utilising modern technology to arrive at a correct picture of land holdings and land parcels and rectification of outdated maps;
- This needs to be accompanied by an existing mechanism for updating land records–which varies from state to state–to be supplanted by an improved and strengthened mechanism which ensures that all future transactions in titles are immediately reflected in the land records. Such a system should be able to detect changes in titles through various means-namely succession, will, partition, survivorships etc. and update land records accordingly;
- The dispute resolution mechanism with regard to land titles needs to be strengthened in order to be compatible with the demands made on it; and
- In case of urban areas, a similar exercise needs to be undertaken especially since measurements and surveys have not been done in many of such areas and even records of titles is not available in most cities.[73]

---

[71] Ibid, p. 140.

[72] Ibid, p. 32.

[73] Ibid, pp. 147–148.

Institutional arrangements for the land records computerisation

The maintenance of land records which covers Record of Rights and cadastral surveys are incorporated under 45th entry of the State List in the Seventh Schedule of the Constitution of India.[74] Though it is a state subject, it is the central government which is the main driving force of the whole project. The rural development ministry provides funds to the state governments for implementation of the two centrally sponsored schemes, i.e., Computerisation of Land Records and Strengthening Revenue Administration and Updating Land Records. Its technical, training and consultancy organisations like Survey of India, National Informatics Centre, Forest Survey of India, National Soil and Land Use Survey, Centre for Development of Advanced Computing (C-DAC), National Remote Sensing Centre, National Institute of Rural Development (NIRD) and Lal Bahadur Shastri National Academy of Administration (LBSNAA) provide technical assistance and evaluation studies for the programmes. The National Informatics Centre (NIC) plays a crucial and integral role in the whole process of policy formulation, design and implementation. NIC 'is providing network backbone and e-governance support' and 'offers a wide range of ICT services including Nationwide Communication Network for decentralised planning, improvement of government services and wider transparency' of central government, state government, UTs, districts and other government bodies.[75]

The scheme of Computerisation of Land Records (CLR) was implemented by Ministry of Rural Development in collaboration with the National Informatics Centre and it also provides training in application software to the revenue officials and technical support for implementation of the scheme.[76] NIC in association with the Ministry of Rural Development has developed a computerised Land Records Information System (LRIS) related to revenue, survey, agriculture, forest, irrigation and land resources. NIC also helps the ministry in formulating the technical guidelines for the deployment of state of art ICTs and conduct LRIS software requirements study. It claims to ensure 'an efficient, accurate, reliable and transparent Land Administration System

---

[74] Hari Charan Behera. 2009. 'Constraints in Land Records Computerisation,' *Economic and Political Weekly*, 20 June, p21.

[75] http://www.home.nic.in, (accessed on May 17, 2009).

[76] S. D. Meena et al. 2005. 'Computerisation of Land Records: National Perspective,' p. 24.

(LAS).' NIC has developed BHULEKH software for the purpose. Some of the Information and Communication Technologies (ICTs) such as Relational Database Management System (RDBMS), FoxPro, Visual Basic, and SQL Server are being used for computerisation of land records. Geographical Information System (GIS) is used to link electronic documents and digitised maps of the area to generate the true GIS and Electronic Document Management System. Other ICTs like simputer, Kiosks and Smart Card, Biometrics are being used at the user's end.[77] The states/UTs are implementing authorities and as such are responsible for periodic monitoring of these schemes and reporting the same to the central government.

Launch of national land records modernisation programme (NLRMP)

The NLRMP was launched by the ministry of rural development in August 2008, after modifying the restructured scheme called National Programme for Comprehensive Land Resource Management (NPCLRM) as some 'disadvantages of the existing schemes' were sought to be redesigned. It was explained that though significant progress has been made by the states and UTs under the two schemes dealing with computerisation of land records and strengthening land revenue administration by putting more emphasis on computerisation and digitisation of old records, less progress has been achieved in 'having a system that maintains accurate and up-to-date record of rights and securely generates such record on demand.' Further, it was realised that the schemes could not integrate textual land records with spatial records and mutation with registration, backend reconciliation of village records and development of a comprehensive land records database across the country 'that is necessary for understanding land and immovable property markets and for efficient administration and policy making in a modern economy'[78] Under the CLR and SRA &ULR schemes, the choice of activities were left to the states and UTs who spent the central allocation in construction of buildings and computerisation of outdated land records. There was absence of 'systematic,

[77] Mantosh Chakraborty and Azad Singh. 2009. 'Land Records Computerisation: An Innovative Approach to Management,' *Informatics*, 17(4), p. 47.

[78] Government of India, *Annual Report, 2008–2009*, Ministry of Rural Development, New Delhi, p. 145–146.

ladder-like approach towards achieving updated land records.'[79] The need for modification of the scheme came from the report of a team under the chairmanship of the secretary, rural development that constituted to consider the modern survey options and their cost and time estimates. The committee in consultation with the technical agencies like National Remote Sensing Centre (NRSC), National Informatics Centre (NIC), Survey of India and a number of states, recommended to adopt 'hi-tech survey instruments' like Global Positioning System (GPS), Electronic Total System (ETS), hybrid method using aerial photography and ground truthing by ETS and GPS and High Resolution Satellite Imagery (HRSI) and ground truthing by ETS in undertaking survey and resurvey by the states. It also recommended adoption of the Torrens system for switching over from the existing land records based on presumptive value to conclusive titling.[80]

The National Land Records Modernisation Programme (NLRMP) was launched in September, 2008 by merging two existing centrally sponsored schemes of Computerisation of Land Records (CLR) and Strengthening Revenue Administration and Updating Land Records (SRA&ULR) of the Department of Land Resources of Ministry of Rural Development. The programme it claimed 'would modernise management of land records, minimize scope of land/property disputes, enhance transparency in the land records maintenance system, and facilitate moving eventually towards guaranteed conclusive titles to immovable properties in the country.' The conclusive land titling system with title guarantee will be based on four principles:

1. A single window to handle land records (including the maintenance and updating of textual records, maps, survey and settlement operations and registration of immovable property);
2. The 'mirror' principle, which refers to the fact that cadastral records mirror the ground reality ;
3. The 'curtain' principle which indicates that the record of title is a true depiction of the ownership of status, mutation is automated and automatic following registration and the reference to past records is not necessary, and

---

[79] Rita Sinha. 2010. 'Modernising India's Land Records Management System,' *Administrator*, 51(1), p. 60.

[80] National Land Records Modernisation Programme-2008, http://www.dolr.nic.in (accessed on June 03, 2009).

4. Title insurance, which guarantees the title for its correctness and indemnifies the title holder against loss arising on account of any defect therein.[81]

The various aspects of NLRMP guidelines are briefly outlined here. It can be argued that the guidelines that also comprise detail technical manuals and management of information system for the states to follow may again subject to change and modification given the past background of the frequent modification of the scheme and development of the scheme. The contents and components of the NLRMP being supported by the central government are given as under:

Scope of the programme

(a) Computerisation of land records;
(b) Survey and resurvey and updating of the survey and settlement records (Including ground control network and ground truthing) using the modern technology options;
(c) Digitisation of maps and integration and integration of textual and spatial data;
(d) Computerisation of registration;
(e) Modern record rooms and land records management centres at tahsil/taluk/circle/block level;
(f) Training and capacity building;
(g) Development of village index base maps by geo-referencing cadastral maps with satellite imagery, for creating core GIS and integration of three layers of data, i.e., spatial data from aerial photography or high resolution satellite imagery; Survey of India and Forest Survey of India maps and GIS ready digitised cadastral maps from revenue records;
(h) Bringing out legal changes such as amendments to the Registration Act, 1908, the Stamps Act, 1899, model law for conclusive titling and other legal changes; and
(i) Programme management and evaluation.[82]

---

[81] Government of India. 2009, *National Land Records Modernisation Programme: Guidelines and Technical Manuals-2008–2009*, Department of Land Resources, Ministry of Rural Development, New Delhi, p. 9.

[82] Ibid, pp. 9–11. See also Government of India. 2011. *Annual Report, 2010–2011*, Ministry of Rural Development, New Delhi, p. 175.

These activities would be carried out by the states and UTs in a 'systematic and ladder-like manner.' The primary ladder will cover activities for reaching the stage for conclusive titling, and the secondary ladder covers archival purposes and strengthening of revenue administration.

Implementation of the programme

Under the NLRMP, the district will be the unit of implementation and the states and UTs will be funded and technical assistance provided by the centre for the initial period of eight years and subsequent funding will be conditional to the submission of project proposals and signing of Memorandum of Understanding (MOU) with the centre. Each state would constitute a Project management Unit (PMU) headed by an officer in the rank of secretary to oversee the implementation of the scheme in its entirety. Outsourcing for meeting the technological gaps and public-private partnership in 'non-sensitive areas' are permissible under the scheme.

Content management (data entry, updation and data verification)

- All spatial data (cadastral map) shall be digitised and textual data including the record of rights (RoRs), mutation data and other land attributes data shall be updated and computerised;
- Manual land records issuance shall be discontinued after a cut-off date and all mutation and updation of data shall be done in the computerised system on an ongoing basis;
- To ensure accuracy of the data entered responsibility of revenue officials would be fixed for checking, verification and validation of the data entered;
- The states/UTs which have authorised Gram Panchayats to pass orders on mutation must ensure their inter-connectivity with the corresponding revenue offices; and
- The land records data base should use UNICODE for data storage and local language display and support and assistance for data conversion should be taken from the CDAC.

Procedural changes and digitisation of maps and integration of textual and spatial data

The states and UTs are to simplify/amend/revise/prepare the land records, laws, rules, manuals, RoRs formats on land records maintenance procedures, standardise the codifications, feature codes etc., in cadastral maps, RoRs and other land attribute data and confer the legal sanctity on computerised land records extracts or copies. Digitisation of maps and integration of textual and spatial data (khatian and cadastral map) and converting the existing paper maps into Geographical Information System-ready digital form in order to facilitate updating of cadastral maps in sync with changes made in the RoRs will be carried forward.

Establishment of tahsil, sub-division and district computer centres

Establishment of computer centre at the tahsil/sub-Division equipped with appropriate level computer system for 'maintaining the village wise property records and easier services to the citizens' and district level data base may be maintained for data analysis, planning, verification etc. at the district level.

State Level Data Centre

For maintaining data repository and back up, each state and UTs would establish a dedicated data centre for the land records data (including map and registration data) at the state/centre level with high-speed processors, switches, fiber optic channels, and software and security devices.

Inter-connectivity among revenue and registration offices

All the land records offices like tahsil, registration offices or equivalent level in the state and UTs will be may be securely connected by local area network or wide area network (WAN) in an appropriate configuration based on the functional and technical requirements.

Survey/re-survey and updation of survey and settlement records and construction of modern record rooms at tahsils

The states and UTs have been advised to undertake survey/resurvey using modern technology of surveying and mapping like aerial photography or high resolution satellite imagery combined with ground truthing using Total Stations and Global Positioning System so as to ensure true ground depiction on cadastral maps and land records that would help them in reaching the stage of conclusive titling.

Computerisation of the registration process

As a major component of the scheme, it is envisaged to make computerisation of registration efficient and hassle-free by integrating land records and registration since the manual registration process involves maintenance of paper copies that often resulted in misclassification of documents, misrepresentation of facts and other losses. Under the NLRMP, the functioning of all the sub-registrar offices in the country will be computerised like land valuation and benchmark rates along with process reengineering, staff training functions and connectivity with the revenue records maintenance system.

Training and capacity building

For effective maintenance and sustenance of the NLRMP, a comprehensive programme for all levels of officials has been prescribed who will be trained for operating the system in making mutation, updating of land records, issue of authenticated copies of RoRs with maps to scale and handling modern survey equipment such as Global Positioning System (GPS), Total Stations and Photogrammetry by technical organisations like National Informatics Centre (NIC), Survey of India, ISRO etc. The capacity building programme should include technical contents, quality procedures, technological advancements, outsourcing procedures, project management, organisation of workshops etc.

Choice of software and standards

The software development and maintenance support would be provided by NIC by setting up core development teams consisting of IT and GIS experts at the central level, supported by state and UT level teams for software customisations and technical coordination.

Data security, user and data authentication

The land records system management gives rise to new concerns and challenges relating to security of information assets and data integrity which are evolving and are dynamic in nature. Further states and UTs have to adopt safety and safeguarding measures for user and data authentication for securing their database in a dynamic environment.

Purchase procedures

The states and UTs shall follow established government's rules and procedures in purchase of services, hardware, equipments, etc. with comprehensive 3–5 year warranty, wherever applicable.

Public-private partnerships (PPP)

The NLRMP document, the government claims to have generated enormous workload on the existing revenue and registration department. The programme is highly technological in nature, and the revenue and registration officials are not trained to handle and apply the technology inputs at every stage. Therefore the central government has planned to implement most of the projects in partnerships with private players or outsource them on turnkey basis. The states and UTs are to outsource or make PPP arrangements on the basis of certain pre-conditions laid down by central government and shall involve NIC in all such technical matters.

Role of panchayati raj institutions and NGOs

The Gram Panchayats can play a significant role in survey and resurvey, and wherever they have been empowered to dispose undisputed mutations, interconnectivity with the tahsils may be worked out by the states with their funds.

Technical support to the states and UTs and implementing agencies

A Core Technical Advisory Group created at the Department of Land Resources (DOLR) consisting of members from national level technical agencies such as the NIC, Survey of India, NRSC, ISRO, C-DAC, Forest Survey of India, Soil and Land Use Survey of India, and experts in the field to render 'necessary technical guidance and hand holding support'.

Monitoring and review mechanism

Three levels of monitoring and review mechanism would be created, i.e., at the district level, state level, at national level to review the progress of the implementation of the scheme. The district level committee shall submit quarterly online monitoring reports to the state revenue department and the state monitoring committee will send quarterly progress of the programme to national monitoring committee at the Ministry of Rural Development, New Delhi.

Evaluation of the programme

To get the impact assessment and feedback about the actual implementation of the programme at field level and suggest the measures for improving the system, the states and central government will get 'concurrent and terminal evaluation' of NLRMP carried out through government training and consultancy institutions such as LBSNAA, Mussorie, NIRD, Hyderabad and state administrative training Institutes (ATIs) etc.

Funding

Funds under NLRMP will be allocated at different scales by the central government and will be restricted to its share based on the estimated cost approved by it and the perspective plans and proposals submitted by the states. The states and UTs are to fix user fees for ensuring 'sustainability of the programme and meeting expenses of the hardware maintenance and obsolescence.'[83]

A study of the central funds utilisation brings out very slow progress in implementation of the various components of the programme. The data on utilisation of the central funds and coverage of districts in the country are very poor. In 2011–2012, only 605.15 crore rupees were released by the central government for implementation of various components of the programme for 243 districts but utilisation of funds about 5 crores rupees could be made possible. Similarly in the financial year 2012–2013, central government released 691.16 crores but utilisation of funds amounting only 12 crore rupees were made by the states. Thus the funding and expenditure pattern amply proves the challenges faced by the state governments and bureaucratic machineries in

[83] Ibid, pp. 11–29.

implementing the techno-managerial solutions to land records management. It is no surprise to find the candid admission of the central government that, 'being a technology driven and complex programme, the physical and financial progress has not been on the expected lines.'[84]

The NLRMP programme thus makes an ambitious step in adding new components like interconnectivity of registry with tahsil, integration of textual and spatial map, option for adoption of modern survey/resurvey of land, GIS mapping, computerisation of registration office, setting up of Project management Unit and NLRMP cells and implementation of some of the programmes through public private partnership mode in non-sensitive areas. Interestingly, the Indian state admits that NLRMP is a 'highly technology driven programme and requires in-depth application of information technology.'[85]

A thorough study of the NLRMP scheme would undeniably drive one to conclude that it is conceived in a very ambitious manner and the success of the complex programme invariably depends on the forging of networks with the intergovernmental, intragovernmental, governmental and private bodies by the state. The programme is purely designed as techno-managerial strategy to go for computerisation of land records within the existing legal and institutional arrangements. By advocating the use of the so-called 'hi-tech equipment' to the states in mapping and digitising their land records uniformly, the states are being encouraged to move in uncharted territories in which neither the state nor the private sector has the requisite knowledge to handle and apply such hi-tech instruments. The objective of NLRMP is thus to modernise India's land records management for better public service delivery and move towards a land titling regime by increasing the security of land records.

Land records management in the context of policy shift from state-led land reforms to neoliberal land policy

The common political economy around the land in India has also deeply influenced the land records management and its modernisation drive. Since economic liberalisation in the 1990s, there has been growing pressure on land

---

[84] See the *Annual Report, 2011–2012*, Ministry of Rural Development, Government of India, New Delhi, pp. 180;235 and also *Annual Report, 2011–2012*, Ministry of Rural Development, Government of India, New Delhi, pp. 179;271.

[85] Parliament of India. 2011. *Fifteenth Report of the Standing Committee on Rural Development*, Lok Sabha Secretariat, New Delhi, August, pp. 42; 44.

for non-agricultural purpose like urbanisation, industrialisation, colonisation, expansion of service and leisure industries and shrinking common property resources. Land reform measures like abolition of tenancy no longer occupy central position in the political discourse of the Indian politics. Rather as we have cited earlier, there has been a strong argument to liberalise the tenancy restrictions and allow the land lease and rental process which could facilitate the growth of land markets.[86] The *Committee on State Agrarian Relations and the Unfinished Tasks in Land Reform* (2009) in its report claimed that land issues had made their forceful 'reappearance as a matter of national discourse after a significant gap.' From the 1950s to the launch of the Eighth Five Year Plan in 1988, land reform had carried symbolic political and economic importance for the planners though state agencies admitted their failure in implementing the radical land redistributive measures. Since the 1990s, the issue of land management, coupled with land records maintenance, has come to occupy a prominent place on the public policy agenda as now 'the land issue of the marginalised was overwhelmed by the shift in the development paradigm towards neoliberalisation.'[87] The present policy reorientation therefore needs to be seen in the context of neoliberal economic policy of the Indian state since the 1990s.[88] As D. Bandyopadhyay has rightly observed that land reform 'has became a forgotten agenda of state policy. Marketers have dominated all segments of governance... They were finding the existing land reform laws that were enacted...in the early 1970s not only unwanted roadblocks but also obnoxious to free play of capital and in the land/lease market.'[89]

Thus it would be useful to understand the present policy shift to land records management as a part of larger strategy of land reforms in the context of neoliberal economic reforms in India and worldwide. The neoliberal reform of land also known as Market Led Agrarian Reform (MLAR) asks states that

---

[86] See Pushpendra and B. K. Sinha. 2009. 'Some Aspects of Tenancy Debate: Implications for Policy Reforms,' in D. Narasimha Reddy (Ed) *Agrarian Reforms, Land Markets and Rural Poor*, Mussoorie: Centre for Rural Studies, LBSNAA, p. 65.

[87] Government of India. 2009. *The Committee on State Agrarian Relations and the Unfinished Tasks in Land Reform*, pp. 144–146; 150–151;154

[88] K. B. Saxena. 2011. 'Land Reforms: Unfinished Agenda or Reversal of Policy,' in *India: Social Development Report 2010; The Land Questions of the Marginalised*, Council for Social Development, New Delhi, pp. 183–185.

[89] D. Bandyopadhyay. 2008. 'Does Land Still Matter,, *Economic and Political Weekly*, March, p. 38.

have long adopted the pro-market economic reforms to create such necessary legal-institutional reforms or environs for the development of private rights to property for the purpose of improving and expanding land market and credit growth and agricultural inputs. MLAR thus means 'a form of land reform that has emerged out of pro-market critique of state- led approaches to agrarian reform.'[90]

The most influential critics of the state-led land reforms are the World Bank experts on land policy like Klaus Deininger and Hans Binswanger who have argued that the state-led land reforms like ceiling on land holding have relied on expropriation and more successful in creating large bureaucracy than serving the interest of the landless. The state-led land reforms according to them are expensive to enforce and resulted in corruption, tenure insecurity and red tape.[91] The World Bank has been vigorously advocating the establishment of secure property rights or land titles as it would lead to growth of agricultural productivity as well as land market. The Market Led Agrarian Reform (MLAR) strategy, as is called by some scholars, has gained prominence since the 1990s as an alternative to that of state-led land reform prevalent from 1950s onwards. It embraces a 'textbook willing seller-willing buyer model' that means seller has secured title and parcel of land the buyer is interested to buy and a range of other policy options like liberalisation of tenancy and land rental market, security of land rights through titling, replacing land ceiling laws, privatisation of non-private lands and a various combination of these policies sequentially or simultaneously. The World Bank's funding of land titling and registration programmes is going on in Latin American, African and Asian countries and the Bank's claim to success is being contested by a growing body of literature. The Bank's land policy strongly advocates abolition of restrictions on land sales and land rentals, allowing for a more fluid land market based on a secured land title policy regime. Its critique of conventional state-led agrarian reform may be summarised in three points viz., state-led agrarian land reform create distortion, poor programme design and excessive cost in implementation.[92]

---

[90] Saturnino M. Borass Jr. 2003. 'Questioning the Market Led Agrarian Reform: Experiences from Brazil, Colombia and South Africa,' *Journal of Agrarian Change*, Volume 3 (3), July, p. 367.

[91] Ibid, p. 368.

[92] Edward Lahiff, Saturnino M. Borass, Jr and Christobal Kay. 2008. 'Market Led Agrarian Reform: Policies, Performance, and Prospects' in Saturnino Borass Jr, Christobal

Securing property rights

It is necessary to discuss some of the policies of the World Bank in order to establish a link with the present land records modernisation programme in India and the neo-liberal policy advocated by World Bank through its policy prescriptions to its aids receiving countries. Firstly, According to the World Bank policy guidelines, secure land tenure would allow people to invest in agriculture, the credit market will grow and land could be put as collateral for investment. Put simply, if self-interested utility maximising individual land owners are provided title guarantees to their land then they would invest and use the land more efficiently. Insecure land tenure, outdated land laws and regulations and dysfunctional administrative mechanisms constrain private investment and undermine the tax base of the governments in many developing countries. Secondly, inequality in land ownerships is due to a state-led land reforms policy that has created inequality among the landowner and landless. Market mechanisms should be used to create new property rights which are distorted by non-market or state-led land reforms with redistributive agenda. State intervention in land reform would send a wrong signal to the landowners who may feel that the connection between property and labour has been severed.[93] Thirdly, the goal of land reform is to transfer land from unproductive people to productive ones. Written land records improve the transferability and property rights of land. Secure and unambiguous property rights allow markets to transfer land for more productive uses and users.[94] Fourthly, 'Improving tenure security and promoting land rental markets (including sales) are good for both equity and efficiency.' As land redistribution involves politicking and political patronage, requires substantial personnel and financial resources to acquire land, compensate and select beneficiaries and then provide credit and agricultural inputs, improving the functioning of land markets and providing greater security of tenures would be a more fruitful area for productive use of land.[95] Fifthly, in India 'unclear land titles combined with unreliable courts'

Kay and Edward Lahiff (Eds) *Market–Led Agrarian Reform: Critical Perspectives on Neo-Liberal Land Policies and the Rural Poor*, London: Routledge, 2008, p. 2–5.

93 Wendy Wolferd. 2007. 'Land Reform in the Time of Neo-liberalism: A Many Splendored Thing', *Antipode, 39*(3), p. 555–556.

94 World Bank. 2008. *World Development Report, 2008: Agriculture for Development*, The World Bank, Washington DC, 2007, p. 138.

95 World Bank. 2006. *World Development Report, 2006*: *Equity and Development*, Washington: A Co-publication of World Bank and Oxford University Press, p, 167.

are identified as the main reason for limited supply of land and discouragement of heavy capital investment.[96] Further tenancy restrictions reduce productivity and equity which needs to be replaced for facilitating land rental that would improve access to land.[97]

The World Bank in its study *India: Land Policies for Growth and Poverty Reduction* (2007*)* has ardently advocated some of the policy reforms that are similar to its present policy approach towards land reforms such as expansion of computerisation and digitisation of textual (*khatian*) and spatial (cadastral) maps; integration of tahsil with registration office; transition towards a system of title registration referred as the Torrens System to make the integration effective; need for political support for legal and institutional changes for the system of title over and above one of deeds registration and provide tenure security; leasing out government land on a long-term basis; legalising land rental, replacing land ceilings, elimination of restrictions on land market and lifting restrictions on transfer of tribal land to non-tribals to facilitate growth of land markets are policy measures expected from Indian state that would promote growth and reduce poverty.[98]

The World Bank's land policy paper have also been analysed by some scholars advocating the liberalisation of land laws and regulations like ceiling of land holding, abolition of tenancy and distributing government waste lands (common property resources). In their arguments, India has the world's largest landless persons and their access to land could be made possible by reconsidering the restricting provisions of the land laws through marketisation and liberalisation. The land policies should be redesigned as 'pro-poor and market friendly.'[99]

NLRMP: a critical perspective

Before critically analysing the National Land Records Modernisation Programme, it would be useful to examine the experience in implementation

---

[96] Ibid, p. 164.

[97] World Bank. 2007. *World Development Report,* 2008, p. 141.

[98] World Bank. 2007. *India: Land Policies for Growth and Poverty Reduction, Report No 38298-IN,* p. vi–xiii.

[99] Tim Hamstad, T. Haque and Robin Nielsen. 2008. 'Improving Land Access for India's Poor,' *Economic and Political Weekly,* March 8, p. 49.

of the CLR programme by the state governments as assessed by the central government. The Government of India in Parliament had sought to explain the poor performance of the programme in an apolitical manner. Interestingly, the ministries of rural development and information technology have approached the problem of the computerisation of land records in their own way. The rural development ministry has explained the poor performance of the CLR programme in the following manner:

- In most of the states, survey/resurvey and settlement operations have not been carried out regularly. Thus, the ground reality like sub-division of plots, up-to-date *Hissa* (shared plot) numbers and village maps are not available. Therefore, states wanted to update their records before undertaking computerisation;
- Due to technological advancements, there have been continuous changes in technologies from DOS (Single User System) to UNIX-FOX Base/ ORACLE (Multiple User) /Windows/ language interface which resulted in delay in the completion of basic data entry;
- Non-availability of private data entry agencies in some states to undertake the mammoth task of data entry in local language;
- Delay in release of funds from the state headquarter to the implementing authority at the district level;
- In some of the states, resistance of revenue staff to take up the task of data verification and validation has hindered the progress;
- Lack of trained staff for undertaking the job of completion of data entry work and managing the computer centres; and
- Lack of effective monitoring mechanism at the state and district level.[100]

The Ministry of Information Technology (MIT) has attributed the poor performance of the CLR programme to the following reasons:

- Diversification of the manual system of land records;
- Delay in release of funds by the states to implementing agencies in remote districts;
- Lack of awareness about the scheme among the operational staff;

[100] See reply to Unstarred Lok Sabha Question No 3643 on 16 December 2005 by A. Narendra, Minister of Rural Development, Government of India at Parliament of India website, New Delhi.

- Shortage of technical manpower; and
- Frequent power failures and low voltage.[101]

For addressing these problems, the MIT advocated two steps like network connectivity from tahsils to district offices, introduction of online mutation, non- repudiation security system for land records database and setting up cyber kiosks for delivery of land records at the grassroots level. Thus one can understand that despite some differences in approaching the implementation of the CLR programme by the two ministries of the central government, the problem has been treated as a techno-managerial matter. The central government explained before the Parliamentary Standing Committee that to 'switch over to a compusterised environment' requires different set-up activities and the states are to be blamed as the choice of activities were left to the state governments who chose to spend the central funds in building construction programmes than updating land records. It also admits that the each activity of the land record modernisation was goal in itself and no integrated and systematic ladder-like approach was followed or suggested by the central government. Technological options like adoption of modern survey and resurvey, GIS mapping and electronic integration with tahsil and registry were not visualised by the government.[102]

Despite the lack of political commitment by the state government leadership to land records modernisation and poor motivation and capacity of the state level revenue bureaucracy, the central government has gone ahead in launching the NLRMP with addition of ambitious programmes like introduction of e-registration and connectivity with tahsil and modern survey. Hardly have we found any comments and discussion on the draft Land Titling Bill, 2011 or the land records modernisation programme (NLRMP) in Parliament or state legislatures or other public domain. Thus the current reforms process in land records management is very much akin to Rob Jenkins' observation that 'manipulative and obfuscatory tactics employed regularly in the implementation

---

[101] Parliament of India. 2003. *Fifty-Sixth Report of Standing Committee on Information Technology,* Thirteenth Lok Sabha, Ministry of Information and Communication, New Delhi, p. 21.

[102] Parliament of India. 2012. *Thirty Third Report of the Standing Committee on Rural Development, 2011–2012*, Fifteenth Lok Sabha, Ministry of Rural Development, Lok Sabha Secretariat, New Delhi, p. 10.

of reform, however, are a much truer representation of the political reality in India.'[103]

The launching of the NLRM Programme underlines the fact that the Indian state's land records modernisation policy is deeply under the influence of the World Bank's land policy. The political nature of state-led land reform measures however is not completely abandoned by the Indian state, thanks to Maoist violence in the countryside and the challenge of meeting the poor's access to land, water, and forest and securing their use of common property resources. However, the advocates of the market-based economic reforms find the land reform policy pursued by the Indian state since the 1950s is a road block to development of land market, land lease and corporate farming in India.[104]

The National Land Records Modernisation Programme (NLRMP) was launched in the backdrop of the steady liberalisation of India's economy. The restructured programme is undoubtedly a highly technology-oriented and complex programme involving application of diverse set of technology for all its components—computerisation of land records and integration of maps, survey and resurvey, use of modern technology such as Total Station, Global Positioning System, Aerial Photography, and High Resolution Satellite Imagery (HRSI). Further the computerisation of registration system and interconnections between registration and land records system, and interconnectivity with revenue offices will require massive efforts in training and capacity building among the officials of both revenue and other departments who have to work in a closely coordinated manner. After the launching of the programme, the central government has started funding for setting up of national and state level institutes and project management units that would deal with the programme implementation, training and capacity building. The ambitious objective of developing and implementing conclusive titling regime entails a very serious financial burden which the central government seeks to meet through public private partnerships. This raises the big question on the capability of the bureaucracy to work with the private sector and protect the public interest given its background of rent seeking, and indulge in various corrupt practices.

---

[103] Rob Jenkins. 1999. *Democratic Politics and Economic Reform in India*, Cambridge University Press, p. 207.

[104] D. Bandyopadhay. 2008. 'Does Land Still Matter?,' *Economic and Political Weekly*, March 8, 2008, pp. 37–40.

The whole exercise of the reform agenda in land records management through ICTs is apolitical and ahistorical in nature. Whether it is a state-led agrarian reform or market-led land policy it is the political factor, i.e., the commitment of political leaderships of diverse spectrum and their political will and ability to act autonomously and forge a broad consensus that will determine the viability and sustainability of the programme.

The history of land reforms in India shows that land and land relations are a political issue and involve power politics. Similarly the historic legacy, complex and bewildering diversity and dynamic nature of land records management, tenurial, customary and class nature of land relations have not been appraised or at best overlooked while designing the policy of land titling programme. The draft Revised Land Titling Bill, 2011, claims as 'model law for consideration by all the state' and provides for the 'establishment, administration and management of a system of conclusive land titles through registration of immovable properties and to further amend the existing laws.'[105] Perhaps had there been a serious, objective and a multi-disciplinary academic study on the impact, achievements and failures of the two interrelated programmes of computerisation of land records and updating land records by the central government on the revenue bureaucracy and public across the country, the highly centralised, top-down and techno-managerial programme would not have been unveiled in its present form.

It was originally claimed that the inefficiencies and corruption prevalent in manually maintained land records could be tackled through computerisation of land records and their online delivery. Unfortunately, the Indian state has not yet undertaken a critical study to look into the formal and informal network of revenue bureaucracy, its rent-seeking attitude and the extent to which its computerisation programme has been able to address the problem.

The NLRMP has looked at land as merely economic resource and the problems of land records management as techno-managerial concerns. It has overlooked its social, cultural and political values and contexts. Till 2007, the programme of Computerisation of Land Records (CLR) was running with the objective of providing computerised and digitised copy of RoRs and map to citizens on demand, providing durable and retrievable land records data,

---

[105] See the Draft Revised Land Title Bill, 2011 at www.dolr.nic.in (accessed on October 23, 2012).

ensuring transparency and accountability, setting up a comprehensive land information system for its utilisation in planning and development explicitly.[106] Since 2008, the programme subsumed under the NLRMP has changed its focus and now promises to develop and implement conclusive title regime by the end of Twelfth Five Year Plan.

The Appu Committee (1995) had looked into the prospects of introducing the land titling system or the Torrens System as forcefully suggested by the Wadhwa Committee (1989) appointed by Planning Commission earlier. The Committee reported that 'considering the heavy load of work, expense and risks involved in introducing the system in a country like India with 97.1 million land owners owning some 500 million parcels of land, we do not recommend the adoption of the Torrens System.'[107] Instead, it recommended the merger of the tahsil and sub-registrar office and empowering sub-registrars to get the averments verified with reference to land records before registering any land transaction. Mutations should be automatically effected after registration.

Conclusion

It is rightly commented that though more than thousand crores of rupees have been spent since the inception of computerisation of land records programme in 1988–89, the performance of the programme has been most unsatisfactory. Various administrative, legal and technological problems have been encountered and out-of-date entries have been made without field verification. In most states, the delivery of the textual land records is being done in a traditional off-line manner. It is found that so far only 16 states have stopped delivering manual land records and placed the computerised RoRs on the website.

The Parliamentary Standing Committee has observed that if the Indian state went into 'deep slumber' after the launching of the land records modernisation programme in the late 1980s, and was not sincere in its implementation as it failed to lay down specific direction of the programme. Unlike the sponsored flagship programmes like MNREGA, JNURM and NRHM where the Indian state allocates billions of rupees in a year, the annual allocation for

[106] Government of India. *Annual Report, 2007–2008,* Ministry of Rural Development, New Delhi: p. 172.

[107] Government of India. 1995. *Report of the Committee on Revitalisation of Land Revenue Administration*, Ministry of Rural Development, New Delhi, p. 37.

the NLRMP programme comes to around 150 crores.[108] The success of the schemes is being assessed in terms of percentage of utilisation of plan outlays and so-called physical targets like data entries of outdated textual records and construction of buildings for officials of tahsils/taluks as admitted by the government. However, it is now justified that the programme was initially not designed with the intent to computerise the correct RoRs. The correct and updated RoRs are virtually nonexistent as in most part of the country survey and settlement operations have not been taken up.[109]

In addition to this, difficulties in applying cutting edge ICTs and their upgradation compounded the problem. The dynamic nature of ICTs and land records with their regional variations, problems of change management, technology obsolescence and bringing land records database of 5000 tahsils/taluks and further integration with spatial records has posed a technological challenge. Mere computerisation and digitisation of textual and spatial land records (RoRs) and even their integration with sub-registration will not bring any change in the functioning in the land records management as both tahsildars and village accountants/patwaris/ revenue inspectors maintain a host of other interrelated land records and registers and forms that have direct bearing with mutation proceedings and these records need constant updating.

Up-to-date land records were perceived as crucial for successful implementation of state-led land reforms and abolition of intermediaries, security to tenancy, ceiling on land holding etc. Now, in the changed 'policy environment' and adoption of pro-market or 'pro-business economic reforms,' it is conclusively stated that 'land reforms seem to have been relegated to the background in the 1990s.'[110] The agenda of land reforms is rightly called market driven land reform and from this context one can very well understand the changed strategy and focus of the recently restructured National Land Records Modernisation Programme (NLRMP) in India which no longer promises better service delivery through adoption of ICTs or strengthening redistributive land reform measures, but rather using it as a tool for evolving a

---

[108] Parliament of India. 2012. *Thirty Third Report of the Standing Committee on Rural Development, 2011–2012*, Fifteenth Lok Sabha, Ministry of Rural Development, Lok Sabha Secretariat, New Delhi, p. 9;16;65.

[109] N. C. Saxena. 2005. 'Is Computerisation Enough?,' p. 317.

[110] Government of India. *Tenth Five Year Plan, 2002–2007*, Planning Commission of India, Volume-II, New Delhi, p. 301.

new policy regime of conclusive titling system which would provide security of land rights, encourage private investment, fewer disputes and conflicts, allow land to be used as collateral, lower transaction costs and corruption and will ensure an efficient market.[111]

The renewed emphasis of the central government to computerise and update land records and integrate mutation of land with registration and its proactive measure to bring out necessary legal and institutional change must be viewed from the context of India's 'pro-business' and 'pro-market' policies pursued since the 1990s.[112] The state however continues as the primary agent and initiator of land reforms setting in motion a series of administrative and legal procedures for affecting existing land laws and regulations in a centralised top-down bureaucratic fashion.[113]

The unequal distribution of property and income and hierarchical social structure based on inequality of assets in land holding forms the basis of agrarian land relations in rural India. Though post independence India took many measures for agrarian reforms and special emphasis was laid on the distribution of surplus land to homesteadless and landless persons, in actuality such reforms have yielded limited success.

The conditions of marginal and small farmers and tribals have worsened and the future trends are also not encouraging. There is no evidence of significant shifts in land relations in the current liberal and market friendly economic reforms. The basic nature of land relations remains in-egalitarian and iniquitous and only some marginal achievements could be noticed.[114] Analysis of household data from forty-eighth and fifty-ninth rounds (1992 and 2003–04) of the National Sample Survey Organisation (NSSO) finds that more than forty per cent of households in rural India do not own any land other than homestead land and more than thirty per cent households neither owned any land other than homestead, nor cultivate on owned homestead land. At the same time, as much as fifteen million acres of land ownership holdings of

[111] Government of India. *Eleventh Five Year. 2007–2012,* Planning Commission of India, Volume-III, Yoyana Bhawan, New Delhi, pp. 29–30.

[112] Atul Kohli. 2006. 'Politics of Economic Growth in India: 1980–2005,' *Economic and Political Weekly*, 8 April, p. 1368.

[113] Thomas Sikor and Daniel Muller. 2009. 'The Limits of State-led Agrarian Reform: An Introduction,' *World Development*, 37(8), pp. 1307; 1309.

[114] Rekha Bandopadhya. 1993. 'Land System in India: A Historical Review,' *Economic and Political Weekly*, 25 December, pp. A149–A155.

more than twenty acres size are found to exist. The inequality of ownerships in land has worsened between 1992 and 2003–2004.[115]

Thus, the centrally sponsored schemes of Computerisation of Land Records (CLR) and Strengthening Revenue Administration and Updating Land Records (SRA &ULR), now restructured as the National Land Records Modernisation Programme (NLRMP), is basically an incremental policy change sought to be carried within the existing land tenure and revenue system. Though it is gradualist in approach, its modest success rate and interstate variations raise many issues of governance which will be discussed in the chapters that follow. The NLRMP policy objectives cannot be understood in isolation from the broader policies of economic and governance reforms that are being carried out at the national level and state level.

More than twenty years of operationalisation of the schemes have brought out a state of change in the revenue administration. First, the schemes outline a new techno-managerial approach for the bureaucracies who are mandated to implement an overoptimistic nature of programme. The revenue officials dealing with revenue administration at the tahsils and sub-registrars offices are required to adhere to the ideas and strategies of New Public Management (NPM) in order to cope with increasing informatisation of the organisation and policy thrust for better delivery of services to the citizens as customers who are now made to pay user fees. Secondly, the programme is undeniably becoming a highly technological and more complex putting question mark on the capability of the revenue officials to handle this technology and complexity.

Continuous upgradation and obsoleteness of ICTs and varied other electronic survey technologies and their implication, challenges of data safety and its cost and the growing importance of IT vendors in the whole process of computerisation of land records and registration as important networks in shaping the policy are adding complexity to the programme. Thirdly, the proposed merger of tahsil and registration work and integration and application of modern survey will inevitably shape the land revenue administration and its policy. Lastly, the very process of implementation of the centrally sponsored scheme through a network of public-private agencies has now created a network mode of governance whose success depend on managing the networks and at the same time securing public interest.

[115] Vikash Rawal. 2008. 'Ownership Holding of Land in Rural India: Putting the Record Straight', *Economic and Political Weekly*, 8 March, p. 43–47.

Atul Kohli has rightly observed that, 'land reforms … have been continuously on India's political agenda.' The 'class bias of the state' is reflected in its inability to implement properly its land ceilings laws and the lack of political autonomy to confront powerful social interests. Land reforms in India highlighted the incapacity of the Indian state to confront the propertied interests and the local bureaucracy and land owners colluded and ensured the failure of land ceiling and other redistributive measures. Even the non-availability of land records could have been answered by the hegemonic Congress Party by mobilising the lower classes in the area that could have helped in identifying the 'surplus' land. The failure of land reforms reflects the failure to institutionalise the interests of lower classes within the state. Since the late 1960s, the state has altered its confrontationist attitude towards landlords and moved to the path of 'agrarian capitalism' by promoting the green revolution.[116] Thus, the ongoing National Land Records Modernisation Programme (NLRMP) needs to be better understood as one of the neoliberal reforms that would develop a land market through the integration of registration with mutation and textual land records with spatial maps as advocated persistently by the World Bank.

The apolitical nature of the NLRMP guidelines that seek wide-ranging governance reforms and redefine the role of the state in land records maintenance (which has hitherto been its exclusive domain) through PPP model and outsourcing to IT vendors an integral part of the programme may not ensure 'good governance' as it may 'ignore the mismatch between the institutions of governance and genuine social demands.'[117]

---

[116] Atul Kohli. 1987. *The State and Poverty in India: The Politics of Reform*, New Delhi, Cambridge University Press and Orient Longman, pp. 3; 63–71.

[117] Niraja Gopal Jayal. 1997. 'The Governance Agenda: Making Democratic Development Dispensable,' *Economic and Political Weekly*, 22 July, p. 410.

4

The Computerisation of Land Records Programme in Odisha

Introduction

The implementation of centrally sponsored schemes of Computerisation of Land Records (CLR) and Strengthening Revenue Administration and Updating Land Records (SRA&ULR) redesigned as National Land Records Modernisation Programme (NLRMP) in Odisha brings forth a number of interesting issues. These issues concern the role of the state, its bureaucracy, other non-formal actors and agencies, the problems of informatisation in public organisations, and the role of the networks involved in the process.

Land records in Odisha

It has been argued that the land revenue administration in Odisha is the most complicated in India. Before Odisha became a separate state on 1st April 1936, Balasore, Cuttack, Puri and Angul were parts of Odisha division of Bihar-Odisha province, and were governed by the Permanent Settlement of Bengal System. Areas like Ganjam, Koraput, and Baliguda subdivision of Boudh district were parts of the Madras Presidency but transferred to Odisha. Similarly, Sambalpur, Khariar ex-Zamindari and the Mahadevpalli police station areas were transferred to Odisha from the Central Province. In January 1948, around twenty-five princely states were merged with Odisha. Thus, the state of Odisha inherited different revenue and tenancy laws, as the princely states and the areas transferred from Bihar, Central Province and Madras presidency had different systems of revenue administration. The common feature among these different systems was the existence of a large body of intermediaries between the state and the tiller of the soil with varying degree of sub-infeudation.[1]

In the late-nineteenth century, B.H. Baden Powell described the land tenure system and the land revenue administration in Odisha as being 'full of interest,' as the 'Odisha settlement was made without any reference to any theory requiring a landlord or a middleman.' Odisha had

> neither exactly a landlord Settlement nor a village Settlement, nor a *raiyatwari* Settlement; but when the survey was made and the details of the holdings were ascertained, the Settlement Officers simply *had to respect to actual facts; they recorded and secured all rights as they found them existing.* Some features of each of the three systems may therefore be traced. A few of the local magnates or chiefs were recognised as landlords, and their assessment was allowed (as a favour) to be permanent.[2]

Such earlier studies have to be borne in mind in any attempt to understand the management of land records for bringing out a regime change in land revenue administration as the historical legacy of the complexities of the land record management is very much present in our contemporary times.

R K Ramadhyani in his *Report on Land Tenures and the Revenue System of the Odisha and Chhattisgarh States, Volume I, General Report* (1945) observed that 'in practically all the Odisha states there is no Agency for the maintenance of land records in an efficient manner' and in many places, he had noticed that the survey marks were missing or defective due to the absence of proper supervision. He had also reported that in the princely estates of Chhattisgarh, the land records maintained by the *Patwaris* were in a better condition. In Odisha, the numbers of entries in the land records were doubtful and defective. In surveyed areas, nevertheless, there 'are more or less satisfactory records with exceptions pointed out in the individual reports,' but in unsurveyed areas rough maps are drawn by eye estimation and 'the records are prepared by either estimation of the area or by reference to seed and plough capacity.'

---

[1] N. C. Behuria. 1997. *Land Reforms Legislation in India: A Comparative Study*, New Delhi: Vikas Publishing House, p. 74.

[2] B. H. Baden Powell. 1894. *A Short Account of Land Revenue and its Administration in British India; With a Sketch of the Land Tenures,* Oxford: Clarendon Press, p. 173.

He had therefore recommended resettlements in some areas where records were totally out of date.[3]

The primary purpose of the provincial survey and settlement operations conducted by the British from 1890 to 1900 was to gain deeper insights into the agrarian structure of the province and make the settlement of revenue and rent. The survey and settlement were conducted only to augment revenue, and the methods of survey and settlement adopted were of little importance as long as it served that primary purpose.[4] Given the varied and multiple revenue laws of tenancy, survey and settlement of rent prevailing then in the areas merged with Odisha, and the absence of laws dealing with survey and settlement in some of the princely states like Keonjhar and Mayurbhanj, Odisha government enacted the Odisha Survey and Settlement Act, 1958 that sought to consolidate and amend the laws relating to survey, record of rights, and settlement operations in the state. The Act lays down provision for 'definite responsibility of the state to provide for the maintenance of record of rights and the cadastral map up to date.'[5] Section 11 of the Act empowers the government to order for preparations of Record of Rights (RoRs) and Section 18 enables the government to direct the settlement of rent in respect of any land where a record of rights was already published. Section 11(5) says that the record of rights shall be comprise of the *khewat* which shall show the character and extent of proprietary interest or the record of rights of the proprietors/landlord/zamindar and the tenure holders and the *khatian* or the record of rights of the tenants/rayaits and the occupants which shall show such details as may be prescribed under the rule. Rule 21 of the Odisha Survey and Settlement Rules, 1962 provides for the following particulars to be recorded in the record of rights namely:

- The name of each tenant or occupant;
- The class to which each tenant belongs;
- The situation and extent of the land held by each tenant or occupant;
- The name of the landlord of each tenant;
- The name of each proprietor and landlord;

[3] R. K. Ramdhyani. 2001.*Report on Land Tenures and the Revenue System of the Odisha and Chhattisgarh States, Volume I--General Report*, Reprinted by The Survey and Map Publication, Board of Revenue, Odisha, Cuttack, pp. 57–58.

[4] B. K. Mishra. 1962. *Land Tenure and Land Reforms in Odisha*, Board of Revenue, Cuttack: Odisha Government Press, p. 145.

[5] Ibid, p. 147.

- The rent and charges for irrigation payable by each proprietor or landlord, tenant or occupant;
- If the rent is gradually increasing, the time at which and the steps by which it increases;
- The use of water for agricultural purposes;
- The special conditions or incidents, if any, of the tenancy;
- Any right of way or other easement attached to the land; and
- If the land is claimed to be held rent free whether or not rent is actually paid, if not paid, whether or not the occupant is entitled to hold land without payment of rent, and if so entitled, under what authority.[6]

Rule 32 authorises the tahsildar to maintain and keep the records up-to-date and Section 34 says that the tahsildar may on application on behalf of any person interested or on receipt of a report from any of his subordinate officers or on receipt of a notice from the registrar or sub-registrar appointed under the Indian Registration Act, 1908, or from a court or on his own motion may order any change of any entry in the record of rights according to the prescribed rules. This procedure of correction is called mutation and is a quasi judicial procedure that involves giving reasonable opportunities to the interested parties of being heard by way of issuing individual notices and general proclamation in the locality and a field enquiry by revenue inspector ascertaining the possessory interest of the land and its present position and a sketch map detailing the boundary of the land in case of mutation of the part plot.

The RoRs and the maps are corrected by the tahsil officials on the basis of the orders passed in mutation case by tahsildar. This is a very important process which makes the dynamic nature of land records up-to-date by reflecting the ground reality. Delay in mutation also makes the land records obsolete. Being a fiscal enquiry which determines the name of the recorded tenant to pay rent or cess, it also confers a prima facie presumptive nature of ownership of land. Under the provisions of sub-Rule (4) of Rule 29 and sub-Rule (4) of 55 of the Odisha Survey and Settlement Rules, 1962, the finally published and republished map and the record or rights shall remain in the custody of the tahsildar.[7]

---

[6] Giridhari Dash and Sapan Chandra Ray. 1996. Law *Relating to Survey and Settlement of Land in Odisha with Circulars*, Cuttack: Cuttack Law House, p. 6; 10; 30. But in practice all these particular information are not recorded in the RoRs.

[7] Government of Odisha. 1966. *The Odisha Land Reforms Manual, 1965, Cuttack*: Odisha Government Press, p. 1.

Problem of land records management prior to computerisation of land records

The actual working of the Act now revealed that large tracts of the tribal inhabited areas in Odisha have been virtually excluded from the survey and settlement process even after coming into force of the statute, and as a result, the tribals living in these areas have been deprived of a prima facie document of record of rights. This matter came to light during the Odisha tribal empowerment and livelihood programme (OTELP) in four districts.

In August 2007, Odisha government decided to undertake survey and settlement operations in Phulbani, Gajapati, Koraput and Kalahandi under the assistance of OTELP covering 392 villages, and 291 unsurveyed villages/tracts have also been notified by the government for survey and settlement operations. In all, 687 villages/tracts/patches of land in Odisha do not have record of rights or remain unsurveyed as per the annual report of revenue department for the year 2009–2010.[8] The latest annual report of the department contradicts its earlier data and states that land records are not prepared or updated in 2318 villages.[9] Thus, there is no complete and correct information on the availability of land records in the number of villages.

The land records of the minor tribes in Odisha like the Dongiria Kondhs have not been done by the settlement authorities. The settlement authorities by adopting plain table method survey have virtually excluded surveying the hilly slopes in the Niyamgiri hills in Kalahandi district that led to catastrophic results against primitive tribals living there for centuries. The land above ten degree slopes were not measured under plain table method and the entire area was declared as unsurveyed area and kept under government land. The 1961 Survey and Settlement operations in the Niyamgiri hills areas only recorded nearly 16 acres as dry and cultivable land and the rent was charged from sixteen *rayaits* only one acre was recorded as grasing land and 6.62 acres were recorded as house site land out of the surveyed area of 2647.32 acres. This can very well explain the reason for the predicament of the primitive tribals,

---

[8] Government of Odisha. *Report on the Activities of Revenue and Disaster Management Department for the Year 2009–2010*, Revenue & Disaster Management Department, Bhubaneswar, p. 6.

[9] Government of Odisha. *Report on the Activities of Revenue and Disaster Management Department for the Year 2012–2013*, Revenue & Disaster Management Department, Bhubaneswar, pp. 17–18.

as the forest areas where they have been living for centuries have not been recorded in their names by the settlement authorities thanks to their poverty, ignorance and illiteracy.[10]

Similarly, the study by Planning Commission of India on landholding system in tribal areas (1991) of Odisha found the lacunae in the operative machinery of land survey and settlement organisations and questioned the validity of the records and the procedure in determining the land records rights of the tribals. The report observed:

> In Keonjhar only 2.48 per cent to 23.50 per cent of land to which tribal communities of the five villages (about which data were obtained from the Settlement Officer) have rights of access of economic use, were found to be recorded in their favour. The data available from Koraput show that in some villages even 1 percent of the lands under actual occupation of the concerned tribal communities have not been recorded in their favour in the record of rights.[11]

The study group further reported that the settlement authorities have recorded hilly and slope lands in Koraput beyond ten per cent gradient as government land which are inhabited by many tribals, and these inhabitants were recorded as encroachers. The community land ownership rights of the tribals did not find their place in the land records of the tribals that led to violation and derecognition of the community land ownership rights of the tribals. It therefore called upon the government to re-examine the land reform policies and questioned the validity of record of rights as it does not take into cognizance the community and communal nature of ownership of tribal lands and landholdings. The study strongly urged the government that a 'thorough study of the effect of the various techniques of survey on the land rights of the tribals and other hill dwelling communities should be carried out in all the hill areas of the country in consultation with the Surveyor General of India.'[12] Poor land records were also the main reason for delayed implementation of the Odisha Estate Abolition Act, 1951 and the process continued till March 1974.[13]

---

[10] B. K. Royburman. 1987. 'Historical Process in Respect of Communal Land System and Poverty Alleviation among Tribals,' *Social Action*, Vol. 37, January–December, pp. 403–404

[11] Government of India. 1991. *A Review of Land Holding Systems in Tribal Areas: Report of A Study Group of the Planning Commission During the Seventh Five Year Plan*, New Delhi: Yoyana Bhawan, p. 52.

[12] Ibid, p. 52.

[13] N. C. Behuria. 1997. *Land Reforms Legislation in India: A Comparative Study*, p. 76.

The Chilika lake has been notified for survey. Nearly 600 hamlets have been declared as villages. Till March 2010, nearly two lakh mutation cases were pending for disposal and nearly 77,000 cases remained pending for correction of RoRs. The information thus reveals that land records problem is essentially a dynamic problem in Odisha.[14] The problem of backlog mutation cases arising out of sale, purchase, succession, land acquisition, leases, grants and gift are recurrent ones and our analysis will show that the dynamic nature of land records management problem has not been addressed by the ongoing land record modernisation drive.

It is common knowledge that in tahsils, thousands of mutation cases are pending and the land records especially the RoRs and the maps have lost their authenticity owing to failure on the part of tahsildars to correct and update land records. The reasons cited by such poor management of land records are the heavy work load on tahsildars and revenue inspectors and their preoccupation with the various revenue and non-revenue matters. The land records computerisation in Odisha has also made no difference to such problem, rather it has made the updating of records and map complicated technological-administrative issue. Delay in processing the applications for mutation by the tahsil officials and the rent-seeking attitude of the officials appeared to have gone hand in hand along the land records modernisation in Odisha.

Before the formation of Odisha state in 1936, there were several tenancy laws in force in different parts of Odisha like the Odisha Tenancy Act, 1913, the Central Province Land Revenue Act, 1881, the Central Province Tenancy Act, 1898 and the Madras Estate Land Act, 1908. Apart from these tenancy acts there were several tenancy regulations prevalent in the princely states.[15] It has been observed that in all the tahsils, RoRs are not regularly updated in time and scores of mutation cases are pending for years to come. The textual land records prepared in low quality paper are torn by frequent use. In many tahsils, the village maps are not available and those available are in a mutilated or brittle condition.[16] The tahsildars are the custodians of land records and as such are responsible for their updating, but it is observed that due to excessive

[14] Government of Odisha. *Report on the Activities of Revenue and Disaster Management Department for the Year 2009–2010*, p. 6.

[15] Ajit Kumar Tripathy. 1992. 'Revenue Laws and Land Administration in Odisha: A Critique,' *Administrator,* Vol. 38, January–March, 1992, p. 116.

[16] Ibid, p. 119.

pressure of varied administrative works on tahsildars like law and order, relief works, elections and attending VIP duties, the record correction has been relegated to the background.

Very often record corrections are done and rents are collected from the tenants after demanding bribes.[17] Many officers of Odisha Administrative Service (OAS) have not shown keen interest in handling revenue cases and are fighting court cases to protect the interest of government. There is steady decline of standards of revenue service due to flawed nature of recruitment from among the subordinate services to Odisha Administrative Services on promotion and selection based on compilation of five outstanding confidential character rolls (CCRs) managed by the non-revenue functionaries like clerks, stenographers, police sergeants and sub-inspectors, junior engineers and livestock inspectors etc.[18] Similarly, revenue inspectors are overwhelmed with overload of duties and responsibilities. A recent World Bank study has observed that the revenue inspectors in Odisha are engaged with various types of revenue, miscellaneous and non-revenue works, which leave a little time for them to attend their primary work of revenue collection and updation of land records. Apart from collection of revenues and their recording in various ledgers and registers, RIs (revenue inspectors) are required to submit reports for initiation of revenue and miscellaneous cases and assist other non-revenue departments in land matters. Therefore, the work of records correction remains almost neglected. The increased scope of revenue and non-revenue works, non-filling of the vacancies of revenue inspectors, amins and revenue collection clerks have virtually overburdened the revenue administration at the revenue inspector circle levels which is also a contributing factors for 'an inefficient land record management system fraught by excessive delays and high potential for rent-seeking.'[19]

At the outset it will be important to mention that computerisation of land records programme in Odisha has not been studied in depth, and very few documents are available to approach the subject unlike the Bhoomi programme

---

[17] Ibid, pp. 121–122.

[18] Ibid, p. 127.

[19] See Robin Mearns and Saurabh Sinha. 1999. *Social Exclusion and Land Administration in Odisha, India, Policy Research Working Paper no 2124,* The World Bank, South Asia Region, Rural Development Sector Unit, May, p. 38. (http://www.worldbank.org.html/dec/Publications/Workpapers/home/html (accessed on November 29,2008)

of land records computerisation in Karnataka whose success and sustainability has caught attention of international donor agencies and NGOs devoted to promote e-governance in developing countries. Nevertheless, in the absence of any primary and secondary materials on the computerisation of land records in Odisha, this study has relied on the proceedings, annual reports, orders and circulars of state government. In addition, the researcher has conducted extensive field studies in some tahsils in different parts of the state, conducted focus group discussions in some villages in coastal and tribal districts and held discussions with and interviewed the officials of revenue and IT departments of the state, in order to analyse the computerisation of land records programme in Odisha, its processes, outcomes and impact on the developmental and governance agendas.

Failure of pilot projects

The pilot project for computerisation of land records in Mayurbhanj district (which was selected as one of the eight districts in India) started in 1989–1990, funded by the central government. Odisha Computer Application Centre (OCAC) was selected for data entry work and it had developed a format for computerised *khatian*. Data entry of outdated *khatians* was started simultaneously in some tahsils of the district and it was targeted to complete the data entry work by 1994. Simultaneously, government also deputed 31 junior clerks in Mayurbhanj district to receive computer training by OCAC for handling the land records computerisation. The format of RoRs in which data entry was made by OCAC was different from the prevailing manual one. The revenue department asked OCAC to prepare the computerised copy of RoRs as per the prevailing format which was not carried out by the IT vendors appointed by OCAC as they did not have the technology or software to comply with the order. Without waiting for completion of data entry, validation and its operationalisation, OCAC in 1997 handed over the incomplete data entry works with computer equipment to the tahsildars in Mayurbhanj district. The reason for handing over an incomplete project was not spelt out by OCAC and consequently the data entry, its validation and updating were also not completed. Later on, the district collector informed the government that the so-called pilot project had come to a standstill after OCAC handed over the computer equipment to tahsildars in the district.

The proceedings of the state level monitoring committee revealed that the reasons for failure of the pilot project of computerisation of land records were manifold, viz. incomplete nature of data entry without its validation and updation, absence of trained manpower to handle computerisation works, the problem of managing different format of RoRs developed by OCAC in deviation of government order and its inability to produce computerised RoRs as per the government order, problem of managing special pay and benefits to the clerical staff deployed in computerisation work, issue of electricity bill payment, problem of supplying computer consumables and other peripherals, lack of training and awareness among the supervising officials like tahsildars and sub-collectors, absence of funds to meet the day-to-day work of computerisation, and absence of technical support of NIC, Odisha. The progress of pilot study of computerisation of land records in the district therefore could not move forward.

The government of Odisha finally asked OCAC to restart the incomplete data entry work by submitting the proposal of revised cost for completion of the work. The OCAC was also asked to convert the data entry software formulated by it in UNIX system to Window system due to software upgradation. In November 2003, OCAC proposed to undertake the data entry work again in Mayurbhanj afresh using the software developed by NIC and update the RoRs data up to 2003 and submitted a proposal of revised cost.[20]

Later on, the computerisation of land records started in other districts in phases funded by the central government and the data entry work was given to IT vendors. NIC provided technical assistance in the project and in some cases provided hardwares through its subsidiary organisation. It also launched district and state level training programme for the clerical and official staff at tahsil level. Odisha government decided to outsource the data entry work to private IT vendors, as NIC expressed its inability to take up data entry work thus reversing its earlier policy of centralised data entry work on the ground of safety and security of land records.[21]

20 See the proceedings of the state level steering committee (SLSC) on pilot project on the centrally sponsored scheme of computerisation of land records in Mayurbhanj district at Director of Land Records and Survey, Cuttack.

21 The decision to outsource the data entry works was taken by the state level steering committee in its meetings in 1995 as it was realised that neither NIC nor the revenue department had the infrastructure to handle such works.

During 1991–1992, a centrally sponsored research-oriented pilot project of modernisation of cadastral survey by using stereophotogrammetry and computer technology was launched in Angul-NALCO area. The project covered demarcation of village boundary, aerial photography, field control work, field verification, photogrammetric plotting, stereo digitisation of landholding, installation of hardwares, developing softwares, and preparation of record of rights and village map. More than 145 lakh rupees were sanctioned by the central government to be spent by Survey of India, Directorate of Land Records and NIC, Bhubaneswar in Angul-NALCO pilot project.

A state level monitoring committee was constituted to review the working of the project. A total of 369 villages were covered under the project. Aerial photography was taken up by Survey of India, but blueprint of village maps prepared under the photogrammetric method were not supplied for the villages surveyed for technical reasons. Due to a long delay in getting a blueprint of maps, a modified conventional system was adopted. Under the analogue method, the survey of India supplied maps on the basis of aerial photography without digitisation or plotting through the computer. The maps prepared under the method had some field problems such as appearance of many artificial ridges including ridges of onion fields as fragmentation of land, and consequently the number of plots increased. The analogue method in which no digitised map is available was not a better substitute to the conventional method of survey.

The second phase of the project was to computerise the land records by NIC, Bhubaneswar for the development of comprehensive land information system. This involved computerisation of data on cropping pattern, irrigation pattern, encroachment on government lands, land distributed under different welfare schemes, ceiling of surplus lands, particulars of dispossession by original land owners, illegal purchase, etc. The target set for photogrammetry plotting could not be achieved due to delay in processing the procurement of modern survey instruments for survey and failure to deploy appropriate technology and software for photogrammetric plotting and reading of coordinates. The survey of India, Hyderabad was the executant of the project and as the programme did not achieve any headway it decided to call off the project on the ground of payment of cost. It blamed the revenue department of Odisha for poor quality of manpower, lack of leadership and supervision leading to failure of the project. The entire expenditure on the project made by the survey of India went futile. Similarly, NIC was allotted a huge amount for purchase of computer hardwares and softwares and deployment of IT personnel in Angul. However, the land records could not be supplied by district revenue administration. Huge amount of public money got wasted in the process.

The failure of the programme highlighted the fact that computerisation of land records is not about purchase of hardware and software, rather a host of important issues such as coordination and organisation of data entry work, provision for infrastructure facilities, issue of providing leadership and ownership to the project and the capacity of the officials to handle such cutting edge technologies. On 22 May 1995, the senior official of NIC, Odisha unit wrote that the failure of Angul-NALCO project brings a lesson that 'until and unless a drastic change in the attitude and overwhelming interest to carry out this project is shown by the DLR&S and Government of Odisha, it is impossible to achieve any result in computerisation of land records.'[22] The failure to carry forward the pilot programme of land record computerisation was formally attributed to the scarcity of trained personnel and professionals within and outside government to conceptualise the schemes, lack of commitment of all levels of administration and circuitous and dilatory nature of release of funds by the state government.[23]

These two pilot programmes have been explained in detail as it would help us understand the reasons for the failure of computerisation of land records programme in Odisha till today. The common grounds for the failure of the two pilot programmes were lack of leadership, ownership and commitment to the projects on the part of top administrative functionaries in the revenue department and lack of capacity of the government officials to deal with such advanced technologies and total absence of coordination and partnership in programme implementation. Further study shows that the state bureaucracy has not learnt from its failure to implement the pilot project, rather the same approach prevails till now in the implementation of land records computerisation and modernisation of revenue administration.

---

[22] See the File No. XL–VIII–1/07 dealing with pilot project on modernisation of cadastral survey at Angul-NALCO area at Director of Land Records and Survey, Cuttack, Odisha.

[23] This was the candid admission of the state of affairs in land records computerisation, strengthening revenue administration, and updating land records on the part of late Dharmalingam, IAS, Director, Land Records, Odisha which continues to be relevant today in studying the land records modernisation drive in Odisha. (File no. XXX–VII-48/93/2616/1993, Board of Revenue, Odisha, Cuttack).

Strategy of computerisation

The process of computerisation of land records was started in a phased manner by taking a group of tahsils and asking the data entry operators to enter the land records as it is recorded in the manual *khatian*. The work was outsourced as the state government did not have the infrastructural base to go for computerisation of land records. The state government decided to create a post of assistant director for looking after the computerisation of land records at Board of Revenue, went in for purchase of computers and other equipment necessary for setting up computer cells in tahsils as per the central government guidelines, set up land records centre (LRC) of NIC at the Board of Revenue, Cuttack, released central funds for training of officials, and set up a survey and settlement training institute at Cuttack. OCAC was given funds for digitisation and updation of land records. It was during this time the decision was taken to develop Bhulekh application software by NIC, Odisha comprising RoRs, mutation, miscellaneous certificate module and query module.[24]

Thus computerisation of land records taken up in Odisha by simply making data entry of the existing entries in the *khatian* (Record of Rights of the rayait/tenant) and the validation was made after comparing with original manual *khatian*. A guideline was issued to private data entry operators to strictly enter the existing data in the land records and not to omit any information or create any information or record that was not originally found in the manually maintained settlement or consolidated land *khatian*. However, errors also entered in the computerised land records.[25] The only issue that

[24] See the proceedings of the State Level Steering Committee (SLSC) from 1989 to 2001 available at the Director, Land Records, Survey and Settlement, Board of Revenue, Odisha, Cuttack.

[25] The problem of erroneous entries in the RoRs have been detected by the researcher himself in some tahsils like Dhenkanal, Cuttack, Berhampur, Malkangiri, Puri and Pipili as well as by the CAG audit report. The main reason for some erroneous entries are due to lack of close supervision and verification after data entry works by the private vendors and the ignorance of data entry operators about the revenue land record entries and the software glitches. It was admitted by S.K. Mohapatra, Senior Technical Director, NIC during my discussion with him on 30 November 2012 that some erroneous entries could have been removed during the data entry and validation phase but the strict guidelines of the Revenue Department to computerise the existing manual RoRs in the present form has resulted many errors in the RoRs. Thus computerisation process was an add-on and not replacement to manual records.

concerned the proceedings of the State Level Steering Committee (SLSC) on Computerisation of Land Records during the period was to arrive at a decision on the approval of tenders put by IT vendors, cost of price to be fixed for data entry and mode of payment to the vendors.

If one goes through the proceedings of the State Level Steering Committee (SLSC)[26] 1998–2001 dealing with computerisation and updation of land records and digitisation of cadastral maps to find out the progress made in the computerisation of land records, one would get an idea that during this period, the state government took very slow and lethargic steps in the computerisation of land records. As stated previously, the work of computerisation of land records, initially started by Board of Revenue, in 1988–1989, first as pilot project in Mayurbhanj district on the funds provided by the centre and implemented by OCAC took nearly 17 years to complete. By that time, the state revenue department had completed the computerisation of land records in most tahsils and started issuing the computer generated record of rights without waiting for the pilot project.

By October 2002, Odisha government had operationalised the tahsil level computer cell for issue of mutation *patta* (RoRs), certified record of rights and a variety of miscellaneous certificates like caste, residential certificates through using Bhulekh software in 43 tahsils out of 171 tahsils. Instructions were issued to tahsildars to issue the computer generated true copy of the RoRs without amending the Odisha Records Manual and copying fees were collected in the shape of court fees stamp.[27] By January 2003, Odisha government could complete data entry work for computerisation of land records in 133 tahsils out of its 171 tahsils and operationalised issue of computerised land records in 53 tahsils.[28] In December 2003, the government decided to reorganise the

---

26 The SLSC formed under the revised guidelines of Computerisation of Land Records (CLR) and Strengthening Revenue Administration and Updating Land Records (SRA&ULR) is to coordinate between different agencies and departments involved in the project and function as 'tender and purchase committee' for the implementation of the two centrally sponsored schemes. The members of the committee are Secretary, Revenue; Revenue Divisional Commissioners; Director, Land Records and Survey; officials from NIC, Bhubaneswar and Odisha Computer Application Centre.

27 Government of Odisha. Board of Revenue Circular No. XXXVIII-33/02-9500/LRS dated 23 October 2002.

28 Government of Odisha. *Annual Activities Report of Revenue Department*, 2002–2003, p. 4.

revenue field administration by integration of settlement and consolidation organisation with tahsils and created 58 additional sub-collector posts who would be looking after survey and settlement matters.

Computerised land records could be made possible in 99 tahsils with the help of Bhulekh software only in February 2004. Similarly digitisation of cadastral maps was going on pilot basis in six tahsils on the funds provided by the centre and state government.[29] In September 2004 and in December 2005, the Odisha government empowered the revenue inspectors to dispose the uncontested mutation cases with the confirmation of tahsildars. The integration of the settlement and consolidation work with the tahsil and the so-called rationalisation of revenue work at the directorate, district, sub-division and tahsil levels were done to 'bring out revenue administration closer to people and for the convenience to the general public.' The integration of the competing institutions of land records management like survey and settlement and consolidation was done in line with the Appu Committee recommendation to enable the tahsil offices to 'function as the single window outlet to provide all services relating to land records to the people and the process of updating the land records would be continuous and much faster.'[30] However, the annual reports of the two years 2002–03 and 2003–04 suggest that hardly there is any perceptible progress except for the huge advances spent on the purpose.

By December 2004, RoRs in 142 tahsils were computerised and digitisation of cadastral survey maps in the so-called pilot projects were going on six tahsils Koraput, Rayagada, Salipur, Narasinhapur, Kendrapara and Bolgada by OCAC but without any mention of their progress and problems being faced during the course of implementation. It was also referred to again in the annual report that computerisation of 13 district registrar and sub-registrar offices and merger of settlement and consolidation wing of revenue administration with tahsil had been carried out as part of the reorganisation of revenue administration in order to bring it 'closer to the people' and for 'providing better and quick delivery of services.'[31]

The annual activities report of revenue department for the financial year 2005–2006 revealed that by December 2005 computerised RoRs in 153 tahsils

---

[29] Government of Odisha. *Annual Activities Report of Revenue Department*, 2003–2004, pp. 6–7.

[30] Ibid, pp. 7–8.

[31] Government of Odisha. *Annual Activities Report of Revenue Department, 2004–2005*, pp. 6–7

out of the total 171 tahsils were made available. The centrally sponsored scheme of uplinking the tahsil, sub-division, district and state level data centre was stayed by Odisha High Court as the tender for such contract was challenged by some IT vendors. The government also decided to introduce land passbook on payment of user charges which could be used as 'authentic document' for availing miscellaneous certificates on caste and residence and may be referred or produced before the competent authority at the time of sale, purchase and mortgage of the landed property.[32]

The annual activities report claimed that Odisha has 'made substantial progress in computerisation of land records' and is in the process of completing it soon. It further claimed that out of 171 tahsils, the process of computerisation of land records has been completed in 167 tahsils and the computerised copies of RoRs are available on demand in these tahsils and 'updated RoRs' are also put on the web for 'easy access' by the general public, which is false and misleading.[33]

In the financial year 2007–2008 and 2008–2009, Odisha government carved out 145 new tahsils from the existing 171 tahsils by making the jurisdiction of each tahsil coincide with the respective block offices. The total number of tahsils thus now stood at 316 in line with the recommendation of the PS Appu Committee on revitalisation of land revenue administration.[34] The state could computerise mostly the old and outdated record of rights in 171 tahsils by 2007–2008 and started issuing certified copies of record of rights and miscellaneous certificates to general public on payment of user fees. One of the annual reports of revenue department claims that 'the main objective of computerisation is to offer maximum benefits to the users with transparency.'[35]

The study of the proceedings of the state level steering committee revealed that teething problem of software development, its installation and updation, lack of technical manpower in the revenue department who could deal with the process of computerisation, problem of digitisation and updation of cadastral maps, and the issue of data safety, have persisted since the initial stage of

---

[32] See the Annual Activity Report of Revenue Department on the website of Odisha Government. http://www.Odisha.gov.in/revenue/activity_rep/activity-report05_06.htm (accessed on March 29, 2010).

[33] Ibid.

[34] Government of Odisha. *Report on the Activities of Revenue and Disaster Management Department for the Year 2006–2007*, pp. 6–7

[35] http://www.Odisha.gov.in/revenue/activity_rep/2007-08.pdf (accessed on March 29, 2010)

computerisation and authorities in the revenue department have not been able to respond effectively to such difficulties till today.

Similarly, the study of the proceedings of the steering committee from 2005 to 2008 found that a lot of interesting issues like managing networks of purchase and supply of computer hardwares and softwares for installation in computer cells at tahsils and data centres at sub-division, district and state level offices, problem of maintenance of computer system and their upgradation and the challenge of imposing user fees dominated the proceedings throughout. The problem of validation of the data entered by the private IT vendors, the decision to computerise the land passbooks, failure of the computer system in the tahsil offices situated in interior tribal areas, the growing problem of backlog mutation data entries and of the subsequently published records of rights in resurvey continued to defy solutions. The monitoring committee was seen busy in finalising, scrutinising and awarding contracts to IT vendors and suppliers for supply of computers and other systems for tahsil computer cells, sub-division, district and state level data centres. It was also found from the proceedings that, hardly the process of data entry of RoRs was over in most tahsils, there arose the problem of upgradation of servers and client servers installed there and the need for purchase of computers of higher configurations for the newly established land records centre by NIC at Board of Revenue was felt too. The centrally sponsored scheme of computerisation of land records has spurred unhealthy competition among the public and private sectors for bagging the lucrative IT contracts for supply, upgradation and maintenance of computer systems at the tahsil, district and state levels. The state level monitoring committee seems to have been happily engaged itself in such contracting tasks than addressing the problems of computerisation process, its long term and short term impacts on the revenue bureaucracies at the tahsil level. Huge amounts were placed with the district collectors under the scheme for Strengthening Revenue Administration and Updating Land Records (SRA&ULR) but utilisation certificates from them have not been forthcoming. Similarly, huge amounts were placed with OCAC for setting up computer cells at the district, subdivisional and tahsil levels funded by the central government, but no information of their progress is available. The proceedings also revealed that till January 2007, the RoRs of as many as six tahsils were left out and it was only in March 2007 Odisha government issued instruction to all tahsildars for stopping the issue of manual RoRs from January 2008. Despite heavy preoccupation with purchase, contracting out the work of computerisation and digitisation of cadastral maps, the Director of Land Records and Survey (DLR&S) did not have detailed information on the ongoing nature of land records computerisation work in the tahsils as well as the need for maintenance and support system for the computers installed in a phased manner in tahsils. [36]

Further study of the proceedings of the state level steering committee (SLSC) between 2008 and 2010 points out that the scheme of computerisation of land records has succeeded in developing a network of governance in which both the formal and informal actors have come to play a significant role in implementing policies. The steering committee sits casually and confines itself almost exclusively to sanctioning funds for purchase of computer hardware and software and awarding contracts. It does not consider it necessary to undertake independent evaluation or study on the process of computerisation of land records, its working, role of officials and their attitude and problems encountered, though the same has been explicitly suggested in the central government guidelines. No discussion on functioning of computer cells in interior areas has taken place. It can thus be argued that as a network of vested interest has taken over the state monitoring cell that wants the committee to get confined with awarding contracts. There is virtually no supervision, leadership, ownership and monitoring of the computerisation of land records programme in Odisha. Thus, the poor performance of Odisha can be understood significantly by studying the proceedings of its state level monitoring committee which highlights as well as conceals the 'official truths' on land records computerisation and modernisation of revenue administration. The proceedings also betray the real motivation of the political and administrative leadership to implement the long years of expenditure driven programme.

Computerisation of Land Records (CLR) in Odisha has been limited to computerisation of existing record of rights in 171 tahsils. It was only in 2007 that the records of rights of all the tahsils were computerised, but record of rights of a good number of villages where survey operations had been completed recently were not computerised due to lack of proper supervision at the time of data entry. The centrally sponsored scheme fully funded the cost

---

[36] See the proceedings of the State Level Steering Committee (SLSC) from 2005 to 2008, available at the Director, Land Records, Survey and Settlement, Board of Revenue, Odisha, Cuttack.

of computerisation of land records and more than 31 crores of rupees were spent by the Odisha government.[37]

The Bhulekh application software is being used on a limited scale, i.e., the generation of certified copies of RoRs (textual data), generation of some notices for correction of RoRs (mutation) and issue of some miscellaneous certificates on payment of user fees. The certified copy of RoRs per holding or *Khata* number is charged 20 rupees and the RoRs as corrected by mutation case per Khata or holding is being charged 35 rupees. The other module of the Bhulekh providing for online mutation is not being followed in any of the tahsils surveyed by the researcher. The reasons cited by the officials were the difficulty in operationalising the application software by the clerical staff, their deliberate avoidance as they perceive that operation of such online mutation will be a burden on them and absence of the technical staff to handle such a system. Further, it was observed by the researcher in the tahsils visited that only a computer-generated mutation number is being provided to the mutation cases and the rest of the works are being done manually. It was officially stated that due to lack of connectivity with the sub-registrar's office, online mutation is not being done but the real problems lie in the computerisation of old records and lack of technical capacity of the revenue officials.[38] It was promised by secretary of revenue department that connectivity would be ensured by September 2009 at a national workshop in New Delhi for the state revenue secretaries, but till today no such development has taken place. There were nearly 12 lakh backlogs of mutation case entries relating to record of rights to be corrected or incorporated into the existing computerised land records database and a target was set for clearing such backlog cases with help of extra personnel in tahsil offices. Manual correction of record of rights and issue of certified copy was yet to be stopped in some tahsils, despite instruction issued by the government.[39]

---

[37] As noted by the Accountant General of Odisha in its Performance Audit, 2008 on CLR in Odisha. The Ministry of Rural Development's *Annual Report, 2007–2008* however records that nearly 40 crores of rupees have been released to Odisha till 31 March 2008 (vide Annexture- XX, p. 277).

[38] The PowerPoint presentation made by G. V. V. Sharma, IAS, Secretary Revenue, Government of Odisha at the National Workshop on NLRMP organised by Department of Land Resources, MORD, at New Delhi on 14 June 2007. Interestingly, this presentation is the only authentic document or "official truth" about the implementation of the programme in the state, not found in any other official documents.

[39] Ibid.

The presentations by the revenue secretary at the national workshop in New Delhi shows that digitisation of cadastral maps have been done on a pilot project basis in six tahsils and the projects were completed without any feedback to the government by the implementing agency although a huge amount was spent both by the central and state governments. The digitisation of cadastral maps have thrown up a number of constraints like non-adjustment of errors and lack of adoption of universal software and problems in training the revenue staff in operationalising the digitalised cadastral maps. Despite facing technical inadequacies and the failure of Odisha Computer Application Centre (OCAC) to successfully operationalise the digitaisation of cadastral maps, what is interesting is that the state government has sent a five-year 'perspective proposal' for funds to the central government for digitisation of all the cadastral maps of the state under NLRMP. This puts the question mark on the real motivation for bagging such huge funds as well as capability of the state government to concretely achieve the objective, given its serious failure to successfully digitise the cadastral maps in six pilot programmes in different tahsils earlier.

The state government has also received full financial assistance from the central government for interlinking tahsil office with subdivisional, district and state data centres, but is yet to make any headway in the matter.[40] The government also has proposed to computerise 1842 Revenue Inspector's circle offices existing in the state and the proposal for funds has been sent to the centre. As said previously, the Odisha government has also created 145 more tahsils with corresponding blocks and the central government has funded the cost of setting up computer cells in all the newly created tahsils. Under SRA&ULR scheme, the state government has gone ahead in utilising the funds by constructing the buildings in tahsil and RI offices, purchased modern survey equipments, and set up a revenue law training institute at Cuttack for its field officials.[41]

Constraints on the computerisation of land records: some findings

The progress of computerisation of land records in Odisha has thus been slow and raises several issues of technical and institutional constraints. As admitted

---

[40] Discussion with Dipak Das, Technical Director, NIC, Land Records Centre, Board of Revenue, Odisha, Cuttack on 15 December 2009.

[41] See Status Report on NLRMP at Director, Land Records and Survey Office, Board of Revenue, Cuttack.

by the revenue secretary, the state does not require any pilot projects for the implementation of computerisation of land records schemes, digitisation of cadastral maps, linking registration office with tahsil for online mutation and uplinking tahsil offices with its subdivisional, district, state level data centres, but needs effective technical guidance and experience sharing on the successful e-governance practices. There is a need for replicable technical specifications for computerisation of the registration process and linking with the tahsil office for integrated and online mutation process as well as the requirement of resources for such computerisation drive, as the state government is unable to release its share of funding to schemes like strengthening revenue administration and updating land records.[42]

The digitisation of cadastral maps was undertaken in pilot projects in six tahsils but the results were negative as the digitisation of the cadastral maps preserved at the survey offices were scanned and digitised and no efforts were made to update such digital maps in the light of numerous changes made in the record of rights since their final publication. It was also confirmed by the officials at the Board of Revenue, Odisha that the private vendors assigned with the digitisation contract did not possess the requisite technology to update the cadastral maps and then hand over the digitised maps to the tahsil officials and train them for regular updation by the staff. In fact the project funds have been spent out without any concrete achievement by the executing officials of the land records directorate and OCAC in connivance with inexperienced IT vendors.[43] This put a question mark on the feasibility of the digitisation of cadastral maps, their correctness and integration with textual land record data like records of rights. It was found in one of the field verifications in Salipur tahsil by the director, land records and survey that the cadastral maps prepared manually contained some errors during plotting and extraction of area of the plots. By digitising the original cadastral maps without their updation, the discrepancy of plot size in map and record of rights are easily incorporated into

[42] The PowerPoint presentation made by G. V. V. Sharma, IAS, Secretary, Revenue, Government of Odisha at the National Workshop on NLRMP organised by Department of Land Resources, MORD, at New Delhi on 14 June 2007.

[43] My discussions with R. K. Sahoo, OAS, Vijayananda Nayak, OSCS, and Section officer Basudev Mallick of land records computerisation cell at the Board of Revenue, Odisha, Cuttack on 8 June 2010.

the spatial database. The end result has been multiplication of errors.[44] In July 2009, revenue department directed all tahsildars to follow online mutation by applying new software developed by NIC (Bhulekh version 3.02) invariably and warned of disciplinary action for non-compliance. The online mutation would be initiated on the basis of Form No 3 (intimations from sub-registrar office on transactions of land) received from the sub-registrar's office on execution of registered sale deed only and not on application by the applicants.[45] But my field visits to all 16 tahsils confirmed me that the so-called online mutation has remained a non-starter due to non-availability of connectivity with registration office and the absence of user friendly software and trained technical staff. In all the tahsils, mutation cases are being initiated manually on the basis of applications by the vendors or recorded tenants, as the intimations from the sub-registrar's office do not reach the tahsils in time.

As discussed previously, computerisation of land records of all the villages in Odisha are not done despite availability of the RoRs in some villages. Our study concurred with audit findings of the Accountant General of India that in most of the tahsils in coastal as well interior areas, the RoRs of few villages have been excluded of computerisation process at the time of data entry due to lack of proper supervision or non-finalisation of survey and settlement operations, and nothing has been done so far in computerising the manually maintained RoRs of these villages. Delivery of certified RoRs and disposal of mutation of land records are being carried out in tahsils without maintaining a queue principle or the first-in-first-out principle and such pick and choose principle of record correction goes directly against the very purpose of land records computerisation. Computerisation of land records has not in any way reduced the discretionary or arbitrary power of the tahsil officials in correction of records through mutation. Sometimes, tahsildars in urban areas like Cuttack, Bhubaneswar and Puri are under pressure from higher political and bureaucratic authorities to attend the mutation applications of some influential persons on priority. The other important reason for discretion is the undue political and

---

[44] Gadadhar Parida. 2008. "Computerisation of Land Records in Odisha: Updating Cadastral Maps" in Ashish Vachhani and N. K. Kumaresan Raja (Eds) *Computerisation of Land Records in India: Achievements and Experiences,* Centre for Rural Studies,LBANAA,Mussorie, p. 132.

[45] See Director Land Records and Survey's letters to all district collectors dated 13 July 2009.

administrative pressure and lure of pecuniary benefits from the real estate companies and firms in getting their mutation and conversion of large chunks of agricultural land disposed early, bypassing others.[46]

As land records computerisation is a multi-agency coordinated work, the single biggest constraint is total absence of coordination and shared interest among the stakeholders like tahsildar, district collector, DL&RS, OCAC, ORSAC and NIC. The main reason for absence of coordination and ownership among the executing agencies is the vendor-driven lucrative contracts executed by one agency to the exclusion of others. My interviews with the officials monitoring the CLR work at the land records directorate and revenue department revealed that they shifted their responsibility to NIC, OCAC and ORSAC for the poor performance and expressed their inability to monitor the work as they placed all the funds with the executing agencies. The land records digitisation being executed by OCAC with the help of IT vendors and the validation being taken up by the map publication officials, not a single cadastral village map digitised by OCAC is validated by the map publication department till today. There is nobody in the revenue department to take up leadership in implementation of the programme. The officials at the land records directorate squarely blame OCAC for slow progress and the mess created in the process, whereas the latter blames the former for 'lack of mindset, ownership and leadership' in the project. An OCAC official dealing with land records digitisation, and construction of modern record rooms in tahsils opined that 'the problem is that DLR&S treats OCAC (the technical directorate of IT) as a mere contractor, only hands over the cheque for spending of the amount, calls for utilisation certificates (UCs) and the sits silently.'[47]

Interviews and discussions with tahsildars in Cuttack, Puri, Kalahandi, Khordha, Dhenkanal, Kalahandi, and Sambalpur districts further revealed that computersation of land records in tahsils are severely constrained by the absence of trained technical manpower like data entry operators, and trained officers of the rank of assistant settlement officer-cum-additional tahsildars who could look after the computer cells exclusively.

---

[46] This unpleasant fact is admitted invariably by all tahsildars as well as tahsil officials at computer cell and record room during my field visits to all the 17 tahsils from 2008 to 2011.

[47] Interview with D. K. Samal, Deputy General Manager, OCAC, at his office on 20 October 2010.

Assistant settlement officers (ASOs) were posted at the computer cell of tahsils after merger of settlement office with tahsil office to deal with computerisation of land records, but later on many of them were promoted to Odisha Administrative Service (OAS), and some retired and the vacancies are not filled up. There are only 30 ASOs to look after computer cells of all the tahsils. What is worse, these ASOs in charge of computer cells are assigned with handling of all types of revenue cases and miscellaneous works. The trained clerks for handling computer cells in tahsils were transferred on promotion thereby leaving the computer cells at the mercy of contractual data entry operators outsourced from vendors.

The data entry operators engaged at the computer cells to assist the additional tahsildar also perform as multi-task clerks by neglecting their primary responsibilities. The preoccupation of the data entry operators in typing various official correspondences, pay bills and monthly progress reports of the tahsils during his visits, and the interviews with the data entry operators clearly confirmed this fact. Such a factor is mainly responsible for huge backlog of old cases of mutation in the computerised land records database and delay in delivery of copy of land records on the same day as promised in the CLR programme.

According to some tahsildars, even if a special drive is taken to clear the backlog cases, more and more cases will pile up as the manpower constraint and the infrastructure problem are not being attended with sincere interest. In tahsils located in interior tribal pockets, sometimes the computers develop technical snag but no service provider is readily available to attend the breakdown of the system. The defunct computer system remains unattended for months together and mutation cases pile up for corrections. So in such a process it would be naïve to expect online delivery of up-to-date land records in Odisha. It therefore creates a fertile ground for rent seeking among the officials. The World Banks' cautious approach that 'the establishment and maintenance of computing facilities is a risk undertaking when insufficiently skilled IT staff is available' is pertinent here as the computer system fails to deliver results credibly.[48] The realtors, deed writers, petty lawyers and other intermediaries looking after their mutation of record cases frequent the tahsil

[48] Edward Cook et al. 2008. 'Information and Communication Technology in Land Administration Projects,' Agriculture and Rural Development, *World Bank, Policy Note No-43556*, Issue 38, February, p. 4.

everyday. These intermediaries however get their work done as they have maintained an informal network by regularly greasing the palms of the tahsil staff.[49]

In many of the newly created tahsils in Sambalpur district, it is but natural that it would take time to construct tahsil buildings and its modern record rooms. However, it is surprising that though basic civil infrastructure like building and electrification has not been readied yet computers and other related equipments have already been supplied by the vendors which lie unused and thereby getting damaged. It only showed total absence of coordination and the vendor driven nature of programme. Even the tahsil in district headquarters like Sambalpur also fails to function during the rainy season due to roof water leakage. Frequent interruptions in power supply or load shedding in tahsils located in rural areas now has become a common constraint for the tahsils in interior or backward tribal areas. In Malkangiri district, the computer cells are defunct in most of the tahsils and manual copies of RoRs are being delivered on payment of user fees.[50]

The district informatics officers (DIOs) of the NIC are the technical consultants of the land records computerisation programme in the district. The DIOs are actively involved from the very inception of the CLR programme implementation as NIC has operationalised its Bhulekh software in tahsils through its district informatics officers and they provide the software support in running the computer cells at tahsils. The interviews and discussions with the DIOs in Kandhamal, Nabarangpur, Balasore, Bolangir, Mayurbhanj, Kendrapara, Sambalpur and Cuttack districts have revealed that tahsildars do not take ownership of the computerisation of land records in the pretext of their preoccupation with administrative and revenue matters. In Balasore tahsil, the huge backlog of mutation cases are not being entered into the computerised database as the tahsildar has a vested interest in awarding contract to an IT vendor which would be obliged to him. At Mahakalpada tahsil in Kendrapara district, in Dharmagada tahsil in Kalahandi, and all tahsils in Malkangiri, the computer cells are virtually defunct.

In tribal-dominated Kandhamal district, the DIO pointed out that demand of bribe for delivery of RoRs on the part of the revenue officials in record

49 The interviews with the tahsildars carried out 2009, 2010 and 2011.

50 Interview with district informatics officer, NIC (DIO) Sambalpur in December 2010 and Malkangiri and Mathili tahsildars in March 2011.

room was a common practice. Even in undertaking repairs in the computer equipment in tahsil computer cells the demand for percentages from the bills of the vendor is a common matter in some tahsils. The DIOs are not actively consulted in choosing the vendors for annual maintenance contract (AMC) by the district collector or tahsildar, and as a result many dubious AMC vendors have bagged lucrative contracts and offer poor services. Computerisation is also not free from corrupt practices like preparing inflated bills towards repair and maintenance and purchase of computer peripherals and selection of IT vendor for entry of backlog data entry of mutation cases. This finding is very interesting, as the tahsildars are generally not interested in devoting their time for proper management of computer cells but when it comes to awarding annual maintenance contracts, purchases of computer peripherals and selecting IT vendors for backlog data entry of mutation cases, they are showing interest for the obvious reason of payoff from purchase or outsourcing.[51]

In districts like Kandhamal, Sambalpur, Kalahandi, Malkangiri and Cuttack, the district level monitoring cells do not hold regular meetings to discuss various matters relating to management of land records computerisation. The monthly district revenue meetings discuss the matter as the last or low priority item in the agenda and naturally the problems concerning land record computerisation are not discussed in depth. District collectors and tahsildars are preoccupied with revenue and administrative work and do not consider the land record computerisation as a primary revenue work. My interviews and discussions with tahsildars and district informatics officers thus revealed that most district collectors are not at all interested in monitoring and coordinating the land records modernisation work as they consider it as a 'dry matter' and no monitoring and leadership on the part of DLR&S and the revenue secretary also has sent a wrong signal to the district collectors to virtually disown the project. User fees are collected but in the absence of clear guidelines and lack of interest and involvement on the part of district collectors as the head of the district level NLRMP cell, the need for purchase of new and replacement of obsolete computers and regular training to data entry operators are overlooked.[52]

[51] Interview with district informatics officers (DIOs) of NIC in Balasore, Kandhamal and Sambalpur district in December 2010.

[52] Interview and discussions with district informatics officers (DIOs) of NIC in Balasore, Puri, Malkanagiri, Kandhamal, Kendrapara and Cuttack from May 2010 to December 2010.

Therefore, given many types of constraints, it sounds logical to argue that the delivery of copies of RoRs are not made on the same day of application in most tahsils though it is possible to generate hundreds of RoRs copies on the day itself. In bigger tahsils in urban areas like Cuttack and Bhubaneswar, the delivery of certified copy of RoRs are being given once or twice in a week thus belying the very objective of land record computerisation and the so-called online delivery of land records. The main reason attributed by these officials for delayed delivery is due to work overload (of both revenue and non-revenue) and lack of trained technical staff, which is at best a partial truth because my interviews with persons waiting for RoRs at the tahsils and focus group discussions with the farmers in some villages clearly revealed that for the middlemen, land mafias and builders, there is no problem in getting a copy of RoRs from the tahsil computer cell on the day of application by paying a good amount of bribe to the officials of computer cell and record room.

Thus, what we find in Odisha at the highest policy making and steering level is an absence of leadership, coordination and accountability and at the bottom level or the tahsil level, the tahsildars are not at all involved in the process of computerisation as they perceive it as non-rent seeking or dry activity. The pressure of non-revenue matters like law and order, conducting elections and VIP visits are offered by tahsil officials as the common convenient excuses for not attending the routine work of land records correction and maintenance. Unlike the lucrative works like conversion of big patches of agricultural land of real estate companies or farms or granting minor mineral leases, the land records computerisation and delivery of RoRs to the public on the same day is not at all a priority for tahsildars, as such works do not result in any payoffs for them.

The programmes for strengthening revenue administration and updating of land records in the last two decades and the computerisation of land records in Odisha and their poor performance has thrown up a number of technical, administrative and managerial constraints.[53] Some of the common constraints are:

- The Bhulekh software is not user-friendly and there is difficulty in its operation. The state government has recently written to NIC

[53] My discussion and interview with the officials at directorate of land records and tahsildars, additional tahsildars and perusal of monthly progress reports and proceedings of district and state level steering committee proceedings helped me understand the technical and administrative nature of the constraints during my field visits between July 2009 and March 2011.

headquarters to develop a user-friendly software for Odisha. The Bhulekh software module has not yet been fully operational in any of the tahsils.

- Connectivity with tahsil and sub-registrar offices has not made resulting stand- alone system of land records management and online mutation process has not been developed.
- Poor maintenance of computer hardware, growing obsolescence of computers and their frequent breakdown, affect the delivery of RoRs in time. Annual maintenance contracts are not being finalised at regular intervals in most tahsils in time as reported in their monthly progress reports.
- Shortage of computer trained clerks as many of them are transferred or posted to other offices on promotion and lack of interest among the clerical staff to learn computers in the absence of incentives.
- Problem in operating Bhulekh software by the less skilled staff leads to frequent breakdown of the Bhulekh system.
- In many tahsils, poor maintenance of buildings and water leakage from roofs have been a problem for smooth management of tahsil computer room and such reporting in monthly progress report by tahsildars highlights the poor working environment in tahsil computer rooms.
- Growing expenditure in maintenance of computer systems in the newly created tahsils in tribal areas of Malkangiri district led to contingency funds being spent in running the computer cells. Similar situations may very well exist in tahsils located in tribal areas where land transactions are low resulting poor collection of user fees. This puts a question mark on the sustainability of the programme.
- Empowering revenue inspectors to dispose mutation cases has created problems in following due procedures in disposal of mutation cases as they are not trained to handle mutation cases involving joint holdings and legal heirs. Their lack of competence and knowledge in legal procedures in disposing mutation cases by issuing of notices to interested parties, hearing them and taking decisions have added problems.
- Given such technical and infrastructural problems in tahsils all over the state, further creation of new tahsil offices in parallel with Panchayat Samitis/ Block Development Offices has added

the problems. The division of tahsils on the basis of Revenue Inspector's Circle and villages has created the problem of separation of computerised RoRs database and the creation of separate computer cells in the record rooms of the newly created tahsils. Hence, it is impossible to go for the so-called online delivery of land records and their correction on demand.

Field observations and findings

My field visits to some tahsils in interior tribal areas like Malkanagiri and Dharmagada tahsil in Kalahandi district revealed that due to frequent breakdown of the computer system, delivery of computerised copy of RoRs is discontinued for a long time and manual copies of RoRs are being issued there.[54] The private vendors who are given the annual maintenance contract are not attending the problem on a priority basis especially in remote or interior areas where the breakdown of the system continues even for nearly a fortnight. Some tahsildars and district informatics officers have informed me that in remote areas, the breakdown of computer systems in tahsils continues for more than a week as the private service providers fail to attend the problem in time. One of the tahsildars commented, 'till the private IT vendors bag contract from us, they run after us, and after they bag the AMC (annual maintenance contract for the computer cell) we run after them for the timely repair and maintenance of tahsil computer cells.'[55]

In major tahsils like Sambalpur, Berhampur, Cuttack and Bhubaneswar, thousands of backlog mutation cases are pending for their entry in the computerised land records database created almost twenty years back due to the absence of technical staff and officers who can exclusively engage in the work of computerisation. The computerised copy of RoRs issued is found to be outdated in many cases as huge backlog of mutation cases are now cited as

[54] My findings were further buttressed by a report of team of officials of DLR&S in July 2012 on the working of tahsil computer cells in Malkanagiri and Nabarangpur district which are backward and tribal-dominated districts. It was found in their report that in Malkanagiri district none of the computer cells were working and in Nabarangpur district except one or two tahsils, no computer cells were functioning due to several infrastructural and technical problems. Land records in the computer database are not updated for longtime in these districts.

[55] Interview with Ajay Tiwari, OAS, tahsildar, Sambalpur on 1 November 2011.

the major reason for failure to bring land records up to date, which thus put a question mark on the prospects of bringing an online mutation system.

In disposal of mutation of cases, computerisation of land records has no effect as the mutation cases are being disposed manually and then sent to record rooms to effect corrections in record of rights manually and thereafter corrections are being carried out in the computer database. Applications for mutation of land on succession, registration as well as the intimation forms sent by the sub-registrar's office are being received manually and then entered in the computer for verification of land records and a mutation case number is made on the mutation case file and individual and general notices and note sheets are also printed out. The non-disputed cases are sent to the revenue inspector who conducts local enquiry, issues notices to the parties concerned in the mutation case, hears the case at his level, records his findings and submits the case records to tahsildar for his confirmation. The revenue inspector, after the end of the statutory period of the individual notice, forwards the mutation cases to the tahsildar for confirmation of his order. The case is confirmed for correction of record of rights after the end of a statutory period of 45 days by the tahsildar, and then the case record is sent to the tahsil record keeper who first carries out the manual correction of land records like the area and name of the recorded tenant to be corrected, the name of the new recorded tenant to be inserted in the village-wise maintained record of rights and the land revenue calculated to be payable by him. He then sends the mutation case record along with intimation slips recording correction to be made to the additional tahsildar/ tahsildar in charge of computer cell for correction of the RoRs as per the mutation order and three copies of RoRs are generated in the process, one for the applicant of the mutation and two other copies to be retained with the RoRs maintained manually at the tahsil and revenue inspector circle offices. Intimation slips reflecting changes to be made in the RoRs are later on despatched by the record keeper to RI circles concerned for effecting changes in the *khatian* as well other registers like tenant registers related to collection of land revenue and water rate at the revenue inspector's offices. The disputed mutation cases are similarly heard by the tahsildar by serving notice on the parties concerned along with the field enquiry reports of the revenue inspector. After the end of the statutory appeal period of 45 days, the case records are similarly sent to the record keeper for manual correction and then correction in the computer database. Then the data entry operator makes arrangement to send the updated land records data in some electronic device like CD or pen drive to the district informatics officer, NIC at regular intervals for uploading the changes in the web.

In bigger tahsils like Cuttack and Berhampur, it takes three months generally to update the land records on the web and in Malkangiri district, the updation of records on the web has not taken place at all since its inception. Thus, one can argue that in Odisha the so-called online updation of land records is buried in myth than in reality. The mutation procedure as followed before computerisation has been kept intact with some minor modifications like empowering the revenue inspector to dispose non-disputed mutation cases and then sending back the case records to tahsildar for confirmation. In some tahsils like Khurdha, the revenue inspectors are not assigned mutation cases on the ground that they delay the process of mutation. Thus, the so-called computerisation of land records and online mutation or correction of records of rights in Odisha is a mere facade and land records maintenance in manually and computerised process goes on simultaneously. The reason for such chaotic and complicated process may be due to inadequate legal and institutional change, legal requirements for hard copy of records as well as need to maintain a backup or fall-back option in the event of total collapse of the computer database.

The delivery of the certified copy of RoRs is also made through application and in many tahsils the records are delivered on the next day or same day. Complaints are raised by most of the public that the delivery of land records and miscellaneous certificates could be available on the same day provided they offer bribe to the officials and the data entry operators at the computer cells.[56] Undoubtedly, such kind of procedure of land record computerisation, management and of delivery of land records has given rise to massive rent-seeking behaviour and corrupt practices. The rent-seeking attitude has been further raised by large-scale vacancies of clerical and field level officials at all tahsils and a few staff are overburdened with different nature of works which increases their indispensability and discretionary power.

Thus in all tahsils, the practice is that RoRs (*khatians*) corrections are made first in manually maintained record of rights and then fed to the computer database, as online system of mutation has not been in practice. Computerisation of land records thus has been an addition and not replacement of the existing

[56] This has been a common complaint in all the tahsils I visited like in Kalahandi, Dhenkanal and Bhubaneswar.

system of correction of record of rights. This has led to duplication work instead of reduction of work and demands deployment of more technical staff. The computerised land record database is not in synchronisation with time, as it has not been integrated to online mutation and the registration system as has been done in Karnataka.

Launch of National Land Records Modernisation Programme (NLRMP)

The National Land Records Modernisation Programme (NLRMP) has been launched in Odisha and it is one of the few states that could submit its 'perspective plan' for five years early to the central government for funds and received large funds from the centre to launch pilot projects in seven districts like Cuttack, Keonjhar, Khordha, Ganjam, Bhadrak, Balasore and Mayurbhanj despite its poor performance in land records computerisation and updation. Without learning anything from its past mistakes or the adverse reports of the Auditor General of India on the computerisation of land records and taking any fruitful measures to clear nearly 12 lakh backlog data entry (RoRs) of mutation cases or devising any feasible software for digitisation of cadastral maps and their integration, Odisha is one of the first states to reconstitute the state level steering committee under the chairmanship of its chief secretary to oversee and monitor implementation of the scheme of NLRMP and request for central funding. The committee consists of IT secretary, revenue secretary, NIC officials, director of land records and survey, and host of other officials dealing with NLRMP scheme. Similarly district level steering committees have been constituted under the chairmanship of collector of the district. The NLRMP as discussed in the earlier chapter consists of various components. The funds are provided to the state government at different scales: computerisation of land records is funded 100 per cent, survey and resurvey funded up to 50 percent, and computerisation of registry funded up to 25 per cent by the central government. Some of the features of the five year perspective plan of Odisha government formulated in line with NLRMP are:

- Online disposal of mutation cases and updation of RoRs and computerised database;
- Digitisation and updation of existing Hal (current) maps to reflect all subdivisions and mutation;
- Interconnectivity among revenue offices at tahsil, sub-division, district, and division level;

- Survey/resurvey and updating of survey and settlement records (including ground control network and ground truthing);
- Survey and settlement of unsurveyed patches;
- Hi-tech survey of lands and digitisation of validated maps;
- Construction of modern record rooms and land records management centres at tahsils; and
- Training and capacity building.[57]

The first proceedings of the state level monitoring and review committee of NLRMP revealed that the foremost task of the committee was to ensure rapid utilisation of funds by several agencies like OCAC and ORSAC and NIC. The governance challenges relating to effecting legal, institutional and procedural changes in the light of experiences gained from last twenty years of implementation of computerisation of land records through IT vendors was hardly discussed at all. In November 2008, Government of Odisha went ahead in amending *The Technical Rule of the Settlement Department Bihar and Odisha, 1927, Volume I* for incorporating Chapter-IIA on survey/re-survey using modern technology of surveying and mapping as per the technical guidelines provided under the National Land Records Modernisation Programme (NLRMP) for facilitating use of high technology equipment in survey works and instructed all settlement officers, collectors to follow accordingly. The amendment was made hurriedly by simply copying out the centrally formulated guidelines of NLRMP without consulting the experienced survey and settlement officials to find out the applicability and suitability of the technical instruments and their guidelines to diverse geographical, physiological locations and human settlements. Further the amendment did not provide any flexibility in application and adoption of so-called hi-tech survey instruments and their local applicability.[58]

According to the *Report of the Committee on State Agrarian Relations and the Unfinished Task on Agrarian Relations,* (2009), mere existence of technology is a matter of fact but it raises questions of 'the state of manpower base of the revenue department, their recognition of the issues that confront the state, their perception of the solutions and above all their commitment to induct these

[57] See the Five Year Perspective Plan for implementation of NLRMP in Odisha available at Revenue Department and Directorate of Land Records & Survey, Cuttack.

[58] See Board of Revenue, Odisha, Cuttack Order no 6540/LRS dated 27 November 2008.

technologies. More important is the commitment of the state government to the people.'[59]

In 2008, nearly twenty years after the launching of the centrally sponsored scheme, the computerisation of old and existing land records in 172 tahsils were completed and hosted on the web. The annual report claims that 'to make the tahsils online, steps are being taken to update the database through backlog mutation entry.'[60] Stating that the main objective of computerisation of land records is to promote transparency, the government claimed that it has already collected more than five crores of rupees as user charges. Under the programme for strengthening revenue administration and updating land records (SRA &ULR), the government has released the entire amount ₹ 935.00 lakh of both central and state government share to the district collectors, but no information on the achievements or failures is available.

Government of India has also provided assistance for setting up computer cells for the newly created 45 tahsils, survey and settlement in eight districts using modern survey instruments, and training of revenue and survey and settlement staff under the National Land Records Modernisation Programme. In two financial years, 2007–2008 and 2008–2009, Odisha government created 145 tahsils on the recommendation of Appu Committee and merged survey and settlement offices with consolidation offices 'with tahsils in order to provide public revenue related services under one roof in public interest.'[61] The uplinking of tahsil offices with sub-divisions and districts and the state government has been initiated. The state has also sent proposal for computerisation of 1842 revenue inspector's office in the Eleventh Five Year Plan. In July 2009, the Odisha government decided to provide broadband connectivity out of user charges to all tahsil computer cells through BSNL network for an e-registration project and BHULEKH website data updation

[59] Government of India. 2009. *Report of the Committee on State Agrarian Relations and the Unfinished Task on Agrarian Relations,* Department of Land Resources, Ministry of Rural Development, New Delhi, p. 186.

[60] The above assertions of the department is in addition to the main problem of not developing the state wide area network and state data centre (SDC) and uplinking the tahsils with sub-division, district and state data centre which is not however mentioned in the annual activities report of the revenue department.

[61] Government of Odisha. *Report on the Activities of Revenue and Disaster Management Department for the Year 2008–2009*, pp. 7–10.

and data transfer to State Data Centre till the Odisha State Wide Area Network (OSWAN) becomes operational.

Role of national informatics centre (NIC)

National Informatics Centre (NIC), Bhubaneswar is the 'technical consultant'[62] to Odisha government for implementing the project. It provides technical supports and testing in purchase of hardware and software for computerisation of land records project and also provides training to the revenue officers and its district level informatics officers at the land records centre (LRC) established at the Board of Revenue premises at Cuttack and coordinates with the directorate of land records and survey in project implementation.[63] NIC has developed and operationalised the Bhulekh software using Visual Basic at front end and SQL Server at back end. The Bhulekh software has four modules: RoRs module which provides certified RoRs copy, plot index and chumbak *khatian*, mutation module that operates mutation data entry, updates the land records and prepares the history report, query module which handles generalised and specific query, and reports module which generates miscellaneous certificates such as residence and caste certificates. National Informatics Centre Services Incorporate (NICSI) set up under NIC aims to provide IT solutions and e-governance services to all government organisations in India.

The Bhulekh software designed by NIC claims to make available RoRs on finger tips, delivery of certified copy of RoRs on the same day, provides loss free data archival and data security, aids in data decision making, and faster grievance redressal, and enables functional integration of sub-registrar office with tahsil. The Bhulekh software aims 'to promote e-governance, expand access to land records information, broadening the civic participation in government and making government services transactable online.'[64] Further the Bhulekh software claims to aid the government officials in the revenue department by providing general information about the revenue department, viewing and printing of cadastral maps and RoRs, and downloading of various forms which can also be delivered at cyber kiosks in future. Contrary to the

---

[62] http://gajapati.nic.in/itscene/landrecords.htm (accessed on March 11, 2010).

[63] The state unit of NIC claims that, "NIC Odisha has been playing a catalytic role in promoting IT culture for effective governance at the state & districts levels." http://as.ori.nic.in/nicosu/default.html (accessed on March 4, 2010).

[64] htttp://as.ori.nic.in/nicosu/Bhulekh_files/files/frame.htm (accessed on 11 March 2010)

tall claims of NIC, the glitches in the Bhulekh software have moved the revenue department to approach NIC headquarters in New Delhi to develop user-friendly software.[65]

Impact of computerisation of land records

The process of computerisation and updating of land records and strengthening revenue administration infrastructure has also spawned a number of legal and institutional changes. To recapitulate our previous analysis, the process of merger of survey and settlement and consolidation organisation of the revenue department with tahsil office took place during 2003–2005. New tahsils (316 in total) were created to coincide with the jurisdiction of blocks and the central government was approached to fund for the construction of the computer cells for the newly created tahsils. The revenue inspectors were empowered to dispose of the mutation cases on uncontested land. Government issued an order giving legal validity to the computer-generated certified copy of RoRs and miscellaneous certificates to public on payment of user fees. Later on it ordered the tahsildars to completely stop issuing the manual RoRs but did not make it invalid. The textual land records were hosted on the website. In 2008, the state government amended the survey manual in line with the technical guidelines of NLRMP to incorporate the provisions for applying modern survey instruments in survey, resurvey and mapping works. The researcher's interviews carried out from 2009 to 2011 with a number of tahsildars and additional tahsildars, revenue inspectors and supervisors revealed that very little organisational change in tahsils has occurred. Though the project is ongoing, only some marginal impacts are discernible:

(a) Computerisation of land records and issue of certified copies of record of rights and issue of miscellaneous certificates have been easier and faster and has helped the staff to reduce their drudgeries at the record rooms. Searching for information on land records or RoRs now become easier and thereby saves a lot of time for the officials.

[65] Dipak Das, the technical director, Land Records Centre of NIC at Board of Revenue on the other hand blames the revenue officials for their inability to operate the application software as stated during my discussion with him. Many additional tahsildars also complained of difficulties in handling the software during my discussion with them and expressed doubts of its complete operationalisation after the net connectivity is provided.

(b) The process of issuing certificates and certified copy of RoRs and mutation RoRs on payment have generated huge user fees in bigger tahsils. But the increased cost in maintenance of hardware and software system of the computer cells is becoming costly day by day. Recently the state government had increased the rate of user fees (October 2011) to make the so-called online delivery of land records sustainable.

(c) Search and query module in Bhulekh software and uploading land records on the web, according to some tahsildars posted in major urban tahsils like Cuttack, Khordha, Sambalpur and Bhubaneswar, helps the real estate agents, builders and land mafia to find out information on record of rights of farmers and other land holders easily and then target these gullible land owners to sell their land at a price higher than the prevailing market rate for their real estate investments.

(d) Interestingly, all the tahsildars, additional tahsildars and revenue inspectors interviewed were convinced that the land records computerisation and hosting them on the web and tight integration of technology with land records will promote transparency and help prevent fraudulent land transactions. Many tahsildars and additional tahsildars are hopeful that in the long run, computerisation of land records and digitisation of maps will increase efficiency in service delivery and will promote transparency. This clearly reflects their techno-managerial perception and beliefs in an apolitical approach to transparency, accountability and corruption.

(e) The delivery of computerised copy of RoRs is a partial one as its corresponding sketch map is not computerised and in tahsils the cadastral maps are not being corrected at the time of correction of RoRs, especially in urban areas due to non-availability of maps or their damaged condition. Hence, there is growing mismatch between the textual (RoRs) and spatial (map) records, creating fertile grounds of land disputes and fraudulent transactions. Even in some tahsils like Puri, Cuttack and Bhubaneswar, though the old cadastral maps are available for some villages, the tahsil officials avoid effecting changes on the cadastral maps of the village in mutation cases on the ground that such changes will be risky as their predecessors have not effected such changes.

(f) The role of data entry operators has become very important after the operationalisation of the Bhulekh application software. Though these data entry operators are contractually appointed and low paid employees, still they play a crucial role in delivery of certified and mutation *patta* (record of rights) and a number of miscellaneous certificates as the tahsil officials are simply ignorant to operate such complex software systems. The data entry operators have been indispensable for running the computer cells in all tahsils. Further, the data entry operators in the computer cells are also preoccupied with other clerical work like typing letters and preparing various monthly progress reports of the tahsils. The data entry operators are also engaged in delivery of different certificates like caste, income and residence certificates from the Bhulekh module. Discussion and interviews with some of the people waiting for a copy of RoRs at the tahsils visited by the researcher revealed that the data entry operators demand bribe for correction of RoRs and delivery of certified copy of RoRs, and the delivery of the latter could be made on the same day if a good amount of bribe is paid; otherwise, the delivery of certified RoRs will be delayed for a few days. Such behaviour among the data entry operators has been a common issue in all tahsils due to their indispensable position and as they are directly dealing with the public in the absence of any personal involvement of the officials in the computerisation work in tahsils.[66] The computer failure or malfunctioning has become a dilatory tactic to demand bribe.[67] In large tahsils like Bhubaneswar, Cuttack and Tangi Chowdar, the additional tahsildars in charge of mutation and record correction and updation are not able to check the records (RoRs) minutely, rather they put their bio-log-in (thumb print) authentication on the records prepared by the data entry operator on the computer screen as they

[66] Interviews with respondents at Bhubaneswar, Dhenkanal, Puri and Khordha tahsils in May 2010 and October 2010.

[67] These findings were made in the course of my visit to tahsil offices in Puri, Dhenkanal, Berhampur and Bhubaneswar and holding semi structured interviews and discussion with the people who have received the certified or mutation RoRs from the tahsil offices during May 2010 to March 2011.

do not find enough time for minute checking of plot and its holding number.[68]

(h) Similarly the lower ranking tahsil officials like record keepers and amins have found that the issue of computer-generated RoRs have reduced their work burden to a large extent. Beyond that, they do not perceive any other changes in the computerisation of land records which is basically partial in nature.

(h) Interviews and discussions with some of the people who came to the tahsil office for obtaining certified copy of RoRs and new RoRs on mutation of land revealed that almost all the respondents feel that the computerisation of land records has made no difference to their problem of getting correction of records. The demand for bribe and delay in disposal of mutation is very much in practice. Almost all the respondents interviewed at tahsils selected for the study opined that without paying bribe to the officials including the data entry operator, it is difficult to get the certified copy of record of rights or its correction.[69] Computerisation of land records (CLR) has not changed the staff behaviour and their arbitrariness, bribe seeking attitude and pick and choose method in initiating mutation or sending the mutation records for correction in computer database.

The very purpose of introducing computerisation of land records initially was faster delivery of copy of RoRs and promoting transparency and accountability in land records management. But in my field studies in 16 tahsils, it was found that it would be a gross distortion of facts to accept that CLR in Odisha has reduced corruption or corrupt practices or promoted a transparent, accountable and efficient land records management. I found a clear response among 203 respondents interviewed at the tahsils who have come from villages and nearby

[68] Interview with additional tahsildars of Cuttack, Bhubaneswar and Tangi-Chowdar tahsil during my field visits in July 2010.

[69] In all 203 persons were interviewed found near the tahsil computer cells waiting for certified copy of RoRs and new RoRs and in total 16 tahsils were visited which were found in all three revenue divisions of Odisha. Twelve focus group discussions were conducted in villages of coastal areas like Khordha, Cuttack and Puri to ascertain the findings made in our field visits. The common findings in the focus group discussions were interestingly found to be similar to the data obtained from interviews and discussion.

towns for collection of copy of their RoRs and mutation of RoRs and conducted seven focus group discussions in seven villages in Cuttack, Bhubaneswar and Puri tahsils and one in Malkangiri district to validate the data collected in a semi-structured interview technique. Interestingly, more than ninety-five per cent of respondents in interviews and focus group discussions have commented that computerisation of land records has in no way reduced the corrupt practices of the tahsil officials in delivery of copy of land records or mutation of land. Rather, computerisation of land records have created new ways and means to demand bribe in issuing of certified copies of RoRs and mutation of land, on the pretext of citing the electrical problem or mechanical troubles of computers. In both the semi-structured interviews and focus group discussions, the farmers and the general public, mostly serving and retired government employees, were asked to narrate their experience in getting their mutation done or time taken in getting a copy of RoRs and certificates like caste or income, etc at their tahsil. A farmer named Sayed Kamaran Alli told me that'even after payment of bribe at each stage of the mutation proceedings, one has to run for several months to get the mutation done.' This was a common response from most of the respondents found at tahsils. [70]

The mutation cases are not disposed on first-in-first out principle or serially on the basis of date of application in any of the tahsils visited. Pick and choose method of mutation favours the rich and powerful applicants like land mafia and builders who get their work done within the stipulated period of time. Most of the respondents (99%) opined that corruption is a business as usual in tahsils and without greasing the palms of the officials, the mutation files would not move. The record keeper demands money for sending a mutation case file to computer cell for delivery of RoRs, and the amins at the record room, who effect correction of manual copy of RoRs and calculate the rent and cess payable by the newly recorded tenant, also demand money for the service. At the computer cell, the data entry operator who corrects and updates the RoRs and gets the same validated by tahsildar and finally generates copies of the same needs bribe. He plays a crucial role from the beginning to the end of the process and, given his preoccupation with multifarious nature of tahsil matters, this low-paid contractual staff needs to be gained over for early delivery of records.[71] At Tangi-Chowdar tahsil, Cuttack district, five farmers

[70] Interview at Bhubaneswar tahsil on 17 December 2009.

[71] This is the general practice in all most app tahsils found out in the tahsils I visited.

who somehow got their new RoRs on mutation of land informed that they had paid bribes in each stage of the mutation process and had to run for 5 to 6 months to get the mutation of their land and correct the RoRs.[72] Similarly, seven villagers of Dudhigadiani in Dhenkanal tahsil who were interviewed by the researcher informed that they could get the copy of their RoRs from the computer cell by paying fifty rupees more than the user fee fixed by the government (charged at rupees twenty per copy). Interviews with them revealed that CLR has not led to better service delivery, or reduction in corruption and delay.[73] At Bhubaneswar tahsil, the certified copies of land records as well as the mutation patta (RoRs) are delivered once in a week on the ground of workload on record keeper and data entry operators.

With the steady growth of the capital city and rapid rise in demands for urban housing, the builders and land mafia have provided spurt in land transaction and conversion of agricultural land around the periphery of Bhubaneswar. It is a common practice on the part of the real estate companies to develop informal nexus with the tahsil staff and officials for their business interest. The real estate agents have appointed their agents to have regular contact with tahsil officials to get their large volume of land transactions (both mutation and conversion of land) done smoothly by resorting to under-the-table means. The tahsil officials are fully aware that their favourable predisposition will enable the builders to get a windfall in the real estate business. Here comes the nature and amount of the rents to be sought by the tahsil officials for attending the lucrative real estate work of the builders. The absence of any queue/serial principle in correction or mutation of land records like first-in-first-out makes it very easy on the part of realtors to gain over the staff and get away with their works. The tahsil officials also pay more attention to the mutation and land conversion works of builders and land mafias for availing higher rent than from the common public.

In the capital city of Bhubaneswar, only well off people can purchase land and buildings and these people find it really hard to regularly visit the tahsil and RI (revenue inspector) office to dispose their mutation application. Hence, they find the deed writers and petty lawyers to get their work done by bribing the officials and in the process pay a hefty amount to the intermediaries. So much is the role of the intermediaries that an additional tahsildar admitted

---

[72] Field visit to Tangi-Chowdar tahsil on 19 October 2010.

[73] Field visit to Dhenkanal tahsil on 27 October 2010.

during interviews that the clerical staff and the field level staff hesitate to initiate any mutation or conversion cases applied directly by an individual. They prefer the intermediaries or petty lawyers to attend their mutation so that they can share the hefty amount of the bribe with the intermediaries safely and get the mutation done in the process. This fact was buttressed by random interviews with eight deed writers and petty lawyers playing as intermediaries in mutation cases found at Bhubaneswar tahsil. All of them informed me that tahsil officials process mutation applications of the intermediaries only and it is very difficult on the part of a common man to get the land mutated on his own due to rampant rent-seeking attitude of the officials.[74] In such environment, the land records computerisation and delivery of RoRs copy on the date of application and time bound disposal of mutation of the general public were relegated to the background by the tahsil officials.[75]

Focus group discussions with some villagers in Cuttack, Bhubaneswar and Pipili (in Puri District) on computerisation of land records and its benefits to the villagers validated my findings made in semi-structured interviews and discussions with district informatics officers and the general public found near the tahsil record room. These areas were chosen owing to their exposure to rapid urbanisation, fast paced conversion of agricultural land for housing and commercial purposes and increasing market value of the land and hence the renewed emphasis on the land records. A disturbing trend is that the villages along the side of national highways in Cuttack, Khurdha, Bhubaneswar and Puri districts are witnessing massive conversion of agricultural land for housing and commercial purposes. The land prices have shot up astronomically. Very few villagers contacted by the researcher have purchased land in the past few years. In seven focus group discussions, it was revealed that more than eighty per cent of villagers have not visited the tahsil for obtaining a copy of RoRs and miscellaneous certificates related to land records and are not aware about its process of availability. A similar focus group discussion was conducted at Malkangiri among the farmers who informed that they were not aware of delivery of a computerised copy of RoRs from the Malkangiri tahsil. Three focus group discussions carried out in villages Poova Sasan and Bileipada, and Nahalpada under Pipili tahsil in Puri district revealed some interesting facts.

---

[74] Field visit to Bhubaneswar tahsil on 10 March 2011.

[75] Interview and discussion with Pabitra Mohan Kanungo, OAS, additional tahsildar, Bhubaneswar tahsil on 30 July 2010.

The villagers in the focus groups virtually ridiculed the idea of computerisation of land records for promoting transparency and accountability in tahsil riddled with corruption and wondered whether the computer system has intrinsic quality to mend the rent-seeking character of the staff. 'Where nothing moves without paying bribe how can computers remove bribe seeking mentality of the tahsil staff? They are not predisposed to rendering service without seeking bribe.'[76] They viewed that computerisation of land records would be better than the manually maintained land records, provided the staff and officials are men of integrity and with no mindset to demand bribes; otherwise such move would suit the interests of the builders who would be easily getting access to the records through internet as well as in collusion with the tahsil staff.

One of the most common points the villagers in all the focus group discussions wanted to make was that at tahsil, even after paying bribe one has to run for umpteen times for getting a certificate, a RoRs copy, land demarcation or mutation done.[77] 'The builders have virtually taken over tahsils and the tahsil officials; especially the tahsildars do not pay attention to the problems of ordinary citizens and are more committed to builders as they are paid handsomely by the real estate business. Tahsildars are also posted after paying bribes.'[78] So much is the rent-seeking tendency that the tahsil clerks were earlier satisfied with 200 to 300 rupees of bribe for disposing the files of

[76] Stated by the village headman at Bileipada village during the focus group discussion on 7 October 2010.

[77] Focus group discussion at Pratap Nagari village under Cuttack tahsil on 22 November 2010.

[78] Focus group discussions at villages Nahalpada and Poova Sasan under Pipili tahsil, Puri district on 8 October 2010. The posting of tahsildar after paying bribes to the top officials of revenue department and chief minister's and revenue minister's offices was also found its reference by some respondents during my interview. One of the district informatics officers at Balasore also informed me that since tahsildars are posted at some lucrative tahsil like Balasore after paying huge bribes to minister, they remain preoccupied how to get the maximum amount of bribes during their tenure. It is also a common knowledge as well as the experience of the researcher who is also a member of Odisha Administrative Service that in Odisha for getting tahsildar posting in some mineral rich areas like Barbil, Sukinda or prawn farming regions like Balasore, Kujang and Krushna Prasad, an officer has to pay handsome amount of bribe to the upper echelons of government. It is but natural that the tahsildars posted in these areas will give low priority to delivery of RoRs copy and timely mutation of records by taking firm action against the errant and corrupt officials.

the villagers and farmers; now they do not bother to pay attention to common people as the hefty bribes by the real estate companies and land mafias have made them favourably predisposed towards them. Tahsildars posted in relatively affluent tahsils like Cuttack, Bhubaneswar and Pipili on the recommendation of the local MP and MLAs or on payment of large amount of bribe work for the builders and real estate companies than for the common public.[79] Some villagers at Bileipada under Pipili tahsil informed me that it was difficult on their part to access the land records or enquire about the status of their RoRs at the tahsil record room, but for builders the staff can get the *khatian* (RoRs of the entire villagers) of a village photocopied surreptitiously in connivance with the tahsil record keeper. At village Nachhipur and Naharkanta, under Bhubaneswar tahsil, 95 per cent of the respondents informed that they have not made a visit to tahsil for getting a copy of RoRs or filing of an application for mutation in the recent past. One of them disclosed that he had paid an intermediary two hundred rupees for getting a copy of his RoRs and his application for mutation of land was lying with the revenue inspector for more than five months as he had demanded money for allowing his mutation. At village Nachhipur, under Cuttack tahsil, in a focus group discussion, a small farmer narrated that he had purchased a piece of land but could not get his land mutated as he did not pay the high bribes demanded by the tahsil staff and he had recently paid 300 rupees to tahsil officials for getting caste certificates for his children. There a retired government employee who got a piece of land mutated after paying 4000 rupees as bribe to the officials informed that without paying such big amount he could not have been able to mutate his recently acquired land.[80]

The villagers during the discussion wondered that whether the government had the capability to rein in the corrupt practices or corrupt officials. Two focus group discussions in village Sisupalgada and Khatua Patna under Bhubaneswar tahsil revealed that though the people appreciate the computerisation of land records policy of government, they are skeptical about its success as the government officials in tahsils are corrupt, and there is need for upright and honest officials to man the computer system; otherwise it would not serve the purpose. A government servant at Khatua Patna village informed me that though he had applied for mutation on purchase of a piece of land in 2008,

[79] My focus group discussions with the villagers at Sisupalgada, Poova Sasan (Bhubaneswar tahsil) on 22 September 2010 and Pratap Nagari (Cuttack tahsil) on 12 October 2010.

[80] Focus group discussion at Nacchi Pur village (Cuttack tahsil) on 5 November 2010.

he gave up the hope of getting the land record corrected in his favour after running for more than two years and paying bribes to the bench clerks and revenue inspector and now continues to possess the land without its mutation. A retired school teacher in the focus group discussion commented sarcastically which was also reiterated by his fellow villagers that, 'computerisation of land records cannot reduce or prevent the corruption or promote transparency in land records management in tahsil, as without greasing the palms of the tahsil officials nothing moves there. Tahsildars and additional tahsildars are posted on payment of huge amount of bribe to their political and administrative bosses and it is but natural on their part to serve the interest of the real estate companies to get their money back with handsome returns. One is forced to pay, otherwise he'll have to run for years together. Ushering in good governance practices like transparency, accountability, fairness and speedy delivery practices are nothing but big jokes as the dominant rent seeking behaviour among the officials are kept intact.'[81] The two focus group discussions were however unanimous that the growing number of dubious transactions of agricultural land for non-agricultural purposes like housing and the entry of real estate companies has made the tahsil the epitome of corruption. One of the unanimous views that ran through in all the focus group discussions was that the delivery of the computerised copy of land records to the general public on the same day is not the prime concern of the tahsil officials; rather it is attending to major land conversion and mutation of the real estate companies or corporates. Computerisation of land records cannot even checkmate the corrupt practices of the staff at tahsils, as the pervasive corrupt practices and general decline of moral standards and crass materialism has seriously affected the moral character of government officials who even justify their rent-seeking practices citing the large scale scams and corruption committed by the political leadership at the top.

Computerisation has in no way reduced the role of middlemen/ intermediaries or agents in delivery of land records to the public. The role of the intermediaries in getting mutation done is widely prevalent in urban areas like Cuttack, Bhubaneswar, Puri and Sambalpur tahsils. More than fifty of the respondents interviewed by me at these tahsils waiting for copy of RoRs or mutation RoRs were deed writers or intermediaries. Interviews with some

[81] Focus group discussions at Sisupalgada and Khatua Patna villages under Bhubaneswar tahsil on 10 October 2010.

of the intermediaries at Dhenkanal and Puri tahsil revealed that as many well-off people purchase land do not have time to negotiate with the long and complicated procedure of mutation requiring several visits, they invariably depend on the deed writers or intermediaries to get the record correction in their name and pay a hefty amount to carry forward their business with the tahsil officials through payment of bribes.

Computerisation of land records: a critical appraisal

Before attempting a critical appraisal of the policy of computerisation of land records in Odisha, it would be more logical to highlight the ICT policy of the state and the institutions involved in implementation of the scheme. The state's ICT policy formulated in the year 2004 seeks to '... to develop a well planned, robust and futuristic IT architecture in the state which will bring about positive change in all walks of life...' The objective of ICT policy includes among other things inexpensive access to information, transparency in governance etc. by reengineering the government procedures. OCAC has been designated as the directorate of the information technology department. It coordinates and implements the ICT policy in government and semi-government sectors. OCAC thus functions as the main agency for computerisation of the state government offices. It is supposed to provide, outsource, organise and coordinate training to new users of computer hardware, software and upgrade the skill level of existing users in the government; design, maintain and host websites of government departments and implement, coordinate and monitor all schemes of the state government relating to IT and ITES.[82] Thus, from the above policy outlines it is clear that OCAC has sought to play the similar role of NIC and NICSI in Odisha and has emerged as a competitor in bagging lucrative contracts related to computerisation, digitisation and uplinking, maintenance and upgradation of computer systems.

From the foregoing analysis of the implementation of the scheme, it can be safely argued that the computerisation of land records in Odisha has been a chaotic exercise and there is complete absence of the administrative and political leadership. The director, land records and survey (DLR&S) rarely

[82] Government of Odisha. 2004, *The ICT Policy*, pp. 3–4; 13–14. (http://www.Odisha.gov.in/information technology/index.htm (accessed on March 31, 2010).

takes personal interest in visiting tahsil offices to review the working of the computerisation of the land records programme.[83] Many tahsildars rarely oversee their computer cells as they do not consider it important, and pass the buck to additional tahsildars. The tahsildars who are expected to play a crucial role in the effective implementation of the scheme are paying mere lip service to the project on the grounds of their pre-occupation with various other revenue and non-revenue matters.[84] There is no accurate figure about the total amount utilised by the state government agencies like OCAC. Its poor performance has gone unnoticed as there is no scope to fix accountability of its performance or monitoring its activities.[85] The directorate of land records (DLR&S) which is the main implementing authority is unable to monitor and coordinate the programme effectively. It is aptly commented by a senior technical director,

---

[83] This post is normally occupied by senior officials from Odisha Administrative Services at their retiring years as it is considered as punishment posting for lacking lucrativeness. Lack of interest in the computerisation of land records was evident when I informed DLR&S during my interview with him on 18 March 2011 about delivery of manual RoRs in Malkangiri and Dharmagada tahsils which he expressed as his ignorance. This was also candidly admitted by G. V. V. Sharma, IAS, ex-secretary, revenue department, Odisha during my interview with him on 29 November 2011 in New Delhi. He said that it was the primary responsibility of the DL&RS to directly monitor, coordinate and supervise the CLR implementation but he had failed to do so owing to his lack of interest and motivation and preoccupation with other works. 'There is no accountability on the part of DL&RS,' he observed.

[84] Many of the additional tahsildars in Khordha, Cuttack, Puri, Pipili, Berhampur, Sambalpur, Tangi–Chowdar and Dhenkanal had complained that their tahsildars do not take interest or responsibility in managing the computer cells and rarely visit to the cells. Similar was the opinion of the district informatics officers (DIO, NIC) about the attitude and response of tahsildars to land records computerisation programme.

[85] The post of director, land records and survey (DLR&S) which is empowered to coordinate and monitor the centrally sponsored scheme is invariably occupied by officers from the state civil services owing to their long experience in revenue administration and the post of chief executive, OCAC is mostly held by Secretary, IT or so-called IT savvy IAS officers. It was pointed out by the assistant director and section officer that the DLR&S lacks courage or inclination to monitor the performance of land records computerisation work outsourced by OCAC under the control of an IAS officer. Further the CEO, OCAC do not feel it proper to keep in touch the DL&RS about the ongoing project. The state level monitoring committee holds its meetings irregularly and as one could see from the proceedings of the committee, the sanction and expenditure of funds are dominating the agenda.

NIC that the CLR project in Odisha is like building one's house through contractors without bothering to monitor the construction work.[86]

The DLR&S confines its role to release proceedings of the state level steering committee meetings, allocates funds as per the decision of the steering committee to the implementing agencies like OCAC, ORSAC and NIC who in turn outsource or contract the work out to IT vendors, collects utilisation certificates from these spending agencies, forwards the same to the ministry of rural development in New Delhi and again demand more central funds from the central government. Interestingly, both the DLR&S and NIC were taking initiatives and interest in the implementation of the CLR scheme so long as they were directly responsible for spending the central allocations until OCAC, the technical directorate of the Odisha government in ICTs, entered on the scene and bagged all the funds for execution of the scheme on behalf of the revenue department with the help of IT vendors.[87] No evaluation study has been done which could have been used as a feedback for finding out the strengths and weaknesses in the implementation process.

Findings from the inside

These findings of my study were interestingly again put to a test when on completion of my research, I was posted as Assistant Director, Computerisation of Land Records (AD-CLR) from July 2011 to October 2011. The posting gave me unique opportunity as an insider to look critically at the working of the CLR programme from a practitioner as well as academician perspective. The entire NLRM Programme run as a vendor driven one with the least involvement of the Director, Land Records and Surveys who are normally state civil service officer at the retiring age. At the time of my joining at the directorate of land records, Odisha, the post of Director was lying vacant and another promotee IAS officer of Board of Revenue was in formal charge. I worked under his supervision and found that as he was in the fag-end of his

[86] Interview with S. K. Mohaptra, senior technical director, NIC, Bhubaneswar on 8 July 2009. He was of the view that posting direct recruited IAS officers would solve many problems of coordination than the promotees at their retiring years.

[87] My interview with dealing assistant, section officer and assistant director at the land records directorate in Cuttack in May 2010 and October 2010. The failure of OCAC to digitise the maps as per NLRMP guidelines has forced it to return the funds to DLR&S which is now executing the work departmentally through IT vendors.

career, he was not interested in taking any initiative in the NLRM programme. The post was later filled up by another promotee IAS officer who was also at the fag-end of his service and obviously was neither interested to go deep into the programme nor inclined to take any initiative for strengthening the implementation and monitoring of the programme. He confined his role to file noting and orders. He was averse to taking up matters like digitisation of land records or construction of modern record rooms with the Secretary Revenue Department and CEO, OCAC which were headed by two senior IAS direct recruit officers. The file works related to the NLRM Programme handled and routed through me only reestablished the facts already analysed in earlier in this chapter.

The main activity of computerisation programme cell at DLR&S office is to compile information on expenditures incurred by executing agencies like OCAC, ORSAC, DDS&MP and district collectors and send them to the Revenue Department. I did not see any scope for supervision, monitoring and coordination on the part of DLR&S in the implementation of the NLRM Programme. Lack of coordination was glaringly evident when the Revenue department unilaterally raised the user fees without consulting DLR&S and communicating the NIC as the former keeps a state level account on collection of user fees and monitors the programme and the latter handles the software matters of the land records. OCAC was found to be going ahead with construction of modern record rooms in some tahsils through contractors/vendors without following central government guidelines. It had to stop the work on my intervention. Many districts never send monthly progress report on collection of user fees on delivery of computerised copy of RoRs. The DLR&S office receives dozens of letters from tahsildars in the monthly report highlighting various software and hardware problems faced by their tahsil computer cells but no follow-up action is taken by the directorate. No training or evaluation study is taken up by the directorate.

The executing agencies like OCAC and ORSAC outsource the computerisation/digitisation works as they lack capacity to handle such works but do not send the progress of the work regularly to the directorate. The officers at the directorate (DLR&S) are both preoccupied in attending other revenue-related works side by side the implementation of the NLRM Programme. The Land Records Information Centre (LRIC) run by NIC also do not have good coordination with DLR&S even though both the offices are located in the same building. On attending various formal and routine works of the NLRM programme as an officer, I found that my role is confined to compiling and sending utilisation certificates on the funds spent by the executing agencies. I also found a casual approach to the observations and findings of AG, Odisha on the failure of the computerisation of land records programme and both DLR&S and NIC were shifting their responsibility in complying the performance audit objections.

As AD-CLR, I was a member in the purchasing committee of OCAC representing DLR&S and in all the committee meetings I found that NIC officials involved in the NLRM Programme were not invited by OCAC. The members were not aware of the latest computer components such as hardware and software aspect and as such they rely on the list supplied by IT vendors. This reveals that in implementing the computerisation programme in land records and choosing appropriate hardware and software system are very difficult given the highly dynamic nature of the ICTs. The capacity of the generalist nature of bureaucracy like IAS and OAS is important concern here to comprehend the techno-managerial aspects of the e-governance programme. Later in my new assignment as Course Director of the five-day and three-day training programmes for tahsildars and other revenue officers from different districts on NLRMP at the State Administrative Training Institute, Bhubaneswar, held in 2012, 2013 and 2014 some interesting facts emerged during the deliberations and panel discussions. Much efforts were needed for securing attendance of a minimum thirty officers in the training sessions as the district collectors were lukewarm to the capacity building exercise.

The participants were asked to share their field experience on the working of computerisation of land records programme in their administrative jurisdiction. During the panel discussion in these training on the working of computerisation of the land records programme, it was found that many computer cells in Odisha are defunct due to the absence of maintenance provision especially in tribal areas and the tahsildars are delivering certified copies manually. The tahsildars admitted that the total land area of the village recorded in manual RoRs and the computerised RoRs vary in many cases due to missing of plots during data entry works. The tahsildars narrated their helplessness in running the computer cells and delivery of land records on demand due to several hardware and software problems. The unreliability/unavailability in teleconnectivity and cost of maintaining the modern record room, demand for regular capacity building exercise for the officials and their preoccupation with other revenue and non-revenue works were cited as constraints in land records modernisation drive in their tahsils. The abolition of the post of additional tahsildars who were trained specifically to run computer cells and their posting as tahsildars at the newly created tahsils has created serious problems in running the computer cells on sustainable basis in the earlier functioning tahsils. [88]

The computerisation of land records programme in Odisha has thus been a rudderless one in the absence of administrative and political will power and leadership in executing the scheme. The study of the proceedings of the state level steering committee on computerisation of land records would reveal that the revenue department has been preoccupied with managing the networks of agencies involved in computerisation and updating of land records, rather than addressing itself to governance reforms.

Allocation and utilisation of funds by the formal and informal actors or agencies involved in the programme has been the most important policy strategy of implementation. The state level monitoring committee hardly discusses important matters like the administrative constraints, the long term and short term effects of computerisation of land records, and charging of user fees from the public for delivery of RoRs copy at a flat rate. The attitude and orientation of the revenue officials to computerisation, their capability and motivation to handle the cutting edge ICTs in land records modernisation and the dynamic problems and challenges like how to ensure data safety and protection, how to deal with IT vendors, and adherence of contractual obligations from them and ensure better delivery surprisingly never caught the attention of the state level monitoring committee members headed by revenue secretary.

The annual activities reports of the revenue department highlight only the so-called 'physical achievements' like the funds released by the central and state governments and utilisation made and installation of computers in the tahsils as token of progress of the programme of computerisation of land records, strengthening revenue administration and updating land records. It also claims vaguely of bringing transparency and revenue administration closer to people through land records computerisation.

In Odisha, computerisation of land records programme thus means spending the entire funds through the IT vendors and sending the utilisation certificates

---

[88] The Department of Personnel and Training (DOPT), New Delhi sponsored training programme on NLRMP was organised at Gopabandhu Academy of Administration, Bhubaneswar , Odisha.

to the central government for availing next tranche of central funds. It is difficult to find from NIC officials at Bhubaneswar any information on the procedures adopted, amount of funds spent and the means through which data entry of land records was achieved. From my repeated interviews and discussions with some of the NIC officials I found that they are not prepared to share responsibility in implementation of computerisation programme. The NIC officials in Odisha play safe and avoid sharing any information on the implementation process of the scheme initiated and executed by them after the damaging criticism of their performance by the C&AG in its report on the CLR programme. It has not accepted accountability for its poor performance and simply shifted the blame to revenue bureaucracy.

Lack of accountability and coordination among the agencies engaged in spending central and state allocations is the hallmark of the execution of the scheme. OCAC gets the lion share of funds, yet it plays the role of a middleman, outsource the works to IT vendors and allocates the funds among them and does not even send monthly progress reports to revenue department. OCAC does not possess any technical expertise to monitor the complex IT contracts nor does it leave any scope in the agreement to fix the accountability on the IT vendors for their failure to deliver in time.

Similarly, lack of transparency in the process of computerisation by IT vendors has led to frequent intervention of Odisha High Court right from the early days of computerisation of land records and data entry operations. The method of selecting IT vendors and the price agreement has appeared as the most contentious issue. Frequent court interventions since 1998 have become a regular feature in the programme; and IT vendors have challenged land records and survey directorate and OCAC time and again for their outsourcing contracts on grounds of various corrupt practices. Uplinking and connectivity among district and subdivision offices have been stayed due to High Court order. The whole process of computerisation and digitisation thus lacks transparency and allegations of corruption in awarding contracts to IT vendors are galore.[89]

---

[89] During my interview with K. P. Das, OAS, outgoing additional secretary, revenue department dealing with NLRMP on 22 December 2009, it was revealed by him that OCAC is simply indulged in vendor-driven approach of computerisation of land records and it does not have technical capacity to monitor the performance of the IT vendors. The officials pocket 10 per cent of money from the IT vendors for providing costly

Total absence of coordination among the central and state agencies in implementation of the earlier programmes like CLR, SRA&ULR and the present NLRMP scheme has resulted in chaos and confusion. As stated earlier, the land records directorate and the revenue secretary do not take ownership and responsibility in implementation of the project. Such approach has given rise to the acute problem of coordination among different agencies like survey, tahsil, NIC, OCAC, ORSAC and IT vendors. The lure of bagging of huge IT contracts involving millions of rupees for implementation of massive land records computerisation and map digitisation and executing them through private IT vendors has led to competition among NICSI and OCAC. National Informatics Centre and its subsidiary NICSI are now out of favour of the revenue department in terms of allocation of lucrative IT contracts and it was natural on their part to play an insignificant role in the implementation of the current NLRMP scheme.[90]

The performance in spatial records or cadastral maps digitisation and their integration with textual records have been a total failure. Initially launched as an integral part of the project on computerisation of land records, central and state government funds were provided for launching of pilot projects in six tahsils. The cadastral map digitisation project was executed by directorate of land records and OCAC with a cost of ₹ 123.26 lakhs. None of the six pilot projects was proved to be successful nor were the experiments or failures made out to public. It was learnt from my visits to directorate of land records that the IT vendors contracted for digitisation of original or mother maps failed miserably as they did not have requisite software to digitise the original or mother maps accurately, not to speak of the handing over of the updated

---

IT contracts. Similarly, ex-director of land records and survey S. N. Panigrahi opined during my interview on 24 May 2010 that the process of high value IT contracts by OCAC lacks transparency and accountability. A focus group discussion was carried out among the survey and settlement field officials at Cuttack major settlement office, Cuttack on 21 June 2010 about the merger of settlement office with tahsil and digitisation of cadastral maps. It was pointed out by all the participants that the process of digitisation of original and old cadastral maps are only meant for 'looting the state exchequer' and huge amount of bribes are being paid to the officials by IT vendors for submitting false validation certificates.

[90] Interview and discussion with S. N. Panigrahi, Former Director, Land Records and Survey, on 24 May 2010.

maps which are to be available with tahsildars' office. However, huge central and state government funds earmarked for the project were spent in collusion with the IT vendors, and utilisation certificates furnished to central and state governments, though the pilot projects failed in its objective.

The annual reports of the revenue department declared that the pilot projects were over but avoided mentioning any results. As described earlier, the state government again received funds for the so-called digitisation of cadastral maps of the four districts under the NLRMP scheme and the same strategy of old and outdated mother maps or original maps are being digitised with the help of IT vendors. When the copy of the digitised maps were sent to survey and settlement offices for verification, it was found that almost all digitised maps were not matching with the original maps. Several complicated errors in the process came up such as grid error, plot errors, boundary line mismatch and errors, mistakes in plot numbers, errors in *alamat* (marking of homestead plots in the map with unique identification mark), errors in rivers and drain identification, errors in showing partitioned and *chaka* (consolidated plot of land) plot numbers and disappearance of narrow water channel, fixing of tri-junction and bijunction in the cadastral map and creation of extra numbers of plots during the process of digitisation.

Such massive errors have raised open question about the feasibility of launching the project and capacity of the IT vendors to produce a correct digitised copy of cadastral map that matches with the preservation maps or mother maps.[91] The digitised version of the cadastral map also records plots in

---

[91] During my visit to deputy director, map publication and survey office at Cuttack, on 21 June 2010, I was informed by the staff and officials that the validation and verification team has returned all the digitised copies of the original maps after checking with to IT vendors for reprint in the light of errors detected by them but till that date not a single copy of reprint has been sent to the team for recheck and verification. The reason attributed to such non-response was that the IT vendors who were going ahead with such digitisation did not have requisite skills and software to produce the replica of a digitised version of original copy. The deputy director B. B. Jagdev also told me of lack of coordination between OCAC authorities and its IT vendors. The non-responsive attitude of IT vendors regarding the problems in checking of digitised maps and absence of adequate technical staff are some of the problems that have arisen in the process of implementation. He apprehended that eventually the erroneous digitised maps would be used for modern survey and there could be serious repercussions on revenue and general administration.

English which is in violation of the basic spirit of the land record digitisation. Even though it was realised by the chief secretary in the first NLRMP state level coordination meeting on review of NLRMP that digitisation of the old and outdated cadastral maps prepared in 1983 would have no meaning, yet the process of digitisation are being carried out through IT vendors on a massive scale.[92]

In 2012, the revenue department decided to take up the digitisation of original cadastral maps for digitisation with the help of vendors in 22 districts at its survey and map publication office as it was not satisfied with the OCACs' performance. The revenue department also ordered for a special audit to find out the poor performance and violation of central guidelines by OCAC in digitisation works.[93] The department also decided to take away the job of construction of modern record room for safe storage of digitised land records from OCAC and implemented the programme through the directorate (DLR&S). The sole motive is to implement a policy that would not address the problem and spend the money without any vision and gain material benefits personally from such long-term lucrative contracts whose meaning and significance is not intelligible to the common public or media.

The merger of survey and settlement and consolidation offices with the revenue department, withdrawal of the field staff and their redeployment in the tahsil office since May 2002 and again resuming of survey and settlement operations in October 2010 after a lapse of 8–9 years has created a chaotic and messy situation in land records management in Odisha. The charge officers and consolidation officers have been redesignated as additional sub-collectors, yet no specific assignment has been provided. Nearly five years after the merger and reorganisation of tahsil office with settlement and consolidation wing of revenue department, Odisha government, in 2008, abolished the settlement and consolidation officers and created equal number of additional sub-collectors post 'with a view to provide effective and quicker services to the people in connection with the revenue related matters and to set up more organised system of land records management.'[94] Throughout the state, the survey and settlement works that were going on locally had come to a grinding halt after

[92] See the proceedings of the first meeting of state level monitoring and review committee for NLRMP 24 October 2009.

[93] Interview with Sumanta Kar, OAS, former AD-CLR, DLR&S office, Cuttack on 11May 2013.

[94] See Revenue Department Notification No.DRC-7/08-16568/ 9 April 2008.

the merger, as the revenue department did not have any strategy or plan of action to utilise the vast reservoir of technical manpower of the settlement and consolidation organisation.

Since 2002, neither the modalities of merger of settlement and consolidation nor the statuses of Odisha Survey and Settlement Act, 1958 and Odisha Consolidation of Holdings and Prevention of Fragmentation of Land Act, 1972 have been spelt out. The settlement and consolidation staffs are deployed in varied routine tahsil tasks. The practical experience and knowledge of settlement and consolidation staff are made of no use. More than eight years have passed after merger of survey and settlement and consolidation organisation with tahsil and sub-collector's office, but the position of land records and its management have not been improved and, on the contrary, getting outdated day by day.[95]

The performance audit of comptroller and auditor general (C&AG) of India, after going into audit inspection of 51 tahsils out of the 171 tahsils randomly, highlights glaring deficiencies of the scheme of computerisation of land records, notwithstanding rhetorical claims made in the successive annual reports of the revenue department and found that:

> Even after 20 years of taking up pilot implementation and ten years of project implementation, deficiencies still exist in the system. As a result, the intended objectives have not been achieved to the extent envisaged and benefits were not commensurate with the expenditure of ₹ 31.60 crore incurred as of July 2008.[96]

Some of the observations of the C&AG, India on the ongoing Computerisation of Land Records (CLR) are:

- Computerisation of Land Records (CLR) programme is going on in the state as a budget plan and not as an approved project by central

[95] Discussion and interview with Sudhansu Sekhar Bhuyan, Additional Sub-Collector, Bhubaneswar on 30 May 2010. He asserted that the survey and settlement of land records of hundreds of villages including some unsurveyed tribal blocks going on locally would have been completed in eight years, had there been no merger of settlement and consolidation organisation with tahsils that had taken place without any strategy, vision and leadership.

[96] Government of India. 2008. *Report of the Comptroller and Auditor General of India for the Year Ended 31 March 2008*, Government of Odisha (Civil), p. 115.

government as required under the CLR guidelines issued by the central government from time to time.

- The pilot project on CLR started in Mayurbhanj District in 1989 took more than 17 years with additional expenditure of nearly fifty lakh and thereby negating the possibility of any benefits accrued to the CLR project which itself was rolled out by 2004 in four phases without benefiting from the project.
- The delayed release of funds for site preparation and procurements of hardwares and softwares for tahsils, huge delay in completion of initial data entry by private firms, and delay in development of Bhulekh application software by NIC, Odisha are some of the factors in delayed operationalisation of computerisation of land records.
- In all tahsils, where the online Bhulekh software system is in operation, the mutation cases are being handled manually and only case numbers were generated from computers. No progress has been made towards online mutation of land records in any of the tahsil checked.
- The Bhulekh software is not being used to issue caste and residence certificates, rather manual methods as existed earlier are being followed as tahsils do not have link with land record database. The caste and residence certificates are being manually typed through MS Word application in all tahsils.
- Though funds were released by central government for providing connectivity or uplinking tahsils with subdivisions, districts and state headquarters, the work is yet to be completed due to insufficient release of funds by the state government, resulting in non-installation of hardwares and softwares at the district and state data centres.
- Digitisation of cadastral maps through specific software developed for the purpose and its integration with Bhulekh software through pilot projects in six tahsils are going on since August 1999 and there is no possibility of its completion and operationalisation in near future. The digitised maps prepared by private firms are not updated and corrected by tahsils and there is no proper supervision and monitoring of the work by the department officials.
- Random check of seven tahsils in July 2008 found that RoRs of as many as 735 villages were not computerised by private data entry operators either due to oversight or damaged *khatians* (record of

rights) or lack of involvement and supervision by the tahsildars and additional tahsildars. Therefore the RoRs in these villages are being issued manually.

- Existence of poor working environment and infrastructural arrangements in some tahsil computer rooms affected the functioning of the computer system though a good amount was allotted for construction of computer cells in those tahsils.
- Poor management of service of computer-trained clerks and officers have adversely affected the operationalisation of the Bhulekh system in some tahsils. As these trained staff are transferred from tahsils to other offices, the correction of records in mutation cases are dislocated and the possibility of making computerised land records database online is difficult to achieve in some tahsils.
- Bhulekh application software did not have provision for the calculation of rent and cess and the same was being done manually and then keyed into the system from the manually maintained mutation case records. There are also errors on a large-scale in rent collection due to erroneous data entry and absence of proper validation. Due to inadequate system design, there is problem in fixation of rent from old landholding to new landholding in the case of sale and purchase of part plots of land. The system of cess calculation is erroneous.
- Though the Bhulekh software has the provision of a query module, it does not have the system to retrieve or trace the history of the land records in details of the transactions on a particular plot in a particular landholding or *Khata*. The tahsildars are therefore depending upon the manually maintained *khatian* first before deciding the mutation case.
- For making minor corrections in vital RoRs, tahsildars were required to open a miscellaneous case under mutation manual which ensures accountability but there is no such provision in the Bhulekh software.
- Lack of proper input and validation control in the computerised land records data is evident in the case of entry of landholding number of RoRs without the tenant's name and allotment of duplicate plot numbers due to data entry and data updation errors. The audit has detected that such mistakes are committed due to deficient input control to check this kind of error. Further in mutation cases, incorrect and inconsistent dates like date of disposal order before institution of

mutation cases were allowed into the system, generation of negative plot area after its transaction for an area aggregating to more than the total plot size, and existence of duplicate and junk numbers in mutation module of Bhulekh software indicated absence of input controls in 46 tahsils out 51 sample tahsils. The deficient system design in Bhulekh required manual intervention and thereby created the possibility of manipulations.

- The Bhulekh software lacks an effective nonrepudiation and audit trails as seen from the analysis of the database in 11,6069 cases in which no dates were stored in the system even after corrections of RoRs were made. In such cases, the accountability for corrections or changes in RoRs could not be fixed.[97]

From the foregoing analysis of the implementation of the scheme, it can be safely argued that the computerisation of the land records programme in Odisha has been a chaotic and messy exercise and there is complete absence of the administrative and political leadership and accountability. The DLR&S does not take personal interest in visiting tahsil offices to review the working of the two decade long computerisation of land records programme.[98] Such lack of interest, motivation, involvement and commitment on the part of the successive directors has created problems of accountability, transparency and coordination in implementation of the programme.[99] The problem could have been addressed by the secretary at his own level, as the head of the state level

[97] Ibid, pp. 115–126.

[98] This post is normally occupied by senior officials from Odisha Administrative Services at their retiring years as it is considered as punishment posting for lacking lucrativeness. The officers continue for a brief period and leave for some other lucrative administrative assignments.

[99] R. K. Sahoo, assistant director, computerisation of land records at board of revenue, Cuttack has stated that the problems and difficulties in land record computerisation and digitisation are manifold and complex. He informed me during my interview on 12 July 2010 that director, land records does not take interest and leadership in coordinating the land record modernisation programme; NIC, Odisha has miserably failed to adopt a user-friendly Bhulekh software since its introduction twenty years back; OCAC does not have basic technical competence to monitor the hi-tech programme outsourced to IT vendors and the state civil service lacks skill, knowledge and expertise to handle such matter. The end result has been buck passing and job-fulfillment nature of duty than any sense of commitment.

steering committee, but there is no sense of ownership of the scheme on the part of secretary. The revenue secretary, given his preoccupation with several important matters, could have given free hand to the DLR&S for effectively monitoring the implementation of the programme. The proceedings of the state level steering committee reveal his role confined to awarding of IT contracts to agencies like OCAC and ORSAC. Such lack of commitment and concern on the part of the revenue secretary has sent a wrong message to district collectors, sub-collectors and tahsildars who hardly take any interest on the complex implementation challenges faced by the scheme and have reduced the importance of the scheme to their routine official job fulfilment.[100]

Conclusion

The progress of computerisation of the land records programme in Odisha has been slow and dismal. The scheme requires collaborative effort among the state and central government agencies that demand a great deal of coordination and commitment to manage it. There is acute lack of political and administrative leadership, commitment and ownership to the implementation of the centrally sponsored scheme. The poor performance can be assessed from the failure of the pilot project that took nearly 17 years to complete in Mayurbhanj district, and the failure of the pilot projects in digitisation of cadastral maps and their integration with record of rights. However, the state has forged ahead in absorbing the central funds and spending with the help of IT vendors without delivering concrete results. This is the most interesting aspect of computerisation or modernisation of land records programme of Odisha viz., how it goes ahead in securing funds from the central government and also commits funds from its budget despite its poor performance in the complex techno-managerial programme.

The Odisha government's executing agency, the directorate of land records and survey, is more preoccupied with managing networks dominated by IT vendors than resorting any viable plan or strategy of collaborative efforts in

---

[100] This fact emerged during my discussions with assistant director, computerisation of land records, R. K. Sahoo; assistant settlement officers Ajit Giri and Vijay Nayak; Basudev Mallick, section officer; Hemanta Nayak, senior assistant at CLR section at Board of Revenue; Dipak Das, technical director, NIC, land resource information centre at Board of Revenue; and S.K. Mohapatra, technical director, NIC, Bhubaneswar between 2009 to 2011.

implementation of the NLRMP projects. Similarly, the NIC unit of Odisha has lacked initiative and motivation to work for user-friendly software for land records computerisation and digitisation of revenue maps. In fact, the interest and initiative of the NIC officials declined steadily with the emergence of state run OCAC as the major executing agency and bagging major IT contracts. The officials of the state unit of NIC also do not show their ownership and commitment to the project. The audit review of Accountant General of India has openly questioned the feasibility of the Bhulekh software in delivery of online land records.

The officials such as tahsildars and revenue inspectors are not sanguine about the computerisation of land records and most of them are not willing to take initiative or ownership in the computerisation process. It is also an unpleasant fact that disposal of mutations and record corrections have only nurtured the rent- seeking condition in tahsils where many tahsildars are posted on payment of bribe or ensure the long continuance of their tenure by greasing the palms of the political and administrative bosses.[101] On the other hand, the so-called state level steering committee is unable to forge a strategy of collaborative or partnership governance among the various formal agencies.

There is apparent failure in adoption of the ICTs in pilot projects of computerisation and digitisation of cadastral maps but that has not deterred the state level monitoring committee to go on awarding IT contracts and outsourcing the works under NLRMP. The DL&RS has utterly failed to provide a semblance of leadership in implementation of the programme. Similarly the commitment and the real motivation of NIC Odisha unit is open to question in view of the teething problems in their software that forced the state government to write to NIC headquarters and DOLR for further development of user-friendly softwares. In other words computerisation of land records programme in Odisha is facing multiple failures.

Though the government claims that e-governance is 'the mantra of good governance' and its computerisation programme will 'provide fair, efficient

[101] The role of corruption in posting and transfer of officials and the pressures on them to be corrupt and to act contrary to the ostensible objectives of their public service offices are vividly analysed by Robert Wade in his article (1985), 'The Market for Public Office: Why the Indian State is not Better at Development,' *World Development*, 13 (4), pp. 467–494.

and transparent services,'[102] the policies and the strategies to achieve this objective, particularly in land records computerisation, lack transparency, accountability and the problem of coordination among the multiple agencies. In the absence of political and administrative commitment and leadership, the land records computerisation programme has turned out to be a vendor-driven programme that serves the interests of IT vendors rather than the interests of public, the central and state government. It may be relevant here to mention Stephen B. Peterson's observation in Africa that the information system fails or underperforms because the saints are few (government reformers), demons (the apathetic officials) are large in number and the wizards (the information system specialists) are inappropriate.[103] But such a framework is inapplicable to Odisha's context. We have conclusively proved that in Odisha we have neither saints nor wizards but only different types of demons who are not only apathetic government officials but also officials with dubious integrity who are out to devour the flow of central and state government funds through vendor-driven computerisation of land records works.

Our understanding of CLR programme in Odisha would be partial or limited if we fail to take into account the nexus between the IT vendors and the executing officials. The success of the computerisation of land records in Odisha is inextricably interwoven with managing the officials and their networks with IT vendors. The miserable failures in digitisation of cadastral maps in six pilot studies have not prevented the state in seeking for central and state government allocations and then outsourcing the entire works to private vendors for digitisation.

Alon Peled's has observed that 'vendors play an influential political role in shaping the vision, build up and deployment of public IT projects.'[104] First, the revenue bureaucracy in Odisha lacks the skill and knowledge to handle the complex techno-managerial programme like land records modernisation. The complete dependence on IT vendors has become inevitable as NPM

[102] Government of Odisha. *Economic Survey*, 2006–2007, Directorate of Economics and Statistics, Planning and Coordination Department, Bhubaneswar, p. 17/11.

[103] Stephen B. Peterson. 1998. 'Saints, Demons, Wizards and Systems: Why Information Technology Fail or Underperform in Public Bureaucracies in Africa,' *Public Administration and Development*, 18(1), pp. 37–60.

[104] Alon Peled. 2000. 'The Politics of Outsourcing: Bureaucrats, Vendors and Public Information Technology (IT) Projects,' *Information Infrastructure and Policy*, 6, p. 209.

and networks approach of implementation strategies like outsourcing and contracting are adopted coupled with the absence of leadership and involvement of the officials. In the days to come, the dependence on the IT vendors will increase and to quote Alon Peled 'we may end up with ever more spectacular public IT failures.'[105]

Secondly, as NLRMP is to be carried forward in collaboration and partnership with private IT vendors, the fundamental challenge before the revenue bureaucracy is how to secure the public interest in such networks setting, given its poor bureaucratic capability and corrupt image. As Kuldeep Mathur has observed that the most important aspect of such mechanism is delineating the accountability procedure in partnership arrangements.[106]

Thirdly, the study also found that despite incremental nature of reforms and reorganisation of revenue bureaucracy, computerisation of land records has failed in promoting governance practices like accountability, transparency and efficiency in land records management as well as in the very process of implementation. At best, the impact is marginal and negligible.

[105] Ibid, pp. 222–223.

[106] Kuldeep Mathur. 2010. 'Governance as Networks: Emerging Relationships among the State, Business and NGOs in India,' *Indian Journal of Human Development*, 4 (2), p. 274.

5

The Computerisation of Land Records Programme in Karnataka

Introduction

The state of Karnataka's revenue administration comprises 29 districts, 176 sub-divisions, 203 taluks, 27,481 revenue villages and nearly 9000 village accountants' offices. The state has inherited a varied and diverse set of regional land revenue systems and tenures owing to the amalgamation of the state of Coorg and regions from the erstwhile states of Mysore and Hyderabad, and the Madras and Bombay Presidencies.[1] According to the *Karnataka Development Report* (2007) the state has in recent years adopted a number of reform measures for 'improving' governance such as the privatisation of government activities by disinvestment, adoption of Public Private Partnership (PPP) model and downsising the bureaucracy to improve 'operational efficiency and productivity in administration.' Successive governments in Karnataka have actively pursued a policy of increasing the use of ICTs for empowering citizens with information and speedy delivery of services. The elements of policy environments that triggered a series of reforms are competitive politics, pressure of globalisation, influence of ICTs, pressure of World Bank and macro-economic reforms initiated by the Government of India.[2]

---

[1] Government of Karnataka. 2008. *Karnataka: A Vision for Development,* Karnataka State Planning Board, Bengaluru: December, p. 1.

[2] Government of India. 2007. *Karnataka: Development Report*, New Delhi: Planning Commission of India and Academic Foundation: pp. 437–438.

In this chapter, we carry forward the analysis of computerisation of land records programme in Karnataka with special reference to the Bhoomi programme.[3] It has been aptly described by James Manor as one of the successful governance reforms in Karnataka.[4] Here we provide an outline on implementation of Computerisation of Land Records (CLR) and Strengthening Revenue Administration and Updating Land Records (SRA&ULR) programmes in Karnataka, and launching of Bhoomi project, the reasons for the success of Bhoomi programme, its impact on public, revenue officials, and taluk offices and the critical appraisal of the programme that has been projected as an ideal model by the central government and World Bank.

Apart from extensive consultation of the relevant secondary literature, we undertook field studies from May 2009 to January 2011. I visited 17 taluks both on southern and northern Karnataka and interviewed village accountants, tahsildars, deputy tahsildars, assistant commissioners, officials at the revenue department and Bhoomi monitoring cell in Bengaluru, survey and settlement offices and the officials of NIC both at the district and state levels. While collecting data on the users of Bhoomi programme, I focused on people found at the Bhoomi front end counters opened at every taluk since Bhoomi has centralised its database and delivery system. The farmers and other landholders who frequently come to the Bhoomi kiosks for obtaining a copy of RTCs, to file application for mutation, and rectification of errors in their RTCs were spoken to as part of the research.

Importance of Bhoomi as an e-governance programme

The Bhoomi project has succeeded in the delivery of Record of Rights, Tenancy and Crop Certificates (RTCs) online and has achieved integrated workflow on mutation cases. The online system of land records delivery, referred as 'data in the RTC database is current at any point of time. Updation of ownership details is embedded into Bhoomi business process itself.'[5] Though the project could not bring out any major institutional and legal changes, it went beyond achieving some of the objectives of computerisation of land records of central

[3] Bhoomi means land, is the project of online delivery of land records in Karnataka.

[4] James Manor. 2009. 'Successful Governance Reforms in Two Indian States,' in Mark Robinson (Ed), *The Politics of Successful Governance Reforms*, London: Routledge.

[5] See Bhoomi website, www.bhoomi.kar.nic.in (accessed on December 16, 2008)

government like quick delivery of tamper proof RoRs. The project has become the model reform strategy for World Bank, UNDP, Planning Commission of India, Ministry of Information Technology, Second Administrative Reforms Commission and the recently released reports of *Committee on State Agrarian Relations and Unfinished Task in Land Reforms* (2009) for its sustainability and noteworthy success of delivery.

The Bhoomi e-governance model has been awarded a silver medal by the Commonwealth Association for Public Administration and Management (CAPAM) in 2002 as it 'has introduced transparency and freed farmers from extortion' and could be replicated in other Indian states.[6] In 2005–2006, the United Nations Public Service award was given to Bhoomi for best practices in innovation as 'it has proven its utility and efficiency' and in providing a fair first-come-first serve treatment to citizens.[7] Its project champion has also been awarded Prime Minister of India award for excellence in public service delivery in 2006–2007.

The Stockholm Challenge, a pioneer among ICT awards and networking organisations that showcase best ICT applications for people and society has listed Bhoomi as one of the finalists at the Stockholm Challenge Awards in 2002 and cited that 'Bhoomi has brought the power of IT to dispel the insecurities of the farmers in 27,000 villages. To ensure authenticity in data management, a Biometric Finger Authentication System has been used for the first time in an e-governance project in India.'[8] Its success in the delivery of online land records has helped it to institutionalize it as a separate branch of the revenue department of the Karnataka government.

Computerisation of land records scheme in Karnataka

Before reorganisation of the state of Karnataka in 1956, there were five different administrative and revenue set-ups, i.e., old Mysore, Madras Presidency, the Bombay Presidency area, state of Hyderabad and state of Kodagu with different systems of maintenance of land records in force. It was only under Karnataka

---

[6] http://www.capam.org/assets/2002%20international%20innovations%20awards.pdf (accessed on June 23, 2009)

[7] http://unpan1.un.org/intradoc/groups/public/documents/un/unpan030517.pdf (accessed on June, 20, 2009)

[8] http:// www.stockholmchallenge.org/project/data/bhoomi/ (accessed on July30, 2010)

Land Revenue Act, 1964 and Karnataka Land Revenue Rules, 1966 that a uniform revenue law was prescribed and Kannada was made the sole official language in which the revenue records like Record of Rights, Tenancy and Crops (RTC) are maintained.[9] The land records in the entire state is built on the basis of original surveys undertaken during 1863–90 in the old Mysore area, 1840–63 in Bombay-Karnataka, 1875–88 in Hyderabad-Karnataka, 1893–1904 in Madras Presidency, and 1806–1816 in the Kodagu areas. After the state reorganisation, an integrated revision settlement was undertaken in 1965 in Karnataka.[10]

The Karnataka Land Revenue Act, 1964 (Karnataka Act 12 of 1964) and the Karnataka Land Revenue Rules, 1966 were enacted after the reorganisation of the state as there was a need for adopting a uniform code for land revenue administration and maintenance of land records. Sections 127 to 136 of Chapter XI of the Act and Rules 38 to 71 of Chapters VIII and IX deal with the record of rights. According to the Karnataka Land Revenue Act, 1964, Record of Rights provides the following:

Record of Rights:

1. A record of rights shall be prepared in the prescribed manner in respect of every village and such record shall include the following particulars.
   (a) The names of persons who are holders, occupants, owners, mortgagees, landlords or tenants of the land or assignees of the rent or revenue thereof;
   (b) The nature and extent of the respective interest of such persons and the conditions or the liabilities (if any) attaching thereto;
   (c) The rent of revenue (if any) payable by or to any of such persons; and
   (d) Such other particulars as may be prescribed.
2. The Record of Rights shall be maintained by such officers in such areas as may be prescribed and different officers may be prescribed in different areas.

---

[9] Subash C. Khuntia et al. 1997. 'Computerisation of Land Records in Karnataka: A Case Study of Gulbarga District,' in Abdul Aziz and Sudhir Krishna (Ed) Land *Reforms in India; Karnataka: Promises Kept and Missed, Volume –IV,* New Delhi: Sage Publications, p. 264.

[10] Ibid, p. 264.

3. When preparation of the record of rights referred to in sub-section (1) is completed in respect of any village, the fact of such completion shall be notified in the official gazette and in such manner as may be prescribed.[11]

The second important land record that is relevant here is the village map that delineates different survey numbers, which is maintained by the survey and settlement department. The register of Record of Rights, Tenancy and Crop Certificate (RTC) prescribed under the Karnataka Land Revenue Rules, 1966 is maintained in Form-16 as a loose leaf register. This important form is a combination of all possible data relating to lands held by an individual or group of individuals such as survey number, land owner's name with extents and land holding number, government rights over the land, area, assessment of land revenue, water rate, classification and soil, number of trees, source of irrigation and the area irrigated, cultivators' details, nature of possession of land whether acquired by registered or unregistered, document by succession, partition, mortgage, liabilities of the owners of the land, tenancy and details of crops grown including seasonal ones, land utilisation, area under mixed crops, etc. Thus the form is a combined document furnishing details about Record of Rights, Tenancy and Crops some of which are dynamic in nature.

In the manual system, the original RTC was maintained by the village accountant and a duplicate copy was available in the taluk office. The RTCs are maintained for each village separately, wherein all the survey numbers, sub-division and partition of survey numbers are entered serially, one page being used for each survey number, sub-division or partition.[12]

Land record itself is a generic term in India and includes all kinds of land and land revenue records and registers, forms maintained in tahsil/taluk and village accountant (Patwari) offices in a parallel and interconnected manner. However, for the purpose of the research we are concerned only with the following: RTC inspection register (Form 16), Khata register (Form 24), Khiridi (Form 25), and mutation register (Form 12), disputed cases register (Form 8), etc. In Karnataka, land records are maintained through manual system by nearly 9,000 village accountants, each serving three to four villages. They maintain eight registers, which cover the following types of information

[11] Karnataka Land Revenue Act, 1964 (Karnataka Act 12 of 1964).

[12] http://www.bhoomi.kar.nic.in/bhoomi (accessed on December16, 2008).

broadly: information on current ownerships of each parcel of land, its area and cropping pattern, disputed mutations, and village maps that reflect the boundaries of each parcel.[13]

It is explained in the Bhoomi website that the manual system of RTCs in Karnataka, as elsewhere, suffers from various problems, which are sought to be addressed in the Bhoomi programme:

- The manual system of 20 million land records (RTCs) was highly opaque and was maintained by more than 9,000 and odd village accountants and no regular updating was being carried out. The village accountants had a virtual monopoly over the maintenance of these records;
- The opaque manual system of RTCs is said to be responsible for fraudulent transaction of government land worth 25 billion rupees in Bengaluru division alone in favour of influential persons;
- The farmers have been subjected to harassment and extortion by village accountant and they were not able to get the RTCs in time as the village accountants were not available when the farmers wanted them most;
- Cumbersome mutation procedure and crop loan mechanism and lack of monitoring mechanism made farmers amenable to pressures from the village officials;
- Non-availability of land records database in time for various administrative purposes; and
- Delay in disposal of civil litigation for non-submission of RTCs in time.[14]

The village accountants are empowered to effect mutation as land records are in their custody. Their inability to dispose the mutations and correct RTC and village maps in time, their rent seeking behaviour, their non-availability in their offices due to mobile nature of their work, and lack of supervision by tahsildars and deputy tahsildars due to their preoccupation with varied nature

---

[13] Subash Bhatnagar and Rajeev Chawla. 2005. 'Bhoomi: Online Delivery of Record of Rights, Tenancy and Cultivation to Farmers in Karnataka' in Wajhat Habibullah and Manoj Ahuja (Eds) *Computerisation of Land Records, (Land Reforms in India; Vol. 10)*, New Delhi: Sage Publications, pp. 48–49.

[14] http://www.bhoomi.kar.nic.in/bhoomi (accessed on December 16, 2008).

of regulatory and developmental works led to several inaccuracies in the old land records and fraudulent land transactions.[15]

Earlier efforts at computerisation

Government of India had launched a pilot project in Gulbarga district of Karnataka in 1991 which was chosen as one of the pilot districts to overcome the problems inherent in the manually maintained land records. The project of computerisation of land records later on was extended to all the districts of the state. It is stated that the centrally sponsored scheme only sanctioned funds for capturing the existing land records but did not clarify its validation and subsequent updation. No funds were allocated for taluks where computerised RTCs could be updated. Some of the deficiencies of the pilot project at Gulbarga were: failure to rectify the data entry errors and update the RTC, no provision of funds for installation of computer system at the taluks after data entry, absence of training to taluk officials for handling the computer system, absence of regular monitoring by the district administration, no availability of stationery and absence of data safety and security provisions. [16]

The project was admitted by the government as a failure as the CLR scheme lacked clarity and strategy with regard to updation of the digitised data, their distribution and the status of manual records. Lack of involvement of revenue officials and the district administration led to wrong and defective database. Therefore, it was claimed that the project 'fizzled out without achieving its objective.'[17]

The innovative efforts of the then additional secretary, revenue department, Rajeev Chawla, an IAS officer, came as breakthrough for redesigning the centrally sponsored scheme with the help of state unit of NIC, Bengaluru in meeting the specific requirements of Karnataka. Karnataka government launched the project called 'Bhoomi—Computerisation of Land Records'

---

[15] Subash Bhatnagar and Rajeev Chawla. 2005. *Computerisation of Land Records*, p. 49. The officials at Bhoomi Monitoring Cell, Bengaluru informed me during my visits in June 2009 that village accountants are responsible for updating of land records. They are found in most cases indulging in rent seeking behaviour that led to growing problems in land records maintenance.

[16] Subash C. Khuntia et al . 1997. 'Computerisation of Land Records in Karnataka: A Case Study of Gulbarga District,' pp. 270–271.

[17] http://bhoomi.karnataka.gov.in/about.htm (accessed on April 7, 2010).

in March 2002, though it was started in 1999 and implemented in all taluks by the end of March 2004.[18] The state government decided to fully support development of 'citizen centric land records system' by spending the central allocation meant for computerisation of land records and bearing other expenditures for the project which are not covered under the scheme. The major objectives of Bhoomi are:

- Facilitating easy maintenance and prompt updating of records;
- Making land records tamper-proof;
- Allowing farmers easy access to their records;
- Collating the information to construct the database regarding land revenue, cropping pattern, land use, etc.,
- Integrating all the land-related activities electronically with BHOOMI so as to achieve single source of ROR data and its updating with minimum or no human intervention.
- Utilising the data for planning and for formulating the development programmes; and
- Enabling usage of this database by courts, banks, private organisations and companies, and ISPs.[19]

Strategy for implementation of Bhoomi

Initially the existing RTCs (legacy data) were computerised and a detailed study was done to develop the comprehensive data entry software to capture all regional aberrations and variations in the land records as Karnataka is divided into four revenue divisions and every division had its own variation in maintenance of land records as well as land tenure system. Some of the variations in land records were removed by administrative orders.

The task of computerising 20 million land records in the face of cynicism and apathy of revenue officials and their preoccupation with administrative affairs was a difficult exercise and the challenge was met by engaging private data entry agencies. Regular interaction with the technical staff of the data entry agencies and their feedback helped further in finetuning of data entry software and land record data preparation in districts. Frequent workshops and trainings

[18] Government of Karnataka. *Annual Report*, 2004–2005, Revenue Department, Bengaluru, p. 43.

[19] Ibid, p. 50.

were organised at the state, division, district levels for the revenue officials like village accountants, revenue inspectors, deputy tahsildars, tahsildars, and assistant commissioners for educating them about the Bhoomi system.

At the district level private consultants were engaged to advise and help the district administration implement the project who also served as eyes and ears to the project champion. To ensure the correctness of the digitised land records data obtained after data entry, all the revenue officials, i.e., from village accountants to deputy commissioners, were asked to verify and check the correctness of computerised land records (i.e., RTCs) and sign as per the percentage of checks fixed by government. Farmers, it was claimed, were given an unsigned copy of their computerised RTCs to point out any discrepancies.[20]

The Bhoomi programme was implemented in a phased and gradual manner through pilot projects at five places. As claimed by the government, such gradual expansion helped in smooth replication of the scheme. The successful pilots had given confidence to the government to ban the manual system of issue of RTCs at the village accountant level and RTCs were issued on user fees payment basis so that the programme could be self-sustainable.

The government made a strategic choice by thwarting off the resistance from nearly 9,000 strong village accountants by appointing young children of these officials to the post of village accountants on compassioned ground at the Bhoomi centres in taluks and imparted necessary computer system training

---

[20] http://www.bhoomi.kar.nic.in/bhoomi (accessed on December 16, 2009). This assertion of the Bhoomi monitoring cell was contested by some of the village accountants who opined during my interviews that the corrections were not properly carried out by the data entry operators after they checked and corrected the draft RTCs. Two of the consultants Sibu S. and Manjunath who still work at the Bhoomi monitoring cell opined during my discussion with them on 29 January 2011 that the higher officials entrusted to carry out the cross-checks resorted to superficial checking and failed to detect the errors in data entries and the village accountants were not at all interested in checking all the RTCs as they still perceived the programme as a threat to their monopoly position in delivery of manual RTCs. The project was carried forward in a time bound manner, thanks to the sincere commitment and predisposition to the project by then chief minister. The recalcitrant officials from the village accountant levels to deputy commissioners in the district were made to fall in line. The hurried nature of the work for meeting the deadline set by government for early launching of the project was also one of the reasons for large-scale errors which constitute nearly 25 per cent of the total RTCs in the state even after ten years of launching of Bhoomi project.

to them for manning the front-end and backend system of the Bhoomi. This strategy succeeded by isolating a large number of village accountants from their colleagues who were agitating against the introduction of Bhoomi system of computerised RTC delivery at tahsil headquarters as hitherto they had the monopoly and discretionary power of issuing of the manual RTCs to the farmers.

The World Bank study has aptly termed the 'strategy and tactic of reformers' as winning over the village accountants that their traditional work of land enquiry related to mutation will be intact and in the new dispensation, their children would be the beneficiaries.[21] This strategy of accommodation and bargaining is a very important factor in successful launching of the Bhoomi project as it yielded some payoffs to the local revenue officials maintaining land records. To allay the fears of revenue officials and field staff a series of state and division level workshops were organised to convince the officials that computerisation of land records would remove the drudgery of maintaining land records manually and the field inquiry functions and the village accountants would be kept intact.

The project champion Rajeev Chawla wrote that 'reducing corruption was not a key message in these gatherings.'[22] Feedback from the workshops was incorporated into the development of Bhoomi software design. Independent consultants were appointed to give reports on the progress of implementation of the Bhoomi programme and the project leader directly consulted the village accountants and was personally involved in the workshops and training programme. The private agencies and independent consultants played a crucial role in various stages of implementation, right from data entry to operationalisation and running the integrated system at the Bhoomi monitoring

[21] World Bank. 2006. *Reforming Public Services in India: Drawing Lessons from Success*, Report No. 35041-IN, 28 February, p. 89.

[22] Rajeev Chawla. 2007. 'Bhoomi: Online Delivery of Record of Rights, Tenancy and Crops to Farmers in Karnataka, India', in Ashok Agarwal (Ed.) *E-Governance Case Studies*, Hyderabad: University Press, p. 94. This admission on the part of the chief executive of Bhoomi is significant as it will help perceptive observers of e-governance practices in India as elsewhere who falsely led to believe by some motivated researchers in their studies that e-governance will lead to drastic reduction of corruption. The technical and political payoffs of computerisation of public services thus have inherent structural constraints as bureaucracy is a political actor and application and adoption of ICTs to reduce the rent-seeking behaviour of the officials would be met with resistance.

cell at Bengaluru. Every district was provided with a consultant who would coordinate between the data entry agency and the district administration.[23]

Features of Bhoomi

Some of the important features of the Bhoomi software designed by NIC, Bengaluru are:

- Fully online system to carry out mutations on land records data;
- Finger print biometrics authentication to ensure foolproof authentication system and to ensure the concept of non-repudiation;
- Facility to scan the field mutation order passed by revenue authorities and the notice served on public;
- Land record centre in each taluk office for public interface;
- Synchronises with the regular fieldwork done by village accountants and revenue inspectors;
- Provision for interfacing of Touch Screen kiosk at taluk office;
- First-in-First-out (FIFO) in mutation process thereby eliminating any favouritism;
- Handles all types of mutations that take place on the land records;
- No major change in the role of revenue officials;
- Built in workflow automation will take of pushing the transactions from one officer to next officer;
- Documents like RTCs, mutation extracts etc. issued are digitally signed;
- The Bhoomi software has a Kannada interface; and
- Software is operated by three important players—clerks/operators, revenue inspectors, deputy tahsildars and Sheristhedars.[24]

---

[23] Ibid, p. 95.

[24] Government of Karnataka. 2004. *Bhoomi 4 Land Records Management System*, Bengaluru: Director, Printing, Publication and Stationery, Published jointly by NIC, Bengaluru and Revenue Department, Bengaluru, p. 2. According to Anil Kumar, an official at Bhoomi Monitoring Cell, Bengaluru, the provision of barcode, hologram and ten digit serial numbers affixed on the RTCs, centralised source of supply of RTC forms, and signature of the authorised person who issues RTCs at the Bhoomi front end counter make the system foolproof and no scope exists for manipulation.

The Bhoomi software provides for printing of land records as and when required. Bhoomi centre has also separate operator-assisted counters that handle the mutation process initiated by sale or inheritance. The system has also developed a crop updation system. Crop updation report submitted by the village accountant is merged with the Bhoomi main database periodically. The mutations of land records are carried out due to various types of transactions like registered ones (sale, partition, gift, mortgage, relinquishment, settlement deed etc.) and unregistered ones (i.e., inheritance, will, unregistered partitions etc.) government grants, regularisations, confirmations of forfeiture of land, court orders on the status of land, pledge and release. The registered documents involving land transactions are intimated by the sub-registrar and in the case of unregistered cases involving transactions, the interested party is required to apply to tahsildar recording his rights on the land he has acquisitioned. The transactions involving ownership changes require statutory notice inviting objection on the interested parties before allowing mutation; and some transactions, like government and court orders on land ownership change, do not require publication of statutory notice.[25]

All the mutations are disposed through Bhoomi system so that the land records data on computer remain up-to-date.[26] The workflow of mutation on computer is a significant feature of the Bhoomi programme that has been made operational without bringing out a major change in the institutional and legal process. In this ICTs-enabled integrated workflow, the Bhoomi Kiosks operators receive suo motu applications for mutation or electronically generated 'J' slips on transactions of land from the sub-registration office and the data will be pushed to the Bhoomi backend counter for processing, verification and preparation of checklist. The data entry operator enters the transactions as per the checklist and the sheristhedar (deputy tahsildar) approves the transaction and refers back to the data entry operator who in turn generates notices and forwards the case records to the revenue inspector for service of notices through the village accountants (Patwaris) on the interested parties for inviting objections if any within thirty days of service of notice.

Each application for mutation received at the front end Bhoomi kiosk at the taluk office and the 'J' slips transmitted electronically assigned with a number can be used by the mutation applicant to ascertain the status of his mutation

[25] See Karnataka Land Revenue Act, 1964.

[26] http://www.bhoomi.kar.nic.in/bhoomi (accessed on December16, 2009).

case. The village accountants conducts the field enquiry and submit report to the revenue inspector, based upon which the revenue inspector may either accept or reject or refer the mutation case for disposal by higher authorities. If the revenue inspector agrees to the mutation request he cannot go back on his decision and he will refer the mutation case to the survey supervisor who verifies the sketch map, assigns new final sub divisional number on the sketch map and make the entries in the survey report sheet. He would assign new landholding numbers to all new owners in the approved mutation and update the survey records like *Akarbandh,*[27] *Tippan*[28] and atlas manually. The survey supervisor thereafter will report that the *Phodi* [29] process is completed and forward the mutation records to the revenue inspector through sheristhedar. The revenue inspector passes the final order for mutation and sends the record for verification by the sheristhedar. The data entry operator enters the mutation details and scans the entire record. The deputy tahsildar (sheristhedar) verifies the records that everything is typed and scanned as per the manual mutation records. The land records are updated as per the mutation order by the deputy tahsildar by using his bio-metric fingerprint authentication. Now the new RTC would be generated for each new sub-division numbers created in Bhoomi and after verification of the RTC the transaction is closed.[30] The contents of changes proposed in the RoRs (RTC) are maintained in the mutation register electronically as well manually.

Apart from RTC copy on accepted mutation cases, old RTCs, mutation extracts and other subsidiary documents to the citizens are available on payment of user fees of fifteen rupees each. The user fees for a copy of RTC have been reduced to ten rupees by the government in November 2010. During the process of the mutation, people can approach the front end kiosk operators of Bhoomi to ascertain about the status of their mutation cases. One of the most interesting features of the Bhoomi system of online delivery of land records is that the information on land records of any land holder can be availed by anybody on payment of user fees by simply visiting to the Bhoomi kiosks and furnishing particulars like name of the land owner, land holding number etc.

---

[27] A register showing the area and the rate of assessment of holdings.

[28] The sketch of a number not drawn to scale but showing the measurements.

[29] It is the process of the re-survey of the land carried out by survey department.

[30] S.M. Jaamdar. 2005. 'Integrated Land Records Management System: A Paradigmatic Change in Karnataka State,' *Administrator*, Vol. XLVIII, December, pp. 46–47.

to the computer operator. It is claimed that the strategy has been adopted to 'prevent' corruption.[31]

The Bhoomi monitoring cell at Bengaluru houses the facility manager who looks after the supply of various items of computer peripherals to all Bhoomi kiosks located in the taluks throughout the state, monitors their functioning everyday, and reports the technical consultant accordingly. A call inventory management system is established in all 29 districts where the technical persons attend to the system failure or the related problems immediately. Delayed service would be penalised by deduction from their monthly payment. The outsourcing for hardware maintenance of the Bhoomi system throughout Karnataka is based on a centralised and competitive bidding and at present Wipro has bagged the contract. Thus the hardware and system problem is looked after by the private IT firms and the software aspect is handled by NIC, Bengaluru and both the activities are monitored at the Bhoomi monitoring cell at Bengaluru.

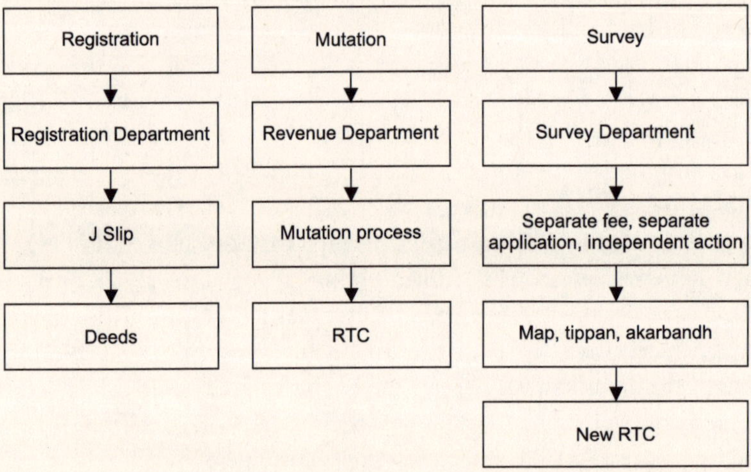

Figure 5.1

Mutation under Old System (manual)

Source: Adapted from S.M. Jaamdar. 2005. 'Integrated Land Records Management System: A Paradigmatic Change in Karnataka State,' *Administrator*, Vol. XLVIII, December, p. 47.

---

[31] See Rajeev Chawla's interview 'Innovation for Successful Societies', An initiative of the National Academy of Public Administration, and the Woodrow Wilson School of Public Affairs and the Boston School of Peace and Justice, Princeton University, 8 June, 2010. (www.princeton.edu/successfulsocieties, accessed on May10, 2011), p. 11.

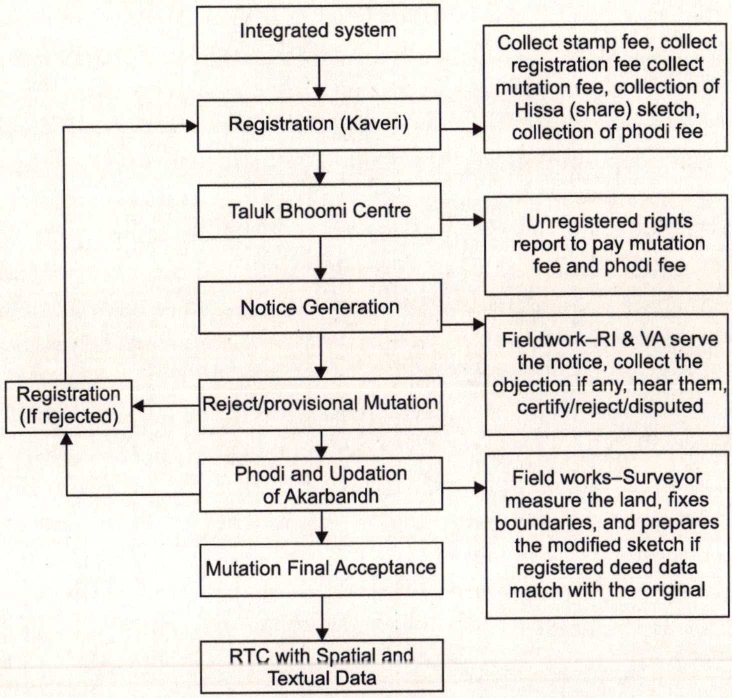

Figure 5.2

Integrated Mutation and Phodi System in Bhoomi System (manual and online)

Source: Adapted from S. M. Jaamdar.2005. 'Integrated Land Records Management System: A Paradigmatic Change in Karnataka State,' *Administrator*, Vol.XLVIII, December, p. 48.

Our understanding on computerisation of land records in Karnataka will be clearer if we make a comparative assessment of the earlier mutation process (manual) and the present online integrated mutation and *Phodi* system. The manual system was based on separate territorial jurisdiction though both the survey and registry had link with the taluk in maintenance and updation of land records. Under the present integrated mutation system, the registry, survey and settlement have been joined by the web-enabled services as well as manual records.

Findings from the Field on Bhoomi System of Land Records Management

The researcher visited 17 taluks in Bengaluru Rural, Bengaluru Urban, Tumkur, Mandya, Mysore, Ramnagaram, Dharward and Kolar districts of

Karnataka in June 2009, May 2010 and January 2011 to assess the functioning of the Bhoomi system and its impact on users. During my visit to these taluk/tahsil offices, I personally observed the working of the Bhoomi system, discussed and interviewed the village accountants, data entry operators and sheristhedars (deputy tahsildars) posted at the Bhoomi centres and interviewed tahsildars, assistant commissioners and deputy commissioners. I did 215 random interviews and conducted 9 focus group discussions among the villagers waiting for RTCs near the Bhoomi kiosks. I focused my study on village areas and taluks of the rural Bengaluru and Ramnagaram districts as these areas witness massive growth of urbanisation and conversion of agricultural lands for housing purposes and consequent increase in the real estate value of the land. I also had semi-structured interviews with the officials of Bhoomi monitoring cell, NIC, survey and settlement in Bengaluru about Bhoomi and other aspects of computerisation of land records in Karnataka. In addition, the state government documents and records relating to Bhoomi were also relied upon. Other stakeholders such as lawyers and bank officials were also interviewed to find out the impact of Bhoomi in land disputes and bank loans. The study was conducted to find out the political context of the Bhoomi project, the reason for its success in operationalisation, short or long term impact on taluk administration, land records management, and the attitude of officials, the farmers etc.

Almost all the respondents (more than 89% of the respondents) especially the farmers and other people like businessmen, real estate agents, middlemen who were interviewed on the delivery of old RTCs at the Bhoomi counters were satisfied with the queue system in getting copy of RTCs easily and smoothly, but some complaints about getting erroneous RTCs and the rent seeking behaviour of the village accountants posted at the Bhoomi kiosks in connivance with the intermediaries also came up.[32]

[32] During my visit to Bengaluru-East, Nelamangala and K. R. Puram taluks in June 2010, I interviewed randomly fifteen persons who received RTCs from the Bhoomi kiosks at these taluks about their perception to the Bhoomi system of delivery of RTCs. Most of the users were satisfied with the lesser time taken (i.e. ten to fifteen minutes) in obtaining the computer generated RTCs by standing in a queue. A focus group discussion conducted at K. R. Puram taluk on 6th June 2009 among the users of the RTCs found that the users appreciated the computerised RTCs available at the Bhoomi kiosks but various complaints like erroneous entries in the RTCs, lack of good behaviour of the persons at the Kiosks, nonrefunding of the exact balance amount on the ground

The overwhelming number of people supported the present system of delivery of land records at Bhoomi kiosks on the ground that the RTCs are available to them within few minutes unlike the earlier system of manual issue of land record by the village accountants which was taking lot of time. They informed that several visits were required to contact him apart from paying bribe. Some of the farmers also informed that RTCs are also available at rural telecentres (Nemmadi). The village accountant was able to tamper with the manually maintained records at his disposal. Moreover, the manual issues of RTCs were erroneous and lacked credibility and authenticity.

After the introduction of Bhoomi, the issue of payment of bribe for getting an RTC copy at the Bhoomi kiosk was not an acute problem. Few persons however opined that the earlier system of manual issue of RTCs as better as they had direct access and contact with the village accountant and could get the manual copy of RTCs on payment of some amount of bribe and the procedure was flexible enough to bring out rectification in the RTCs at the level of village accountant which is not possible under the Bhoomi system based on tight electronic integration and biometric finger print authentication for nonrepudiation of data. The problem of travel cost and time cost and occasional technical failures in Bhoomi kiosks were also cited as other problems.

The speed in delivery of RTCs which are utilised for availing agricultural subsidy, seeds, instruments on subsidised rate, crop loan and its renewal, sale and purchase of land etc is the prime reason for overwhelming appreciation by the general public for the present system of taluk-based delivery of computerised copy of RTCs. Interestingly, the farmers by and large come directly to the Bhoomi kiosks at taluks without visiting or consulting village accountants on their survey number required for obtaining an RTC printout.

In some Bhoomi kiosks like in Mysore, Dharward, Kolar, Tumkur and Ramnagaram, I observed that it took normally five minutes to get a copy of RTC in case there was no rush. In this way, the monopoly or discretion of the village accountants in issue of RTCs and possibility of manipulation have

---

of shortage of change, demanding bribes for mutation and long delays in mutation and rectification of mistakes/ errors in RTCs have cropped up. Some also complained that the cost of obtaining RTC copy is now higher as they had to travel to the taluk by paying bus fare. At Anekal taluk under urban Bengaluru district and Devanhalli and Doddaballapur taluk in rural Bengaluru district I heard a lot of complaints about the middlemen who were collecting the RTCs on behalf of the farmers by charging extra ten rupees during my visits to these taluks in January 2011.

been considerably reduced or weakened under the new system. The search and query module of Bhoomi software enable the villagers to find out their survey number and landholdings instantly by telling their name and their father's name and of their revenue village to the village accountant on a small piece of paper at the Bhoomi front end kiosks and also help the land owners ascertain the status of their mutation or conversion of land case. However, when it comes to the matter of mutation or correction of erroneous entries due to wrong entry of data at the time of computerisation,[33] almost all respondents including farmers (nearly 97 per cent) took a very negative attitude to integrated mutation process for delays, widespread rent-seeking behaviour among the officials and taking excuse of delay by blaming on the software designs and hardware problems of the Bhoomi system.

The taluk officials have shifted the blame to the government for adopting such hierarchical and cumbersome mutation process that has taken out the discretion of the village accountants and play safe before the farmers and the general public. Interestingly, some educated respondents during my interviews opined that the existing computer system could not be faulted but the staff involved in manning the system are to be blamed for their rent-seeking attitude as computer system cannot check the immoral and greedy nature of the government officials seeking bribe.

The problem of correction of wrong entries in the computerised RTCs like the name of the tenant, the extent of land holding, classification of soil and the mismatch between the total land holding and the extent of share in the joint holding have been found to be acute in all the taluks visited by the researcher. The earlier manual procedure allowed the village accountant and tahsildars to carry out the changes in the RTCs easily by taking into account the views of the farmers and field enquiries. Under the Bhoomi system, there is an elaborate bio-log in the authentication system to prevent tampering of the records.

The power to rectify errors in the RTCs has been given to the assistant commissioners located in sub-divisional headquarters. The farmers are required to apply to tahsildars with supporting documents citing erroneous entries

33 When interviewed the village accountants at Kolar taluk about the erroneous entries of names, extent and area of land in the computerised RTC, they pointed out that the private data entry workers engaged for the purpose were not given proper supervision and the data entered in the computer were checked by them but the errors pointed out by them were not rectified in the Bhoomi database. The AG in its audit report has also pointed out the problem similarly.

and the applications are verified and enquired by the village accountants and revenue inspectors and then submitted to tahsildar for his approval and forwarding the papers to the assistant commissioner (sub-divisional magistrate) for consideration. This procedure has been adopted after launching of the Bhoomi as tahsildars were found to be vulnerable to corrupt practices like manipulation and fraud while dealing with changes in the entries in the RTCs in the name of rectification.[34] This procedure takes a long time as the application for rectification of errors in RTCs would pass through several stages and this has given rise to corruption in taluk offices. The respondents also informed me that the rich farmers or builders and land mafia and other powerful individuals got their work done by paying handsomely to taluk officials but for the poor it was a nightmarish experience. The farmers of Dudhinalli, Raabnalli, Gopalli and Buddigere villages found at Devanhalli taluk during a focus group discussion observed,

> If you pay a good amount of bribe at each stage of processing of your application for correction, your work will be immediately attended. The computerised RTC is not a good measure as it has made the process of rectification of RTC very rigid and the farmers are unnecessarily being harassed in running for correction of wrong entries for the fault of data entry operators and the officials. [35]

The Bhoomi system of rectification of errors in the RTCs have made it difficult and complicated for the poor farmers. In the new process, Assistant Commissioners have been given the authority to order/consider rectification of errors application forwarded by tahsildars in the RTC to prevent malpractice at the taluk office.

> 'Except delivery of RTC copies at the taluk headquarters, Bhoomi has not changed the corrupt practices in mutation and rectification processes of RTC. It's business as usual. If you pay the bribe as demanded by the officials, your work will be attended on priority. Otherwise, you'll be made to run for months together.'[36]

---

[34] Interview with Rajeev Chawla, IAS, the project champion of Bhoomi, on 7 May 2010 in Bengaluru. The Assistant Commissioner, Bengaluru urban district informed me this during my interview with him on 29 January 2011.

[35] Focus group discussion on 21 January 2010.

[36] Focus group discussion on 24 January 2010.

This was the common response of the farmers from Mandya taluk during my three focus group discussions with them in January 2011. At Yelhanka taluk, I interviewed nine farmers and three deed writers acting as middlemen about the Bhoomi. Their response was similar to the views of farmers of the taluks visited by me earlier.[37] Thus there is no doubt that the delivery of much sought after RTC copies has virtually reduced corruption. The cumbersome mutation and rectification process and tightly integrated electronic workflow adopted in the Bhoomi system may provide, technically speaking, transparency, but has increased delay in the process and corruption. My study thus established that not a single farmer is found happy or to have trust the claim of transparent process of integrated mutation and rectification of errors of Bhoomi manned by the taluk officials.

As the mutation process passes through several stages under the conventional procedure retained under Bhoomi, the role of village accountants, revenue officials, sheristhedars and tahsildars remained intact. These officials are required to give their thumbprint approval in the biometric log in system of authentication in the disposal of mutation cases based on seniority principle of first-in-first-out. The allegation that these officials demand bribe and if not paid by the farmers delay the process of mutation is a common matter of fact found in my visit to all the taluks. Even after payment of bribe, all the respondents, who had applied for mutation of land records in the taluks, informed me that they had to run several times and days to get their work done on mutation and correction of RTC. Further, these respondents also alleged that the survey officials who were functioning in tahsil after the merger of survey and settlement branches of the revenue department were not allotting new survey number and correcting the map in mutation proceedings without bribes. There were also serious complaints by the farmers against the private licensed surveyors engaged for preparing pre-mutation sketch map of the land to be registered, for demanding huge bribes for preparing the sketch maps.[38]

The first-in-first-out (FIFO) system which is an anti-corruption device to checkmate the corrupt practices like pick and choose style in mutation of land by tahsildars is being circumvented by citing a mutation as disputed and thereafter the mutation was taken out of the FIFO-based queue system and

[37] Field visit to Yelhanka taluk on 19 January 2011.

[38] Focus group discussions with the farmers at Doddaballapur and Anekal Taluk on 28 and 20 January 2011, respectively.

thereby facilitate the next mutation case in the queue which might be filed by a real estate company or politician for early disposal. As described earlier, apart from the political pressure, the petty officials like most of the village accountants and the data entry operators were vocal in lifting the seniority and queue principle of FIFO.[39]

Focus group discussions among the persons who have come for obtaining a copy of their RTCs at Dharward taluk, Chhanapatna taluk in Ramnagaram district and K.R. Puram taluk in Bengaluru rural district revealed that one had to pay huge sums of money to all the staff involved in the mutation case as it moved in stages and had to run for several months to get his work done. Therefore ICT application in Bhoomi has not made any difference in the existing rent-seeking structure of land records correction and whatever positive image earned by the revenue department in online delivery of RTC copies at Bhoomi counters is negated in the so-called integrated mutation process. Rent-seeking behaviour among the taluk staff and the failure of the tahsildars to rein in such tendencies are the main reasons.[40]

Some of the farmers at Chhanapatna taluk and Doddaballapur taluk waiting for ascertaining the status of their mutation and application for rectification cases were interviewed by me and many of them showed me of their mutation case number or application for rectification of wrong entries in RTCs case numbers pending for disposal dating back eight months to one year. When enquired whether they had approached the tahsildar for their delayed mutation process, nearly ninety per cent of the respondents informed that the tahsildar

39 Interviews with three village accountants at Nelamangala taluk, four village accountants at Kollar taluk, two village accountants each at Chhanapatna, Nelamangala and Devanhalli taluks and two village accountants at K. R. Puram taluk carried out from 2009 to 2011 revealed that these village accountants squarely blamed the FIFO principle for causing huge delay in disposal of mutation cases which could be done manually by the earlier system with less time.

40 This finding is based upon my interview and focus group discussion with the general public and officials of taluk including the project leader Rajeev Chawla who admitted, during my interview with him in May 2010, the prevalence of such corrupt practices and contended that computer cannot cure the immoral and greedy nature of the staff and it is not a panacea. Mr Chawla also informed me that the demands for revocation of FIFO have come from MLAs, MPs and some vested interests like real estate companies and he apprehended that if FIFO system in Bhoomi would be removed, the system would lose its credibility and collapse.

used to blame the FIFO system of Bhoomi and was unable to take any prompt action against the corrupt staff as he had unholy nexus with the officials of the taluks and he gets percentages of bribe from them. They reasoned that, since the tahsildars are posted in important taluks on payment of huge money to the ministers and MLAs, their only mission is how to amass the bribe amount within few months of posting 'to get the return' on their investment. So the allegations of the farmers against the taluk officials for delay and harassment fall on deaf years.

Other respondents informed that the nexus between the tahsildar and the staff were so strong that even after they complained against the rent-seeking attitude of the staff there would be no strong action and the staff in turn would harass them, further delaying their work by putting up frivolous objections. More than 95 per cent of the respondents found near the Bhoomi counters replied that the process of rectification of errors crept in their RTCs after computerisation is very cumbersome and the taluk officials demand bribe for the rectification work.[41]

The Record of Rights, Tenancy and Crops (RTC) covers comprehensive information on rights of land, tenancy and crops. The RTCs delivered at the Bhoomi kiosks provide information on record of rights over the land, and ownership details including joint holding. But the tenancy columns of the RTCs under the manual system remain empty. Though 'colluded tenancy' or 'concealed tenancy' in practice exists, the detection of tenancy and their recording in RTC is very troublesome job on the part of village accountant. The practice of tenancy is banned in Karnataka and even the detection mechanism of such practices and their enforcement is very weak. Interestingly, in the taluks visited by me, the columns in the computerised RTCs showing information on crops cultivated by the land owner in most cases are found to be empty or at best the entries are made long back. The reason for non-updation of crops including the seasonal crops in the RTCs is that the village accountants are not furnishing the information in time as their monopoly in the maintenance of RTCs has now gone.

---

[41] These data were collected during my visits to the taluks from 2009 to 2011 during my interviews with the farmers found near the Bhoomi kiosks at the taluks. They informed that they had met the tahsildars and highlighted their grievance about the delay in processing their works but nothing concrete was done by tahsildars and they believed that tahsildars were hand in gloves with their officials due to their corrupt nature of transfer and posting.

The Bhoomi monitoring cell has outsourced the private agencies to conduct the survey on crops cultivated in taluk-wise areas and accordingly update the information on crops in the RTCs of farmers. It appears that the earlier exercise of providing simputers to the village accountants for recording crops have not been successful. Such outsourcing to the private agencies for crop data updation was not appreciated by the district level statistical officials. The farmers who were interviewed informed me that the manual RTCs issued by their village accountants contained some partial information on crops, as village accountants used to ask them the crops being cultivated. The bank officials at Mandya, Kolar, Chhanapatna and Anekal informed me that they relied on the information furnished by their filed officers, and not the information contained in the RTCs submitted by the farmers while sanctioning crop loans.

The poor information in nine-fold classification of crops in the RTCs delivered at the Bhoomi counters was further supported during my interviews with the senior official at the state's directorate of planning and statistics, Bengaluru. He informed that the total cropped area of a village as recorded by the village accountants did not match the total geographical area. Bhoomi database on crops has not collected information on gross cropped and net cropped areas, areas cropped once and more than once, irrigated land, and information on seasonal crops in village-wise or taluk-wise.

The rapid decline of agricultural land due to conversion for non-agricultural purposes is also not taken into account by the taluk officials and the old data on crops are retained without their proper field verification and updation. The nine-fold classification of crops found in the RTC is simply left vacant, as it requires massive exercise in coordination with various other agricultural branches like horticulture, sericulture, pisciculture for collecting information on crops and areas covered and not by the private agencies for field base survey.

The role of the village accountant is crucial as a revenue functionary in updation of data on crops but after the centralised delivery of RTCs the village accountants' role in updation of crops is replaced by that of private agencies.[42] Thus much acclaim given to Bhoomi for comprehensive information on crops for their utilisation in developmental planning is not factually correct and the problem of recording information on crops persists after its operationalisation.

---

[42] Interview with K.V. Subramanian, Joint Director, Directorate of Economics and Statistics, Bengaluru on January 18, 2011 and District Statistics and Economics Officer, Mandya on 24 January 2011.

It also raises the challenge as well as limits to the extent of automation or informatisation that could be allowed in managing complicated and dynamic nature of land records, tenancy and crop details in partnership with other agencies.

The Bhoomi online land record management has been an addition and not a replacement of the existing manual-based land records as it has covered the RTCs from 2000 onwards. My repeated visits to the taluks confirmed that the reasons for long queue in the counters dealing with delivery of manual records are manifold. There are usual queues in any of the taluks or its adjoining record rooms in both rural and urban areas for getting copy of the old manual records. The old records detailing the historical background of the land size and its ownership records and transfer have not at all lost their relevance after the implementation of the Bhoomi system due to growing pressure on land for real estate and other non-agricultural purposes as well as land disputes and frauds.

In Yelhanka and Anekal taluks, I came across some people waiting outside the record room counters to get the old land records of the plots which they intended to purchase from real estate companies for ascertaining the original owner of the land and the background of the acquisition of the rights over the land by the vendor of the land. In many other taluks in rural areas, farmers collect the old records for filing correction of wrong entries in the records and fighting court cases. I was also informed by the farmers in Ramanagar and K. R. Puram taluks that the old RTCs prior to computerisation under Bhoomi are also in demand for various legal purposes like settling a land dispute, preserving the copy of valuable old records as security against future land disputes or making a land transaction. In these cases the village accountants also demand some bribe to deliver the copy of old manual RTCs prior to Bhoomi. Thus the demand for resurvey of old records continues to grow along with the computerised RTCs at the Bhoomi counters as well as the demand for bribe in searching these records and delivering photocopies of the records. The Bhoomi system of computerised land records database would have been very effective, had it been launched after resurvey and settlement in the state afresh. Instead it was launched by computerising the already old records, surveyed and settled in the year 1965.

Response of the officials

The tahsildars and village accountants support the delivery of land records from Bhoomi kiosk on the ground that such a system delivers the land records speedily, tamper proof and legible, FIFO system of mutation promotes transparency, the land records are in the public domain, and the discretion of lower officials in affecting correction and maintenance of land record is reduced. They are hopeful that the tamper-proof nature of land records under Bhoomi which requires thumb approval (bio-metric log in with non-repudiation) of all the field level functionaries from village accountant to tahsildar will prevent fraudulent manner of settlement of government land. All tahsildars interviewed by the researcher highlighted about the poor quality of training to the Bhoomi kiosks operators, software and hardware problems and obsolescence of the computer system, shortage of trained staff, and the centralised nature of computer maintenance system that leaves few options before them to undertake repairs immediately.

Their lack of administrative control over the private hardware and software consultants/vendors attending the problems of Bhoomi kiosks at taluks, the delay in mutation attributing to the seniority principle of the FIFO system, the corrupt practices of private licensed vendors in submitting false and erroneous reports, large-scale errors in the RTCs such as name of the recorded tenant, extent of landholding, classification of land due to lack of proper validation during the data entry process, and the long time taken in correction of such mistakes are some of the important and common administrative constraints faced by Bhoomi. All the tahsildars, however, stress that the delivery of RTCs at the Bhoomi counters have greatly reduced the earlier corrupt practices like fraudulent correction of records, settlement of government land illegally, and in the long run the erroneous entries in the RTCs would be cleaned up but admit the prevalence of corruption in the lengthy procedure of mutation and correction of errors in RTCs.[43]

The statutory period involving disposal of mutation is thirty days from the date of publication of proclamation but in practice it takes minimum four months normally to complete the mutation process apart from paying bribes at each stage of the mutation case disposal. The tahsildars blame it on the very process of the Bhoomi system particularly the FIFO system of the seniority principle (first come first serve) in disposal of mutation cases which has simply taken out their discretionary power of the pick-and-choose method of mutation and also on the middlemen and real estate companies

[43] Interviews carried out with tahsildars, deputy tahsildars and village accountants of Kolar, Ramnagaram, K. R. Puram, Tumkur, Belgaum, Nelamangala, Yelhanka, Shimoga, Doddaballapur and Mysore taluks in May 2010 and January 2011.

for creating mess in the system and exploiting the general public who have turned to them for help. Some tahsildars are however critical of the very centralised nature of the Bhoomi system, dilatory process of Bhoomi, their lack of control over the hardware and software consultants and licensed private surveyors, and cumbersome mutation process of the Bhoomi.[44] Thus barring a few, most of the tahsildars responded that they have tended to believe that the techno-managerial approach to land records management would promote 'good governance' agendas like transparency and accountability and reduce the corrupt practices of petty officials.

Innovations and further developments in the techno-managerial programme

According to Rajeev Chawla, the chief executive of the Bhoomi programme, several challenges pertaining to Bhoomi like maintenance of equipment at 203 taluk centres, mitigating the problems of farmers who have to travel for a long distance for obtaining an RTC copy at Bhoomi kiosks, poor quality of crop updation data and problem faced by illiterate farmers in filing mutation forms for online disposal have been overcome successfully and new innovations have been introduced as the programme has proved to be sustainable.

The Bhoomi project has been operationalised in all the 177 taluks of Karnataka since 2002. It means that in every taluk, Bhoomi centre has the server with the local database stored on the server. The RTCs are also available at 800 rural telecentres/cyber kiosks catering to about 3–4 villages. This facility helps to the rural populace by saving their travel cost and time required for visiting taluk offices. In 2005–2006, the government set up an exclusive Wide Area Network (WAN) for the Bhoomi application using a dedicated V-SAT based network. All the taluk offices are connected through this network and Bhoomi data are linked centrally to the state data centre and the database is thus centralised in Bengaluru. The land records data in a dynamic mode gets replicated at the state data centre in Bengaluru. [45]

All the 177 Bhoomi servers have been upgraded with new servers which are fully remote controlled through scripts and on-line enabled UPS, for the

[44] Interviews with tahsildars Anekal and Yelhanka and ex-tahsildars of Shimoga and Doddaballapur during my field visits in January 2011.

[45] This fact was also explained to me by the officials of Wipro IT firm serving at the Bhoomi Monitoring Cell, Bengaluru.

first time in India, as claimed by Bhoomi officials at the Bhoomi monitoring cells. 'So much is the extent of automation that an application running at the data centre switches on the UPS and the HP servers for taking data backups during the night after which the servers and UPS are switched off' due to erratic power supply system in some taluks located in rural areas that prevents transmission of data. [46]

The state data centre (SDC) is also used for electronic data interchange with the 'Kaveri' programme which is software for the computerised registration process. The Kaveri and the Bhoomi programmes have been fully integrated for operationalisation of the integrated mutation process. The Kaveri applications using the web services at the state data centre sends daily registration of deeds to the state data centre from its 220 locations which are then forwarded to the respective Bhoomi locations in the taluks through the Wide Area Network (WAN). The officials at the Bhoomi centre at taluks handle these transactions on First-In–First-Out (FIFO) principle after comparing the copy of registered deed sent by sub-registrar with the XML copy in the computer. This principle, adopted later, is an anti-corruption device where the mutations are disposed on a seniority basis and tahsildars cannot bypass a mutation case to favour others. The Bhoomi online land records system now uses integrated mutation process where the textual and spatial (map) land records data get updated simultaneously.

It is claimed by the project executive that every year, approximately 1.6 to 1.8 crores people are served through Bhoomi centres and the project earns nearly ₹ 25–30 crores as revenue. More than ten to fifteen lakh mutation cases are handled every year through the Bhoomi software, and land records in Karnataka therefore remain updated. The constant feedback process has further led to limiting the role of tahsildars and deputy tahsildars.

The project champion has asserted that nearly ten to fifteen lakh of mutations are handled by the Bhoomi online system which is in contrast to five lakh mutations handled under the manual system.[47] The Bhoomi project champion

[46] Rajeev Chawla. 2007. 'Bhoomi: Online Delivery of Record of Rights, Tenancy and Crops to Farmers in Karnataka, India,' p. 83.

[47] Subash Bhatnagar and Rajeev Chawla. 2005. *Computerisation of Land Records*, p. 85. The total number of cases of mutation is not available as there is 'no need to watch and observe the system' said Anil Kumar, tahsildar, Bhoomi Monitoring Cell, Bengaluru during my field study in June 2010.

also claims that annual mutation cases (involving correction of records) have been increased three fold. Such tall claims of the chief executive are, however, not supported by any comparative quantitative data, depicting the number of mutation cases instituted and disposed per year under a manual system and the number of mutations disposed under the Bhoomi system. A comparative quantitative analysis of the record corrections in pre and post Bhoomi periods of five years each would have been useful for the project champion as well as for central and state governments to showcase the performance of Bhoomi. The repeated efforts of the researcher to collect the data on yearly disposal of mutations in the pre-Bhoomi period and mutations now being disposed under the post-Bhoomi period (since 2001) were not successful as the officials at the monitoring centre as well as the revenue department failed to provide such basic data on the ground that such information is not maintained. It was surprising to find that despite the much acclaimed and narrated success story of the Bhoomi, neither its highly centralised monitoring cell nor the revenue department documents, records, or builds such a basic data to justify the adoption of a costly and complex computerised land records management system.

The Karnataka government has introduced some recent changes in land records management like online integration of land transaction index data of registration with Bhoomi, merger of the survey and land records branch with taluk office, empowering tahsildars to simultaneously manage both mutation and *Phodi* (process of resurvey of the land carried out by survey department), mandatory requirement of the sketch map (in Form 11-E) before every mutation is initiated either by inheritance or through registration in all cases of sub-division of lands, and preparation of sketch by licensed surveyors, which make the land record updating process a dynamic one. It is also claimed that Karnataka government has become the first state in India to introduce an integrated mutation process.[48] For every transaction on a parcel of land, a pre-mutation sketch is to be compulsorily presented before the sub-registrar for registration of all registered transactions, and before the tahsildar in applications for mutations of all non-registered transactions like inheritance, family partition, government grants, conversion etc. In the

[48] S. M. Jaamdar. 2005. 'Integrated Land Records Management System: A Paradigmatic Change in Karnataka State,' pp. 40–41.

integrated mutation process (IMP), the survey number, the extents and rights of a land parcel are updated simultaneously and recorded in the corresponding documents. The manually prepared sketch and mutation order are scanned and linked to RTC and stored in the Bhoomi database. In the integrated mutation process, every new owner gets a single owner RTC and is assigned with a new survey number.[49] Over a period of time, the integrated process is expected to enable every owner of land to get a single owner RTC as this mechanism will individualise the landed property and greatly increase the real estate or market value in contrast to joint holding of landed properties with unclear share in land and its boundaries. It would prevent disputes over land and be useful for creating a separate RTC integrating the textual and spatial land records. Electronic integration of Bhoomi with survey, registry and land acquisition and banks has also been achieved and it is claimed that such process would keep the land records updated. Recently a web-based monitoring system has been developed by the Bhoomi monitoring cell, Bengaluru to review the performance and pendency in disposal of mutation cases and the reasons for rejection of mutation cases. The process involves 'drilling down' to the individual transactions to ascertain the status of the mutation process.[50]

The chief architect of Bhoomi programme, Rajeev Chawla claims that it has achieved some of the techno-managerial governance practices like speedier delivery of services, accountability, transparency, fair and equal delivery of services etc. First, Bhoomi empowers the rural poor to access the land records online at cyber kiosks and the land records can be collected online. Status of mutation can be tracked online. Land records in Karnataka are now in the public domain so much so that anybody can access anybody's RTCs by paying user fees without furnishing any identity proof.[51] Poor and

[49] See Government of Karnataka. Revenue Department, Government Secretariat, MS Buildings, Bengaluru Circular no. RD39MPR 2005 dated 11 July 2007.

[50] Rajeev Chawla, B. V. Sharma and P. V. Bhatt. 2008. 'Bhoomi: Key Learnings & New Initiatives,' in Ashish Vachhani and N. K. Kumaresan Raja (Eds). *Computerisation of Land Records in India: Achievements and Experiences,* Mussorie: Centre for Rural Studies, LBSNAA, Mussorie, p. 48.

[51] Bashir Ahmed, deputy tahsildar, K. R. Puram opined that the Bhoomi system is transparent and not prone to manipulation by village accountants as was happening earlier under the manual system during my discussion with him at his office in June 2009.

illiterate farmers can get RTCs on payment of user fees as they need not have to file application.[52]

Second, Bhoomi has inbuilt security and accountability system such as bio-login procedure, the use of encryption and public and private key system to ensure file tracking and non-repudiation system. The first come and first serve basis system as well as empowering the deputy tahsildar to pass the mutation order in case the revenue inspector fails to do so within a stipulated period are expected to prevent corruption at lower level.

Third, in terms of costs and benefits, Bhoomi has been a self-sustainable e-governance programme and generating good amount of revenue. Fourth, Bhoomi land records database offers many potential benefits for developmental planning and implementation of land reforms.[53] Fifth, Bhoomi will help improve the investment climate in real estate and land sale and land rental market by maintaining clean records of land ownerships in urban and rural areas.[54] The corruption in crop insurance market will be reduced as the RTC will not be prone to manipulation. Sixth, the open access to data and transparent and traceable mutation records will help settlement of disputes. Petty corruption in facilitating or hindering the retrieval of mutation records will be reduced. Seventh, after computerisation of land records, the request for mutation of land records has shown rapid growth. According to the Bhoomi officials, the change in mutation application has indicated the level of approval of the new

[52] Anil Kumar, tahsildar, Bhoomi monitoring cell, Bengaluru commented that the Bhoomi system is such that if somebody pays he can get the RTCs for the entire villagers. Thus 'there is no question of helping the rich farmer only.' Another important feature is that any person can access the stage of disposal of his mutation process at any stage. At Nemmadi centres (cyber kiosks delivering common services) people can access their land records and need not come to taluk office. Sh C. N. Sreedhara, deputy director, survey and settlement Bhoomi monitoring cell told me during discussion that mutations are disposed in a time-bound manner in the Bhoomi system and 'corruption has been reduced to nil.' He even claimed that one can get his work done by sitting at home. These officials were interviewed by me in June 2010 in Bengaluru.

[53] Rajeev Chawla. 2007. 'Bhoomi: Online Delivery of Record of Rights, Tenancy and Crops to Farmers in Karnataka, India', pp. 90–92.

[54] According to Ravikumar, village accountant posted at Nelamangala taluk, in the Bhoomi system no addition and deletion is possible in RTCs without permission from higher and competent authorities.

system.[55] Eighth, Bhoomi programme has the potential to be extended to rural cyber kiosks and can bridge digital divide in rural areas.

Lastly, the dynamic land records management and integration with registration will eventually update the textual and spatial land records due to its constant usage and openness of the land records and will help Karnataka government move ahead on the path to conclusive title regime as envisaged in the National Land Records Modernisation Plan (NLRMP).[56] The reason for such modest nature of reforms in the Bhoomi system, according to Rajeev Chawla, was the 'need to balance the potential benefits of the system against the risk of implementation failure in deciding how much reform (re-engineering) to tackle any point of time' and this appears realistic.[57]

Constraints of Bhoomi

The ICT-enabled Bhoomi system, however, faces a number of challenges for its sustainability. The most significant one is the technological one. During my discussion with the officials of government and WIPRO company at the Bhoomi monitoring cell, Bengaluru it was informed that the need for constant upgradation of hardware and software components is challenging one. There is also pressing need to train the newly recruited village accountants posted at Bhoomi office further to handle the upgraded versions of hardware and software aspects of the Bhoomi back end and front end operating system. The facility manager and the technical support team everyday receive calls to attend to various teething problems like hard disk and operating system failures, network connection problem, mother board problem etc. The dynamic issues of data safety and protection from virus attack have cropped up. These problems have to be addressed in coordination with NIC unit in Bengaluru and the private IT farms assigned with the task of maintenance of Bhoomi network system. The chief executive of Bhoomi says that the NIC, Bengaluru has been

---

[55] Rajeev Chawla. 2007. 'Bhoomi: Online Delivery of Record of Rights, Tenancy and Crops to Farmers in Karnataka, India', pp. 86–87. Some of these benefits are expected to be accrued in future like lowering disputes over land and reducing the fraudulent land deals, etc. My discussion with some lawyers at Kollar and Mandya district court complexes in May 2010 and January 2011 also revealed that some of the expected benefits will take time to materialise.

[56] Ibid, p. 99.

[57] Ibid, p. 97.

constantly improving the Bhoomi software applications and addressing the loopholes in the system. At present, the Bhoomi computer system is running the version 4.5 of the software application in the taluk offices.[58]

Some tahsildars at Ramnagaram, Kolar, Tumkur, Dharward, Anekal, Nelamangala and K. R. Puram taluks pointed out the shortage of technical staff like data entry operators and software personnel to handle the complicated software system of Bhoomi and its front end and back end counters. The demand for regular updation of crops cultivation, the increased travel cost on the people for availing of RTCs at the taluk level, filing application for correction of wrong entries in their RTCs and mutation at taluk level, lack of trained manpower, the delayed process involved in mutation and correction of wrong entry in RTCs, and partial nature of land records database created by Bhoomi are some of the constraints noticed by in my field studies.[59] The comprehensive software of Bhoomi is 'over dependent' on proprietary software of Oracle and Microsoft which are costly and the need for open source software is there in order to reduce the cost of running the Bhoomi system.

The role of National Informatics Centre

The National Informatics Centre in Karnataka in close coordination with the Bhoomi management team played a central role in developing the Bhoomi software specific to the state's need. The earlier software created by NIC Bengaluru in 1992 for data entry was unable to handle all the variations in land titles. The state government worked closely with NIC for developing data entry software with back end Bhoomi software, and due to the team efforts of technical professionals and the feedback from the field officials, the Bhoomi software could be developed and operationalised. My discussion and interviews with officials at NIC, Karnataka unit at Bengaluru found that the close coordination forged by Rajeev Chawla, the team leader of Bhoomi monitoring

---

[58] Rajeev Chawla, B. V. Sharma and P. V. Bhatt. 2008. 'Bhoomi: Key Learnings & New Initiatives,' p. 45.

[59] It was learnt from field visits that Bhoomi kiosks are providing the RTCs entered in the computer database since 1999 and the land records prior to 1999 are not entered and validated. The manually maintained record room very much exist in taluk offices. Also see Roger Harriss and Rajesh Rajora. 2006. *Empowering the Poor: Information and Communication Technology for Improving Governance and Poverty Reduction*, UNDP-APDIP ICT4D Series, Bangkok, pp. 48–53.

cell, with the state NIC unit in developing the Bhoomi software that focused exclusively on the requirements of the farmers and other landholders, and in-house study of the land records system and its dynamic nature of entries by the NIC's IT professionals were the key to the successful launching of the Bhoomi system. The said strategy of collaboration is being followed till date in running and innovating the system.[60] During my repeated visits from 2009 to 2011 to both NIC and Bhoomi monitoring cell at Bengaluru I could observe very close and constant coordination between the two agency officials in managing the online land records delivery system.

Present position of computerisation of land records

Computerisation of RTCs in Karnataka has been completed in all districts, their manual issues have been stopped in the entire state, legal sanctity to computerised copies of RTCs have been accorded, and the RTCs are placed on the internet. Digitisation of village maps and scanning of parcels of maps as envisaged under the centrally sponsored scheme of Strengthening Revenue Administration and Updating Land Records (SRA&ULR) are going on. The figures on achievements by SRA&ULR are, however, almost negligible. Except setting up of two survey training institutes, it has nothing to report or highlight as compared to its achievements on Bhoomi. Its performance in launching so-called modern land survey and settlement in the entire area of Belgaum district has been unsuccessful due to several administrative, technical and political factors.[61]

Impact of computerisation of land records

The success of the Bhoomi programme in delivery of computerised land records copy and online mutation and integration with registration has drawn attention from various quarters, and the project champion Rajeev Chawla's contribution has been recognised in all studies. The Centre for Rural Studies, LBSNAA, Mussorie, has conducted an impact assessment study of computerisation of

---

[60] Interview and discussion with Samartharam, Technical Director and Suresh Babu, Scientist-C, NIC, Bengaluru on 2nd May 2010 at Bengaluru.

[61] Discussion with Mrudurangappa and C. N. Sreedhara, Settlement officials at M. S. Buildings in Bengaluru in January, 2011.

land records in all the ten taluks of Gulbarga district (2002) of Karnataka. The field study covered one hundred villages of Gulbarga district and collected data from 1,478 respondents. Gulbarga district was selected by the central government as one of the pilot project districts for computerisation of land records programme and the work started in 1992 but due to some technical and legal problems the programme could not be implemented. It was only since 2001 computerised copies of RTCs were being delivered to the people in that district. Some of the important findings of the study are:

- In 2002, it was found that 85 per cent of the respondents were aware of the computerisation of RTCs at taluk headquarters and an overwhelming majority of the persons who obtained computerised RTCs opined that the present system was less time consuming than the old manual system where one had to search for the village accountant. Problems like power supply and absence of kiosks operator has also caused delays in obtaining RTCs. The study revealed that only 59.7 per cent of the farmers were getting RTCs on the same day.
- Only 44.2 per cent of the respondents were quite sure of the accuracy of computerised land records and less than half of the respondents (43.8 per cent) have opined that the computerised system was not free from any type of harassment, due to delays caused by power failure and the increased travel cost.
- All the tahsildars opined that the accuracy rates of RTCs and updating have become higher after computerisation and the arbitrary and discretionary powers of the village accountants in issuing RTCs have been reduced.
- The wealthy farmers were against the Bhoomi system as their hold over the village accountants that facilitated their works had changed.
- About 51.80 per cent of farmers paid actual user fee charges fixed for obtaining computerised RTC and the remaining 48.20 percent farmers paid more than fifteen rupees for obtaining that document at the Bhoomi counter which implied that petty corruption was prevalent even at the initial years of the launching of the Bhoomi project.
- Farmers are found to have engaged village accountants or other persons in obtaining computerised copy of RTC on their behalf by sharing the travel cost as the system of obtaining any farmer's RTC is made open for all at Bhoomi counter by furnishing information on

the land survey number as there is no restriction on getting others' land records. For getting an RTC in Gulbarga district, the study found that a farmer, on an average, has to spend nearly fifty rupees and four hours and thirty minutes.

- Computerisation of land records (RTC) has not led to any change in revenue administration and any impact on implementation of land reforms legislation.
- Computerisation of only textual land records (RTC) without spatial map has not contributed significantly in reducing the land disputes and detecting the concealed tenancy as the data entered in the computer is the same as the manual one.
- Around 63 per cent respondents found it easier to obtain a loan after computerisation of land records.
- Computerisation of land records has helped conveyancing of property. Overall 97.29 per cent of respondents have been able to get information on land for sale and purchase purpose within a day.

Some of the problems found by this initial study which are still relevant for understanding the Bhoomi system of land records management like frequent power failure in tahsils located in rural areas, difficulty in issuing RTCs with current year's crop information, glitches in Bhoomi software related to transfer and inheritance of land, increasing travel cost for obtaining RTCs, more time lost in making corrections in the computerised RTCs, and dependence of illiterate farmers on village accountants to first obtain their survey number and then go to computer kiosks to collect RTCs.[62]

Though the computerisation of land records has increased the transparency and accessibility to information on land records and has reduced the workload of village accountants, it would be inappropriate to say that it has not left any room for manipulation of records and malpractices. During my field study in June 2009, I had come to know that Bhoomi monitoring cell had set deadlines for mutation case for all tahsildars of Karnataka and accordingly programmed its remotely controlled software so that back dated application for mutation would not be allowed after the deadline is passed. The reason was that some tahsildars are resorting to fraudulent practice in order to get some mutations

[62] Manoj Ahuja and A.P. Singh. 2006. 'Evaluation of Computerisation of Land Records in Karnataka: A Study from Gulbarga District,' *Economic and Political Weekly*, 7 January, pp. 69–77.

of influential politicians and builders disposed in backdate with malafide intention.[63] This corrupt tendency and frailties on the part of tahsil officials and their networks with non-formal actors/agents clearly highlights the limitations of the ICT-enabled public service delivery mechanism to deliver a transparent and manipulation-free service. Interestingly, the project champion was candid enough to admit the prevalence of corruption in the integrated mutation process. 'You would not be able to wipe it out. After all, IT systems cannot take away crookedness of the mind of the people.'[64]

The assessment of the benefits by users of the computerised land records system in Karnataka by Public Affairs Centre, Bengaluru gives a clean chit to the Bhoomi project by calculating statistically some so-called tangible benefits and non- tangible benefits. This study, funded by the World Bank's governance sharing programme, concludes, on the basis of sample survey of respondents of Bhoomi kiosks users and those users under the manual system, that Bhoomi system has rendered tangible benefits like saving man-days required under manual system for repeated visits to patwari's (village accountant) office and amount spent on bribes there. And also it provided intangible benefits in terms of shorter queues and less number of officials to be met, error-free RTCs, timely action on complaints and better staff behaviour than under manual system.[65] The most interesting aspect of the study is that the bribe paid under the previous manual system was to the tune of 66 per cent of cases, whereas at the Bhoomi kiosks at taluk it reduced to a meagre 3 per cent.[66] This uncritical finding was contradicted by my studies of Bhoomi users in some taluks like K. R. Puram and Nelamangala where I came to know that the front end Bhoomi kiosks operators invariably do not tender the exact amount on the pretext of

---

[63] This was revealed to me by Anil Kumar, tahsildar, Bhoomi monitoring cell, and Bengaluru as he was busy in sending fax messages to tahsildars on disposal of mutations within the deadlines during my visits to the office in May, 2010.

[64] See interview with Rajeev Chawla by David Hausman on 8 June 2010 on 'Innovations for Successful Societies', An initiative of the National Academy of Public Administration and the Woodrow Wilson School of Public and International Affairs and Bobst Center for Peace and Justice, Princeton University, 83 Prospect Avenue, Princeton, New Jersey, 08544, USA, p. 12. (www.princeton.edu/successfulsocieties (accessed on May 10, 2011)

[65] Albert Lobo and Suresh Balakrishnan. 2002. *Report Card on Service of Bhoomi Kiosks: An Assessment of Benefits by Users of the Computerised Land Records System in Karnataka*, Bengaluru: Public Affairs Centre, November, p. 9.

[66] Ibid. p. 9.

nonavailability of exchange money. Some agents of builders and real estate firms who frequent to Bhoomi kiosks for obtaining the RTCs of a number of farmers for purchase of their land leave a good amount of money for the kiosk operators as tips.[67]

The audit review by Comptroller and Auditor General of India (2008) on Bhoomi throws significant light on built-in 'data integrity, security of data, systems and other IT assets apart from assessment of the efficiency and effectiveness of the system in achieving the stated objectives and adequacy of good practices of IT governance'. The C&AG in its performance audit of the Bhoomi project undertook to 'test-check' of records at Bhoomi monitoring cell, Bengaluru and seven taluks observed the following deficiencies which are important issues and problems that would enable us to better analyse the governance challenges in the context of ICT adoption in land records management.

- Inadequate arrangements for backup land records data could lead to avoidable loss of data and time in case of crashes. Periodic test of retrievability of backup data is not carried out independently;
- Inadequate backup power supply arrangements could affect the health of the servers and replication of databases at State Data Centre via V-SAT;
- There was no well-developed business continuity and disaster recovery plan or guidelines to take care of IT assets in case of disasters;
- Payments made by district officers for data entry work by private agencies without adequate supervision resulted in many discrepancies and errors in the database. A total of 2,89,489 applications for corrections were received in seven districts soon after the creation of Bhoomi database which put a question mark on the reliability of land records data.

---

[67] At Bengaluru East Taluk in May 5, 2010, I noticed an agent of a property dealer is getting printouts of hundreds of copies of RTCs on payment but the Bhoomi front end operator could not explain satisfactorily the reason for such large number of printouts of RTCs by a single person. Similarly interview with the Vijay Kumar, a staff of a real estate company on May 6, 2010 revealed that he used to come to K. R. Puram taluk for obtaining the RTCs of other persons as desired by his company for real estate purpose and the staff at Bhoomi front end kiosks demand bribe for the delivery of RTCs of farmers and other landholders.

- It was observed that there was no second level check of making crop updation and authentication of collection of crop data submitted by village accountants.
- The Bhoomi system lacked various controls to ensure complete data accuracy and reliability. The audit findings in three taluks revealed that the name of land owners in 99,186 cases and khata (landholding) numbers in 53,055 cases were recorded as junk characters.[68]

Others have taken a critical assessment of the whole project in the context of application of ICTs in the discourse of development. Amit Prakash and Rahul De in their studies found that the computerisation of land records programme or redesigned Bhoomi is the third but successful attempt to computerise the land records in Karnataka. The earlier attempts in 1991 failed with the explanation given that the size and scope of the project was not designed properly and the second attempt to computerise the land records also failed due to non-anticipation of land records digitisation and subsequent updating requirements correctly. In designing the Bhoomi, the lower rung officials were generally excluded from the design process and the village accountants had resisted implementing the system but due to the political support from then Chief Minister S.M. Krishna it could be implemented. Some of the findings in their studies are quite relevant to our studies.

First, Bhoomi has helped easier sale and purchase of land and mutations in the periphery region of Bengaluru metropolis which has witnessed rapid urbanisation. Bhoomi has not added significant increase of agricultural credit in rural areas. The big landholders in areas like Chitradurga and Shimoga taluks are able to access the RTC certificates with ease and in a transparent manner. In the contemporary pro-business and pro-market policy environment, Bhoomi has undoubtedly emerged as a 'model project of ICT for development' as the objective is now bringing greater efficiency and productivity in government service delivery in the application of ICTs, but not increasing the freedom and capability of the poor and marginal farmers. Though Bhoomi helps in improving the transparency and access in getting a copy of RTC for farmers, nevertheless it has enabled the real estate agencies to access the land records easily and target the farmers through various means for buying out their land.

---

[68] Government of India. 2008. *The Report of the Comptroller and Auditor General of India (Civil)*, Government of Karnataka, pp. 88–100.

Getting a copy of RTC for poor farmers entail wage lost and travel cost as the Bhoomi centres are located in taluk headquarters only. Bhoomi has reduced the role of village accountants in the delivery of RTCs and mutations, but the interest of the small farmers and marginal farmers have not been furthered in the process; rather the big landholders and real estates and builders have been benefited. Their study rightly concludes that the 'Bhoomi project appears to adopt an essentially neo-liberal view of technology use.'[69] This critical finding is significant for our study of computerisation of land records analysed in the context of neoliberal techno-managerial reforms.

A critical appraisal of Bhoomi system of land records management

These findings on Bhoomi and also my field studies have helped me arrive at certain conclusions on the working of the Bhoomi system of land records management, which could be summarised as follows:

1. Bhoomi is a comprehensive software which enables the administrators to generate various kinds of useful reports related to land classification, soil type, ownership, crops pattern, possession of land, liabilities, tenancy, source of irrigation, area assessed etc. Given its steady upgradation and innovation, the role of technical personnel in land record management in taluk offices has become integral to its operationalisation. Bhoomi has made the complex nature of land records system more complicated, cumbersome, costly and technology-dependent. It has also contributed in the growth of a new bureaucratic structure like 'front-end' and 'back-end' offices, entry of technical professionals such as data entry operators or kiosks operators or computer-trained village accountants, hardware and software consultants, and tahsildars' total dependence on them in manning the Bhoomi system. Neither tahsildar nor the deputy tahsildar is able to handle the operating systems of Bhoomi. Similarly, at the state level monitoring cell, it is both the hardware and software consultants who virtually control and monitor the Bhoomi system.

[69] Amit Prakash and Rahul De. 2007. 'Importance of Development Context in ICT4D Projects: A Study of Computerisation of Land Records in India,' *Information Technology & People*, Vol. 20 (3), pp. 271–274.

The Bhoomi system thus has added further complexity, cost, demand for high skill and specialisation in land records management through an online system. It is very difficult to assess the impact of such ICT application, adoption and management of such information system on the efficiency of the tahsil officials as it has covered only a small part of land records. The other vital parts of land records like sketch map and various land registers, maintained both at tahsil and village accountant levels, are not covered under Bhoomi.

2. The sustainable operation of Bhoomi and its monitoring cell at Bengaluru is an example of the techno-managerial approach to solve the vexed question of land records updation and management. This approach relies on the assumption that ICT-enabled land record management system is value neutral and can serve all sections of society on client-oriented principle and will promote transparency and accountability. The Bhoomi's perspective to land records management is based on the assumption that ICTs are the 'easiest way to promote transparency' and is 'unquestioned good' which is quite debatable as it negates or overlooks the political and power relations of the taluk bureaucracy who are also political actors in the system. The informal networks of the local bureaucracy, the village accountants and revenue inspectors in running the everyday affairs of the everyday state is at best not understood or overlooked. The technical and political payoffs to the taluk bureaucracy would invariably determine the political sustainability of the Bhoomi system. The virtuous role of ICTs and its professionals and the villainous role of the taluk bureaucracy that underlies the Bhoomi's approach to land records management is problematic as it seeks to steadily alienate itself from the generalist bureaucratic control over land records management by adopting more and more tightly integrated centralised electronic and information technology based innovation system. One can thus say that the 'political marriage of information technology and bureaucracy' has not been perfect or gone down well in the land records modernisation system of Karnataka state.[70]

[70] Theodore J. Lowi. 1992. 'The Political Marriage of Information Technology and Bureaucracy,' in Larry B. Hill (Ed) *The State of Public Bureaucracy*, London: Me Sharpe, Inc., pp. 203–208.

3. Bhoomi system of online delivery of land records and integrated mutation process is an addition to land records management as it has not replaced or changed the existing institutional structure in land record management. Ironically, its business process or system architecture does not replace the need for manual records as so-called backup or security against the uncertainty of the online system. The roles and responsibilities of the revenue functionaries have not undergone radical change and their rent-seeking behaviour remains intact. The village accountants continue to maintain many vital land records and registers manually and are vested with power and responsibility to conduct field enquiries in mutation and other revenue and non-revenue cases. Mutation records are being kept manually and scanned for record and non-repudiation.
4. Discussion and interviews with a large number of village accountants revealed that their attitude to Bhoomi remains hostile right from the beginning of the project, as Bhoomi took away their monopoly in maintenance and delivery of manual land records like RTCs and reduced scope for rent seeking. Many of them (80 per cent) have argued that the process of mutation has become cumbersome and dilatory and as a result people end up paying more bribes than was prevalent under the manual system. Electronic integration and connectivity with survey and settlement and registration offices and appointment of private licensed surveyors have further diminished their role. In the changed set-up or institutional arrangement, the village accountants are now able to play as intermediaries and manage to collect some rents in helping the farmers or rural people in getting their RTCs and mutation of their land done at taluk offices. Some village accountants have engaged privately helpers (*sahayaks*) to collect bribes from the farmers for getting their miscellaneous works at taluk office done.
5. The role of the central government in the development of Bhoomi software by way of funding and providing technical assistance through NIC has been overshadowed by the commitment, devotion and leadership shown by then Chief Minister S. M. Krishna and the project executive Rajeev Chawla. It has been discussed earlier that the central government has treated computerisation of land records in India as a mere expenditure-driven scheme and varied nature of achievements in the scheme has been left to the states to explain.

At the same time it also consciously pushes its agenda of achieving uniformity in land record management by applying the UNICODE principle. Bhoomi's success shows that the uniform and top down scheme of computerisation of land records cannot be succeeded, as the failure of the early phase of computerisation in Karnataka revealed.

6. The Bhoomi system of land records management cannot prevent the fraudulent or benami land transactions, as its primary objective has been improvement of service delivery and up-to-date maintenance of land records with the help of ICTs. Moreover, the present objective of the Bhoomi is not to promote land reforms agenda or redistributive strategy, but confined to a clientele-oriented approach of service delivery on user fee basis to farmers and other sections of people.
7. The land records of poor and marginal farmers or anybody's land records can be easily bought by paying user fees, as the Bhoomi system has made no bar in getting the land records of others simply by informing the survey plot number and paying user fees to the kiosks operators. Such mechanism will no doubt be exploited to the hilt by the real estate companies and land mafias.
8. Bhoomi system of land records management has led to increase in the size of bureaucratic structure at the taluk level and expansion of accountability in online land record management by including assistant commissioners, surveyors and kiosk operators apart from tahsildars, revenue inspectors, sheristhedars and village accountants who were in the manual system.
9. Bhoomi model of land records management claimed by NIC, Bengaluru as 'the first e-governance project successfully implemented for the benefits of common man jointly by government of Karnataka and NIC, Karnataka' [71] can be accepted as an innovation in public service delivery imposed or initiated strategically from higher administrative and political leadership of the state rather than an outcome of citizen demands.
10. The land records delivery and mutation system has been automated in such a way that despite the preoccupation by tahsildar and deputy tahsildar in important non-revenue activities like conducting local and general elections, relief operations, and law order problem in a taluk,

[71] www.kar.nic.in.bhoomi.html. (accessed on July 12, 2010)

the Bhoomi counters deliver the RTCs and other related records to the farmers and other landholders.

11. The tight integration of Bhoomi and Kaveri (computerised registration system) and mandatory submission of pre-mutation sketch before registration of any parcel of land or mutation application in case of all unregistered transactions in land has led to the increased rent-seeking activities and role of the middlemen in mutation. My interviews, discussions and focus group discussions with the farmers have revealed a common response that corruption, delay and harassment to farmers have increased in the integrated mutation process under Bhoomi. Some of the respondents at taluks in rural Bengaluru areas like Doddaballapur, Anekal, Devanhalli, Yelhanka, Chhanapatna and Mandya in January 2011 informed me that in mutation of one acre of registered land, one has to spend nearly fifty thousand rupees as bribe to all the officials and the private licensed surveyors as the procedure is very complicated and cumbersome. The FIFO system of seniority of mutation cases moves only when the interested parties contact the officials and pay bribes. The FIFO is reduced to a sham by the corrupt taluk officials by putting various objection or queries in the mutation and striking of the mutation application from the serial. The private licensed vendors deployed to prepare pre-mutation sketch are demanding huge amounts of bribe for their service and there is no direct accountability and control over their activities by the tahsildars. Focus group discussions with the farmers at Mandya, Chhanapatna, Doddaballapur and Devanhalli taluks revealed that the survey supervisor in connivance with the private licensed surveyors resorted to dilatory tactics in correction of survey maps for demanding more bribe.[72]
12. The success of the integrated mutation process requires commitment of the tahsildars. Most tahsildars and assistant commissioners interviewed by me responded that the first-in-first-out principle in mutation, the pre-mutation sketch and uploading the land records on the web would promote transparency in land records management and reduce corruption and fraudulent settlement of government land and tampering of records by village accountants. Such assertions of

[72] The field studies to these taluks were conducted in January 2011.

the tahsildars and Bhoomi officials are debunked by the farmers and other general public found at the taluks visited by the researcher. It is interesting to note that except for the delivery of the copy of RTCs at the Bhoomi kiosks, the application for mutation and rectification of errors have proved to be a nightmarish experience for them. Some farmers at Chhanapatna and Devanhalli taluks during my focus group discussions in January 2011, observed that 'if you pay a good amount as demanded by the taluk officials, all your works will be immediately attended and disposed, like paying a big amount for immediate *darshan* (an occasion in which one is permitted to see a god or a holy person); otherwise they will force you to keep coming to taluk office till your shoes wear out.' Similarly, given the pervasive corruption in taluk office, the first-in-first-out principle does not cause any problem for the builders, land mafia, and other rich and powerful persons as they pay heavy bribes and carry forward their work in collusion with the taluk officials through informal networks. Many of the respondents at Mandya taluk informed me that they on some occasion had complained before the tahsildar who took the matter lightly, expressed his helplessness, and blamed the integrated mutation system and assistant commissioners for the delay. Some others informed that complaints and allegations against the taluk officials before the tahsildar have not been effective as the farmers were afraid that they would be harassed further by the officials at the taluks and may reject or delay their mutation/ rectification application on some frivolous grounds.

One of the common findings from my interviews and focus group discussions that emerged was that the farmers have lost their faith on the capability of tahsildars to redress their grievances as they were perceived or suspected to have unholy nexus with the corrupt officials, builders and land mafias as their postings are being made on payment of money to ruling politicians or through their contact with them. The amounts of bribe in posting of tahsildars in urban or fast urbanising areas are heavy. Therefore, tahsildars pay more attention to the land transactions of real estate companies for the obvious reason of getting huge material benefits. The role of the revenue department in deciding the transfer and postings of the tahsildars are peripheral like 'post office' just to sort out and despatch letters as everything is decided at the level of the chief minister or revenue minister. [73] The negative public perception to the officials in my studies has led me to analyse the launching of land records computerisation in the context of massive urbanisation in Karnataka especially in urban fringes of metropolitan Bengaluru and consequent growth of real estate activities and their networks with the taluk officials. The tahsildars who are posted at highly lucrative tahsils in urbanising areas like Anekal, Ramanagar, Doddaballapur, Hoskote and Devanhalli after paying huge bribes to their political masters obviously go for return of their investment in 'market for public office,'[74] and for them managing the cumbersome mutation process for the so-called common man is just the routine job fulfilment than any personal involvement.

13. The role and discretion of the village accountants and tahsildars have not declined in any significant manner. Contrary to the widespread claim that the discretion of the village accountants has been reduced to a large extent due to delivery of RTCs at the tahsil level as well as *hobli* levels (the territorial jurisdiction of revenue inspector circle formed by a cluster of villages), the finding of the study is not generally supportive of such beliefs and assumptions. Even at the *hobli* level, the village accountants are authorised to issue a copy of RTC by putting their digital signatures. One has to keep in mind that the village accountants continue to maintain as many as 13 land records related registers and collect land revenues from the landholders in addition to a number of miscellaneous revenue and non-revenue works like submitting enquiry reports and identifying beneficiaries in various social welfare schemes. His original power to conduct local enquiry in mutation cases remain intact. The village accountants continue to play a crucial role in the developmental activities and the everyday revenue administration affairs of state like issue of various miscellaneous certificates such as caste and income certificates, crop inquiry and crop loss certificates for claiming crop insurance

[73] Interview with the section officer dealing with transfer and postings of tahsildars at the revenue department, Bengaluru in January 2011.

[74] See Robert Wade. 1985. 'The Market for Public Office: Why the Indian State is not Better at Development,' *World Development*, 13(4), pp. 467–494.

etc. Narayan Gatty's study of village accountants' role after Bhoomi has brought out interesting facts. The village accountants act as the 'grassroots authority' between the farmers and the state. Due to multiple dependencies on the village accountants by the farmers, the village accountants command, not demand, bribe from farmers. The bribe amount fixed by the village accountants is matter and person specific. The farmers feel obliged to bribe village accountants as a reciprocal act for the 'official favour' shown by the latter in conducting various enquiries and furnishing reports and in order to keep good will due to their frequent contacts with him on various matters apart from the land records. So the allegation against the village accountant for demanding bribe in an issue of manual RTC and other certificates are rare. Neither the villagers nor the higher officials challenge or confront the rent-seeking attitude and the authority of the village accountants who serve as a link between the 'distant state' and the villagers. At the village accountant level, the boundaries between the state and society are blurred and matters like bribe by the village accountant therefore become irrelevant.[75] The farmers invariably depend on village accountants for obtaining crop loss certificates for claiming crop insurance, loan waiver and other relief measures of the government. A good relation with village accountant would enable the farmers to fetch/claim higher compensation by showing partially cropped plot area as full crop area. Similarly the rich persons or big landholders of the village who lease out their land to tenants also like to have good relations with village accountants as there is risk that village accountant may book police case as tenancy is banned. The village accountant also keeps a watch on encroachment of government land and illegal conversion of government land. So it is rightly observed that 'farmers adopt the strategy of compromises, alliances and deals, and they tend to judge the village accountants by their ability to get things done as an agent of the state.' [76]

[75] Narayan A. Gatty. 2009. *Information Technology for Governance Reforms: Land Records Computerisation in an Indian State*, Unpublished PhD thesis submitted to the Institute of Development Studies, University of Sussex, pp. 128–138.

[76] Ibid, p. 156.

The village accountants in my field study are found to be working also as intermediaries or have in some cases engaged helpers who act as middlemen on their behalf in getting mutations of the farmers done through the complex FIFO system of Bhoomi, which corroborate the findings of Narayan Gatty.[77] As the mutation case requires field enquiries and serving of notices on the interested parties and thumb print approval by the village accountants, and several visits are to be made on the part of farmers, the role of the village accountants are vital here. His visits to taluk offices at regular intervals for attending his varied nature of official work there also are utilised by the farmers to save their travel and time cost to some extent. At Kolar, Tumkur, Dharward, and K. R. Puram taluks I came across many village accountants frequently entering the back end office of the Bhoomi and ascertaining the status of many mutations queued up in the FIFO system from the computer trained village accountant, noted down by them on a piece of paper, and also obtaining copies of RTC of others on payment of user fees. Obviously, the village accountants must be taking some amount of rent for getting the work done thanks to their complete access to the Bhoomi back end and front end offices and the taluk officials.[78] The village accountants, due to their critical role in identifying beneficiaries like landless and homesteadless persons, and in issuing ration cards, old age pension and other social welfare schemes, also maintain a symbiotic relationship with the local political representatives including MLAs.

The village accountants also play an enviable role in maintaining the 'informal side of running state administration's day to day practice' like bearing the expenditures incurred in food and drinks during the visits of higher officials like district collectors, department secretaries and political leaders like ministers. As they 'finance the informal functions of formal state agencies' of the everyday state, the higher officials even being aware of the village accountants' corrupt practices are unable to take corrective or deterrent measures as they maintain a very delicate relationship with the village accountants.[79] Thus the role and responsibilities of village accountants as laid

---

[77] Ibid, p. 157.

[78] Narayan A. Gatty has also cited this intermediary role as one of the reasons for increased rent seeking under the online integrated mutation system.

[79] Narayan A. Gatty. 2009. *Information Technology for Governance Reforms: Land Records Computerisation in an Indian State*, pp. 170–171.

down in the Karnataka Land Reforms Act, 1964 are different when we find the real role and working environment of the village accountant as an agent of the everyday state at the village level. Narayan A. Gatty's observation that '... paying bribe to the village accountant as a part of the land transaction is an instrument of the larger strategy of survival of farmers instead of merely being a way of avoiding potential trouble for mutation' is pertinent to understand the role of the village accountants in the village life and the tall claims of the Bhoomi about reducing the discretionary power of these street level bureaucrats.[80] For the policy elites, the purpose of Bhoomi has been served as it has been financially sustainable and online delivery of copy of RTCs across the state is taking place, but behind the glass and steel world of Bhoomi counters lie the harsh reality of the farmers and the landholders who face a number of difficulties while encountering formally and informally the taluk officials which cannot be tackled by ICTs alone. The project leader's assertion that, 'Karnataka is tearing up 20 million land records (manual). That has delighted farmers, angered the accountants' and 'gone are those days when village accountants would be able to dole out farmers on extraneous considerations'[81]thus requires critical examination in the context of political and administrative role of the village accountants in local governance.

The tight electronic integration of the Bhoomi system and the strategic move by the Karnataka government for gaining over the support of the village accountants in introduction of online delivery of land records has ironically helped retain the scope for rent seeking by the village accountants. As we have described, despite careful process of reengineering in the Bhoomi system of land records management, the everyday state actors like the village accountants have survived and readjusted their role.[82]

Bhoomi and the politics of governance reforms

The prime reason for success of the Bhoomi project is the support from political leadership particularly the then Chief Minister S. M. Krishna and

---

[80] Ibid, p. 159.

[81] Rajeev Chawla. 'Freedom in the Fields', Power Point Presentation, http://unpan1.un.org/intradoc/groups/public/documents/UN/UNPAN023395.pdf (accessed on May 10, 2010)

[82] Ibid, pp. 173–175.

the commitment of the project champion, Rajeev Chawla, a senior Indian Administrative Service officer. Karnataka chief minister and revenue minister highlighted the importance of the Bhoomi project in many public forums and personally reviewed the progress of the programme. The project champion Rajeev Chawla admits that it was a sort of chance and luck factor to have S.M. Krishna as chief minister who supported the online delivery of land records. 'He was able to see the use of computerising the property records. We took his help to demonstrate to the village officials that political will was there in place.'[83]

Narayan Gatty's study of land records computerisation attributes the chief minister Krishna's support to computerisation of land records programme to a shrewd political strategy to buy back rural political support base of his party which was feeling being neglected in his favourably disposed promotional polices towards information technology and biotechnology sector that served the interest of urban middle class. Krishna was also blamed by his partymen for steady alienation of farmers and by-election defeats of his party due to his pro-urban and IT policy, favouring urban people. Krishna thus found, in the programme for online land records computerisation and delivery of RTCs, to farmers presented by an IT savvy bureaucrat, political potential as through this programme he could send a message to his party's rural support base that his government's IT policy serves also the needs for rural people. 'With Bhoomi, the chief minister was able to covey to the urban middle class that the government was keen to make governance more transparent and less corrupt and to rural farmers that IT was here for everyone.'[84]

The continuance of the project champion and stability of his tenure was critical for success of the Bhoomi project that took nearly seven years for operationalisation.[85] Bhoomi project is claimed to have been embraced by all parties in Karnataka and it has therefore gained political acceptance and political sustainability.[86] The demand for extension of Bhoomi to sub-taluk

---

[83] See Rajeev Chawla's interview 'Innovation for Successful Societies' – An initiative of the National Academy of Public Administration, and the Woodrow Wilson School of Public Affairs and the Boston School of Peace and Justice, Princeton University, 8 June, 2010. (www.princeton.edu/successfulsocieties, accessed on May 10, 2011), p. 5.

[84] Ibid. p. 104.

[85] Subash Bhatnagar and Rajeev Chawla. 2005. 'Bhoomi: Online Delivery of Record of Rights, Tenancy and Crops to Farmers in Karnataka,' pp. 93–94.

[86] Ibid.p. 85.

level by the farmers, elected representatives and district officials is taken as evidence of the programme's 'unqualified success.'[87]

However, the Bhoomi project leader has admitted some major limitations. Bhoomi has not reduced the discretionary power of the officials dealing with the mutation process and much of the old mutation process remains unaltered. It has to some extent reduced the discretionary power of officials by introducing a provision for online registration of the request for mutation of land.[88] Given the complex and diverse system of RTCs in Karnataka, it took seven years for the Bhoomi project to develop the software for application. But Bhoomi cannot provide security to tenancy or title.

The Second Administrative Reforms Commission (ARC) viewed the Bhoomi as 'a noteworthy effort... (which) sets an example for other projects in its approach towards piloting a project as well as its rolling out and sustenance.'[89] The ministry of information and technology has accepted Bhoomi 'as national model for computerisation of land records' for replication in the country.[90] The Second ARC has opined that the reasons for the success of the Bhoomi model of e-governance are a well conceptualised and executed business process reengineering, total political support, continuity of the project management team, adoption of holistic approach to e-governance, and a system of strong backup.[91] The Commission's observation is a sketchy one as it relied upon the government sources to arrive its findings. The Commission did not look at the impact of Bhoomi's consumer service-oriented approach to public service delivery on democratic accountability and the increasing vulnerability of small farmers to the real estate developers, as anyone can take out the computerised printouts of RTCs from a Bhoomi counter by referring a land survey number.

The evaluation of Bhoomi as e-governance model has been made by some scholars in the context of larger political and economic changes in India. It is argued that Bhoomi programme has not succeeded in reducing corruption rather it has made costlier the process of obtaining an RTC from a taluk office. Life of poor and marginal farmers have become worse due to Bhoomi as their

[87] Ibid.p. 87.

[88] Ibid. p. 97.

[89] Government of India. 2008. *Second Administrative Reforms Commission-Eleventh Report on 'Promoting e-Governance: The Smart Way Forward,'* New Delhi: December, p. 34.

[90] Ibid.

[91] Ibid.

land records are on the website and now easily accessible for big realtors, IT companies, agro-business corporate houses and big capital.[92]

In contrast to the uncritical findings of Public Affairs Centre, Bengaluru, Solomon Benjamin and others have in their studies shown that the post-Bhoomi situation has increased corruption levels as the people have to make several visits to taluks to get their works like mutation done and to avoid the travel and time cost and uncertainty of getting RTCs on the same day due to power failure and system breakdown, they invariably depend upon the intermediaries or agents who have emerged as new power centres. Here the bribe amount depends upon size of land in transaction and nature of work involved.[93] The Bhoomi project has helped the growth of land markets dominated by builders in a big way. The small and marginal farmers stand in no way to get benefited from the project. Many landless and small farmers lost land, as they have been cultivating various customary lands which (*Peda* land) have been classified as *Sarkari* (government) land as Bhoomi has homogenised variegated nature of rights of tenancy and sub-tenancies into a computerised format of RTC.[94]

The World Bank's study on Bhoomi is influenced by its approach to development of land market. It has viewed Bhoomi as the 'best practice' as it has implemented innovative solutions in a decentralised manner under the leadership of a 'project champion.' The success of Bhoomi is attributed to outsourcing of data entry, validation and operationalisation with the help of private IT vendors. The delivery of computerised land records from the taluk offices have significantly eliminated petty corruption of lower ranking officials like village accountants, simplified transactions, and promoted positive attitude towards the bureaucracy. Further, the Bank's findings revealed that Bhoomi has succeeded in abolishing manual records, promoted positive attitude to bureaucracy and is self-sustainable due to improved collection of user charges, and most importantly, it provided scope for the integration of tahsil data with registry, and enabled access to registration officials before registration of land records.[95]

---

[92] Solomon Benjamin et al. 'Bhoomi: 'E-Governance' or Anti Politics Machinery to Globalise Bengaluru,'?, pp. 4–6. (http://www.casum.net/downloads/Bhoomi%Report.pdf (accessed February 20, 2010)

[93] Ibid, pp. 18–22.

[94] Ibid, p. 33.

[95] World Bank. 2007. *India: Land Policies for Growth and Poverty Reduction, Report No-38298-IN*, 9 July, pp. vii; 15.

Similarly, the collaborative study by Planning Commission of India and UNDP's Human Resource Development Centre (2002) describes Bhoomi initiatives as one of the best practices 'that have successfully achieved their intended goals and made signal contribution to improvement in governance and implementation practices.' The reasons pointed out are the sustainability, relevance to the poor, benefits to maximum number of people, potential for productivity enhancement of the participating populations, potential for replication, and well documented governance practices.[96] The study has viewed that Bhoomi has succeeded in making a major effort to make land records 'completely transparent and revenue officials accountable.'[97] The claims that the 'records are available free of human arbitration' and 'farmers are freed of harassment from government officials, touts, middlemen and village level leaders'[98] are bits of exaggeration as they cover up ground reality of Bhoomi which has been analysed by us.

The *Karnataka Development Report* (2007) claims that e-governance projects like computerisation of land records, registration and treasury (Bhoomi, Kaveri and Khajane) have made governance more transparent and citizen-friendly; speed money for issue of RTC is eliminated; corruption and harassment have declined.[99] Such findings and observations are due to uncritical acceptance of the ICTs as a panacea for all the administrative inefficiencies in service delivery and due to considering the bureaucracy as apolitical institution. What is missing in these studies and reports is their inability to understand the application of ICTs design and development and operationalisation in the context of specific historical and political trajectories of development process and thinking.

It is rightly viewed that IT implementation projects cannot be seen in isolation from historical, organisational and economic circumstances from which they emerge.[100] The Bhoomi programme needs to be seen in the context of the currently 'hegemonic or near hegemonic' model of neo-liberal economic

---

96 Planning Commission of India and United Nations Development Programme. 2002. *Successful Governance Initiatives and Best Practices: Experience from Indian States*, New Delhi: pp. vi–vii.

97 Ibid, p. 183.

98 Ibid, p. 185.

99 Government of India. 2007. *Karnataka: Development Report*, New Delhi: Planning Commission of India and Academic Foundation: p. 462.

100 Prakash, Amit and Rahul De. 2007. 'Importance of Development Context in ICT4D Projects: A Study of Computerisation of Land Records in India,' p. 263.

development across the world and in India.[101] What is not highlighted in the array of writings on Bhoomi is that the Bhoomi model of e-governance could be seen as an attempt to reinvent the public service delivery by adopting the cutting edge information and communication technologies on managerial and client-oriented mode run on business principle. The problem of land records management is viewed solely in terms of a technical and managerial issue, not a political one.[102] The reason why the political leadership in India does not give priority in maintaining a correct and up-to-date land records, conduct regular surveys and settlement operations does not find its place in the literature on land records management. Rather in the whole discourse of land records management, the petty officials like the village accountants/ revenue inspectors are presented as villains in the current problems of poor land records management in India. The complex problem of land records and their management and governance is sought to be dealt through the application of ICTs, modern surveys and mapping, and in the whole process the question of land records management becomes depoliticised and the real motive for such political or policy choices are thus covered up. We would however make a detailed analysis of the depoliticisation of land records management in our concluding chapters.

Bhoomi as a model of network governance

Robert Agranoff and Michael McGuire have noted that the dramatic rise in 'organisational interdependence' in public and private bodies has given rise to networks in which multiple actors, both formal and informal, are involved. To them networks are 'social structures that permits inter-organisational interactions of exchange, concerted action and joint production' and are based on a specific policy arena. As multiple actors are involved in the networks organised in horizontal-vertical manner, it cannot be guided by a single organisational goal. But the problematic aspect of the networks is

---

101 Atul Kohli. 2006. 'Politics of Economic Growth in India, 1980–2005, Part-II, The 1990s and Beyond,' *Economic and Political Weekly*, 8 April, p. 1368.

102 The Bhoomi web site claims that the online land records management '...provides transparency in land records management with better citizen services and takes discretion away from civil servants from the operating levels.' http://www.bhoomi.karnataka.gov.in (accessed on April 6, 2010)

that all participants are accountable to networks manager or government functionary but none appears to be absolutely accountable for failures in network performance. It is therefore difficult to assess the accountability in networks.[103]

Bhoomi's online land records delivery has been successful due to a partnership and network among the public and private agencies. The operationalisation and sustainability of the Bhoomi e-governance programme has created a network setting revolving around it the actors who have developed a vested interest to see that the Bhoomi system should get going. The workload of the village accountants have been reduced but their rent-seeking behavior in mutation of land records remain intact; the integration of mutation with registration and survey has created job opportunities for more than 3,500 private licensed surveyors who prepare sketch maps for the land to be registered and mutated and earn a good amount of bribe; the tahsildar's responsibility in managing the Bhoomi system is reduced by the centralised monitoring cell and his subordinates like deputy tahsildars and revenue inspectors are empowered to handle integrated mutation process and the rent-seeking potential of these officials have not decreased; the assistant commissioners have been empowered to rectify errors in the RTCs which has increased the scope for rent seeking at their level; there is keen interest among top IT firms to bag the outsourcing or contracting of sales and service of the Bhoomi's computer systems and networks; the further innovation of the Bhoomi by enabling nearly 800 rural cyber kiosks are run by private IT vendors to download the distribution of land records; the builders and real estate firms now take the real advantage of gaining access to the details of government and private lands placed on the website for development of their real estate business; the World Bank officials commend the success of Bhoomi as 'best practice' for promoting techno-managerial reforms and facilitating land markets and title security; the agents or middlemen now take the advantage of the centralised delivery of the RTCs at taluks and serve the farmers by providing them RTCs and charge extra money; and finally the politicians do not perceive the Bhoomi as threat to their support base. In such networks, it is difficult to fix accountability on the actors involved and so too in the whole process of Bhoomi system of land records management.

---

[103] Robert Agranoff and Michael McGuire. 1999. 'Managing in Network Setting,' *Policy Studies Review*, 16(1):18–41, reprinted in Mark Bevir (Ed.) *Public Governance*, Vol.-IV, London: Sage Publications, 2007, pp. 102–103; 112.

The networks, according to B. Guy Peters are 'conceptualised as a central component of the capacity for governing within the governance framework' based upon the notion that 'surrounding every policy area there are a set of organisations and actors, generally including a number of government organisations, that shape the politics within that policy area.' These networks are said to be self-organising and self-interested and exist autonomously not with the intention to serve public purpose but 'exist in large part to circumvent or even elude the state, rather than to serve it.'[104] The claim that the networks exist autonomously of the state is not correct if applied to the Bhoomi model of e-governance. The networks that revolve around the Bhoomi project are not totally autonomous from their actions and operations. Rather they are linked to the government and its authority that provide them the stamp of legitimacy of their operation and thereby they are able to get the benefits and attend to their self-interest. In the Bhoomi model of e-governance, we found that there exist 'some amount of mutual cooptation between public and private actors, with each side of the policy equation needing the other in order to be successful.'[105]

The important question is whether or not the Bhoomi model of e-governance has enabled a growth of some special interest or social actors that will be able to strengthen the democratic governance in the long run. The delivery of public services on client-oriented mode by adopting ICTs with the help of private IT companies and professionals and charging of user fees from citizens as consumers of public services have inevitably raised the question of genuine democratic impact of these linkages. This network-centric business-oriented model under the firm control of a committed project leader and senior administrator will be beneficial to the social actors within the network but not the poor and marginal farmers who do not have the presence or access in the network. This approach of network governance is accepted as the best practice as it meets the interests and demands of particular social groups. The involvement of the special social interest group or framing a policy that has been more beneficial to those well-off and powerful sections like real estate companies would impact adversely the process of democratic accountability of Bhoomi. No doubt the involvement of these special social groups or actors in public service delivery will open up the bureaucratic structure and enhance their

104 B. Guy Peters. 2004. 'Governance and Public Bureaucracy: New Forms of Democracy or New Forms of Control'? , *The Asia Pacific Journal of Public Administration*, Vol. 26 (1), pp. 6–7.

105 Ibid, p. 7.

control in the policy arena, but this cannot be equated with the participation of citizens in general. It will obscure the process of policy formulation, implementation and accountability.[106] For example, during my visit to the revenue department and department of e-governance in Bengaluru in 2009, 2010 and 2011 for collection of data on Bhoomi, I was asked by the officials of these departments to contact the project leader only for information and they expressed their inability to share information for the research.

Bhoomi as a metaphor for 'good governance'

Bhoomi, the online mutation software for land records management, was designed and developed by NIC, Bengaluru. It is claimed that Bhoomi has demonstrated '... the benefits of making government document more open so that citizens are empowered to challenge the arbitrary actions.'[107] The project champion claims that the Bhoomi e-governance programme is the first successful rural e-governance programme that has sustained for more than 10 years.[108] Similarly, Deepa Narayan of the World Bank writes that the lesson learnt from the Bhoomi programme is that it fulfills the critical need of the people at large; it was launched in phased manner by taking change management process and sustainability of the programme into account and continuity of the leadership of the project champion. Though Bhoomi is not a land redistribution programme, according to her, it still has been able to free 'farmers from the tyranny of village accountants, whom they had to beg, cajole, bribe, and chase down for their land records.'[109] Such a techno-managerial approach to governance limits their argument by saying that putting land records on the website promotes transparency and accountability and reduces discretion and corruption of petty officials like the village accountants and

[106] Kuldeep Mathur. 2008. *From Government to Governance: A Brief Survey of the Indian Experience*, New Delhi: National Book Trust of India, p. 110.

[107] National Informatics Centre. 2005. *Good Governance Through ICT*, New Delhi, p. 38.

[108] Rajiv Chawla and Samartharam NR. 2013. 'Using ICTs Enable Better Land Administration: Bhoomi System of Karnataka, India as A Case for the Study,' p. 4. (www.conftool.com/landandpoverty2013/.../Chawla-409_paper.pdf?./ accessed on June 2,2013)

[109] Deepa Narayan. 2004. 'Field Visit to Karnataka: The Bhoomi Programme,' http://info.worldbank.org/etools/docs/reducingpoverty/doc/117/file/India-FV-Facilitator%20 Report.pdf (accessed on March 28, 2010)

thereby promotes good governance agenda. This understanding gives a narrow approach to governance problem and seeks apolitical solution to the complex issues related to promoting and ensuring administrative accountability. Similarly, the *e-Governance Strategy for Karnataka Government* asserts that the Government of Karnataka firmly believes in e-governance which will 'demystify the role of government' and 'bridge the gap between the rich and poor and between more developed and less developed'[110] and this is based on a techno-managerial perspective.

The ICT-enabled Bhoomi system may have given better access to the poor small and marginal landholders in getting land records (only RTCs) easily, but to argue that such access has led to the development of their capability to raise their socio-economic standards sounds illogical. My study on the delivery of online RTC copy and mutation process revealed very strange and interesting findings, which unfortunately are not highlighted by the studies conducted by World Bank. Though delivery of land records or RTCs from taluk Bhoomi counter has been made easier and reduced corruption, the mutation process and rectification of errors in the RTCs has become cumbersome after the introduction of Bhoomi. As described earlier, the mutation process initiated by the village accountants manually lacked transparency and no queue procedure or serial/listing was maintained in disposal of mutation. Statutory period of notice inviting objection from the interested parties in a mutation case was not strictly adhered to and there were many cases in which the village accountants had issued notices inviting objection in a backdated manner. After the Bhoomi system in operation and the introduction of first-in-first-out principle, the mutation cases are being disposed in a tight integrated manner in which the earlier process of manipulation has been almost reduced. ICT application in mutation has ensured transparency but resulted in delays, increased travel and time cost for the applicants, and the worst aspect is increased corruption since mutation has to pass through several stages (euphemistically 'several tables') and a number of officials are involved in the process. Thus while the manual system was lacking transparency and riddled with corruption, the online integrated mutation process is beset with delays, increased cost in mutation, difficulties for the applicants of mutation and increased scope for corruption. The project champion was candid enough to admit that, 'in the distribution of records there is no bribe, just very simple, but in mutation, in spite of people,

[110] Government of Karnataka. (n.d.) *E-Governance Strategy for Karnataka*, Department of Information Technology & Biotechnology, Bengaluru, p. 8.

in spite of lots of checks, I'm sure people still demand money although it may be on a decreased scale… You would not be able to wipe out it. After all, IT systems cannot take away the crookedness of the mind of the people.' He also admitted that the notwithstanding the existence of a centralised database of Bhoomi in Bengaluru, the correctness of land records and data safety depends on the integrity and commitment of the officials.[111]Interestingly, the limitation of this techno-managerial approach is seldom highlighted by the so-called evaluative studies on best practices of 'good governance.'[112] My interviews with some assistant commissioners (empowered under the Karnataka Land Revenue Act to act as appellate authority to dispose the appeals arising against the mutation orders of tahsildar) of Mysore, Bengaluru Urban, Dharward, Kollar and Mandya revealed that the Bhoomi system has only a mixed impact on the growth of mutation appeal cases compared to previous mutation cases done manually. They were hopeful that, in the long run it might lead to a reduction of appeal cases.[113]

The Bhoomi system of enabling the access to the land records and its impact on providing transparency in the land records management to the landholders and farmers can be understood in the background of failure of the populist nature of land reforms in Karnataka and its marginal impact on poverty reduction. Atul Kohli's study on the land reforms and the role of state showed that the Urs regime in Karnataka only brought a 'mildly redistributive tenancy reforms' and the land reforms were nothing but a 'sham' and the regime acted more for 'preservation of basic class structure' and private enterprises than effecting a radical change in the inequitous agrarian social order in Karnataka. Despite adopting a high ownership of land ceiling limit (up to 54 acres in different classes of land), the state could distribute only 0.2 per cent of cultivated agricultural land among the poor and landless. The small farmers were not benefited from the land reforms. The landholders of above the ceiling

---

[111] See Rajeev Chawla's interview 'Innovation for Successful Societies', An initiative of the National Academy of Public Administration, and the Woodrow Wilson School of Public Affairs and the Boston School of Peace and Justice, Princeton University, 8 June, 2010. (www.princeton.edu/successfulsocieties, accessed on 10 May 2011), pp. 12–14.

[112] See for example World Bank. 2006. *Reforming Public Services in India: Drawing Lessons from Success*, Report No. 35041-IN, 28, February.

[113] Interview with the Assistant Commissioners of Kolar, Mysore, Bengaluru Urban and Mandya in January 2011.

limits were not touched by the revenue administration. Tenancy reforms failed to abolish the tenancy and nearly 50 per cent of the tenanted land exists.[114] Others have also studied the administration of land reform measures and its impact on the beneficiaries. It was observed that in Gulbarga district, the implementation of land reforms failed as the landed elite wielded the political power to circumvent the land reform measures and there was no countervailing pressure from the poor landless persons.[115]Therefore the ceiling surplus land distribution was marginal.[116] Interestingly, the Bhoomi project champion is also quick to admit that the project cannot bring out land reforms and detect the concealed tenancy.[117] At best, to put in World Bank's language, the Bhoomi e-government strategy only facilitates and simplifies the land transaction and reduces petty corruption (not the systemic and embedded nature of corrupt practice) in land administration. Thus, the claim that, Bhoomi would lead to better land reform or change the inequitous land relations is a far-fetched one. Even its project champion's assertion in his writings that Bhoomi has led to reduction of land disputes is not supported with any data. My studies on the functioning of the Bhoomi revealed that it is basically confined to delivery of services on client or business principle mode, and given the increase in corruption in integrated mutation process and the growing pressure on agricultural land for real estate and other non-agricultural purposes, it would be very difficult to predict or arrive at a conclusion that operationalisation of online delivery of land records has led to reduction in disputes over land.

Bhoomi is closely identified with its chief architect Rajeev Chawla, who can be said as a strong entrepreneurial bureaucrat. Chawla has a firm grip over the Bhoomi monitoring Cell. During my frequent visits to the cell, I have closely observed its corporate working style and ambience. Surprisingly, the young and directly recruited officers of KAS are not found, instead two retiring promoted officers of the state civil service, few clerks and IT consultants work there. During my interviews and discussions with the officials and consultants, I

---

114 Atul Kohli. 1987.*The State and Poverty in India: The Politics of Reform*, New Delhi: Cambridge University Press & Orient Longman, pp. 165–187.

115 S. V. Deshpande and Vijaykumar Torgal. 1994. 'Administering Land Reforms in Karnataka,' *Economic and Political Weekly*, 13 August, pp. 2132–2134.

116 S. V. Deshpande and Vijay K. N. Torgal. 2003. 'Land Reforms in Karnataka: Impact on Beneficiaries,' *Economic and Political Weekly,* 1–7 November, pp. 4647–4649.

117 Rajeev Chawla. 2007. 'Bhoomi: Online Delivery of Record of Rights, Tenancy and Crops to Farmers in Karnataka, India', p. 99.

observed that they never forgot to repeatedly harp on the strong autonomous leadership of Rajeev Chawla, Bhoomi's bulging user fees deposits running over 100 crores of rupees, and getting international and national awards and recognitions for the innovation in delivery of land records.

During my visit to the revenue department and department of e-governance at Bengaluru, I wanted to know the details of Bhoomi programme but the officials of these two departments advised me to contact Rajeev Chawla, the project champion, for information as the revenue department of the government did not have information on Bhoomi e-governance programme. Here, the image of the chief executive as public entrepreneur identified with autonomy, innovation, personal vision for the future, secrecy and risk taking is in contrast with democratic governance based on citizen participation, accountability, and open policy-making process. Such an image according to Larry D. Terry 'cultivates and perpetuates an overly romantic view of public administrators' as 'heroes and conquerors' who have the ability to transform the public organisation and act as a guardian of public interest.[118] The autonomous and managerial style of functioning of Bhoomi monitoring cell also explains the reason for non implementation of NLRMP in Karnataka as the state is yet to submit the proposal for funds for execution of several components of the programme to the central government.

Bhoomi and ICT for development and digital access

It is put forth logically that an e-governance project like Bhoomi is a developmental project that is made possible due to the intervention of the state and it has some impact on the lives of the people. But what is significant here is that when viewed from the developmental perspective, the success or failure of Bhoomi becomes a contested one. There is no evidence to prove that the computerised delivery of RTCs at the taluk headquarters to farmers has enabled them to access agricultural credits easily and raised their economic standards which was not possible during the manual method of delivery by the patwaris. Rather it has been proved that the easy accessibility of land records on the web has helped the 'land sharks' who target the poor and vulnerable

[118] Larry D. Terry. 1993. 'Why We Should Abandon the Misconceived Quest to Reconcile Public Entrepreneurship with Democracy,' *Public Administration Review*, 53(4), pp. 393–395.

farmers to purchase their lands for the real estate companies. Bhoomi has been a success in terms of public service delivery programme but to view it from the developmental or capability expansion goals it will be problematic to accept its claim of success.[119] Hence application of ICTs in public service delivery needs to be seen as a tool for enhancement and empowerment of people's capabilities. The policies or steps for providing digital access or service delivery at the local level cyber kiosks may not help the poor to improve the entitlements and the rights of the common citizens. Robin Mansell has rightly put that 'the bias of new media configurations favours the minority of citizens, those who are best positioned to live their lives in an intensely technologically mediated world.'[120] To him, new media technologies should deepen and broaden the capability of larger sections of common people and help them live in the social world of online spaces. The plan to extend the delivery of RTCs through cyber kiosks in rural areas will benefit the rich farmers more than the poor and marginal farmers and tenant cultivators, as such delivery of records will be of marginal effect in improving their socio-economic condition and enhancing their capability to acquire skills necessary to 'approach their problems on their own with courage and freedom.'[121]

The Bhoomi model of e-governance has improved the citizen interaction in a limited way that is beneficial to those wealthy and highly educated farmers and other real estate firms having high stake in land markets. The Bhoomi project champion's article and other uncritical studies' argument that centralised delivery of RTCs will be beneficial to the farmers for securing agricultural loans by putting his land as collateral is not factually correct.

My interviews with some of the nationalised bank officials at Kolar, Nelamangala, Mandya, Chhanapatna, Anekal and Devanhalli taluks revealed that the bank requires only certified or authentic land records be it manually written or computer generated and therefore to argue that computerised RTCs will help more agricultural credit is not based on ground reality. The banks follow their own procedure in sanctioning and renewing agricultural loans.

---

[119] Rahul De. 2006.'Evaluation of E-Government Systems: Project Assessment Vs Development Assessment,' in M A Winner et al (Eds) *EGOV 2006, Lecture Notes in Computer Sciences* (LNCS) 4084, pp. 317–328.

[120] Robin Mansell. 2002. 'From Digital Divides to Digital Entitlements in Knowledge Societies,' *Current Sociology*, Vol. 50 (3), May, pp. 408–411; 423.

[121] Amartya Sen. 1999. *Development As Freedom, New* Delhi: Oxford University Press, p. 63.

However, the bank officials interestingly informed me that as RTCs are available easily at taluk headquarters, many farmers are resorting to multiple loans on the same agricultural land from different nationalised banks as their requests to tahsildars for entering the borrowings of the farmers on their RTCs are not being followed up.

Bhoomi and institutional change

The Bhoomi model of delivery of RTCs and integration of registration with mutation system and merger of survey and settlement wing with tahsil office, the banning of manual RTCs and the plan to allow private run cyber kiosks to deliver RTCs in rural areas have brought out some partial nature of change in the institutional arrangements of taluks. The adoption of ICTs in the computerisation of land records has not been a one-way process. Though the institutional arrangements have been exposed to change, the nature and structure of institutions and its actors have also shaped the ICT strategies in the process. The whole process of computerisation of land records has an incremental nature and it does not envisage any radical change or new institutional arrangements by reversing or altering the power and responsibilities of the taluk officials. The role of the institutional actors like village accountants and tahsildars and the statutory provisions governing the revenue administration in the taluk remain unaffected. The content of manual RTC and computerised RTC copy or the manual process of updation of land records and now the so-called online process absolutely have no difference.

When the pattern of recruitment, posting and transfer of tahsildars is steeped in corruption, it is simplistic to assume that techno-managerial approaches like Bhoomi would remove political and systemic concerns like corrupt practices in land records management and promote accountability, transparency and efficiency in land records management at taluks. Such perspective ignores or covers up the non-technical factors in corruption and inefficiencies in land records management or bureaucratic malfeasance. Bureaucratic performance and reforms for enhancing their accountability and efficiency are quintessentially political phenomena and to find their solutions through centralised, tightly integrated and controlled ICTs systems in partnership with public and private agencies is apolitical and partial one. The Bhoomi system has so far no effect on the rent-seeking behaviour of taluk level officials.

Conclusion

The Bhoomi model of online delivery of land records have spawned a new techno-managerial model of governance based on five aspects: centralised and tight integration of electronic and manual based system of land records, importance of a committed techno-managerial bureaucrat as project champion, political support to the innovation, creating a sustainable environment for innovation and slow but strategic reform placating the interests of all the stakeholders like village accountants, cyber kiosk operators, political elites, landed castes, and real estate interests.

The central premise of the Bhoomi system of computerised land records management is that the land records maintenance manually by village accountants are inefficient, corrupt and opaque as lot of human discretion is involved. The corrupt practices of the petty officials like village accountants, but not the role of powerful officials like tahsildars, assistant commissioners, district collectors and politicians, have been cited as the prime reason behind poor land records management and the land frauds. The techno-managerial strategy to reduce the discretionary power of petty official like patwari/ village accountant by developing a centralised electronic delivery of land records and management is however fraught with problems and challenges. Because more and more electronic and ICT-enabled innovation in Bhoomi would only take away the power and position of the generalist revenue bureaucracy and vests them with techno-managerial professionals.

The political and bureaucratic problems of land records management are reduced to some hardware and software concerns. Bhoomi has sought to add not replace the manual system of land records management. Our studies based on both primary and secondary data revealed that it has failed to address comprehensively the problems of land records management and in the process it has become an addition not replacement of the existing land records management. It gives more emphasis on the techno-managerial strategy of public service delivery than on developmental concerns like participation, land reforms, empowerment and equity in land records management. It has no way reduced the rent-seeking attitude of the officials like village accountants (patwari) and the tahsildars and their informal networks that sustains their corrupt activities.

The Bhoomi system has overlooked the informal networks of land revenue bureaucracy representing the everyday state. Therefore, it is wrong to assume or expect that adoption of ICTs in land records management would remove corruption in the system. Interestingly, it reduced marginally their discretionary power in managing the land records updation and delivery by facilitating the entry of IT professionals and vendors but made difficult to enforce accountability in such multiple agency networks. The delivery of RTC copy and placing the land records on the web has promoted techno-managerial notion of transparency but intriguingly its tightly integrated mutation process combining both manual and computerised process has led to massive increase in corruption, harassment and delays. The tahsildars do not take ownership of Bhoomi system managed on NPM principles of contracting out and outsourcing. Thus, Bhoomi has institutionalised itself as well as the corrupt practices.

James Manor has rightly observed that the Bhoomi programme in Karnataka could succeed as it did not envisage radical institutional and legal changes that would have affected the political support base of the ruling Congress party. Moreover Bhoomi prescribed incremental change and did not affect change in the existing agrarian relations. The Bhoomi project of delivery of RTCs was successful as it was comparatively easier to pursue and enjoyed political support from state chief minister, as he perceived that Bhoomi would be advantageous for gaining political support.[122]

Further, the strategic alliance with the patwaris (village accountants) by assuring them that their original power in field works would not be done away with and the purpose of Bhoomi was to facilitate the transaction in land records management and reduce their drudgery, and not removal of corruption, with the help of cutting edge ICTs, succeeded in selling the Bhoomi project. The banning of issue of manual RTCs was a great leap forward for Bhoomi as it signalled the administrative and political will power of Karnataka government. Further, charging uniform user fees of fifteen rupees for computer generated RTCs (now ten rupees) made Bhoomi programme a financially sustainable and viable project. The Bhoomi project is no longer the financial liability to the state exchequer. Therefore, it is not surprising to find the boastful claims of its project champion as well as officials at the Bhoomi monitoring cell that Bhoomi project has 'earned' a good amount of user fees after meeting the cost in operating the ICTs-enabled system. Such notion on Bhoomi unfortunately

---

[122] James Manor. 2009. 'Successful Governance Reforms in Two Indian States: Karnataka and Andhra Pradesh', in Mark Robinson (Ed) *The Politics of Successful Governance Reforms*, London: Routledge, pp. 25; 31.

limits its potential to a mere ICT-enabled public service delivery and has reduced the role of citizens as mere passive consumer of service delivered by Bhoomi from cyber kiosks than playing itself as one of the means to planning, development and socio-economic equity.

The ICT architecture of Bhoomi has transformed the present landlord (state)–tenant (citizen) relationship to landlord-consumer (tenant) relationship. In such a model of land records management driven by New Public Management and network governance principles, its accountability to citizens is open to question. Managerial autonomy and discretion and functioning in network setting of private-public agencies are the hallmarks of the Bhoomi system. The most interesting aspect is the New Public Management (NPM) style of the Bhoomi system controlled by the centralised Bhoomi monitoring cell (BMC) under the leadership of a senior IAS officer Rajeev Chawla (transferred recently after nine years of service and posted again recently in November 2010), functioning autonomously free from the day-to-day regulation of the revenue department of Karnataka, which is not found elsewhere in the country. His return to Bhoomi management underlines the complex networks that need to be managed on the so-called entrepreneurial or business principles for running the ICT enabled system which was difficult for his successor.

My field observation of the functioning of Bhoomi shows that it has been successful in evolving itself into identifiable stages simultaneously in the development of e-government, unlike the popular perception that e-government will evolve in stages like launching of the website containing informational contents then move into interactional or transactional stages.[123] It simultaneously started transaction base e-government with the public by delivering their RTCs on payment of user fees and later started integrated mutation workflow by connecting to the Kaveri system of registration at sub-registrar's office. In this process it will be erroneous to presume or conclude that the street level bureaucrats have been replaced by system level bureaucrats or the monopoly power and discretion of the field officials have been displaced by Bhoomi kiosks operators.

Though Bhoomi has reduced the work burden and monopoly power of the pretty officials like village accountants in delivery of RTCs and processing mutation, it has at the same time spawned a network of agents or intermediaries

[123] Christopher G. Reddick. 2004. 'Citizen Interaction with e-Government: From the Streets to Servers, ?' *Government Information Quarterly*, 22, pp. 38–57.

who are now out to gain from the process as the mutation and rectification processes are cumbersome and centralised at taluk offices.

Further, close study of the Bhoomi programme has shown that the programme could forge ahead of other states due to innovative measures planned by its project champion which deviated from the uniform nature of the centrally sponsored scheme of computerisation of land records of the central government and devised the Bhoomi software that specifically suited to the land records system of Karnataka. The reason why the World Bank has highlighted Bhoomi's success as 'best practice' and a role model for other states is due to its advocacy for liberalising and opening up land markets, integrating tahsil with registration, and securing tenurial rights through computerisation and digitisation of land records fits perfectly with the Bhoomi e-governance project. This approach only focuses land as an economic resource devoid of social, cultural and political meanings.

Lastly, the recent innovations like integrated workflow in the Bhoomi system, providing web connectivity to banks and other financial institutions, allowing private cyber kiosks operators to deliver digitally signed RTCs for information and remote controlled monitoring of Bhoomi operation at the Bhoomi Monitoring Cell, Bengaluru point out that this ICT-based innovation will further go on and more and more IT professionals and IT vendors who have bagged the contract for operating the integrated Bhoomi ICT system will play important roles in the network of the e-governance policy making and implementation. Kenneth Kernaghan and Justin Gunraj have rightly observed that the use of ICTs by public organisations will 'predispose' them to change in a particular way as ICT has certain inherent predispositions like its requirements of skills, innovation and investment on a continual basis and this will pave the way for change in the organisation and management by increased dependence on the private sector.[124]

[124] Kenneth Kernaghan and Justin Gunraj. 2004. 'Integrating Information Technology into Public Administration: Conceptual and Practical Considerations,' *Canadian Public Administration*, Vol. 47 (4), pp. 525–546.

6

The Computerisation of Land Records Programmes in Karnataka and Odisha

A Comparative Study

Introduction

The CLR and SRA&ULR programmes started simultaneously in Karnataka and Odisha and in other parts of India as centrally sponsored schemes. We analyse here the different trajectories in achievements and constraints encountered by these states by comparing the processes, outcomes and impacts of these schemes which would broaden our understanding. The factors behind the success of computerisation of land records and online delivery of land records in Karnataka and the poor and dismal performance in Odisha will be analysed by comparing their administrative and institutional aspects in policy implementation and the capacity of the political and administrative elites to deliver the results.

In India, a wide variation among the states exists in terms of their political, administrative and economic performances and social and cultural composition. All the states show different trajectories of development during the British period as well as after Independence; the political, economic and cultural variables have been the determining factors in shaping the regime performances. In the macro context, we see different political issues at the central government level and at micro level, we perceive the political, social, economic and cultural issues among the states as varying. These differences have widened after Independence. The decline of the Congress party's dominance, the rise of regional parties, coalition governments at the centre and in some states, the rise of lower and the intermediate classes in the political arena, uneven socio-economic and regional developments, assertion of regional and ethnic identities, and the economic liberalisation policies pursued both at central and state government levels have been the crucial factors in shaping the inter-state differences in India.[1] Although there is absence of a 'general theoretical framework' for studying the political and administrative developments among the states, yet the states in India continue to operate in an 'independent political space.'[2]

To Myron Weiner, our very understanding of the Indian political system depends upon the pattern of political developments across the states. Despite existence of some commonalities among all the states in India, like common constitution and common legal and administrative system, but in terms of socio-economic and political developments, there are wide variations among the states though each state is a political constituent of the Indian state. Thus, Indian polity can be described as a socially and politically segmented system and each state government and its administration 'mirrors the kind of societies in which they function.'[3] One of the interesting observation of Myron Weiner is that despite the existence of unusual microcosm and macrocosm of political developments, it is the central government which takes all the initiatives for economic and administrative reforms and innovation as the state government lacks skill and initiative. For example, land reform measures were initiated by the state governments under the pressure of the central governments, but the state governments and their administrative machinery did everything to water down the legislation and implementation.[4] Iqbal Narain's edited volume on *State Politics in India* (1976) dealing with political developments across the Indian states in the aftermath of decline of one party system of congress party

---

[1] Sudha Pai. 2000. *State Politics: New Dimensions*, New Delhi: Shipra Publications, p. 6.

[2] Ibid, pp. 3; 259.

[3] Myron Weiner. (Ed). 1968. *State Politics in India*, Princeton: Princeton University Press, pp. 3–7; 53–56.

[4] Ibid, p. 57. It is noteworthy that, the computerisation of land records and strengthening revenue administration and updating land records and later on redesigning as National Land Records Modernisation Programme (NLRMP) are initiated by the central government. The process has gained momentum since the mid eighties.

also carried forward the original premises of Weiner and it even asserted that study of the state politics in India would help in the development of theory of state politics. His observation that in India the states are themselves both a 'whole' and 'part,' both a system and sub-system, implying their distinctive socio-cultural and historical development and legacies as well as a part of the Indian state system. The political system of a state serves as 'point of confluence' for the regional, national and local politics and it is only by taking studies of state politics and also focusing on the intra-regional differences within the state, raising many politico-economic and socio-political issues, that we can fruitfully understand the complex working of the Indian political system in a micro context. Iqbal Narain has forcefully noted that 'state politics is a key variable in the context of the nature, performance and behaviour of the Indian political system and its various subsystems.'[5] This perspective remains relevant till the date and starting point for many of the justifications for the comparative studies of state politics in India.

The socio-political processes in the states in federal India invariably affect their policy making and implementation. Influenced by growing literature on the caste and class dominance in the power structure in the state politics, John Harriss argues that the differentiation among political regimes across the Indian states in policy formulations and implementation of anti-poverty schemes and decentralisation of power to lower class/caste groups can be understood if we take into account the balance of caste-class power and the nature of party organisation within those states.[6]

The justification for comparative studies of Indian states was perhaps first laid by Atul Kohli in his study of state government performance in land reforms in some states like Uttar Pradesh, Kerala, West Bengal and Karnataka where he found that the 'federal nature of the Indian polity allows for a disaggregated and comparative analysis within India.' The variations among the Indian states about the nature of political rule and different types of regimes, different bureaucratic performances in implementation of public policies such as land

[5] Iqbal Narain (Ed.) 1967. *State Politics in India*, Meerut, Meenakshi Prakashan, pp. xvi; xix; 590.

[6] John Harriss. 1999. 'Comparing the Political Regimes across Indian States: A Preliminary Essay,' *Economic and Political Weekly*, Vol. 34 (48), 27 November-3 December, p. 3376.

reforms create different outcomes in very comparable context. The big size of some of the states and their populations equaling some of the developing countries, are the reasons for such comparative studies which help us develop broader understanding on the nature of Indian political system or state.[7]

Recent works such as Rob Jenkins' book highlights four key areas or practice of 'actually existing democracy,' viz. economic policy making, subaltern politicisation, civic engagement and political leadership as areas of comparison. The authors in that book have sought to adopt analytic approach in making a two-state comparison 'within the confines of a single nation state' which, it is claimed, can contribute to understanding the political and social change in India. To Jenkins, the puzzles in similarities and divergences and outcomes can be understood by adopting a two state comparison, as India's federal system has created 'mini democracies' (i.e. state governments) which function on 'almost identical institutional infrastructures.' Further, the common variables offer an opportunity to study and analyse the convergences and divergences in the policy outcomes as the 'federal system provides a laboratory of democracy.'[8] Aseema Sinha's work describes several factors like the structure of state bureaucracy and political environment that are responsible for inter-state variations. Such variations, according to her, offer an ideal context to analyse how a 'common global policy takes a variety of forms as it intersects with different environmental and political processes.' The variation between Gujarat and West Bengal in terms of attracting industrial investment despite taking a similar promotional industrial policy by the two states is sought to be explained in terms of a complex interplay among ideas, interests and institutions.[9]

Commenting upon the intra-state variations in efficiency and administration, C. P. Bhambhri has argued that actions of the states 'are an epiphenomenon.' Due to the existence of specific socio-economic structure of society and forces of colonial and feudal, such historical legacies and experience have to be kept in mind while making a comparative study of the public administration among

---

[7] Atul Kohli. 1987. *The State and Poverty in India: The Politics of Reform*, Cambridge University Press, pp. 3–4.

[8] Rob Jenkins. (Ed). 2004. *Regional Reflections: Comparing Politics across India's States*, New Delhi: Oxford University Press, 2004, pp. 3–7.

[9] Aseema Sinha. 2007. 'Idea, Interests and Institutions in Policy Change: A Comparison of West Bengal and Gujarat,' in Rob Jenkins (Ed) *Regional Reflections: Comparing Politics across India's States*. New Delhi: Oxford University Press, pp. 66–108.

the states. The administration at the state or sub-national level operates in the context of national uniformity and local diversity.[10]

The recent study in inter-state variations in delivery of five basic public services such as primary education, public transport, Public Distribution System (PDS), drinking water and healthcare among ten states show wide gap and disparities between the states in terms of access, use, reliability and user satisfaction.[11] A comparative study of e-readiness among the Indian states is being carried out regularly by Department of Information Technology (DIT) of central government and National Council of Applied Economic Research (NCAER), New Delhi.

Such e-readiness among the states are measured by taking into several indicators like political and regulatory infrastructure and market environment that promote the spread and usage of the ICT, readiness of different stakeholders of the economy like individual, and government, and business readiness and degree of usage by the stakeholders. Readiness is understood in terms of the educational achievements or training in IT of individuals or players like government and business that enable them to respond to an information age environment. E-readiness is a multidimensional concept which measures the state's ability to participate in an increasingly networked world. The role of the state government in promoting e-readiness and e-governance is of critical importance. According to *India: e-Readiness Report*, 2008, Karnataka continues to occupy a position as one of the leaders in e-readiness and Odisha continues to occupy a place of average achiever among the states. The report has noted that Karnataka is the only state in India to have a secretary level official heading the e-governance wing.[12]

Here, there is an attempt to explain not only the *process* of computerisation of land records in the two states but also the different *outcomes* of the two schemes. Though the two states initiated the centrally sponsored scheme through pilot projects as per the common guidelines issued by the central government, the Karnataka government forged ahead of Odisha and claimed to have developed

---

[10] C. P. Bhambhri. 1976. 'Contextual Framework of Public Administration in Indian States,' *Indian Journal of Public Administration*, 23(3), July-September: pp. 330–348.

[11] Samuel Pal et al . 2004. 'State of India's Public Services: Benchmark for the States,' *Economic and Political Weekly*, 28 February, pp. 920–933.

[12] See *India: e-Readiness Report,* 2005, 2006 and 2008 published by Department of Information Technology, Government of India and NCAER, New Delhi.

an e-governance model of land records management for its replication in other states, whereas the performance of Odisha is dismal and slow leading to several factors like the role of its political and administrative leadership, the institutional arrangements and the role of network management. The P. S. Appu Committee (1995) has reported that, notwithstanding variations among the states in the structure of revenue administration and the designations of revenue functionaries, the basic features of the revenue administration across India except in permanently settled areas remained same.[13] Why then the remarkably similar nature of revenue administrations in Karnataka and Odisha generated two different processes and outcomes? What are the factors that helped Karnataka to operationalise the Bhoomi application software through pilot projects and introduced online mutation system in phased manner successfully in seven years? Why has Odisha not been able to computerise the land records completely and ban the issue of manual record of rights? What are the reasons for success of Bhoomi and the failure of Bhulekh system of land records management? We seek to find out the interesting but 'puzzling regional contrasts within a centralist nation state' and 'sub-national institutional variation'[14] and the reasons for such differential nature of progress and its future implication in the land records modernisation programme including the goal to achieve the land title regime. However, this study is not limited to identifying the divergences, but also finds growing convergences in the public policy changes between the states.

An examination of allocation of central funds from 1987 to 1992-1993 by central government for implementation of the CLR and SRA&ULR programmes for Karnataka and Odisha shows that it is the latter which has received larger flow of funds, but when it comes to delivery of results it is the former that has performed better. The data on release of fund for implementation of CLR programme since 1988 (since inception of the scheme) till 2006-2007 revealed also the same trend viz. Odisha government has received more central allocations for implementation of CLR programme than Karnataka.[15]

---

[13] Government of India. 1995. *Report of the Committee on Revitalisation of Land Revenue Administration,* Ministry of Rural Development, New Delhi, p. 1.

[14] Aseema Sinha. 2003. 'Rethinking the Developmental State: Divided Leviathan and Sub-National Comparison in India,' *Comparative Politics*, 35(4), p. 460.

[15] Government of India. *Annual Report, 2006–2007,* Ministry of Rural Development, New Delhi, p. 261.

Table 6.1

Allotment of central funds for implementation of CLR and SRA&ULR from 1987 to 1992-1993 (Rupees in Lakhs)

State	*CLR*	*SRA&ULR*
Karnataka	107.50	7.5
Odisha	245.215	52.00

Source: Ministry of Rural Development, Government of India, New Delhi. (L.N.14015/15/28/5/1993)

Structure of revenue administration and the functionaries

The land records management system in post independent India as we have described earlier, is the legacy of colonial land revenue administration. Despite the common objective and significance of land records, the nature of land records management widely varies among the states. In India, three systems of land revenue administration broadly existed during the colonial period. These were the zamindari system (the land lord based intermediary system), ryotwari system (cultivator based system) and the mahalwari system (village based system). The post independent land revenue administration is broadly divided into four main institutions which is also a colonial practice. The survey and settlement department undertakes survey and settlement works at periodic interval and is responsible for preparation of both textual and spatial records and mapping. The revenue department under which tahsil/taluk function, maintains the land records prepared by survey and settlement department, collects land revenue, updates land records necessitated due to registered sale deed at sub-registrar office. The tahsil/taluk offices are assisted by revenue inspectors/village accountants/ patwaris/kanungos who function at revenue inspector's office/circle comprising group revenue villages. The department of stamp and registration is responsible for registration of sale deeds and collection of stamp duties and preservation of registered deeds on landed properties. These three institutions come under state revenue departments.

In many states, local bodies like municipalities and development authorities/town planning bodies and village Panchayats (councils) also keep register of land records for collection of property holding taxes, approval of building plans/layout plans. In some state like Andhra Pradesh, the sarpanch (head of the village council) is empowered to resolve local disputes on land. In Rajasthan, the sarpanch is authorised to approve mutations on registered sale deeds sent by sub-registrar. In states like UP, Punjab, Haryana and Rajasthan, the management of wastelands are done by the village panchayats. The centrally sponsored scheme computerisation of land records programme are being carried out by the states in India by their revenue departments by digitising the existing entries in manual RoRs / RTCs and maps in tahsil/ taluk and the registered deeds containing the transfer/sale details at sub-registrar offices.[16]

Both Karnataka and Odisha have inherited heterogeneous tenancy laws prior to their formation as separate states. The Karnataka Land Revenue Act, 1964 and the Odisha Survey and Settlement Act, 1958 and Odisha Land Reforms Act, 1960 have sought to provide a unified revenue administration in Karnataka and Odisha respectively. The revenue administration of Karnataka is headed by the Secretary (Revenue). The regional commissioner heads the revenue division comprising some districts. At the district level, the deputy commissioner heads the district revenue administration followed by assistant commissioner at the subdivisional level. The taluk is headed by a tahsildar, hobli villages are headed by revenue inspectors and the sub-taluk office is manned by village accountant, the lowest functionary in revenue administration, who looks after the maintenance of land records and other revenue and non-revenue works of a small group of villages.

Similarly in Odisha, the secretary, revenue department is the administrative head and the revenue divisional commissioners are the divisional or regional head of three revenue divisions. At the district level, the collector is the head of the district revenue administration followed by sub-collector and additional sub-collector at the subdivisional level. The tahsildar heads the tahsil administration and revenue inspector is at the revenue circles comprising groups of revenue villages. The hierarchies of officials as described in the two states also deal with computerisation of land records and its implementation.

[16] The World Bank. 2007. '*Land Policies for Growth and Poverty Reduction*,' Agriculture and Rural Development Unit, India Country Management Unit, Report No-38298–IN, July 9, pp. 6–7, Rekha Bandopadhya. 1993. 'Land System in India: A Historical Review,' *Economic and Political Weekly*, 25 December, A149–A155 and Government of India. 2009. *Report of the Committee on State Agrarian Relations and the Unfinished Task in Land Relations*, p. 169;171.

In Karnataka, Rajeev Chawla acted as special secretary, Bhoomi, the post created to head a state level Bhoomi online land records management, also known as Bhoomi Monitoring Cell (BMC) at Bengaluru that took the charge of bringing out an innovative land records management by application and adoption of ICTs. On the other hand, in Odisha, the programme of computerisation of land records and strengthening revenue administration and updating land records are being dealt by director, land records and survey (DLR&S), the post that earlier existed to deal with land records management.

The revenue administration in Odisha comprises 30 districts, 58 sub-divisions and 316 tahsils, 1842 revenue inspector's circles. In Karnataka, the revenue administration comprises 27 districts, 58 sub-division, 203 taluks including special ones (tahsils), 745 hobli (revenue inspector's circles) and 8000 village accountant offices. It may be thus stated that though geographically Karnataka is larger than Odisha and has more population, it is the latter that has a larger bureaucratic structure in revenue administration.[17] A comparative allocation of funds, their utilisation, and the progress made in land records computerisation by the two states are provided in tables that would enable us to analyse the performances of the two states.

Table 6.2

Releases and Utilisation of Funds towards Central Share under the Centrally Sponsored Scheme for SRA&ULR as on 31 May 2008 (Rupees in Lakhs)

State	*Release during Eighth Five Year Plan*	*Release up to Ninth Five Year plan*	*Release during Tenth Five Year Plan*	*Eleventh Five year Plan, 2007-2008*	*Total release since inception*	*Percentage of utilisation*
Karnataka	404.37	826.47	65.00	1298.88	2190.35	31.12
Odisha	355.62	355.62	467.50	700.35	1523.47	16.51

Source: Department of Land Resources, Ministry of Rural Development, Government of India.

[17] The total number of tahsils before the launching of computerisation of land records was 172 and later on the number of tahsils were increased to 316 as the state government claims to have implemented Appu Committee Report (1989) on strengthening revenue administration.

Table 6.3
Release and Utilisation of funds under CLR as on 31 May 2008, since inception in 1989 (Rupees in Lakhs)

State	*Release up to Eighth Five Year Plan*	*Release up to Ninth Five Year Plan*	*Release during Tenth Five Year Plan*	*Eleventh Five Year Plan, 2007-2008*	*Total release since inception*	*Percentage of Utilisation*
Karnataka	311.00	1874.43	1807.00	150.28	3831.71	69%
Odisha	522.50	1759.12	1857.90	704.05	4321.07	67%

Source: Department of Land Resources, Ministry of Rural Development, Government of India.

The data on release and utilisation of the central funds for the two centrally sponsored schemes shows that both the states, despite differential nature of their revenue administration and the size and extent of landholdings, have shown surprisingly some convergence in utilisation of the central funds in SRA&ULR and CLR programmes. Karnataka government developed innovatively the Bhoomi model of online land records delivery and land records management with nearly spending 69% of the central funds and has become the role model for other states to follow or replicate. Odisha government, despite having received more amounts of funds and nearly spent the similar percentage of central allocations, has shown disappointing results. This has made one ponder the nature, process, outcome and direction of the land records computerisation programme in the state.

The comparative performance by the two states (Table-5) shows that though there appears similar nature of progress, Karnataka has gone ahead of Odisha in actual operationalisation of the project. For instance, Odisha is yet to complete computerisation of the land records, as the record of rights of scores of villages are left out due to various reasons like lack of supervision and monitoring at the time of data entry. Karnataka has started providing computerised sketch map of parcels of land by integrating textual with spatial maps in many tahsils. The integration of registry with tahsil office and uplinking has not been provided and the pilot project of digitisation of maps and their integration with record of rights has not been successful in Odisha. In contrast, such progress was part and parcel of the Bhoomi system of land record management in Karnataka.[18]

[18] It can be said here that the Bhoomi model of computerisation of land records is a state specific programme and it did not follow the central guidelines on land record guideline, rather the broad objectives were adhered to.

Table 6.4

Comparative performance of implementation of the scheme of Computerisation of Land Records in Karnataka and Odisha

State	*RoRs Data entry/re-entry*	*Status of issue of manual RoRs*	*Legal sanctity to computerised copy of RoRs*	*Placing RoRs on the web*	*Scanning and digitisation of maps after pilot project*	*On-line mutation*	*Tahsil Computer cell*	*State data centre*	*Sub-division and district level data centre*
Karnataka	completed	Stopped	Yes	done	Going on	already done	yes	yes	No
Odisha	Not yet Back log cases pending	Not completely stopped as many places tahsils computer cells are defunct	Yes	Done partially	Pilot project not successful but digitisation with help of vendors going on	No	computer cells in newly created tahsils are under construction	No	No

Source: Information provided by Bhoomi Monitoring Cell (BMC), Bengaluru and Director of Land Records & Survey (DLR&S), Cuttack, as on 31/4/2010

The land records like RTC, mutation extracts, and sketch map of the plots are delivered online at the taluk level Bhoomi counters, whereas in Odisha, in many tahsils, the delivery of copy of RoRs takes at least two to three days owing to various reasons, and in some tahsils in Malkangiri district, manual delivery of RoRs is continuing till the date.

Political and administrative leadership

The Bhoomi project, as has been analysed in this book, owes its success to the political commitment and support that the administrative leadership has shown at the highest bureaucratic level. The political support of the then IT savvy Chief Minister S. M. Krishna was crucial to the successful launching of the Bhoomi pilot project. Narendra Pani writes that Krishna presented himself as an 'icon of reforms' in Karnataka. He developed 'an image as a reformer' and 'chose to build his image on what is perhaps best described as a modernist platform. He not only promised development but also identified with its entirely advanced technology.'[19] The opposition made by nearly 9000 strong village accountants to the Bhoomi pilot project was politically managed by Chief Minister and revenue minister by assuring the village accountants that Bhoomi would reduce their drudgery and their original power in land records maintenance would be kept intact. The young children of the deceased village accountants were also rehabilitated in the Bhoomi counters after imparting to them necessary IT training as a tactical measure. S. M. Krishna's political support for Bhoomi stems from two factors, according to James Manor. First, to avoid the impression that he was much preoccupied with the support for IT in Bengaluru and second, to avoid his pro-urban bias that had risked the alienation of his caste support base. Thus, the Chief Minister found the computerisation of land records programme to deliver the rural people their most sought after document through ICT adoption. His open support and public articulation in favour of Bhoomi gave important backing to Rajeev Chawla, the IAS officer and the project leader.

The Bhoomi project, as James Manor has said, was easy to operationalise for two reasons: the logistical support the government possessed such as vast revenue bureaucracy and its competent officials and availability of IT companies

---

[19] Narendra Pani. 2006. 'Icons and Reform Politics in India: The Case of S. M. Krishna,' *Asian Survey*, Vol. 46 (2), pp. 242; 247.

and vendors in Bengaluru; and secondly, the political support provided at the highest level as the programme did not entail a radical change. Bhoomi succeeded as it did not affect the political interest of the ruling parties and threaten the interest of the ruling alliance. Therefore, insulation from politics would not have helped the Bhoomi programme to be successful in an open democratic society. The political gain of Bhoomi has been so immense that political successors found hard to abandon it.[20]

Mark Robinson argues in a similar vein. He says that the fate of governance reforms depends upon how the existing formal and informal institution shapes the incentives for risk taking in relation to reforms. The incentives to politicians are those which would not put an end to rent seeking or their political support base and in the long run would rather help to garner support to new political and social support groups. The reforms that threaten the existing social interest or the established procedure of functioning will be resisted by bureaucrats and mid-level staff.[21] Even after accepting this perspective of no radical change, we find it difficult to understand the problem of delay in computerisation of land records programme in Odisha. The objective of the land records computerisation in Karnataka or in Odisha is the same and it in no way threatens the political base of the ruling parties, as it entailed only incremental changes in the delivery of public services. Why did the political leaderships in Odisha not evince interest in the centrally sponsored scheme of land records computerisation and updating of land records that do not adversely affect the interest of their political support base? Did the land records computerisation and modernisation of revenue administration threaten the support base of the political leaderships in Odisha? Did the revenue administrators in Odisha fail in projecting the incentives and risks involved in carrying forward land records computerisation and updation before the political leadership? Did the revenue administrators in Odisha take up leadership in the implementation of the land records computerisation?

In Odisha, neither the political leadership nor the administrative leadership has the vision or understanding on the need for computerisation of land records, as we have shown clearly in the previous chapter on the state. The political

[20] James Manor. 2009. 'Successful Governance Reforms in two Indian States: Karnataka and Andhra Pradesh' in Mark Robinson (Ed) *The Politics of Successful Governance Reforms*, London: Routledge, pp. 44–46.

[21] Ibid, pp. 2–4.

support could have been own, if the state administrative leadership in revenue department would have provided a viable programme of action and strategy of implementation, as the bureaucratic leadership has shown in Karnataka, Tamil Nadu, Maharashtra and Gujarat in implementation of computerisation of land records. Neither the bureaucratic leadership of revenue department in Odisha has any commitment nor does it have any inclination to innovate while implementing the centrally funded scheme. It has rather confined its role to promoting a vendor driven programme implementation. Interestingly, the bureaucracy in revenue department in Odisha has shown its ability to secure the flow of central fund, spend through IT vendors by distributing contracts, and promptly send utilisation certificates to central government. The head of executing agency, the post of director, land records and survey, is viewed as punishment posting for the senior officers of Odisha administrative service (OAS) or promoted IAS officers at their retiring years and the incumbents are routinely transferred even before completion of a year or they themselves find some other lucrative postings and manage to leave the post. Obviously, there is no stability of tenure in the post and hence no involvement or ownership among the successive directors to the computerisation of land records programme.

The World Bank's study on some 'successful innovations of public service delivery across India' and how they worked as some form of institutional reform on the other hand offers some plausible explanation to understand the reason for success of Bhoomi, despite the bureaucratic complexity, lack of accountability and transparency, lack of civil society and citizen involvement, and prevalence of official secrecy. The Bank's study found that the success of Bhoomi is due to support from the political leadership and political support across the party lines; empowering the civil service through stability of tenure, managerial autonomy, and high-level access of the bureaucracy to political decision makers were crucial factors in the success of Bhoomi programme.[22]

The restructuring of the agency like reengineering the intra-organisational process, empowering the senior managers through creation of centralised monitoring system, improving intra-agency coordination, developing more effective linkages with the civil society, and a strong management team were

---

[22] World Bank. 2006. *India: Reforming Public Services in India; Drawing Lessons From Success, Report No. 35041–IN,* 28 February, pp. I-III. Also see Vikram Chand. 2006. 'Institutional Innovations in Public Service Delivery Lessons' In Vikram Chand (Ed) *Reinventing Public Service Delivery: Selected Case Studies*, New Delhi: Sage Publications.

critical strategies for success of Bhoomi. The objective was cast strategically in terms of improving citizen convenience and elimination of drudgery, and not curbing corruption.[23] Such strategy is important in the context of neoliberal reforms that aim at only procedural reforms through incrementalist way than planning for any structural change in the existing institutional set-up.

The leadership of Rajeev Chawla, a senior IAS officer in Karnataka and his innovative ideas could provide political incentives to the Chief minister S. M. Krishna. He is rightfully called the project leader or champion of Bhoomi, which took nearly seven years to operationalise in the state. His continuance as the head of Bhoomi programme for more than ten years was crucial for successful launching of the project and its stabilisation through phased manner in collaboration with NIC, Bengaluru and private IT vendors and software companies. After a brief transfer from his post as a special secretary Bhoomi in 2009, he was again posted as chief executive Bhoomi monitoring cell in December 2010, as his successor was incapable to manage the network settings of the Bhoomi system designed by him.[24] Today, the Bhoomi programme has become financially sustainable and it has been institutionalised as a branch of the revenue department and it is on the path towards more and more innovation through adoption of ICTs. Rajeev Chawla was selected for the 'Prime Minister's award for Excellence in Public Administration' for the year 2004-2005, in recognition of his 'extraordinary and innovative work done.'

The achievements of the Bhoomi programme bring home the point that in the contemporary neoliberal governance reforms, it has become 'axiomatic that there existed a need for competent and confident managers with the leadership capabilities required to enhance their organisation's performance within the newly emerging politico-managerial environment.'[25]

In contrast, Odisha lacks both political and administrative support and leadership to carry out the programme of computerisation of land records. The pilot programme of computerisation of land records took nearly 17 years for completion and additional amount was spent for the purpose, but hardly

---

[23] Ibid, p. 27.

[24] Interview with Anil Kumar, KAS, Bhoomi monitoring cell, Bengaluru on January 18, 2011.

[25] Andrew Korac Kakbadse. et al. 1996. 'Leadership in Public Sector: An Internationally Comparative Benchmarking Analysis,' *Public Administration and Development*, Vol. 16, p. 394.

any feedback or experience was gained by the implementing agency of the state government. The director land records and survey, secretary, revenue department, the CEO of Odisha Computer Application Centre (OCAC) and the NIC officials do not demonstrate commitment or personal interest in computerisation of land records programme. In fact, these officials of the programme passed the buck to others for poor performance. The irregularly held proceedings of the state level steering committee confines the discussion to sanction and approval of the contracts for IT vendors to execute the work and never engages itself to monitor the programme. Similarly, the political leadership in Odisha has not shown interest in the computerisation of land records and its political payoff unlike the then Karnataka Chief Minister S. M. Krishna. Thus, it was because of the political support that the state bureaucracy under the leadership of Rajeev Chawla could implement Bhoomi programme in an innovative manner that was different from the central government's guidelines despite the resistance from the lower rung taluk officials of online delivery of land records programme.

Institutional arrangements

The land records computerisation in both Karnataka and Odisha have taken place in two different institutional arrangements. In Karnataka, the *pahani* or the Record of Rights, Tenancy and Crops (RTC), and in Odisha the Record of Rights (RoRs) or *Patta* have the similar contents and features. However, the important difference is that the RTC document in Karnataka is a broader one and covers important features like owner and cultivator details, utilisation of land under various categories, details of crops grown seasonally that are updated at regular interval, tenancy and cultivation details, and land utilisation and crop details. Therefore, the importance of RTC for farmers to avail crop loan and insurance or concessional seeds and fertilisers is very high. The RTCs were issued by the patwaris or village accountants and the prime reason for the introduction of Bhoomi was to reduce the discretion of these petty revenue officials in issuing the RTCs. In Odisha, on the other hand, the certified copies of record of rights are issued, even prior to computerisation of land records, only by the tahsildars centrally and the revenue inspectors are not authorised to issue such documents. Moreover, the revenue inspectors are not authorised to make any entry in the record of rights or map available in their circle offices without intimation from the tahsildar.

The institutional arrangements that dealt with the land records management and maintenance are similar. In the early phase of computerisation of land records, the revenue department of Karnataka had implemented the scheme and also the pilot project in Gulbarga district in 1991. The Bhoomi model of online land records management and delivery was developed through pilot projects under the leadership of Rajeev Chawla, special secretary, e-governance. A state level monitoring cell was created for rolling out the Bhoomi application software. The special purpose institutional arrangement was created to function autonomously without necessitating major administrative changes. The earlier computerisation of land records programme in Karnataka fizzled out as the programme did not have a clear cut objective and lacked leadership and collaborative effort as has been the case in Odisha. One of the reasons for success of the Bhoomi programme is that it started on business principles and developed a solid partnership or collaborative effort with the help of various stakeholders like NIC, revenue officials including village accountants, and IT consultants.

On the other hand, in Odisha, initially the Member, Board of Revenue headed the land records computerisation project for more than a decade and owing to his poor performance, the revenue secretary was asked to head the computerisation of land records programme. The director, land records and survey (DLR&S) continues to function as the main authority to oversee the implementation and coordination of the programme with the technical assistance of NIC, Bhubaneswar. After the merger of the two centrally sponsored schemes into NLRMP, the Chief Secretary of the state now heads the programme of computerisation of land records, but the proceedings of the state level monitoring and review committee revealed that the vendor driven approach to implementation continues as usual, which defeats the purpose of computerisation of land records. The IT vendors have become the real beneficiaries in bagging lucrative contracts, as the main objectives of computerisation have got confined to the purchase of hardwares, softwares and some crash training courses to unwilling or disinterested tahsil officials by the executing agencies like OCAC.

The state run Odisha Computer Application Centre (OCAC) executes the computerisation of land records projects through private IT vendors. In Odisha, there is a network of formal agency involved in the CLR project but as we have analysed in the previous chapter, serious problem of coordination, partnership and leadership in implementation of land records computerisation have become an endemic feature of the land records computerisation project in Odisha.

Policy designs and implementation through networks

In understanding the computerisation of land records programme, the role of policy design must be taken into account as it helps in explaining the sustainability or failure of particular policy in different states in India. Aseema Sinha says that few studies have been conducted on explaining the 'multilevel character of states' and 'variation within the developmental states, whether they are strong or weak.' She argues that 'the policy framework of growth may not be centrally guided but is a joint product of central rules, provincial strategic choices, and sub-national institutional variation.'[26] The role of policy design and strategy is important here to understand differential outcomes among the Indian states. Policy design, according to Anne L. Schneider and Helen Ingram, 'refers to the content and substance of public policy—the tools, instruments, and other features or 'architecture' of policy.' The designing of policy and processes in which it is produced cannot be understood in isolation of the product that has been produced. Policy design, no doubt reflects the ideas, interests, and goals, definition of problem and identification of problem, rules, tools, rationales, and implementation structures.[27] The role of ideas, institutions and interests in public policy design and implementation can be better approached through study of policy networks in which both the formal and informal partnerships between government and private agencies are formed for policy formulation and implementation.

Interestingly, in Odisha, the proceedings of the state level steering committee that monitor the implementation of the land records computerisation programme in the state reflects the strategies and procedures adopted and decisions taken, but in Karnataka, such proceedings are not available or held. One can find a series of publications of Bhoomi Monitoring Cell detailing strategies, guidelines and instructions to be followed in running the integrated mutation process. The thrust in Bhoomi's business model is on output and

---

[26] Aseema Sinha. 2003. 'Rethinking the Developmental State: Divided Leviathan and Sub-national Comparisons in India,' *Comparative Politics*, Vol. 35 (4), July, pp. 459–476.

[27] Anne L. Schneider and Helen Ingram. 2008. 'Policy Design', *Encyclopedia of Public Administration and Public Policy,* New York: Taylor and Francis, pp. 1477–1481.

no records found the process of adoption of Bhoomi model. Discussion with the officials of the Bhoomi monitoring cell revealed that the organisation runs on the leadership and direction of its chief executive, Rajeev Chawla. No records are readily available on the monthly disposal of mutation cases or correction of RTCs after the Bhoomi system was in operation and prior to the operationalisation of Bhoomi. The Bhoomi monitoring cell is identified with its project director and his brief transfer and reinstatement only clearly reinforce his NPM style management, autonomous of government control and regulation.

Odisha government's implementation policy strategy clearly reveals that it has been blindly following the broad policy guidelines of CLR programme for the achievement of so-called physical and financial targets rather than any redesign of the central guidelines to suit its needs. The reason is the absence of political and administrative leadership and lack of bureaucratic commitment and ownership. Neither the NIC nor the DLR&S has any plan or vision to implement the computerisation of land records programme.

The Karnataka experience, on the other hand, is basically a top-down executive-led reform initiative 'which was formulated after careful study of the requirements of public, identification of the problem, finding a solution and smoothing or assessing political path to reform process by administrative elites and later on appropriated by political leadership.'[28] The Bhoomi design team set the reform agenda, evolved strategies for implementation, and dealt with the kind of conflicts that would meet the proposal for change. The role of innovation and policy design was crucial to the success of the Bhoomi system as could be seen in its integrated mutation that linked mutation process with registry and survey branch without bringing in a large scale legal and institutional change or reversal of power of revenue officials. But in Odisha, computerisation has not made any difference to the mutation process as was prevalent earlier.

Karnataka government has effected out some legal changes in the Karnataka Land Revenue Act, 1964 that completely banned the issue of manual RTC by the village accountants. The phase-wise implementation of programme through pilot programmes with the backing of the state's political leadership, setting

---

[28] Merilee S. Grindle. 2000. 'Designing Reforms: Problems, Solutions and Politics,' *Faculty Research Working Paper Series, RWP01–020*, Kennedy School of Government, Harvard University, November, pp. 6–7

up a separate and autonomous Bhoomi monitoring cell for implementation of the Bhoomi system on New Public Management principles, delivery of computerised RTCs (new and old) and variety of other records related to mutation at the Bhoomi kiosks on payment of user fees, leadership of a devoted administrative officer, close partnership with NIC, Bengaluru for web enabled constant upgradation of services, introduction of FIFO principle of integrated mutation process, and the financial sustainability of the programme have sent a clear signal to the taluk officials that the Bhoomi system of land records management has come to stay and is not reversible. On the other hand, Odisha presents a picture of chaotic and messy situation in implementation of the centrally sponsored schemes. Lack of coordination, partnership and leadership has removed any space for innovation and facilitated a vendor driven approach.

ICTs, network governance and politics of public service delivery reform

The success of Bhoomi model of land records management by application of ICTs and the dismal performance of the land records computerisation in Odisha can be understood from the perspective of network governance. The land records computerisation, integration with registry, survey and resurvey, digitisation, scanning and integration with record of rights by the revenue department requires the active participation and support of many other formal and informal agencies. The role of the project leader in providing leadership, his ability and capacity to develop networks of relationship among the public and private sectors for efficient implementation of the project is of vital importance.

During the implementation phase of the Bhoomi system, the state government officials of Karnataka worked closely with NIC officials in Bengaluru and devised the back end and front end software of Bhoomi after taking feedback from the taluk level officials.[29] The Bhoomi system of online land records management has gone out of the direct control of the tahsildars.

[29] Interestingly, NIC, New Delhi in its website has proudly hosted some of its 'most noteworthy projects to offer the viewers/citizens... influencing the lives of citizens of India,' which includes the Bhoomi project. It has projected a number of such initiatives which it claimed to have conceptualised and implemented in many states and central government departments but not a single e-governance project from Odisha has found a place. See http://home.nic.in/nicportal/projects.html (accessed on July 31, 2010).

One could see the kiosk counters at tahsils in Karnataka run its routine activities of delivery of RTCs and other records and receive applications, along with the pre-occupation of tahsildar and deputy tahsildar with other duties like elections, relief operation and law and order problems. But in Odisha, the Bhulekh system is totally dependent on the officials like tahsildar and additional tahsildars. Their pre-occupation with non-revenue works means stoppage in delivery of RoRs copies from the computer cell for days. Both NIC, Bhubaneswar and revenue officials at the directorate blame each other for the present mess in computerisation of land records.

The sustainability and national and international recognition in application of ICTs in online delivery of land records in Karnataka has brought forth some lessons for the execution of the e-governance projects and the politics of administrative reforms. According to Rajeev Chawla, the project leader of Bhoomi and B. V. Sharma and P. V. Bhatt, the NIC officials at Bengaluru, the reasons for successful delivery of public service by Bhoomi application software are:

- Citizen-centric e-governance projects that reduce delay, provide accountability and bring transparency are sustainable as they get public and political support.
- Process of re-engineering may be started in a phased manner to avoid resistance from the officials.
- By incorporating business rules such as first-in–first-out and the delivery of RTCs at cyber kiosks, the discretion available to officers can be controlled.
- Intensive, well organised and regular training to willing and motivated staff to operate e-governance applications and collection of feedback and suggestions from these staff involved in e-governance projects and ensuring secure data-base are prerequisites for any successful e-governance project.
- The manual system of public services needs to be replaced or stopped by the e-governance system for its success.
- Necessity to provide legal support for the procedures and formats of e-governance system.
- Imposition of user charges needed for better service delivery and making the e-governance system sustainable and enabling further reinvestment to upgrade and improve the system.

- E-governance system critically needs the project leader who can take up ownership, monitor and guide the project closely.
- Need monitoring of the project by regular and close interaction with the officials involved and taking in feedback and suggestions.[30]

These experiences gained in the operationalisation of the Bhoomi programme can be compared with the dismal performance of computerisation of land records programme in Odisha. The administrative leadership of Rajeev Chawla in Karnataka could convince the political leadership about the political benefits of Bhoomi without bringing any radical change in the legal and administrative system or upsetting the political coalition of the ruling party. Regular training, interaction and feedback from the willing and motivated staff in taluks and with IT vendors helped the Bhoomi team fine-tune the application software and operationalise it.

In contrast, Odisha has neither shown administrative leadership nor political willingness to implement the land records computerisation innovatively despite central flow of funds and the existent institutional arrangements. Odisha has made some legal and administrative reforms and restructuring of revenue administration in the wake of computerisation of land records but it could not deliver the results as has been done by Karnataka. The network formed by the Bhoomi monitoring cell was able to deliver the land records, meet the needs and interests of stakeholders and implement online and integrated mutation process, and hence was more effective than the vendor-driven network system involved in computerisation of land records in Odisha. The cooperative and inter-organisational networks have, according to Provan and Brinton, a common mechanism for delivery of public services; it becomes effective only when it provides essential services. Public sector networks are effective when they are able to solve the problems of the organisation by enhancing its capacity to solve the problems and the interest of clientele.[31]

---

[30] Rajeev Chawla, B. V. Sharma and P. V. Bhatt. 2008. 'Bhoomi: Key Learnings and New Initiatives' in Ashish Vachhani and N. K. Kumaresan Raja (Eds) *Computerisation of Land Records in India: Achievements and Experiences,* Centre for Rural Studies, LBSNAA, Mussorie, pp. 44–47. These key learnings are quintessentially techno-managerial approaches that rely on the rational solutions through application and adoption of information and communication technologies.

[31] Keith G. Provan and Brinton Milward. 2001. 'Do Networks Really Work? A Framework for Evaluating Public Sector Organisational Networks,' *Public Administration Review,* July-August, 61(4), pp. 419–422.

Growing convergences in policies

States in India have similar nature of administrative set up including revenue administration, notwithstanding several inter-state institutional variations. Both Karnataka and Odisha, like other states, went ahead in implementation of the two centrally sponsored schemes in their own way. The convergences in policy outcomes between the states as found in this study would grow over the time as the techno-managerial strategies and instruments adopted by the policy elites of the two states are similar in nature.

There exists a striking similarity between the two states in implementation of the SRA&ULR programme. In the absence of political support and administrative leadership, the programme for strengthening revenue administration and updating land records was simply confined to scanning of cadastral maps, construction of buildings, setting up training institutes, and purchase of some cutting edge survey instruments that were kept in the store rooms. The programme was basically reduced to a vendor driven one. Interestingly, the performance audits of the Auditor General of India on the working of computerisation of land records programmes in some important states like Uttar Pradesh (2007), Bihar (2009) and Tamil Nadu (2009) bring out some common problems and limitations of technological solutions to India's diverse land records management practices. The audit reports revealed that the problems of hardware, deficient software, lack of trained personnel, erroneous data entry, lack of validation of data, and input controls, tardy progress due to lack of supervision and poor data safety standards have constrained the progress of land records modernisation works in these states. Thus, while highlighting about the positive contributions of ICTs in public service reform, one cannot sweep aside the formidable challenges of adopting ICTs that calls for emergence of 'new patterns of intergovernmental relationships' and 'new order of competence, viability, and innovativeness' among the public officials at taluk/tahsil levels of revenue administration.[32]

The neoliberal techno-managerial strategy of land records modernisation aims at only piecemeal procedural and systemic changes. Both the states have not been able to provide a transparent and corruption free land records management system notwithstanding the techno-managerial solutions offered

[32] Ida R. Hoos. 1966. 'Automation, Systems Engineering, and Public Administration: Observations and Reflections on the California Experience' *Public Administration Review*, 26 (4), December, pp. 311–319.

under the computerisation of land records because of the political compulsion for not adopting the radical reform that would checkmate the 'sources of corrupt income.' It is rightly observed that despite the initial enthusiasm to adopt ICTs, 'the actual benefits offered to citizens are constrained in many cases by persistent efforts to retain access to a rich source of corruption' in the form of bribes paid by the citizens to avail public services.[33]

Both Karnataka and Odisha, despite wide variation in performance of CLR programme implementation, have been able to partially achieve some of the objectives of the scheme. Interestingly, both the states have adopted some of the broad strategies of New Public Management (NPM) and network governance like outsourcing, contracting, partnership arrangements, and charging of user fees in implementation of the programme. Both the states' approach to computerisation has similar apolitical perception that ICTs are value neutral and their adoption and management in land records would offer rational solutions to land records management like enhancing the bureaucratic capacity and efficiency and also promote the techno-managerial notion of transparency and accountability without disturbing the existing land relations and the bureaucratic structure. In delivery of computerised land records on client oriented principle by charging user fees from the farmers and other landholders, the status of citizens/farmers in these mechanism have been reduced to consumers of public service with passive role in the implementation of the programme. As such it is not surprising to find that the success of the programme is evaluated by the amount spent in the execution of the programme, user fees collected and copies of land records delivered.

The generalist revenue officials of Karnataka and Odisha like tahsildars and district collectors do not undertake personal involvement or leadership in the land records computerisation programme, as it does not provide any technical and power payoff. In both the states, computerisation of land records as our studies revealed, has not led to reduction of corruption in mutation and rent seeking behaviour of the taluk/tahsil officials or reduction in the role of intermediaries in land records management or delivery. Computerisation has also failed to reduce the discretionary power of the village accountants/patwaris/revenue inspectors and tahsildars in land records management. Computerisation of land records has been an addition, not replacement of

[33] Jennifer Bussell. 2012. 'E-Governance and Corruption in the States: Can Technology Serve the Aam Aadmi?' *Economic and Political Weekly*, June 23, p. 78.

the existing manual system of land records management in both states and thereby the process of land records management became more complex and cumbersome. The concern for land records data safety, managing the networks of IT vendors and professionals, and coordination with central government agencies like NIC have thrown up new challenges for the capacity of the state bureaucracy to handle such cutting edge technologies. The real estate businesses were more benefited by such computerisation, more than by the common man, as placing the land records on the web helped the builders and real estate companies access the land records of others for acquisition. Anyone can obtain the land records of other landholders by paying user fees, as there is no requirement of the identity proof on such delivery.

The land records computerisation in both the states have taken place through the existing revenue structure without effecting any change in the status and power of tahsildars, revenue inspectors and village accountants. Moreover, the existing old land records, i.e., record of rights and maps have been computerised and digitised without verifying their authenticity. It is therefore not surprising that the problems of erroneous entry of land records data, as pointed by the AG audits, persist in the two states. This provides the revenue functionaries scope for rent-seeking while initiating rectification of such deliberate errors.

The expectation that such computerisation will further the agenda of land reforms is a misconceived notion. The process of computerisation and digitisation of land records with the help of IT vendors and charging of flat user fees in both the states has given a new direction to the public service deliveries. Both the states have adopted a 'client-centred public service delivery' inherent in e-governance concept and in the process storage of information on land records in electronic databases have opened up several possibilities. The application, adoption and management of ICTs in their land records system has given rise to new networks of interdependent relationships among IT vendors, government officials, programme administrators and technical specialists. The states are heavily dependent on consultants for implementing new systems and technology enabled programmes and services.[34]

In such network setting, my comparative study revealed that it is very difficult to enforce accountability and transparency in management of land records computerisation works, even in running the day today works of the

[34] David Brown. 2005. 'Electronic Government and Public Administration,' *International Review of Administrative Sciences*, 71(2), pp. 247–250.

computer kiosks at the tahsil/taluk offices. Partnership with private IT vendors and autonomous style of management has obfuscated the clear costs and benefits of ICT intervention in the Bhoomi system and led to the poor performance and accountability in the vendor driven approach in Odisha.

A comparative analysis of the land records computerisation in two states brings out a critical issue that the so-called best practices of IT enabled service delivery cannot be replicated in other states because of the simple reason that the land records, their institutional arrangements and political-bureaucratic systems are contextual. The Karnataka model is projected as a role model and an instance of best practices in service delivery for other states by the central government. It is interesting to note that Karnataka state is going ahead of its own variant of land records computerisation by adopting its specific tight electronic integration of registry with tahsil in a sustainable basis without seeking regular central assistance whereas Odisha is one of the first states to claim and secure central government funds to implement various components of NLRM Programme despite poor performance on several counts.

Conclusion

The unequal political and economic developments among the states in India have become a matter of 'exciting and important enterprise' for academic pursuits; according to Yogendra Yadav and Suhas Palsikar, the dynamic nature of state politics provides 'a mixed balance sheet of possibilities and anxieties.' To them, the state politics have become autonomous of national politics and each state has developed its particular political culture and vocabulary of politics.[35] The performance of state governments varies and even within the state it varies among the regions. Thus, such different trajectory of Indian states within nation states offers a useful scope for study of a complicated subject like land records which has remained in the State List under the Indian constitution but the central government continues to be a driver of policy reforms. The study of land records computerisation or modernisation across the Indian states brings out the role of political and administrative leadership, ideas, interests and institutions like bureaucratic performances closely. James Manor's advice for

[35] Yogendra Yadav and Suhas Palsikar. 2008. 'Ten Theses on State Politics in India,' *Seminar*, 591. http://www.India-seminar.com/2008/591/591_y_Yadav &_s_palsikar.htm. (accessed on February 13,2011)

the Indian scholars to focus on the 'inspiring, exasperating and vastly complex democracy by doing comparative studies of the different states in the federal system' thus finds relevance in our study.[36]

A comparative study of the land records computerisation in Karnataka and Odisha yields a good source of information on the role of innovative ideas in policy design, interests, institution, administrative and political leaderships, and networks in the process of implementation of the scheme. Some convergence and divergences in terms of implementation of policy and agencies involved help us grapple with challenges of achieving a uniform land records information system as envisaged under the National Land Records Modernisation Programme (NLRMP). Both the states have similar types of problems in land records management, but both have adopted different paths and different policy solutions to deal with the problem. The comparative study of computerisation of land records between the two states revealed puzzling interstate variation in land records management and differential performance levels in implementation of land records computerisation. Karnataka has not sought funds for implementation of NLRM Programme since its inception in 2008-2009 to 2002-2013 and goes ahead in land records modernisation programme on its own funds whereas Odisha has received huge funds from the central government.[37] It challenges the optimism of central government to evolve a uniform coding system of land records and crops and make the land records of the country online and thereby paves the way for land titling to facilitate the growth of land market.

In Karnataka, for example, computerisation of land records has marginally reduced the monopoly of village accountants in initiating mutation of land and issue of RTCs. But in Odisha, this has led to vesting more powers to revenue inspectors like deciding some mutation cases and enhancement of their pay scale. Similarly, the implementation of computerisation of land records has led to the institutionalisation of the Bhoomi monitoring cell, a separate department in Karnataka. In Odisha, the implementing agency, viz. the directorate of land records and survey (DLR&S) has lost its nodality in the process to vendor driven approach to computerisation of land records by OCAC.

---

[36] James Manor. 2010. 'What do they Know of India who Only India Know? The Uses of Comparative Politics,' *Commonwealth and Comparative Studies*, 48(4): November, p. 513.

[37] See *Annual Report, 2012–2013*, Ministry of Rural Development, New Delhi, p. 271.

The divergent outcomes in the computerisation of land records in Karnataka and Odisha led us to conclude that, in Karnataka, a network governance has been successful to deliver some visible results owing to adoption of 'the business rules into the e-governance system' and the administrative leadership and innovation provided by the project leader. In Odisha, the networks that run the process of land records computerisation is more IT vendor driven than led by a project champion or network manager. There is perceptible lack of coordination, trust, and leadership among the major network partners comprising central and state public sector organisations. Computerisation of land records programme is basically an expenditure driven programme in Odisha. This approach will also help us understand why despite being a role model for the online delivery of land records, Karnataka could launch the National Land Records Modernisation Programme (NLRMP) without depending on funds from the central government, whereas Odisha has been one of the states to secure early release of funds for implementation of its vendor driven NLRMP scheme and go ahead in spending the huge allocations without any leadership, coordination and direction. A study conducted by IIM, Ahmedabad on the impact of computerisation of land records in ten states has found that each state government has implemented computerisation of land records (CLR) in their own way without following the best practices of the other states. In Odisha, the land records computerisation has not resulted in any significant impact on the transformation of tahsil administration, rather the amount of bribe money, the role of agents/intermediaries, the number of trips to tahsil offices by the customers and the waiting time to get copy record of rights have only increased.[38]

The differential nature of land records computerisation process in the two states and their achievements underline the fact that the technocratic approach proved to be failure or as a limited success. If viewed from the perspective of the multiple objectives of computerisation land records of the central government, both the states have made differential nature of progress. The central government has taken a very optimistic and uncritical view of the achievements of the centrally sponsored scheme. The Union Rural Development Minister,

[38] Government of India. 2008. *Impact Assessment of e-Governance Projects*, Department of Information Technology, Ministry of Communication and Information Technology, New Delhi, pp. 45–50 ;57.

overlooking the varied nature of achievements, constraints and problems faced in implementation of the CLR programme, even claimed in Parliament:

> The programme of computerisation of land records is a successful application of information technology, which has succeeded in converting a particularly non–transparent system into a transparent system. It has brought accountability in revenue administration, checked corruption and reduced delay and harassment of the people and ensured easy availability of land related data to all concerned.[39]

In Odisha, my study found that the computerisation of land records has in no way reduced the corrupt practices or rent seeking behaviour of the tahsil officials. Computerisation of land records and vesting power in revenue inspectors to dispose mutation has also increased their rent seeking behaviour. In Karnataka, we have found that corruption in delivery of RTC copies has almost been reduced, but introduction of cutting edge ICTs in the integrated mutation process has led to increase of corruption and rent seeking behaviour of the tahsils/taluk officials. Ironically, adoptions of ICTs have thus helped in increasing transparency in land records management as well as corruption in mutation process.

Though Bhoomi has taken a techno-managerial approach, yet it has been able to garner the political support across the party lines and its sustainability has encouraged the government to expand the delivery of land records in rural telecentres. Mark Robinson in his study of some successful governance reforms in India, Brazil and Uganda has observed that three crucial conditions for successful institutional reforms are political support and leadership, bureaucratic and technical competence that enjoy political support, and the incremental process which would enable the political leadership to garner new support base.[40] Innovations in land records management and administrative reforms that are necessary for computerisation of land records need political and bureaucratic champions as well as careful planning, designing, study and

---

[39] See reply to Starred Lok Sabha Question Number 41 on 25 November 2005 by Raghuvansh Prasad Singh, Minister Rural Development at Lok Sabha. (www.parliamentofindia.in accessed on January 5,2011)

[40] Mark Robinson. 2009. 'The Politics of Successful Governance Reforms: Lessons of Design and Implementation,' In Mark Robinson (Ed) *The Politics of Successful Governance Reforms*, London: Routledge, pp. 119–120.

research. Most approaches to public sector reforms need to be addressed to specifics of bureaucratic system and redesigning to fit to local conditions as one has to take into account administrative ecology or a shifting combination of history, culture, politics, economics, sociology, ideology and values of each state in formulating the strategies of reforms.[41] This perspective has immense importance for our comparative approach to study the land records modernisation across the states in India. To Fred Riggs, a comparative study in developing countries would be a fruitful exercise if we take into account politics and administration ecologically. Ecological approach is construed as 'relating the patterns of interaction between the subject of the study and its environment.'[42] Non-administrative factors like geography, history, social structure, religion, etc. are to be appreciated and 'administration and politics are also included as part of the total system.'[43]

The role of administrative leadership is also a critical factor in the successful implementation of complex and highly technical computerisation of land records. Like Karnataka, few other states of Tamil Nadu, Gujarat and Maharashtra have done well in implementation of computerisation of land records scheme. The role of senior bureaucrats in the execution of innovation-oriented public service delivery like computerisation and digitisation of land records has been recognised widely. Peterson has observed that 'the most important factor in the process of an information system is a progressive senior officer who is willing to shoulder the risk of changing the organisation and nurture the information system until it is revered and feared.'[44] The poor development and performance of ICT applications in African bureaucracies is therefore a personal, contingent and vulnerable process. Richard Heeks has observed that in India, majority of ICT projects have ended up with either partial or total or replication or sustainability failures due to 'ignore and idolize' approach. It combined the ignorant approach of senior public

---

[41] Gerald E. Caiden and Pachampet Sundaram. 2004. 'The Specificity of Public Service Reform,' *Public Administration and Development*, 24, pp. 373–376.

[42] Fred W. Riggs. 1962, 'Trends in the Comparative Study of Public Administration' Reprinted in *International Review of Administrative Sciences*, 2010, 76(4), p. 756.

[43] Ibid.

[44] S. B. Peterson. 1998. 'Saints, Demons and Wizards and Systems: Why Information Technology Reforms fail or Underperform in Public Bureaucracies in Africa,' *Public Administration and Development*, 18 (1), p. 44.

servants to information technology and information system who do not consider the role of IT in administrative reform but idolize the approach in which the island like e-government projects succeed due to the role of a project champion and on his transfer, the project collapses due to the absence of the original champion.[45]

[45] Richard Heeks. 2000. 'The Approach of Senior Public Officials to Information Technology Related Reform: Lessons from India,' *Public Administration and Development*, 20, pp. 199–204.

Conclusion

Beyond Techno-Managerial Governance

Land continues to be the most crucial resource for an agrarian economy like India. It has regained importance as India is heading towards massive industrial-urbanisation and more and more agricultural land is being acquired for non-agricultural purposes. The importance of correct and up-to-date land records therefore cannot be underestimated. In addition to this, it is urgent in the context of granting forest land rights to the tribals and forest dwellers, inheritance rights to women, and vanishing common property resources across the country. However, the computerisation of land records programme clearly reveals that the schemes for modernisation of land records are being taken up for an incremental policy shift to facilitate the growth of land market and title regime. The overall performance of computerisation of land records has been a disappointing one if viewed from broader perspectives.

The *National Knowledge Commission Report* (2009) has aptly observed that many of the e-governance programmes are vendor driven and, 'simply digitising the existing government processes merely adds an additional layers of expense, complexity, delay and confusion.'[1]

ICT, public sector reforms and neoliberalism

It has been explained in the theoretical framework that the move towards reinventing government organisations on business principles like New

[1] Government of India. 2009. *Report to the Nation, 2006-2009*, National Knowledge Commission, New Delhi, p. 159.

Public Management and application and adoption of ICTs has its theoretical foundation in the contemporary neoliberal economic policies pursued by the states across the world. India is no exception to this trend. The sole objective of neoliberal structural reforms is to institutionalise the political agenda of a free market. The dominant concern of the administrative structure under the neoliberal economy is to promote the primacy of market values by adopting 'techno-managerial practices and values.'[2]

Since the 1990s, there has been a re-emphasis on the central role of the state and the complementariness or embeddedness of the state and market. The role of the state is now to focus on creating necessary conditions for securing and promoting market and property reforms apart from techno-managerial initiatives. It is therefore natural to expect international donor agencies like World Bank to promote neoliberalism as its sole policy objective with the help of multilateral aid agencies. The role of the state, in World Bank's governance prescription, is to facilitate the growth of private property and free market economy or known as 'pro-market governance.'

The World Bank is currently engaged actively in promoting the adoption of land title regime to facilitate the growth of private property in India. This could be evidenced from the policy shift of computerisation and updating land records for facilitating state-led agrarian change to market base land reform. The main task of the reform of legal institution and laws governing the land relations and transactions is to remove legal restrictions for market-led land transaction and development of private property rights. The objective of the NLRMP is to achieve the conclusive title regime which will formalise the private property rights in India. Such formalisation of property structure in developing countries like India will facilitate investment and growth of land market. [3]

The adoption and application of ICTs has not led to a radical improvement in service delivery and reform of governance in the land records management. The reasons for such limited and slow progress may be analysed and explained with the help of some of the influential writings on the impact of ICTs in

---

[2] Garry Rodan. 2005. 'Neo-Liberalism and Transparency: Political Versus Economic Liberalism' in Richard Robinson (Ed.) *The Neo-Liberal Revolution: Forging the Market State*, New York: Palgrave –Macmillan, pp. 214-215.

[3] Ioannis Glinovas. 2008. 'Neoliberal Law: Unintended Consequences of Market Friendly Law Reforms,' *Third World Quarterly*, 29(6), pp. 1087-1092.

government and governance structure and process. *The Economist* in its special report has noted that:

> Selling new technology to government has brought private contractors a bonanza of many tens of billions of dollars in the past ten years... 'e-government'—using the interactivity and speed of the internet to provide public services has so far mostly meant high cost and poor returns.[4]

An assessment of the empirical research published in more than 1000 issues of recent research journals (published between 1987-2000) on ICTs impact found that though the study reveals that there are substantial information benefits such as improved data access and quality of information for both public administrators and citizens, all empirical studies offer little evidence on the transformative impact of ICTs on the major redistribution of values and power in the public sector or the interaction pattern among officials.[5]

Computerisation of land records: an overall assessment

Based on findings from the comparative study, field work and extensive consultation of literature on this subject, some of the following constraints, impacts and developments have been experienced in land records computerisation and digitisation.

1. The progress of computerisation of land records has been very slow and varies across the states. The states like Karnataka and Tamil Nadu have achieved notable progress in terms of computerisation of land records, digitisation and integration with registry while states like Odisha and Bihar have fared badly in achieving the objective. The Committee on *Unfinished Task in Agrarian Relations (2*009) has rightly estimated that it would take at least 15 to 20 years to complete computerisation of land records in all the states.[6]

---

[4] See 'The Electronic Bureaucrat,' *The Economist*, 16 February, 2008, p. 13.

[5] James N. Danziger and Kim Viborg Anderson. 2001. 'The Impact of Information Technology on Public Administration: An Analysis of Empirical Research from the "Golden Age" Transformation,' *International Journal of Public Administration*, 25(5), pp. 591-627.

[6] Government of India. 2009. *Report of the Committee on State Agrarian Relations and Unfinished Task in Land Reforms*, Ministry of Rural Development, New Delhi, p. 163.

2. Computerisation of land records is being implemented in all states in an isolated manner and has no relation with other supporting programmes of many other departments and branches both at centre and states like drinking water, animal husbandry, soil conservation and agriculture. These departments have developed their own land database without depending on the main land records of the revenue department as there is no linkage among the departments for creation of an integrated database. Even in Karnataka the comprehensive database on land holding, tenancy, ownership, crops and soil type developed by Bhoomi is yet to be used by other line departments.
3. Computerisation and updating land records schemes are being carried out within the existing tahsil/taluk administrative/institutional setups and the much hoped for modernisation of land revenue administration and land records management is yet to be materialised. The attitude of tahsil/taluk officials in Karnataka and Odisha towards digitisation and computerisation of land records remain ambiguous and non committal. Experiences with implementation of land records computerisation and digitisation reveal that the systemic inefficiencies or structural limitation of land records management cannot be addressed partly through computerisation of only RoRs and digitisation of old maps or electronic integration of registry with tahsils. There is a need for looking beyond the techno-managerial approach and address other problems like the capacity and motivation of the revenue officials especially the tahsildar, deputy tahsildar, revenue and survey inspectors and the reorganisation of the taluk/tahsil administration based on purely the insiders perspective of these stakeholders like reducing their regulative and supervisory nature of duties and work burden rather than imposing the vague concept of government process re-engineering. The brief in-service training to revenue officials by information technology and system professionals who are not well acquainted with intricate revenue laws rules and regulations would in no way improve their capacity. This study in Karnataka and Odisha revealed that the tahsildars do not own up the computerisation of land records programme due to their work load as well as absence of any payoff. The centralised monitoring system and outsourcing of the maintenance of running the Bhoomi kiosks in Karnataka has removed any role of the tahsildars to play

in computerisation of land records. The national level committee on *Unfinished Task in Agrarian Relations* (2009) has noted that the more than two decade old computerisation of land records has not been able to impel a change in the attitude of the managers and officials of the programme. 'The moment this change comes about there will be a major revolution in the land management system.'[7]

4. Computerisation of land records has not led to improvement of land records management and reduction of corrupt practices in general. The study in Karnataka has shown that though there has been a reduction of bribe at the Bhoomi kiosk at taluks where copy of RTCs are delivered on demand, but in mutation, and correction of errors in the RTCs, payment of bribe has been widespread and usual. Similarly in Odisha, RoRs are not delivered on demand and it takes at least two days to deliver copies of RoRs in most tahsils and seven days in some bigger tahsil like Bhubaneswar due to various administrative and technical reasons. Mutation cases are disposed of on a pick and choose method in tahsils. Computerisation of land records has only expanded the network of rent-seeking activity to the computer cell and the role of middlemen has been increased who have developed an informal network with the staff at the tahsil office. In a way, one might say that computerisation of land records and mutation has not led to the removal of intermediaries who are the real beneficiaries in the cumbersome and complex mutation process. The techno-managerial approach of land records modernisation has failed to address the problems of land records management like complexity, inefficiency, corruption and unaccountability. The reasons for lack of transparency in land records management also equally lie in non-technical and political factors or grounds which technical solutions cannot address. For example, computerisation has not reduced the rent-seeking attitude of the taluk/tahsil officials as the non formal sources and contacts of the tahsil bureaucracy as agents of 'everyday state' with land mafias, middlemen and real estate firms have remained intact. The non-transparent process of recruitment, posting and transfer of tahsildars and other officials also explains one of the major reasons for rent-seeking activities in tahsils.

[7] Government of India. 2009. *Report of the Committee on State Agrarian Relations and Unfinished Task in Land Reforms*, p. 163.

5. Computerisation of land records may have helped in faster delivery of land records, search and retrieval of land information but it has not led to rationalisation of work load and improved delivery of services. For example, in Odisha, after the delivery of RoRs in mutation cases, intimation slips are required to be sent to the revenue inspector for correction and assessment of land revenue of the newly recorded owners. Record keepers in taluks of Karnataka deal with manual copy of RTCs and mutation extracts of pre-Bhoomi period and in Odisha, the record keeper first effects manual correction in the RoRs (*khatian*) of the mutation case with the help of Amin (a field staff) and sends the case to computer cell for correction and updation of RoRs and generation of computer copies of RoRs. The case records are then sent back to record keepers by the computer cell staff for preservation and issue of intimation slips to revenue inspectors to correct land records and collect land revenues accordingly. The so-called uploading of records on the web takes place a few months later. Computerisation and digitisation of maps are only a part of the important multifarious functions of tahsildars. Many a time it has been observed that the tahsildars either in Karnataka or Odisha remain preoccupied with important nature of non revenue works like law and order, election, relief and rehabilitation, VIP duties and do not give proper attention to the correction of land records at their computer cells and the mutation cases are practically disposed of by the clerical staff and field officials. Even after computerisation of land records and online mutation system in Karnataka, we find the same trend continues and the clerical staffs, the computer trained young village accountants and field level functionaries play a decisive role in the mutation process notwithstanding the introduction of first-in-first-out system in mutation. These petty officials' discretion power is not reduced.
6. The objective of land records computerisation is narrowly focused on techno-managerial strategies and it does not address other burning political-economic issues that are intricately interwoven with land. For example, the NLRMP policy document does not lay out the roadmap in addressing the challenges of tenancy rights, concealed tenancy, reverse tenancy, migration of agricultural/ landless labourers and securing the rights of women in land records which could be a

'great step towards faminisation of agriculture.'[8] Computerisation of textual land records in Odisha, Karnataka and elsewhere has not helped in the detection of benami and other illegal land transaction. Its present policy design of recording the existing landholders and owners excluding other interest holders on the land like the tenants and sharecroppers will in no way help in the detection and regularisation or abolition of tenancy/share cropping in cultivation and other aspects of land reforms like detection of ceiling surplus land. Computerisation of land records will certainly be a bulwark against land frauds, provided its land database of both RoRs and maps remain correct and continuously updated and secure.

7. Computerisation of land records in Karnataka and Odisha has not been able to promote transparent and accountable administration and reduced corruption. My field visits to Karnataka and Odisha has led me to observe that introducing some supply side and vendor driven ICT innovation in land records delivery in a multifaceted and multipurpose office like tahsil would not remove institutional barriers. It may lead to reduction of petty corruption and simplification of transaction like delivery of existing RTC/RoRs rather than providing transparent land records management. The problem of land records management is more a political than a techno-managerial matter. My study of the computerisation of land records (CLR) in the two states has revealed that computerisation could have reduced corruption provided a simple mechanism was devised in the correction of land records or mutation process which would have discouraged choosing a corrupt practice and establishment of a monitoring mechanism which could have increased the likelihood of being penalised.[9] In both the states, the computerisation of land records software is a very comprehensive and complicated one which is beyond the comprehension of the generalist tahsildars and deputy tahsildars

[8] Government of India. 2006. 'Towards Faster and More Inclusive Growth: An Approach to Eleventh Five Year Plan,' Planning Commission, Yoyana Bhawan, New Delhi, December, p. 29.

[9] Murali Patibandla and Amal Sanyal. 2009. 'Corruption: Market Reform and Technology' in Rajesh Kumar and Murali Patibandla (Eds) *Institutional Dynamics and the Evolution of the Indian Economy*, New Delhi: Palgrave-Macmillan, p. 122.

and could be handled only by the specially trained computer system operators and consequently there is absence of direct monitoring of the computerised delivery of land records on the part of these key officials. The computerisation of the land records offers a partial solution to the multifaceted problem of corruption and lack of transparency in the land records management.

8. Computerisation of land records has led to a speedier delivery of textual land records (RoRs) in Karnataka and Odisha though rent-seeking behaviour has not been eliminated altogether. The data entry operators in Odisha and the computer trained young village accountants in Karnataka have emerged as the new petty rent-seeking agents in the process due to their critical position in running the computer cells.
9. It is too early to find partial nature of land records computerisation in Odisha and Karnataka has led to reduction of litigation and land disputes given the growing pressure on land for non agricultural purposes, granting of forest rights to forest dwellers, recording rights of women in land records, growth of tenancy and concealed tenancy, reverse tenancy and persistence of corrupt practices in tahsils/taluks.
10. Computerisation of land records in Karnataka and Odisha has not helped in the reduction of monopoly or discretion power of the revenue officials like village accountants and revenue inspectors and it would be naïve to say that corruption has been eliminated or reduced on the whole in the delivery of computerised land records. The 'street level bureaucrats' like the village accountants/revenue inspectors, play an important role in the execution of policy and enforcing regulations; they deal directly with an agent of the 'everyday state' and exercise substantial discretion in implementation of policies related to dynamic nature of land-agrarian relations that cannot be turned into 'system level bureaucracy or screen level bureaucracy.' The field based decision-making processes of the revenue bureaucracies, their professional knowledge and discretions are too difficult to be routinised and programmed into the computer's software design. This would seriously affect the wide-ranging nature of the decision making power of the field-level public functionaries. The street-level bureaucrats can be made accountable to justify their decisions or grounds of consideration, but transparency and accountability does not develop easily, neither in the algorithms of the computer process

nor in the discretionary power of the system level bureaucracies dealing with the data and information and processed into decision.[10] In Karnataka, the complicated and integrated mutation process has led to increase in rent-seeking behaviour and growth of a new network among the village accountants, middlemen, kiosk operators and other revenue officials. In Odisha, computerisation has not led to reduction of corruption either in delivery of RoRs or mutation cases. Rather the monopoly and discretion power of both tahsildars and revenue inspectors have been expanded under the new mutation rule that empower the revenue inspectors to dispose uncontested mutation cases and tahsildars to confirm such cases.

11. Computerisation of land records has improved the transparency in land records by putting these on the websites and the tampering of the records has been reduced but the safety of land records database still depend a lot on the type of data safety standards maintained by NIC and the integrity of tahsil officials empowered to effect changes in the RoRs. In Odisha, the tahsildars and additional tahsildars do not find enough time to minutely check the RoRs to be corrected before putting their thumb print authentication (bio-metric log-in) due to their preoccupation with other works and depend on the data entry operators to do the critical work of correction.
12. Partial nature of the computerisation of land records has not led to transition from the so-called street level bureaucrats in land records management to system level bureaucrats dominated by IT professionals. Rather there is growing interdependence between the revenue officials and the data entry operators, software and hardware professionals both in public (NIC) and private sectors (IT vendors) in delivery of land records and mutation. The dynamic and complex nature of land records and software on land records mutation has raised important problems of coordination and accountability between the IT professionals and the revenue officials dealing with manual system and the capacity of the latter to handle such cutting edge

[10] Mark Bovens and Stavros Zourdis. 2002. 'From Street Level to System Level Bureaucracies: How Information and Communication Technologies is Transforming Administrative Discretion and Constitutional Control,' *Public Administration Review*, 62(2), March-April, pp. 175-183.

technologies. Moreover the land records computerisation cannot be a substitute to manual system of land records management difficult tasks like field verification of land use, measurement, detection of encroachment, survey and settlement, ground truthing exercise and settlement of boundary disputes require field works which cannot be handled by the computer hardware and software system. As it is aptly observed that 'excessive dependence on sophisticated tools may help us to make an impact in meetings and seminars, but does not improve the ground situation.'[11]

13. In these techno-managerial reforms, the role of administrative leadership in the whole process of computerisation, digitisation and interlinking of land records is vital. The role of the project champion who continued nearly ten years to oversee the implementation of Bhoomi system of online delivery of land records in Karnataka and his return to the said post after his brief transfer; his relative stability of tenure in institutionalising the Bhoomi model of e-governance and his interest in bringing out innovations in ICT applications with the help of NIC and consultants in Karnataka proved crucial in the successful operationalisation of Bhoomi. This also explains the reasons for poor nature of achievements in Odisha although it has secured more funds from central government than Karnataka. Computerisation of land records and its interrelated works demand a great deal of partnership, ownership and coordination on the part of project leader. But the implementation of CLR programme in Odisha has revealed that the post of the director, land records has been treated as a non-rewarding post or what has been aptly referred as a 'dry post.'[12] The role of administrative leadership is important

[11] Naresh C. Saxena. 2005. 'Updating Land Records: Is Computerisation Sufficient?,' *Economic and Political Weekly*, January 22, p. 319.

[12] Interview and discussion with Mr Rajeev Chawla, IAS, Ex-Special Secretary, Bhoomi, on 15 May 2010 in Bengaluru. He also wondered as why an IAS officer like him would come and work hard and take ownership in this highly complicated institutional and legal system in land record management as the post of land record director is a 'dry and not a lucrative' one. Similarly N.C. Saxena, IAS (Retd.) has observed that the post of Director, Land Records in Bihar is considered as a 'punishment posting' meant for those who fall out the political favour. See Naresh C. Saxena. 2005. 'Updating Land Records: Is Computerisation Sufficient?', p. 317.

as he designs the implementation of the programme by involving a variety of central and state government agencies and departments and other stakeholders and convinces the political leadership in the state of the political payoffs for its acceptability.

14. The land records modernisation programme has involved spending of huge amounts of public resources mostly through partnership or outsourcing to private IT vendors which appeared as 'vehicle of choice' for execution of complex and dynamic ICT strategies in the states. More than two decade old programme of computerisation of land records has also raised concern over the capacity of the state bureaucracy to manage the complex, dynamic, and often multi-partner relationships that involve considerable sharing of authority, responsibility, financial resources, information and risks with the private IT vendors. It has also thrown up challenges in management like establishing right partnership arrangements with private vendors and firms, finding right partners and management of relationship with partners in a network settings and securing public interests thereby as delivery of land records depends on successful partnership with private and public agencies.[13]

    Implementation of the CLR programme in Odisha has brought out a network of IT vendors and top revenue officials and IT department who have seised the opportunity in maximising their self-interest as the complex programme involves huge lucrative contracts to IT vendors on a long term and sustained basis. The Bhoomi model of online land records system could see the light of the day due to an innovative policy design of an IAS officer who could manage to secure the political support as it entailed an incremental reform and politically beneficial. The village accountants in Karnataka were not supportive to the project still they could be made to fall in line due to the strategic policy design, political support by the state Chief Minister and administrative leadership by the project champion.

15. The National Informatics Centre has been playing a crucial and integral role right from the beginning of conceptualisation and

[13] John Langford and Yvonne Harrison. 2001. 'Partnering for e-Government: Challenges for Public Administrators,' *Canadian Journal of Public Administration*, 44(4), Winter, December, pp. 393-416.

implementation of the land records computerisation programme. Initially the computerisation of land records was confined to the RoRs but was later on extended to digitisation of maps of villages and more complicated phase of integration of textual and spatial map integration. The performances of NIC in the later phase of works of computerisation such as digitisation of maps, integration with textual records and updating are not successful. In Karnataka, the Bhoomi model succeeded in online delivery of land records due to a robust and close partnership built by the revenue department of Karnataka and the NIC unit Bengaluru and its continuous standardisation is a proof of the extent of partnership and networking between the central and state government agencies. In Odisha, on the other hand, a different picture of lack of coordination and trust between the two implementing agencies emerged. The NIC has confined its role primarily to a technology service provider and has failed to take up ownership role in the vendor driven computerisation programme initially laid out by it. Despite its long experience and domain knowledge in handling the government projects, NIC lacks the capacity to develop user-friendly software for land records computerisation, updation, online mutation and integration of map with RoRs of state specific land records which could be easier for the direct supervision and monitoring by tahsildars. The organisation boasts of the land records computerisation as one of its most successful e-governance initiatives but the poor documentation of its so-called success and lack of cooperation to the research works raise an open question mark over its capability. Perhaps aware of the dismal performance in its costly and complicated nature of the computerisation programme through the IT vendors, its officials at the state and national levels always interpret their role as a mere technical consultant of the programme like land records modernisation and shift the blame to revenue officials for the poor performance. The technocrats of NIC lack basic understanding or underestimate the importance of non technical factors in adoption of ICTs that impede their so-called technical prescription thanks to their poor social science perspective in the politics of democratic governance and policy process in a pluralistic society like India. That the bureaucracy is a political actor and to bring out an organisational reform or change through adoption of technology is quintessentially a political matter which cannot be addressed by software or hardware packages is sadly beyond the comprehension of NIC's information technology and system professionals. Many of its technical staff at the district informatics centres and state informatics centre in Odisha lack creative knowledge and innovation in improving the user-friendly software on land records mutation.[14] The NIC's technical personnel are to be blamed for designing client oriented software for delivery of land records; reducing the role of the citizen as a mere consumer in availing services from the state run land records kiosks or counters; its failure to devise strategies innovatively to reduce the growing dependence on IT vendors and information system professionals and its inability to control their growing influence in the computerisation of land records programme design.

16. The central government has been a driving force in implementation of the land records computerisation and modernisation programme since its formulation and conceptualisation in the 1980s to this date though the subject matter of land record management falls under the State List of the Constitution of India. The central government has been playing a vital role in the implementation and further expansion of the land records modernisation programmes by way of issuing guidelines, financing, providing training to the officials and rebuilding the state level training institutions through its agencies like DOLR, NIC, Survey of India, National Remote Sensing Centre, Forest Survey Institute and C-DAC. It has undertaken evaluation studies to find out the problems and achievements of the programme. By and large, the central government encourages the state to go for expenditure driven progrmme implementation without bothering to study the long-term and short-term impact on governance process and system. It has not yet undertaken multidisciplinary studies on modernisation of land records. The proceedings released at the national level review meetings and workshops on NLRMP end up in the exhorting of states to spend the allotted funds in time so that

[14] Interviews with the additional tahsildars in charge of record rooms in Talcher, Berhampur, Malkanagiri, Dhenkanal, Khordha and tahsildar of Tirtol tahsil in Jagatsingpur in October 2010.

it could secure more funds for them from the finance ministry. It is frequently seised up with deciding the uniform cost to be borne by the states and the Union government in computerisation, digitisation and application of modern survey equipment in land records updation. Such strategy of implementation has led to the development of a vendor driven approach to the land records modernisation as has been found in Odisha. The central government admits that NLRMP is a 'difficult and complex high-tech programme' yet it shies away in undertaking continuous independent and critical evaluation of the programme. Interestingly, we find the similarity in approach to implementation in land records computerisation programme of both the Central government and Odisha government. Both the governments' departments only focus the progress of land records modernisation in terms of funds spent and the quantitative targets achieved with the help of vendors. Despite the complex nature of the programme, there is low priority in monitoring the implementation of the programme on some of the parameters like financial viability, ease of use by the officials, assessment of in-house capacity, volume of transactions, appropriateness of technological solutions, adequacy of process reengineering, generalist officials ability and motivation to manage difficult and dynamic technological solutions in network with private IT vendors. Such monitoring would have provided critical inputs for further streamlining the policy. Similarly, critical policy evaluation studies have not been under taken focusing upon how far the techno-managerial solutions/strategies in land records management have been able to attain its objectives and promoted bureaucratic efficiency.

The central government has projected before the departmental Parliamentary Standing Committees as well as in Parliament that CLR is a demand driven scheme and the states are responsible for implementation of the programme and it releases funds to the states depending on their demands to such funds within the guidelines formulated by it. Though it has shifted the responsibility to the state for poor performance in implementation, yet it does not take 'hands off' attitude in the process. It has recently prepared a draft land title policy and it is also taking steps to go ahead in implementation of the programme in Union Territories. By periodic holding of national workshops in cooperation with the World Bank's so-called experts on the land records of India, such as in 2006 and 2010 and organising national conferences of state chief ministers, revenue ministers and revenue secretaries, the central government has been able to shape and redesign the policy of land records computerisation in the country. It has gone ahead with providing the oft repeated 'hand-holding' support to the states implementing the programmes. It has shown its determination in forcing the states to undertake 'hi-tech surveys' of land (survey with modern equipment) for switching over to the new land title regime. The central government has gone ahead in organising the technical fairs of NLRMP and playing the role as a facilitator in advocating the state governments to adopt modern survey equipment in their land records out of the funds provided by it. In short, the central government has not remained confined to the 'catalyst or coordination' role. Rather it is vigorously pursuing the states to go ahead to modernise their land records and revenue administration[15] without affecting the existing iniquitous land relations so that the states could be able to embrace the neoliberal policy of the land title guarantee regime. The central government also aims at development of a national land records database for multiple uses in investment and planning and with the help of the National Informatics Centre, it has taken steps to develop a UNICODE system for the land records in India.

Both the National eGovernance Plan (NeGP) and the National Land Record Management Plan (NLRMP) are top down initiatives by the policy elites of India and the techno-managerial design of these policies have based on premise of ushering in the neoliberal agenda of 'good governance.' This approach is based on the assumption that application and adoption of cutting edge ICTs will be able to remove deficiencies and constraints of the Indian bureaucratic structure as ICTs are viewed as a neutral tool. For example, the World Bank in its report on *Reforming Public Institutions and Strengthening Governance:*

[15] Interviews and discussions with Rita Sinha, IAS, Secretary, on 22 July 2010 and Mr Chinmay Basu, IAS, Additional Secretary on 21 March 2010, Department of Land Resources, MORD, GOI, New Delhi. See also the Lok Sabha Question no 1718 answered on 10 December 2010 and Question no 1602 answered on 8 March 2002 by Minister, Rural Development in Lok Sabha web site.

> *A World Bank Strategy (2000)* has noted that application and adoption of ICTs especially the internet will promote accountability, cut red tape and corruption, harassment and enhance access to public information and services leading to transparency and equity. The report is however silent over the recurrent cost of such initiative.[16]

Beyond techno-managerial reform

The centrally sponsored scheme of land records modernisation in India (CLR/SRA&ULR /NLRMP) drives home to the point of the limits of apolitical techno-managerial initiatives that do not address to its divergent land records. Rather it has added to the problems of complexity, cost, duplication, bureaucratic leadership, motivation, and capability. Computerisation of land records process have been irreversible but managing further advance like constant upgradation of hardware, software, electronic equipment, training and capacity building of the bureaucracy and a network of generalist revenue officials with IT vendors and system specialists equally bug down the process. The World Bank's observation on ICTs in land administration merits a reference here, 'The application of high-tech solutions to a critical legal system such as land register should only be done once the capacities to maintain are ensured full.'[17] Thus ICT application has not been able to change the silos of the existing structure of multiple institutions responsible in the land records management. The state in India however has succeeded in depoliticising the land records management that reflects unequal economic, social and political relationships and reduced NLRMP as a techno-managerial initiative for consumer citizens. The Indian state's apolitical strategy to the land records modernisation initiatives also explains the main reason for its poor performance. Implementation of e-government or e-governance strategy crucially depends upon the commitment and a broad agreement among the political leadership in a democratic country. Similarly, the policy shift from the presumptive nature of land records and state-led land reform regime to market-led agrarian reform and conclusive title system needs a massive political consensus for its success.

---

[16] World Bank. 2000. *Reforming Public Institutions and Strengthening Governance: A World Bank Strategy*, Washington: November, p. 28.

[17] Edward Cook et al. 2008. 'Information and Communication Technology in Land Administration Projects,' Agriculture and Rural Development, *World Bank, Policy Note No-43556*, Issue. 38, February, p. 3.

The ongoing land records modernisation programme's success in a few states and their varied nature of performance in the implementation of the centrally sponsored schemes has clearly revealed the importance of the state level political leadership in India. On the other hand, the NLRMP is designed as a highly technological programme to 'make all land records computerised, easily available, accurate and real time i.e. accurate at any given time' overlooking the historically diverse and complex nature of land records and political and economic implication of such policy. It is also falsely claimed that as textual land records are put on the web and digitisation and integration of textual and spatial maps are being taken up, the age old deficiencies inherent in the land records will be removed in the process. [18]

The application, adoption and management of ICTs have several implications, challenges and constraints. The poor performance of Odisha in implementation of the scheme and relatively better performance of Karnataka and the overall slow progress in land records computerisation in other states of India need to be seen in the context of state specific political and administrative factors. The Karnataka model of computerisation of land records also has several bottlenecks like managing the complex ICTs application in networks with private vendors and pervasive corruption in correction of land records, and lack of involvement of revenue officials in outsource driven programme. It may be added that the difficulties found in the process of computerisation and digitisation of land records in the two Indian states can be generalised as similar problems faced by other states. The need for political and administrative leadership support and their full fledged commitment and involvement; minimising the risk of critical projects; complete awareness of capabilities to handle complex digitisation and technical nature of information; removal of cultural barriers in the minds of public managers about access to information; convincing the stakeholders of an open approach to the adoption of new technology; maintaining a continuous communication between top and bottom up hierarchy and open mind for feedback from the below; involvement of frontline or lower level officials in designing the innovation; incremental nature of adoption; addressing the interdependence of the organisations and its level of red tape are some of the challenging issues in computerisation of land records.

---

[18] See 'NLRMP: An Integrated Approach to Land and Property Management' an interview with Rita Sinha, IAS, Secretary, Department of Land Resources, MORD, GOI, in *Informatics*, 18(1) July,2009, p. 8-9, by Vinay Thakur, Director, NLRMP cell of NIC.

The problem of sharing information on the land records to civil society and market organisations are also posing a difficult challenge to data security and safety. The management of public IT projects is very challenging in nature due to its prohibitive cost on man, machine and infrastructure, the budgetary constraint, and the growing number of failed e-government projects. Further, as land records are computerised and uploaded on the web for online delivery on demand, the problem of risk in securing information and maintaining safety and privacy arises. The risk of managing information and trust of public on land records in the information age has become an important issue. [19]

The earlier review of literature on e-government studies tell us that ICTs are not value neutral tools and high level of technological emphasis has been its great limitation as well as the main reason for its failure. Techno-managerial design in the computerisation of land records cannot provide transparency, accessibility, accountability and democratic participation rather it reinforces the status quo and benefits the wealthy and powerful. The computerisation of land records and its online delivery require more thrust on politics of coordination and network than techno-managerialism.[20] Such approach has been proved wrong in many of the studies on e-governance. Most of the studies highlight the reinforcing of the pre-existing institutional-political structures and practices by the e-government initiatives.[21]

---

[19] See Miriam Lips et al. 2005. 'Public Administration in the Information Society: Essays on Risk and Trust', *Information Polity*, 10, pp. 1-9., David Landbergen and George Wolken Jr. 2001. 'Realising the Promise: Government Information System and the Fourth Generation of Information Technology' *Public Administration Review*, March-April, 61(2), pp. 206-208., Nada Korac Kakbadse and Alexander Kouzmin. 1996. 'Innovation Strategies for the Adoption of New Information Technology in Government: An Australian Experience,' 16, *Public Administration and Development*, pp. 317-330., William Cats-Baril and Ronald Thompson. 1995. 'Managing Information Technology Projects in Public Sector,' *Public Administration Review*, 55(6), November-December, pp. 559-566.

[20] See for example Jonathan Davies. 2009. 'The Limits of Joined-up Government: Towards A Political Analysis,' *Public Administration*, 87(1), p. 94.

[21] See for example Vincent Pina et al. 2007. 'Are ICTs Promoting Accountability?: A Comparative Analysis of e-Government Developments in 19 OECD Countries,' *Critical Perspectives on Accounting*, 18, pp. 583-602. Wilson Wong and Eric Welch. 2004. "Does E-Government Promote Accountability? A Comparative Analysis of Website Openness and Government Accountability," *Governance: An International Journal Policy, Administration, and Institutions*, 17(2), pp. 275-297.

Taking a cautious approach, David Coursey and Donald F Norris have suggested that instead of expecting dramatic results from e-government we have to contend with incremental changes. Studies and experiments show that e-government is 'what it is not what it was predicted to be.'[22] The overemphasis on the techno-managerial approach and underestimating of other variables like human and political factors result in building oversold and overoptimistic assumption about the capacities of institutional transformation by ICTs in public service delivery. Silvia Bolgherini has aptly observed that massive technological application and adoption will in no way reinvent the government rather the political, cultural barriers, administrative culture, as well country specific traditions play decisive role in the failure and success of e-government initiatives.[23]

The emerging challenges in the computerisation of land records

Some of the emerging issues which have theoretical as well practical relevance have come to the fore in the process of policy implementation. These are issues institutional change, network governance, democratic governance and consumer citizenship, role of central government, the capacity of the bureaucracy to implement modern land records system, emerging concept of private property and the neoliberal policy of the state. It may be argued here that the comparative study of the computerisation of land records with three variables like state, ICTs and governance cannot be confined to narrow evaluative approaches which are being resorted by some so-called research and consultancy organisations.[24]

---

[22] David Coursey and Donald F. Norris. 2008. 'Models of E-Government: Are they Correct? An Empirical Assessment,' *Public Administration Review*, 68(3), May-June, p. 534.

[23] Silvia Bolgherini. 2007. 'The Technology Trap and the Role of Political and Cultural Variables: A Critical Analysis of the E-Government Policies,' *Review of Policy Research*, 24(3), pp. 259-274.

[24] Some of these institutions like LBSNAA, Mussorie has done only evaluative research by figuring out some of the quantitative data on the number of computerised copies issued and the waiting time taken. Other critical theoretical and substantive issues intricately related to the 'information age' reform appear to beyond their conception and understanding.

It is interesting to note that the state in India has been playing a critical role in the process of governance reforms through modernisation of revenue administration and land records management. The governance process and system is state centric in which the state in India decides and formulates policy and in the second aspect, the state again enables and facilitates the growth of network governance to implement the complex and challenging programme of land records modernisation as it lacks technical skills and knowledge in adopting the cutting edge technologies in land records modernisation.

(i) Institutional change

The application and adoption of ICTs, new organisational arrangements, new policies of service delivery and reform of the existing institutions for implementation of the CLR programme may affect the internal and external institutional relationship, networks of influence and power relations in the institutions but such changes will be incremental and imperceptible. The change is understood as 'complex interdependent' process. The public institutions as well the public bureaucrats are political actors and share features of new institutionalism and are resistant to change. [25] New institutionalism acknowledges the role of technical factors in institutional change but not as a determinist way. Douglas North writes—

> It is the combination of the constitutional rules with the associated moral and ethical codes of behaviour that underlies the stability of institutions and makes them slow to change. The combination produces ingrown patterns of behaviour which like the capital stock, tend to be changed only incrementally.[26]

The new institutionalist perspective of institutional change will help us to understand the complex nature of change in computerisation of land records

[25] Lawrence Pratchett and Melvine Wingfield. 1996. 'Petty Bureaucracy and Woolly minded Liberalism? The Changing Ethos of Local Government Officers,' *Public Administration*, 74(4), pp. 639-656; Anil Hira and Ron Hira. 2000. 'The New Institutionalism: Contradictory Notions of Change,' *American Journal of Economics and Sociology*, 54 (2), April, pp. 274-275.

[26] Douglas C. North. 1981. 'A Theory of Institutional Change and the Economic History of the Western World' in *Structure and Change in Economic History*, New York: W. W. Norton & Company, p. 205.

which is deep rooted in history, culture and custom. Although computerisation of land records has led to the speedy delivery of tamper-proof land records, but it is difficult to perceive any institutional transformation or change.

(ii) Land records, democratic governance and consumer citizenship

There has been a growing concern among the scholars that e-governance model only reduces the citizen to the status of a mere consumer, as the architecture of the system is based on the client oriented business principle. In the Bhoomi model of land records management in Karnataka and the Bhulekh model of land records management in Odisha, we have shown that the delivery of the land records are being made on payment of uniform user fees by the land owners to make the services sustainable. The state is now playing the role of service provider and the role of political leadership is uncertain and unclear in the market and consumer orientation of service delivery (which is one of the characteristics of NPM). Such techno-managerial initiative based on NPM principle, according to Aberbach and Christensen, will have a profound effect on the way the role of citizen in the democracy is defined and will depoliticise the public decision-making process.[27]

The NPM model of public service, it is rightly argued, will make for passive citizenship.[28] We may agree with Richard C. Box, who has forcefully argued that the movement for introducing market model in delivery of public service like land records at tahsil/taluk computer kiosks, has resulted in the 'loss of citizen self determination in the creation of public policy and operations of public organisations' because the notion is revolved around the 'idea of happy citizens rather than involved citizens.' Government is not a business rather it involves a collective efforts and involvement of citizens in running its affairs. [29] There can be no dispute about the fact that citizens appreciate the quicker delivery of services but that does not preclude their right to exercise their

---

[27] Joel D. Aberbach and Tom Christensen. 2005. 'Citizens and Consumers,' *Public Management Review*, 7 (2), pp. 225-246.

[28] Robert Kraemer. 1999. 'Weaving the Public into Public Administration,' *Public Administration Review*, 59 (1), pp. 89-92.

[29] Richard C. Box. 1999. 'Running Government like a Business: Implications for Public Administrations Theory and Practice,' *American Review of Public Administration*, 29(1), March, p. 35.

option to participate and determine the policy and monitor its implementation. This notion of democratic governance goes beyond the steering role of the government (policy decision) and rowing role (policy implementation) of non-state actors like market and civil society. At the heart of citizenship lies the governments choice to adopt some efficient business methods for proper delivery of services but, the involvement of citizens, public officials and politicians should be the foremost requirement instead of the public service professionals and IT vendors'. [30]

There is no disagreement with the idea that the application of ICTs may improve the public service delivery of land records useful for all citizens but it is now reasonably apprehended that the client orientation of e-government architecture will cause a fundamental impact on the relationship between the state and citizens in a democratic country like India. The question is whether such preoccupation with consumer oriented public service delivery will be able to serve the interest of India's common men and women who constitute more than three fourths of its population and 86 percent among whom are illiterate and vulnerable. The challenges that the advocates for NPM style administrative reforms avoid to deal are: what values and models of democratic governance does the electronic delivery of services carry or is embedded with? Does this electronic service delivery favour the notion of passive citizenship and frustrate the democratic ideals of active citizenship? Thus, the new mode of service delivery tied to NPM principles definitely requires critical studies in terms of its impacts on democratic accountability, representativeness and citizen protection. [31]

The online delivery of public services like land records on customer driven philosophy of e-commerce at public sector organisation like tahsil is unworkable and may not provide democratic empowerment and citizen participation. Robert B. Denhardt and Janet Vinzant Denhardt have made a powerful attack on NPM's normative model of redefining public administration and delivery

---

[30] Ibid, p. 40.

[31] Victor J.J.M Bekkers and Stavros Zouridis. 1999. 'Electronic Public Service Delivery in Public Administration: Some Trends and Issues,' *International Review of Administrative Sciences*, 65, pp. 183-195; Arjun Sengupta et al. 2008. 'India's Common Man: Who are They? How many are They? How do They Live?' *Economic and Political Weekly*, March 15, pp. 49-63; J. L. Perry. 2007. 'Democracy and the New Public Service,' *The American Review of Public Administration*, 33(1), pp. 3-16.

of public services for using market mechanism and terminology. According to the Denhardts, public servants do not deliver customer service but they deliver democracy. They have suggested New Public Service in place of NPM in which the citizen and public interest is central to any public policy.

> We argue…that in a democratic society, a concern for democratic values should be a paramount in the way we think about systems of governance. Values such as efficiency and productivity should not be lost, but should be placed in the larger context of democracy, community and public interest.[32]

Such an approach emphasises the democratic and public interest over the marketisation of public service as relevant for India's democratic governance. In more than six decades of its working, Indian democracy it has been following the path of 'selective availability' of its resources; has failed to consolidate basic conditions of procedural democracy and made deviations from its avowed path of welfare, equity, justice and development. The state's apparatus for social transformation, it is argued, is inclusive and open to the rich and powerful but exclusive to the poor and less powerful. 'The core projects of the state are rendered differently open to negotiation' and the democratic state in India suffers from inauthenticity and unrepresentativeness.'[33]

Notwithstanding the claim to provide citizen services at the doorstep or open to citizen feedback, the cyber kiosk model of public service delivery is based on the principle of customer-business relationship with little scope for the participation of public. We have argued in the earlier chapters that the modernisation of land records (CLR) programmes are imposed by the policy elites and such policy objective is driven by NPM principle of techno-managerial approach rather than any explicit egalitarian concern like land reforms. The wholesale and uncritical adoption of market mechanism and redefinition of citizen as a consumer, corporatisation of public service delivery agencies and charging of user fees are guided by market principles. Treating citizens as customers in delivery of public services contradict their rights and duties as a citizen when pitted against consumer of services. Citizens'

---

[32] Robert D. Denhardt and Janet Vinzant Denhardt. 2000. 'The New Public Service: Serving rather Than Steering,' *Public Administration Review*, 60(6), p. 557.

[33] Niraja Gopal Jayal. 2001. 'The State and Democracy in India or What happened to Welfare, Secularism and Development' in Niraja Gopal Jayal (Ed) *Democracy in India*, New Delhi: Oxford University Press, pp. 219-221.

role go beyond mere passive consumer of services to their inherent right to decide what the government should do for them and exercise their choice in availing the services. It also harms the citizenship of the poor and weak for whom the universal nature of public service is no longer free or nominally charged. The values of consumer oriented society will ultimately replace constitutional democracy.[34] Thus the rules of the democratic interactions between the e-government service recipients and government is unworkable and not attractive as the current e-government architecture is based on business principles and customer relationship management.[35]

(iii) Capability approach to development and computerisation of land records

According to Amartya Sen, the primary objective of development should be expansion of capabilities and removal poverty, social and economic constraints, deprivation, neglect of public facilities, repressive state machinery etc. The 'primary aim and principal means' of development is the expansion of freedom. Capability approach for Sen, 'sees human life as a set of 'doings and beings' we may call them functionings...' Capabilities here refers 'to choose a life one has reason to value' and the concept of 'functionings...reflects the various things a person may value doing or being.' [36] He has pointed out five types of 'instrumental freedoms' of interconnectedness and mutually reinforcing nature like economic opportunities, political freedoms, social facilities, transparency guarantees and protective security. Therefore, to view development as the process of expansion of the freedom or capability, it needs to be focused on the aims of the developmental projects or public policies that aim to achieve the promotion of the instrumental freedoms stated before. People need to be involved in the formulation of policy not as mere passive recipients of state led

---

[34] Joseph A. Regnato. 1997. 'Is Citizen A Customer?,' *Public Productivity and Management Review*, 20 (4), June, pp. 397-404 and John Kane and Haig Patapan. 2006. 'In Search of Prudence: The Hidden Problem of Managerial Reform,' *Public Administration Review*, September-October, p. 716.

[35] Patrice A. Dutil. et al. 2007. 'Rethinking Government- Public Relationships in a Digital World: Customers, Clients or Citizens?,' *Journal of Information Technology and Politics*, 4(1), pp. 283-84.

[36] Amartya Sen. 1999. *Development As Freedom*, New Delhi: Oxford University Press, pp. 74-75.

developmental programme. Sen has forcefully putforth that 'what people can possibly achieve is influenced by economic opportunities, political liberties, social powers, and the enabling conditions of good health, basic education, and the encouragement and cultivation of initiatives.' [37] Amartya Sen asserts that to view capability approach as person's freedom to choose between different ways of living it can be accepted as an alternative route to evaluate public policies instead of utility based approach which 'fails to a person's real deprivation.'[38] Thus, the capability approach can be taken as an important determinant of the developmental policy goals of National Land Records Modernisation Programme.

It is necessary to examine whether delivery of online land records or its updation by the cumbersome computer system will help the farmers deal with the social, political and economic constraints in their lives so that they can lead a life which they find worth pursuing. The role of the land records modernisation programme in increasing human capabilities, its direct importance to the wellbeing, economic production and capacity of the people, its indirect role in influencing social change like promoting land reforms must be taken into account while examining the tall and oversold claims of the cyber optimist bureaucrats and technocrats. Surely, the delivery of the computerised land records or online mutation will have no meaning for the poor farmers if their social, political and economic constraints are not addressed beforehand. Running for several months to get mutation of a piece of land even after paying bribes at all stages of the tahsil hierarchy and finally seeing the land records on the web in no way enables the farmers to enhance their capability.

(iv) Capacity of bureaucracy

More than two decades of implementation of the computerisation of land records programmes has raised an important question on the capacity of the Indian bureaucracy to perform, given its historic failure in implementation of the land reforms from 1950s to the late 1990s. Its lack of active association with the programme run on outsourcing and contracting procedure seriously

---

[37] Ibid, p. 5.

[38] Amartya Sen. 'Development As a Capability Expansion' In Sakkio Fukkuda Parr and A. K. Shiv Kumar (Eds) *Readings in Human Development*, New Delhi: Oxford University Press, pp. 4-6.

affect their capability to supervise and monitor the programme. Further, the programme for modern surveys and complex integration of cadastral maps with RoRs and electronic integration with sub-registration, managing modern record rooms and land title regime being implemented under NLRMP raise a question about the capability of the tahsildars in India to handle the highly complex technical nature of the work. The lower and middle level bureaucracy is not enthusiastic about the programme of modernisation of land records. They find it burdensome and an addition to their routine which does not even provide a payoff. The capacity of the generalist nature of bureaucracy like IAS, KAS and OAS officers and their autonomy of action in protecting the larger public interest in the present IT vendor-driven network will inevitably determine the extent of ICT adoption, application, and management in land records system. Strangely, the central government has been organising many national level workshops for the revenue secretaries and state level NIC officials and confine themselves to the so-called 'physical achievements' without even deliberating the capability of the officials at tahsil level offices to implement the complex technological programme and attend the goals.

The problem of the capacity of bureaucracy is very important factor in the success of the computerisation and digitisation of land records.[39] Further, the emergence of network governance or public-private partnerships in implementation of the highly complex nature of land records modernisation programme also raise a question on the bureaucracy's ability to deal with the IT vendors and evaluate the provision of the contracted out service. The influence of the private IT service providers and firms on government determines the performance of computerisation of public sector.[40] The issue of taking

[39] The process of computerisation of land records started in Keonjhar district in 1999 by digitising the existing old and outdated khatians (RoRs) by the IT vendors and I was given a brief training as tahsildar and Record Room in charge, by the NIC officials at Cuttack. I remember that I could not give priority to monitor the computerisation of land records work in the tahsil and sensitised the revenue officials due to preoccupation with various revenue and administrative assignments. Hardly the district collectors and sub-collectors discussed the matter in the monthly revenue meetings with the revenue officials or shown their personal interest on the progress of the work. Nobody was there in the district to take the leadership in implementing the project.

[40] P. Dunleavy et al. 2006. *Digital Era Governance-IT Corporations, The State and E-Government*, New York, Oxford University Press, pp. 256-257.

responsibility or ensuring accountability in such works and preventing the rent-seeking behaviour of the government officials involved in the programme has assumed challenging problems. The problem of bureaucracy in India has been observed in general perspective by some scholars. Its inability to reform and enhance its efficiency, accountability and transparency of its performance and its ability to develop informal networks with IT vendors have put a big question mark on the capability of bureaucracy to deliver. [41]

The current land records modernisation programme would in no way alter the entrenched position of the bureaucracy or would bring about fundamental change in land records management and the discretion of the revenue officials. Rather, the reform launched in the wake of India's neoliberal economy 'could even provide the new opportunities for earning illegally and strengthening support bases.' The vendor-driven and expenditure oriented land records modernisation thus viewed will be 'business as usual' for the Indian bureaucracy like IAS and the state administrative services.[42] Interestingly, in the current Twelfth Five Year Plan the Indian state belatedly admits the emerging challenge:

> The most critical bottleneck that is likely to arise is in the capacity building of human resources. There is need to both strengthen the profile of the personnel deployed, as also to train those currently in service, whose skill sets are currently completely out of sync with the demands posed by the radically new architecture visualised for NLRMP.[43]

(v) NLRMP, network governance and democratic accountability

The networks or to put simply implementing complex public policies through interactive, interorganisational and intergovernmental framework based on interdependence, negotiation, trust has assumed importance in the writings of the scholars on network governance. The liberal democratic scholars have

---

[41] Kuldeep Mathur. 2004. 'Administrative Reforms in India: Policy Prescriptions and Outcomes' in Surendra Munshi and Biju Pal Abraham (Eds) Good *Governance, Democratic Societies and Globalisation*, New Delhi: Sage Publications, p. 229.

[42] S. K. Das. 2005. 'Reforms and Indian Administrative Service' In Jos Mooji (Ed) *The Politics of Economic Reforms in India,* New Delhi: Sage Publications, pp. 193-194.

[43] Government of India. 2013. *Twelfth Five Year Plan(2012-2017) Volume-I*, Planning Commission of India, Yoyana Bhawan, New Delhi, pp. 200-201.

taken critical stand against the growth of networks approach to governance as they believe that the networks structure blur the line between state-society boundaries, undermine representative institutions, lack transparency and accountability.[44] Sorensen and Torfing while agreeing to the anti-democratic nature of networks governance have suggested for 'democratic anchorage' over the networks since they have become indispensable in the complex, fragmented and multilayered societies, by facilitating the entry of elected politicians in the networks for securing the interest of public in the policy design and implementation.[45] This prescription of allowing network governance to function highlights the utter weakness of the model of governance and its unsuitability and harmfulness to an open democratic polity like India.

One of the running themes in our study of the land records computerisation is that the schemes are being implemented in a complex intergovernmental and government-private mode. We have mentioned in our study that the complex and tricky issue like the computerisation of land records has been sought to be implemented despite the absence of the technical capability of the state governments even to do basic data entry of land records. The implementation of various schemes of land records modernisation like computerisation and digitisation of RoRs and maps, e-registration, modern electronic surveys are being taken up on a massive scale across the country with the help of private IT vendors and survey companies. The real challenge is how to reconcile the profit motive and maximisation of business interest and return on invested capital of the private sectors with the interest and values of public administration in the networks or partnerships venture where cooperation and trust has been the basis of such motive. It is observed that 'there has been widespread impression that networks have been the cases of privatisation by 'stealth' and the bargains have been made or worked out in general more favourable to corporate interests.'[46] Such problems have raised accountability and transparency issues in dealing with private sector participation.

---

[44] Eva Sorensen and Jacob Torfing. 2005. 'The Democratic Anchorage of Governance Networks,' *Scandinavian Political Studies*, 28(3), pp. 195-199.

[45] Ibid, pp. 210-211.

[46] Kuldeep Mathur. 2010. 'Governance as Networks: Emerging State, Business and NGOs Relationships in India,' (mimeo) Centre for Democracy and Social Action and OXFAM, March 2010, Gurgaon, India, p. 7. Also reprinted in *Indian Journal of Human Development*, 4(2), 2010, pp. 253-279.

In the partnerships venture, the private and public interest is blurred and the bureaucrats and politicians are not uncomfortable to secure material benefits from such network for themselves which in the process weakens the public servant's power to defend, bargain and secure public interest. The network's approach to governance thus raise the vital question of the capacity of government bureaucracy to negotiate with the private actors and agencies in the networks for promoting and securing social and public interest and democratic accountability. Thus it will not be out of place to say that the approach of governance for multiple actors and agencies, has led to the weakening of the critical role of the Indian states in implementation and delivery of public service.

The network's approach to land records modernisation has raised a challenging issue of the state capacity and the capability of the bureaucracy to secure public interest while negotiating a deal with big IT corporates. The investment of funds by the private sectors in land records modernisation are to be repaid with profit to the private sector by charging user fees on the citizens who are to be treated as service users and consumers and the universality of the public service has to be diluted.

The experience of implementation of e-government projects in America has been closely studied by Jane E. Fountain, the author of *The Virtual State* (2001). She has noted that as outsourcing activities for building virtual state in America has increased and the need for public–private policy networks grew, consequently there has been a massive rise of 'an industry of e-government vendors' who are out to play critical role in designing, developing, managing and controlling the virtual state.[47]

As ICTs application, adoption and management in public sector are outsourced, the management of information as powerful instruments of governance and the public policy making of the virtual state is also effectively outsourced. This has very serious repercussions on the capacity of the public servants to secure public interest and the safety of the public records preserved in the databases.

The 'growing trend on of governmental outsourcing' of e-governance programmes, the evolving power dynamics of bureaucrats vis-a-vis IT vendors, IT consultants in both formal and informal relations, the 'the political' role

[47] Jane E. Fountain. 2001. 'The Virtual State: Transforming American Government,' *The National Civic Review*, 90 (3), Fall, 2001, p. 250.

played by IT vendors in influencing the shaping of ICT based public service delivery would be important emerging areas of research.[48]

(vi) Neoliberal state and land records

Unequal landholding and access to land and widespread concealed tenancy continue to be the primary elements in the agrarian relations in India. Yet the possibility of radical land reforms have appeared remote as the policy objective under the NLRMP is to provide secure land title and property rights for facilitating the growth of land market. It is the clear indication of the state's inability to 'foster equitable economic growth' through radical distribution of landed property. [49] Computerisation and digitisation of land records is an attempt to reinvent the governance with the help of ICTs and depoliticise the land records management. The political choice of such policies is not brought by the state to the public sphere for debate and deliberation. Rather, the whole problem of land record management is portrayed by the policy elites of India as a techno-managerial issue and implemented in a top-down policy framework. [50]

Some policy suggestions

Finally, it will not be out of place to provide some policy recommendations for the ongoing implementation of NLRMP scheme having closely studied the policy design and the strategies of implementation from both an insider and outsider perspective. First, the present vendor-driven approach to computerisation of land records and supply side approach of installation of hardware and software should be completely dispensed with as the capability of the generalist revenue bureaucracy and capacity of the revenue administration to adopt such complex information system and their ability to secure and protect the public interest in public service delivery in partnership with IT

---

[48] Alon Peled. 2001. 'Outsourcing and Political Power: Bureaucrats, Consultants, Vendors and Public Information Technology,' *Public Personnel Management*, 30(4), pp. 495-523.

[49] Atul Kohli and Rani D. Mullen. 2004. 'Democracy, Growth, and Poverty in India', in Atul Kohli et al *States, Markets and Just Growth: Development in the Twenty First Century*, New Delhi: UN University Publications and Rawat Publications, pp. 219-224.

[50] Rahul De. 2008. 'Control, Depoliticisation and the eState' in M A Wimmer et al. *EGOV2008*, Lecture Notes in Computer Series (LNCS), Heidelberg: Springer-Verlag, pp. 61-72.

vendors is overlooked. This means the capacity of the generalist nature of tahsil bureaucracy needs to be critically assessed before going for application and adoption of cutting edge ICTs and electronic survey equipment for land records updation and survey.

Tahsil administration and its bureaucracy will continue to serve as the agents of the state at the grassroots level in the present local governance structure and the private players cannot replace the multiple nature of regulative and welfare oriented works of tahsildar. Simply installing hardware and software through IT vendors without involving tahsil officials will no way help in modernisation of land records. The land records computerisation works should not be handed over on a platter to the private IT vendors. Lack of knowledge, involvement and motivation of the revenue officials have reduced the whole exercise of CLR to a vendor driven one. The land records modernisation programme, to quote John Kane and Haig Patapan, have created scope for 'greater opportunities for straight forward criminal conduct' due to the involvement of the officials in outsourcing and contracting works. There is also crisis of accountability in networks involving public and private agencies.[51]

The modernisation of land records of the Indian state has been left with two options. The governance paradigm that advocates private sector to replace or substitute or shape public service delivery may either lead to better efficiency 'through coordination of responsibilities' or may lead to 'outright corrupt practices' by depending on the private sector who may resort to state capture.[52] Our study finds that the latter has been the prominent emerging trend as no importance is given by the policy elites to the concerns of new ethical imperatives for the public officials working in network/partnership with IT vendors involved in profitable land records modernisation contracts.

Second, the top administrative officials heading NLRMP projects in the states should have sufficient knowledge and exposure to the uncertainties, risks and constraints in applying, adopting and managing the ICTs in public administration and its serious implication on democratic governance and citizenship as web-enabled service delivery is run on business and client oriented principle where the citizen or say a land holder is reduced as a mere passive consumer of electronic services.

---

[51] John Kane and Haig Patapan. 2006. 'In Search of Prudence: The Hidden Problem of Managerial Reform,' *Public Administration Review*, September-October, pp. 717-720.

[52] Claus Offe. 2009. 'Governance: An Empty Signifier'? *Constellations*, 16(4), p. 553.

Third, it is not the so-called citizen centric or supply side approach of ICTs but equally the complete adoption of the open source software will lead to less dependence on IT vendors who are out to grab long term lucrative markets and ensure permanent dependence of the public organisations on them. Fourth, the powerful officials in the state administrative services like OAS and KAS, revenue inspectors and village accountants should be constantly involved in any policy design and implementation as these officials constitute the backbone of the computerisation of land records and their sense of commitment and involvement is vital for the sustainability of the programme.

The present policy of top down initiative involving state revenue secretaries and retiring director of land records will radically yield results, if the middle and lower officials regularly associated themselves at all stages of policy design and implementation. There is an absence of responsibility among the tahsildars as they feel that the vendor-driven and outsourced approach to computerisation of land records has no scope for them to participate. Fifth, the success of NLRMP critically depends upon the highly motivated direct recruited IAS officers with stable tenure, who can take up leadership of the project, maintain high degree of integrity and transparency in dealing with IT vendors and lucrative IT contracts, be able to work hand in hand with the state administrative service officers like OAS and KAS and the vast army of patwaris, revenue inspectors who have developed a formidable network with local level politicians and vested interest to upset any top-down plans and strategies. The command and control driven mentality of IAS officers with an attitude to shirk away responsibility of failures is simply unsuitable to run the multiagency centred and complicated programme of NLRMP.

Sixth, the tahsildars, deputy tahsildars, revenue inspectors, village accountants and the clerical staff may be given regular training for enhancing their capability and removal of the misgivings and prejudices. The feedback and suggestions received from them or their professional associations need to be given the utmost importance in further development of simplified and user-friendly software as these officials at the tahsil level occupy a critical and enviable system in ensuring the smooth functioning of the hardware and software system in the record room.

Seventh, technical officials of the National Informatics Centre need to appreciate and acquire the social science perspective of the complexity of democratic governance practices, policy processes and citizenship which would help them to understand the demand side needs of ICTs architecture rather than guided by techno-managerial and quick-fix solutions to complex politico-administrative problems of the land records. It is a fact that many IT personnel of NIC harbour the dangerous notion of customer driven bureaucracy, replicating the so-called best practices overlooking the administrative ecology, the value neutrality of computers and its operators and lessening the personal contact of the public with public servants as the solution for administrative inefficiency and malpractices.

Eighth, we must have a common consensus regarding the extent to which the land records be computerised and to what extent the modern survey of land to be permissible in the lights of the failure to digitise the maps and integrate these with RoRs and conducting land surveys with modern equipments given the limited capacity of the bureaucracy.

James Scott's advice to the carriers of high modernist ideologues, planning for the abstract and standardised citizens is quite relevant as the Indian state move ahead in its gigantic efforts to map and digitise the land records of its subject population. His rules of thumb is taking small steps, stand back and observe and take next small steps, favour reversibility that can be of help if mistakes or plan surprises arise that may allow accommodation of unforeseen situations. A scope for human inventiveness will to improve the design, and turn out to be immensely useful for the techno-managerial mindsets dominating the implementation of NLRMP. [53]

[53] James C Scott. 1998. *Seeing Like A State: How Certain Schemes to Improve the Human Condition Have Failed,* New Haven: Yale University Press, p. 345.

Select Bibliography

Aberbach, Joel D. and Tom Christensen. 2005. 'Citizen and Consumers,' *Public Management Review*, 7(2): 225-246.

Abrams, Philip. 1988. 'Notes on the Difficulty of Studying the State,' *Journal of Historical Sociology*, 1(1), March; 58-89.

Agranoff, Robert and Michael Mcguire. 1999. 'Managing in Network Settings,' *Policy Studies Review*, 16(1):18-41. Reprinted in Mark Bevir (Ed) *Public Governance*-Volume III, London: Sage Publications: 102-116.

Ahuja, Manoj and A P Singh. 2006. 'Computerisation of Land Records in West Bengal,' *Man and Development*, 28(1):59-77

———. 2006. 'Evaluation of Computerisation of Land Records In Karnataka: A Study from Gulbarga District', *Economic and Political Weekly*, 7 January: 69-77.

Alternative Survey Group. 2008. 'Decline of Developmental State,' Alternative Economic Survey, India-2007-2008, Delhi: Danish Books, September.

Antiroiko, Ari-Veikko and Malkia, Matti (Eds.) 2007. *Encyclopedia of Digital Government*, Hershey PA (US): Idea Group Reference.

Appu P.S. 1975. 'Tenancy Reforms in India', *Economic and Political Weekly*, 10 (33, 34, and 35): 1339-1375.

———. 1996. *Land Reforms in India*, New Delhi: Vikash Publishing House.

Argyriades, Demetrious. 2006. 'The Rise, Fall and Rebirth of Comparative Administration: The Rediscovery of Culture,' *Public Administration Review*,66(2),April-May:281-284.

Avgerou, Chrisanthi. 2001. 'The Significance of Context in Information Systems and Organisational Change,' *Information Systems Journal*, 11: 43-63.

———. 2002. *Information Systems and Global Diversity*, New Delhi: Oxford University Press.

Baden, B. H. Powell. 1894. *A Short Account of the Land Revenue and Its Administration in British India with a Sketch of the Land Tenures*, Oxford Clarendon Press.

———. 1974. *The Land Systems in British India, Volume-I,* London: The Clarendon Press.

Bagga, R. K, Kenneth Kenniston and Rohit Raj Mathur (Eds). 2005. *The State, IT and Development*, New Delhi: Sage Publications.

Bandopadhya, Rekha. 1993. 'Land System in India: A Historical Review,' *Economic and Political Weekly*, 25 December: A149-A155.

Bandyopadhyay, D. 2008. 'Does Land Still Matter?,' *Economic Political Weekly*, March 8:37-42.

Banguara, Yusuf and Larbi, George, A (Eds). 2006. *Public Sector Reforms in Developing Countries: Capacity Challenges to Improve Services*, New York, Palgrave Macmillan and UNRISD Publications.

Barber, Benjamin R. 2001. 'The Uncertainty of Digital Politics: Democracy's Uneasy Relationship with Information Technology,' *Harvard International Review*, Spring: 42-47.

Basu, Subhojit and Richard Jones. 2005. 'Indian Information Technology Act 2000: Review of the Regulative Powers under the Act,' *International Review of Law, Computers and Technology*, 19 (2): 209-230.

Beeson, Mark and Ann Firth. 1998. 'Neo-Liberalism as a Political Rationality: Australian Public Policy Since the 1980s,' *Journal of Sociology*, 34(3):215-231.

Behera, Hari Charan. 2009. 'Constraints in Land Records Computerisation,' *Economic and Political Weekly*, 20 June: 21-24.

Behuria, N C . 1997. *Land Reforms Legislation in India: A Comparative Study*, New Delhi: Vikash Publishing House.

Bekkers, Victor and Vincent Homburg. 2007. 'The Myths of E-Government: Looking Beyond the Assumptions of a new and Better Government,' *The Information Society*, 23(5):373-382.

Bekkers, Victor JJM and Stravos Zourdis. 1999. 'Electronic Service Delivery in Public Administration: Some Trends and Issues,' *International Review of Administrative Sciences*, 65:183-195.

Bellamy, Christine and John Taylor. 1992. 'Informatisation and New Public Management: An Alternative Agenda for Public Administration,' *Public Policy and Administration*,7(3):29-41.

———. 1994. 'Exploiting IT in Public Administration–Towards An Information Polity,' *Public Administration*,72(1), Spring:1-13.

———. 1999. 'Joining-Up Government in the UK: Towards Public Services for an Information Age,' *Australian Journal of Public Administration*, 58(3): 89-96.

———. 2000. 'Implementing Information Age Government: Principles, Progress and Paradox,' *Public Policy and Administration*, 15(1), Spring: 29-42.

Benjamin Solomon et al. 2007. 'Bhoomi: 'E-governance' or An Anti-politics Machinery Necessary to Globalise Bengaluru? (http://www.casumm.net.downloads/ Bhoomi%Report.pdf.(accessed 20 February 2010)

Bert and Michael Mcguire. 1999. 'Managing in Network Settings', *Policy Studies Review*, 16(1):18-41. Reprinted in Mark Bevir (Ed) *Public Governance-Volume.III*, London: Sage Publications: 102-116.

Bevir, Mark, (Ed). 2007. *Public Governance*, London: Sage Publications.

Bhambri, C. P. 1976. 'Contextual Framework of Public Administration in Indian States, *Indian Journal of Public Administration*, 22 (3), July-September: 330-348.

Bhatnagar, Subash. 2004. 'Public Service Delivery: Does E-Government Help?' In Sadiq Ahmed and Suman Berry (Eds) *Annual Bank Conference on Development Economics*, 2003, New Delhi: The World Bank and NCAER, New Delhi.

———. '*E-government and Access to Information*' (http:// www.urpan1.un.org/intradoc/groups/public/documents/urpan008435.pdf (accessed December 4,2008)

———. 2004. *E-Government: From Vision to Implementation: A Practical Guide to Case Studies*, New Delhi: Sage Publications.

Boas, Jr. S M, Christobal Kay and Edward Lahiff (Eds). 2008. *Market led Agrarian Reforms: Critical Perspectives on Neo-liberal Land Policies and the Rural Poor*, London: Routledge.

Boas, T, T Dunning and J Bussell. 2005. 'Will the Digital Revolution Revolutionise Development? Drawing Together the Debate,' *Studies in Comparative International Development*, 40(2):95-110.

Bolgherini, Silvia. 2007. 'The Technology Trap and the Role of Political and Cultural Variables: A Critical Analysis of E-Government Policies,' *Review of Policy Research*, 24(3):259-275.

Borass Jr, Saturnino M. 2003. 'Questioning the Market Led Agrarian Reform: Experiences from Brazil, Colombia and South Africa,' *Journal of Agrarian Change*, Volume 3 (3), July: 367-394.

Bourgeon, J. 2008. 'The Future of Public Service: A Search for New Balance,' *The Australian Journal of Public Administration*, 67(4):390-393.

Bovens, Mark and Stavros Zourdis. 2002. 'From Street level to System level Bureaucracies: How Information and Communication Technologies is Transforming Administrative Discretion and Constitutional Control,' *Public Administration Review*, 62(2), March-April: 452-465.

Box, Richard C. 1999. 'Running Government like A Business: Implications for Public Administration and Theory,' *The American Review of Public Administration*, 29(1), 19-43.

Box, Richard et al. 2001. New Public Management and Substantive Democracy,' *Public Administration Review, 61*(5), September-October: 608-619.

Bretschneider, Stuart. 2003. Review: Information Technology-Government and Institutional Change,' *Public Administration Review*, November-December: 738-741.

Brewer, Gene A et al. 2006. 'Designing and Implementing E-Government Systems: Critical Implications for Public Administration and Democracy,' *Administration and Society*, 38(4):472-499.

Brown, David. 2005. 'Electronic Government and Public Administration', *International Review of Administrative Sciences*, 71(5): 241-254.

Brown, Wendy. 2006. 'American Nightmare: Neo-Liberalism, Neoconservativism and De-Democratisation', *Political Theory*, 36 (6), December: 690-734.

Bussell, Jennifer. 2012. 'E-Governance and Corruption in the States: Can Technology Serve the Aam Aadmi?' *Economic and Political Weekly*, June 23:77-85.

Caiden, Gerald E. and Pachampet Sundaram. 2004. 'The Specificity of Public Sector Reform,' *Public Administration and Development*,24 :373-383.

Caiden, Naomi and Demetrios Argyriades. 2006. 'The Rise, Fall and Rebirth of Comparative Administration: The Rediscovery of Culture,' *Public Administration Review*, 66(2), April-May: 281-284.

Calista, Donald J. and Melitski, James. 2007. 'E-government and E-Governance: Converging Constructs of Public Sector Information and Communication Technologies,' *Public Administration Quarterly*, 31(1): 87-100.

Carter, Michael. 2004. 'E-Governance-Transforming India,' The World Bank, February, 17 (http://go.worldbank.org/10BBYV9M 90 (Accessed 17 July 2010)

Caseley, Jonathan. 2004. 'Public Sector Reform and Corruption,' CARD Façade in Andhra Pradesh,' *Economic and Political Weekly*, March 13:1151-1156.

Castells, Manual. 2000. 'Materials for an Exploratory Theory of Network Society,' *British Journal of Sociology*, 51(1):5-24.

———. 2000. 'Toward Sociology of the Network Society,' *Contemporary Sociology*, 29(5), September: 693-699.

———. 2004. 'An Introduction to the Information Age,' In Frank Webster (Ed) *The Information Society Reader*, London: Routledge.

Cats-Baril, William and Ronald Thompson. 1995. 'Managing Information Technology Projects in the Private Sector,' *Public Administration Review*, November-December, 55(6):559-566.

Cecchini, Simonne and Christopher Scott. 2003. 'Can Information and Communication Technology Applications Contribute to Poverty Reductions?' Lessons from Rural India,' *Information Technology for Development*, 10:73-84.

Chadwick, Andrew and Christopher May. 2003. 'Interaction between States and Citizens in the Age of Internet-Government in the United States, Britain and the European Union,' *Governance: An International Journal of Policy, Administration and the Institutions*, 16(2): 271-300.

Chaganti, Sruti. 2003. 'Information Technology Act: Danger of Violation of Civil Rights,' *Economic and Political Weekly*, August 23: 3587-3595.

Chakravorty, Mantosh and Azad Singh. 2009. 'Land Records Computerisation: An Innovative Approach to Management,' *Informatics*, 17(4):46-47.

Chand, Vikram K. (Eds). 2006. *Reinventing Public Service Deliveries in India: Selected Case Studies*, New Delhi: The World Bank and Sage Publications.

Neera Chandhoke. 1996. 'Limits of a Comparative Political Analysis,' *Economic and Political Weekly*, 31(4), January 27:PE2-PE8.

———. 2005. 'Seeing the State in India, *Economic and Political Weekly*, 40 (11), March 12:1033-1040.

Chandrasekhar, C.P. 'Aspects of India's Engineered Traverse to an Information Society,' http://www.itforcharge.net/poleco_is.html. (accessed on September 23,2008)

Chatterjee, Partha. 2008. 'Democracy and Economic Transformation in India,' *Artha Vijnana*, L (1), March: 1-20.

Chaturvedi, M. K. 1971. 'Commitment in Civil Service', *Indian Journal of Public Administration*, 17(1):40-46.

Chawla, Rajeev, B. V. Sharma and P. V. Bhatt. 2008. 'Bhoomi: Key learnings and new initiatives' in Ashis Vachhani and NK Kumaresan Raja (Ed) *Computerisation of Land Records India: Achievements and Experiences, Centre for Rural Studies*, LBSNAA, Mussorie.

Chawla, Rajeev. 2007. 'Bhoomi: On line Delivery of Record of Rights, Tenancy and Crops to farmers in Karnataka, India' in Ashok Agarwal (Ed) *E-governance Case Studies*, Hyderabad: University Press.

———. 'Freedom in the Fields', Power Point Presentation, http://unpan1.un.org/intradoc/groups/public/documents/UN/UNPAN023395.pdf (accessed on May 10, 2010)

Chawla, Rajeev and Samartharam N.R. 2013. 'Using ICTs Enable Better Land Administration: Bhoomi System of Karnataka, India as A Case for the Study,' p. 4. (www.conftool.com/landandpoverty2013/.../Chawla-409_paper.pdf?./ accessed on June 2,2013)

Chibber, Pradeep, Sandeep Shastri and Richard Sisson. 2003. 'Federal Arrangements and the Provision of Public Goods in India,' *Asian Survey*, 44 (3): 339-352.

Chowdhury, T. H. 2002. 'Information Technology for Development: Necessary Condition,' *Economic and Political Weekly*, September, 21:3886-3889.

Ciborra, Claudio. 2005. 'Interpreting e-Government and Development: Efficiency, Transparency or Governance at a Distance,?' *Information Technology and People*, 18(3):260-279.

Clark, David. 2002. 'Neo-liberalism and Public Service Reform, Canada in Comparative Perspective,' *Canadian Journal of Political Science*,35(4), December:771-793.

Clemens, Elisabeth S. and James M. Cook. 1999. 'Politics and Institutionalism: Explaining the Durability and Institutional Change,' *Annual Review of Sociology*, 25:441-466.

Cook, Edward et al. 2008. 'Information and Communication Technology in Land Administration Projects,' Agriculture and Rural Development, *World Bank, Policy Note No-43556*, Issue. 38, February

Corbridge, Stuart, Glyn Williams, Manoj Srivastava and Rene Vernon. 2005. *Seeing the State: Governance and Governmentality in India,* Cambridge University Press.

Corrizales, Tony. 2009. 'The Internet Citizenry: Access and Participation,' *Public Administration Review*, March-April: 350-353.

Coursey, David and Norris, Donald F. 2008. Models of E-Government: Are They Correct? An Empirical Assessment,' *Public Administration*, 68(3), May-June: 523-536.

Christensen, Tom and Per Laegreid. 2012. 'Governance and Administrative Reforms,' in David Levy-Faur (Ed) *The Oxford Handbook of Governance,* Oxford University Press.

Crawford, Gordon. 2006. 'The World Bank and Good Governance: Rethinking the State or Consolidating Neo-Liberalism' in Alberto Paloni and Maurizio Zanardi (Eds) *The IMF, World Bank and Policy Reform*, London: Routledge.

Curtis, Bruce. 1995. 'Taking the State Back Out: Rose and Miller on Political Power,' *The British Journal of Political Sociology*, 46(4):575-589.

D'souza Nafisa Goga. 1991. 'Landholding Systems in Tribal Areas', *Social Action*, July-September, 41(3): 345-350.

Danziger, James N. and Kim Viborg Anderson. 2002. 'The Impact of Information Technology on Public Administration: An Analysis of Empirical Research from the Golden Age Transformation', *International Journal of Public Administration*, 25(5):591-627.

Das, S. K . 2005. 'Reforms and the Indian Administrative Service' In Jos Mooji (Ed) *The Politics of Economic Reforms in India*, New Delhi: Sage Publications.

Dasgupta, Shimanthi. 2008. 'Success, Market and Ethics: Information Technology and the Shifting Politics of Governance and Citizenship in the Indian Silicon Plateau,' *Cultural Dynamics*, 20(3):213-244.

Dash, Giridhari and Sapan Chandra Ray. 1996. *Law Relating to Survey and Settlement of Land in Orissa with Circulars*, Cuttack: Cuttack Law House.

Davies, Jonathan. 2009. 'The Limits of Joined-up Government: Towards A Political Analysis,' *Public Administration*, 87(1):80-96.

Dawes, Sharon S. 2008. 'The Evolution and Continuing Challenges of E-Governance', *Public Administration Review*, 68 (Spl. Issue): S86-S101.

———. 2009. 'Governance in the Digital Age: A Research and Action Framework for an Uncertain Future,' *Government Information Quarterly*, 26:257-264.

De, Rahul. 2006. 'Evaluation of E-government Systems: Project Assessment Vs Development Assessment' In M A Wimmar et al(Ed) *Egov 2006,Lecture Notes in Computer Sciences,4084*:317-328.

———. 2008. 'Control, Depoliticisation and the eState' in M A Wimmer et al. *EGOV 2008*, Lecture Notes in Computer Series (LNCS), Heidelberg: Springer-Verlag, p. 61-72.

Deininger, Klaus and Hans Binswanger. 1999. 'The Evolution of the World Bank's land Policy: Principles, Experience and Future Challenges,' *The World Bank Research Observer*,14(2),August:247-276.

Deininger, Klaus. 2008. 'A Strategy for Improving Land Administration in India' Agriculture and Rural Development Notes, Land Policy and Administration Report No-42694, Issue 33, February. http;//www-wds.worldbank.org/external/default (accessed September 13, 2009)

Deleon, Linda and Robert b Denhardt. 2000. 'The Political Theory of Reinvention,' *Public Administration Theory*, 60 (2): 89-97.

Denhardt, R. B. and J. V. Denhardt. 2000. 'The New Public Service: Serving Rather Than Steering,' *Public Administration Review*, 60(6), November-December.

Deshpande, S.V. and Vijay Kumar Torgal. 1994. 'Administering Land Reforms in Karnataka, *Economic and Political Weekly*, August 13:2131-2134.

———. 2003. 'Land Reforms in Karnataka: Impact on Beneficiaries,' *Economic and Political Weekly*, November, 1-7: 4647-4649.

Downs, Anthony. 1967. 'A Realistic Look at the Final Payoffs from Urban Data Systems,' *Public Administration Review*,27(3):204-210.

Drucker, Peter. 2001. 'The Next Society', *The Economist*, 3 November.

Dubashi, P. R. 1971. 'Committed Bureaucracy,' *Indian Journal of Public Administration*, 17(1), January -March: 33-39.

Duggal, Pavan. 2005. 'Cyber Laws and Its Implementation in India' In R K Bagga, Kenneth Kenniston and Rohit Raj Mathur (Eds) *The State, IT and Development*, New Delhi :Sage Publications.

Dunleavy, P et al. 2005. 'New Public Management is Dead: Long Live Digital Era Governance,' *Journal of Public Administration and Theory*, 16:467-494.

Dunleavy, P. Margetts, H and Bestow, S. 2000. 'The Advent of Digital Government: Public Bureaucracies and the State in the Internet Age' paper to the Annual conference of the APSA downloaded on 24-3-2009(http://governmentontheweb.net/downloads/papers/APSA_2000.pdf dated March,24,2009).

Dutil, Patrice A. et al. 2007. 'Rethinking Government-Public Relationships in A Digital World: Customers, Clients or Citizen?', *Journal of Information Technology and Politics*,4(1):77-90.

Evans, Peter B. 1992. 'Indian Informatics in the 1980s: The Changing Character of State Involvement,' *World Development*, 20(1):1-18.

Finger, Mathias and Thomas Landenberg. 2007. Electronic Governance 'In Ari-Veikko Antiroikko and Matti Malkia (Eds) *Encyclopedia of Digital Government*, Hershey: Idea Group Reference.

Fisher, Eran. 2012. 'E-Governance and E-Democracy: Questioning Technology-Centred Categories,' in David Levi-Faur (Ed) *The Oxford Handbook of Governance*, Oxford University Press.

Foley, Paul and Ximera Alfonso. 2009. 'e-Government and the Transformation Agenda,' *Public Administration*, 87(2): 371-396.

Fountain, Jane E. 2001. 'The Virtual State: Transforming American Government,' *National Civic Review*,90 (3),Fall :241-251.

———. 2001. *Building the Virtual State: Information Technology and Institutional Change*, Washington DC: Brookings Institution.

——— 'Prospects for the Virtual State'
http://www.j.u.tokyo.ac.jp/coeps/pdf/040710.pdf (accessed 14 May, 2009)

——— 'Central Issues in the Development of the Virtual State', http://www.umass.edu/digitalcenter/research/pdfs/jf_portugal2005_centralissues.pdf (accessed 26 May 2009)

Freeman, Chris. 2007. 'The ICT Paradigm' In Robin Mansell et al *The Oxford Handbook of Information and Communication Technology*, Oxford University Press.

Freedman, Des. 2002. 'A Technological Idiot'? : Raymond Williams and Communication Technology,' *Information Communication & Society*, 5 (3): 427-442.

Frissen, P.H.A. 1992. 'Informatisation in Public Administration: Introduction,' *International Review of Administrative Sciences*, 58:29-41.

——— 1997. 'The Virtual State: Post Modernisation, Informatisation and Public Administration,' in Brian Loader (Ed) *The Governance of Cyberspace: Politics, Technology and Global Restructuring*, London: Routledge.

———. 1999. *Politics, Governance and Technology: A Post Modern Narrative of the Virtual State*, Cheltenham: Edward Elgar Publishing Housing Limited.

Frykenberg, Robert Eric. 1967. 'Studies in Land Control in Indian History: A Review Article,' *Economic Development and Cultural Change*, 15 (3): 347-353

——— (Ed). 1969. *Land Control and Social Structure in Indian History*, Madison: The University of Wisconsin Press.

Fuller, C. J. and Veronique Benei. 2000. 'For An Anthropology of Indian State' in C J Fuller and C J Harriss (Eds) *The Everyday State and Society in Modern India*, New Delhi: Social Science Press.

Fuller, C. J. and Haripriya Narsimhan. 2007. 'Information Technology Professional and the New-Rich Middle Class in Chennai,' *Modern Asian Studies*, 41(1):121-150.

Gamble, Andrew. 2006. 'Two Faces of Neo-liberalism' in Richard Robinson (Ed) *The Neo-Liberal Revolution; Forging the Market State*, New York: Palgrave Macmillan.

Gasco, M. 2003. 'New Technologies and Institutional Change in Public Administration', *Social Science Computer Review*, 21(1):6-14.

Gatty, Narayan A. 2009. *Information Technology for Governance Reforms: Land Records Computerisation in an Indian State*, Unpublished Ph D thesis submitted to Institute of Development Studies, University of Sussex, The UK.

Giovanneti, E. and M. Kagami and M. Tsuji (Eds). 2003. *The Internet Revolution: A Global Perspective*, Cambridge University Press.

Glinovas, Ioannis. 2008. 'Neoliberal Law: Unintended Consequences of Market Friendly Law Reforms,' *Third World Quarterly*, 29(6):1087-1099.

Goodsell, Charles T. 1993. 'Reinventing Government or Rediscover IT,' *Public Administration Review*,53(1), January-February:85-87.

Government of India. *Annual Report,2004-2005, 2006-2007, 2007-2008, 2008-2009, 2009-201, 2010-2011,2011-2012 and 2012-2013* Ministry of Rural Development, New Delhi.

Government of India. India: *E-Readiness Assessment Report, 2003, 2005 and 2008.* Department of Information Technology and NCAER, New Delhi.

Government of India. 1951. *First Five Year Plan*. Yoyana Bhawan, Planning Commission of India, Yoyana Bhawan, New Delhi.

———. 1956. *Second Five Year Plan,* Yoyana Bhawan, Planning Commission of India, Yoyana Bhawan, New Delhi.

———. 1961. *Third Five Year Plan,* Yoyana Bhawan, Planning Commission of India, Yoyana Bhawan, New Delhi.

———. 1969. *Fourth Five Year Plan*, Yoyana Bhawan, Planning Commission of India, Yoyana Bhawan, New Delhi.

Government of India. 1974. *Fifth Five Year Plan*, Yoyana Bhawan, Planning Commission of India, Yoyana Bhawan,New Delhi.

———. 1980. *Sixth Five Year Plan*, Yoyana Bhawan, Planning Commission of India, Yoyana Bhawan, New Delhi.

———. 1985. *Seventh Five Year Plan*, Yoyana Bhawan, Planning Commission of India, Yoyana Bhawan, New Delhi.

———. 1992. *Eighth Five Year Plan*, Yoyana Bhawan, Planning Commission of India, Yoyana Bhawan, New Delhi.

———. 1995. *Report of the National Committee on Revitalisation of Land Revenue Administration*, Ministry of Rural Development, New Delhi.

Government of India. 1996. 'Action Plan for Effective and Responsive Government,' Department of Administrative Reforms and Public Grievances, New Delhi. Reprinted in *Indian Journal of Public Administration*, Vol. XLIV (2), April-June, 1998:626-660.

———. 1999. *Ninth Five Year Plan, 1997-2002*, Planning Commission of India, Yoyana Bhawan, New Delhi.

———. 1999. *Report of National Task Force on Information Technology and Software Development*, New Delhi.

———. 2000. *The Information Technology Act, 2000*. The Gazette of India, Part-III, Section-I, New Delhi, Friday, June 9, Ministry of Law, Justice and Company Affairs (Legislative Department),New Delhi.

———. 2001. *Report of the Working Group on Convergence and E-governance for the Tenth Five Year Plan, 2002-2007*, Planning Commission of India, Yoyana Bhawan, November, New Delhi.

———. 2002. *Report of the Committee on India Vision 2020*, Planning Commission, Yoyana Bhawan, December.

———. 2002. *Report of the National Commission to Review the Working of the Constitution*, New Delhi.

Government of India. 2002.*Tenth Five Year Plan,2002-2007*, planning Commission of India, Yoyana Bhawan: New Delhi.

Government of India. 2002. *Successful Governance Initiatives and Best Practices: Experience from States*, Planning commission of India and UNDP, New Delhi.

———. 2005. *Report of the Committee on Computerisation of Land Records*, Department of Land Resources, Ministry of Rural Development, New Delhi.

———. 2005. *Good Governance Through ICTs*, National Informatics Centre, New Delhi.

———. 2006. *Report of the Working Group on Land Relations for Formulations of the Eleventh Five Year Plan*, Planning Commission of India, Yoyana Bhawan, New Delhi, July 31.

———. 2006. 'Towards Faster and More Inclusive Growth: An Approach to Eleventh Five Year Plan,' Planning Commission of India, Yoyana Bhawan, New Delhi, December.

———. 2007. *Proceedings of the Civil Services Day*, Department of Administrative Reforms and Public Governance, Ministry of Personnel and Public Grievances and Pensions, 21 April. New Delhi.

———. 2007. *Karnataka Development Report,* Planning Commission of India, New Delhi, Published by Academic Foundation, New Delhi.

———. 2008. *National Task Force on Information Technology and Software Development*, 2008, New Delhi. Basic Background Report-I. http://ittaskforce.nic.in/bgrlz.htm. (accessed July, 10, 2009)

———. 2008. *Eleventh Five Year Plan*, Planning Commission of India, Yoyana Bhawan, New Delhi.

———. 2008. *Audit Report (Civil) of the Comptroller and Auditor General of India for the Year ended 31st March 2008* (for Karnataka) Comptroller and Auditor General of India, New Delhi.

———. 2008. *Audit Report (Civil) of the Comptroller and Auditor General of India for the Year ended 31st March 2008* (for Orissa) Comptroller and Auditor General of India, New Delhi.

———. 2008. *Eleventh-Report of the Second Administration Reforms Commission of India*, New Delhi on '*Promoting e-Governance: The Smart Way Forward*,' December, 2008.

———. 2008. *Impact Assessment of e-Governance Projects*, Department of Information Technology, Ministry of Communication and Information Technology, New Delhi.

———. 2008. *Second Administrative Reforms Commission-Eleventh Report on 'Promoting E-Governance: The Smart Way Forward*, New Delhi, December.

———. 2009. *National Land Records Modernisation Programme: Guidelines and Technical Manuals-2008-2009*, Department of Land Resources, Ministry of Rural Development, New Delhi.

———. 2009. *Report of the Committee on the State Agrarian Relations and the Unfinished Task in Land Reforms*, Department of Land Resources, Department of Land Resources, Ministry of Rural Development, New Delhi.

———. Ministry of Information Technology n.d. Working Group on information Technology for Masses, National Informatics Centre. http (accessed May10, 2009)

———. *Report of the Working Group on Information Technology, Eleventh Five Year Plan,2007-2012,*Department of Information Technology, Ministry of Communication and Information Technology, New Delhi.

———. 2010. *Change Management for e-Governance Projects,* Department of Administrative Reforms and Public Governance, Ministry of Personnel, Public Grievances and Pensions, November, New Delhi.

———. 2010. *Report on Business Process Reengineering for e-Governance Projects*, Department of Administrative Reforms and Public Governance, Ministry of Personnel, Public Grievances and Pensions, November, New Delhi.

———. 2010. *Economic Survey, 2009-2010*. New Delhi: Oxford University Press.

———. 2011. *Mid-Term Appraisal of Eleventh Five Year Plan,2007-2012*, New Delhi: Oxford University Press.

———. 2013. *Twelfth Five Year Plan. 2007-2012,* Planning Commission of India, Volume-I & II Yoyana Bhawan, New Delhi: Sage Publications.

Government of India. *Report of the Working Group on Information Technology Sector, Twelfth Five Year Plan (2012-2017)*,DIT, Ministry of Information and Communication &Information Technology, New Delhi.

Government of Karnataka. *Karnataka Land Revenue Act, 1964.*http://www.karnataka.gov.in/dpal/pdf_files/LANd%20REVWNU%20ACT%20(page-434-555)%20(122)%20(BM).pdf(accessedApril 6, 2010)

Government of Karnataka. (n d) *E-Governance Strategy,* Department of Information Technology & Biotechnology, Bengaluru.

Government of Karnataka. *Annual Report, 2004-2005*, Revenue Department, Bengaluru.

———. 2004. *Bhoomi 4: Land Records Management System*, Revenue Department, Bengaluru.

———. 2008. *Karnataka at a Glance: 2007-2008* Directorate of Economics and Statistics, Bengaluru.

———. 2008. *Karnataka: A Vision for Development,* Karnataka State Planning Board, Bengaluru.

———. 2004. *The ICT Policy, 2004.* Department of Information Technology, Bhubaneswar.

http://orissa.gov.in/informationtechnology/index.htm (accessed June 29, 2009)

Government of Orissa. *Economic Survey, 2006-2007*, Directorate of Economics and Statistics, Planning and Coordination Department, Bhubaneswar.

Government of Orissa. *Proceedings of State Level Steering Committee (SSLC) on Computerisation of Land Records (CLR) and Strengthening Revenue Administration and Updating Land Records (SRA&ULR),* Board of Revenue, Orissa, Cuttack.

Government of Orissa. *Report on the Activities of Revenue and Disaster Management Department for the Year 2003-2004, to 2012-203.*Revenue and Disaster Management Department, Bhubaneswar.

Government of Orissa. *The Orissa Land Records Manual, 1965.Board* of Revenue, Orissa, Cuttack.

Greenspan, Anna. 2004. *India and the IT Revolution: Networks and Global Culture*, New York: Palgrave Macmillan.

Grindle, M. S. 2001. Designing Reforms: Problems, Solutions and Politics', KSG, Faculty Research Working Paper Series, RWP01-020, November.

(http://web,hks.harvard.edu/publications/workingpapers/citation.aspx?Publd=217(accessed July 4 2010)

Gronlund Akke and Annika Anderson. 2006. 'E-Gov Research Quality Improvements Since 2003: More Rigor, but Research (perhaps) Redefined', in M A Winner et al (Eds) *EGOV2006*, LNCS 4084:1-12.

Gronlund, Ake. 2007. 'Electronic Government' in Ari Veikko Antiroikko and Matti Malkia (Eds) *Encyclopedia of Digital Government*, Hershey: Idea Group Reference.

Gupta, Akhil. 1995. 'Blurred Boundaries, the Discourse of Corruption, the Culture of Politics and the Imagined State,' *American Ethnologist*, 22(2),May, p. 375-378

Habibullah, Wajhat and Manoj Ahuja. 2005. (Eds) *Land Records in India: Computerisation of Land Records, Volume-X,* New Delhi: Sage Publications.

Hamstad, Tim, T. Haque and Robin Nielsen. 2008. 'Improving Land Access for India's Poor,' *Economic and Political Weekly*, March 8:49-56.

Hand, M. and B. Sandywell. 2002. 'E-Topia as Cosmopolis or Citadel: On the de-democratising Logic of the Internet, or, toward a Critique of the New Technological Fetishism,' *Theory, Culture and Society*, 19:197-225.

———. 2002 'E-Governance in India: Its Impacts on Relations among Citizens, Politicians and Public Servants,' *International Review of Administrative Sciences*, 68, June: 231–50.

———. 2007. 'Revisiting the New Public Management', *Public Administration Review*, 67(1), January-February: 179-182.

Harriss, John. 1999. 'Comparing Political Regimes Across Indian States: A Preliminary Essay', *Economic and Political Weekly*, 34(48), 22 November-3 December: 3367-3377.

Hariss, Roger and Rajesh Rajora. 2006. '*Empowering the Poor: Information and Communication Technology for Governance and Poverty Reduction*,' UNDP-APDIP ICT4D Series, Bangkok.

Hartman, Yvonne. 2005. 'In Bed with Enemy: Some Ideas on the Connections between Neoliberalism and the Welfare State,' *Current Sociology*, 53(1): 57-70.

Harvey, David. 2007. 'Neoliberalism as a Creative Destruction,' *The ANNALS of the American Academy of Political and Social Science*, 610, March: 22-44.

Hausman, David. 2010.'Innovations for Successful Societies,' An Interview with Rajeev Chawla on 8 June, An initiative of the National Academy of Public Administration and the Woodrow Wilson School of Public and International Affairs and Bobst Center for Peace and Justice, Princeton University, 83 Prospect Avenue, Princeton, New Jersey, 08544, USA. (www.princeton.edu/successfulsocieties (accessed on 10 May, 2011)

Hearn Greg and Thomas Mandeville. 2005. 'How to be Productive in the Knowledge Economy: The Case of ICTs,' In David Rooney et al *Handbook on the Knowledge Economy, Cheltenham*: Edward Elgar.

Heeks, Richard (Ed). 1999. *Reinventing Government in the Information Age: International Practice in IT enabled Public Sector Reform*, Routledge, New York.

———. 2000. 'The Approach of Senior Public Officials to Information Technology-Related Problem: Lessons from India,' *Public Administration and Development*, 20:197-205.

———. 2002. 'I-Development Not e-Development,' *Journal of International Development*, 14(1):1-11.

———. 2006. *Implementing and Managing eGovernment: An International Text,* New Delhi: Sage Publications.

———. 2007. 'Analyzing e-Government Research: Perspectives, Philosophies, Theories, Methods and Practice,' *Government Information Quarterly*, 24:243-265.

Hira, Anil and Ron Hira. 2000 . 'The New Institutionalism: Contradictory Notions of Change,' *American Journal of Economics and Sociology*, 54(2), April: 267-282.

Holden, Stephen H., Donald F. Norris and Patricia D. Fletcher. 2002. 'Electronic Government at the Grassroots: Contemporary Evidence and Future Trends,' Proceedings of the 36th Hawali International Conference on System Sciences, IEEE (HICSS'03).

Holliday, I. 2001. 'Steering the British State in the Information Age', *Government and Opposition*, 36(3):314-329.

Homburg, Vincent and VJJM Bekkers. 2005. 'E-Government and NPM: A Perfect marriage?,' in VJJM Bekkers and Vincent Homburg (Eds) *The Information Ecology of E-Government*, Amsterdam : IOS Press.

Homburg, Vincent. 2008. 'Red-Tape and Reforms: Trajectories of Technological and Managerial Reforms in Public Administration,' *International Journal of Public Administration*, 31(7):749-770.

———. 2006. 'The Tools of Government in the Information Age' in Michael Moran, Martin Rein and Robert E. Godwin (Eds) *The Oxford Handbook of Public Policy*, Oxford University Press.

Hoos, Ida R. 1966. 'Automation, Systems Engineering, and Public Administration: Observations and Reflections on the California Experience,' *Public Administration Review*, 26 (4), December, pp. 311-319.

Howard, M. C. and J. E. King. 2008. *The Rise of Neo-liberalism in Advanced Capitalist Economies: A Materialist Analysis*, Houndsmills: Palgrave Macmillan.

Hudson, John and Stuart Lowe. 2007. *'Understanding the Policy Process: Analyzing the Welfare Policy and Practice,'* Jaipur: Rawat Publishers.

Hudson, John. 1999. 'Informatisation and Public Administration: A Political Science Perspective,' *Information, Communication and Society*, 2(3):318-319.

Huff, Richard F. 2007. 'Governmentality' In Mark Bevir (Ed) *Encyclopedia of Governance*, London :Sage Publications.

Iqbal Narain (Ed) 1967. *State Politics in India*, Meerut: Meenakshi Prakashan.

Jaamdar, S.M. 2005. 'Integrated Land Records Management System: A Paradigm Change in Karnataka State', *The Administrator*, XLVIII, December: 34-53.

Jalan, Bimal. 2005. *The Future of India: Politics, Economics and Governance*, New Delhi: Viking.

Jannuzi, F Thomas. 1994. *India's Persistent Dilemma: The Political Economy of Agrarian Reform*, Boulder (USA): West View Press,

Jayal, Niraja Gopal. 1997.'The Governance Agenda: Making Democratic Development Dispensable,' *Economic and Political Weekly*, 22 July,32(8):407-412

———. 1999. *Democracy and the State: Welfare, Secularism and Development in Contemporary India*, New Delhi: Oxford University Press.

———. 2001. 'Reinventing the State: The Emergence of Alternative Models of Governance in India in the 1990s' in N.G. Jayal and Sudha Pai (Eds.) *Democratic Governance in India: Challenges of Poverty, Development and Identity*, New Delhi: Sage Publications.

———. 2001. 'The State and Democracy in India or Whatever Happened to Welfare, Secularism and Development' in Niraja Gopal Jayal (Ed) *Democracy in India*, New Delhi: Oxford University Press.

Jayal, Niraja Gopal and Pratap Bhanu Mehta. 2010. *The Oxford Companion to Politics in India*, New Delhi: Oxford University Press.

Jayaprakash Narayan. 2005. 'Governance: Virtual to Real' In R K Bagga et al (Eds) *The State, IT and Development*, New Delhi: Sage Publications.

Jenkins, Rob. 1999. *Democratic Politics and Economic Reform in India,* Cambridge University Press.

———. (Ed). 2004. *Regional Reflections: Comparing Politics across India's States*, New Delhi: Oxford University Press.

Jordan, Andrew et al. 2005. 'The Rise of New Policy Instruments in Comparative Perspective: Has Governance Eclipsed Government?', *Political Studies*,35: 477-496.

Joseph, Sara. 2007. 'Neoliberal Reforms and the Democratic Agenda in India,' *Economic and Political Weekly*, August 4, 2007.

Judge, Paramjit Singh. 1989. 'Role of Patwari in Land Reform,' *Mainstream*, 14 October: 11-14.

Kakbadse, Andrew Korac et al. 1996. 'Leadership and the Public Sector: An Internationally Comparative Benchmarking Analysis,' *Public Administration and Development*,16: 377-396.

Kakbadse, Korac, Nada, Alexander Kahzmin and Andrew Korac Kakbadse. 2006. 'Information Technology and Development: Creating 'IT Harems,' Fostering New Colonialism or Solving Wicked Policy Problems?' *Public Administration and Development*, 20(3):171-184.

Kakbadse, Korac, Nada, Alexander Kahzmin. 1996. 'Innovation Strategies for Adoption of New Information Technology in Government: An Australian Experience,' *Public Administration and Development*, 16(3):17-30.

Kalam, A. P. J. Abdul. 2005. 'A Vision of Citizen Centric Governance in India' in R K Bagga et al (Eds) *The State, IT and Development*, New Delhi: Sage Publications.

Kamarck, Elaine C. 2005. 'Government Innovation around the World' in Bidyut Chakrabarty and Mohit Bhattacharya (Eds) *Administrative Change and Innovation*, New Delhi: Oxford University Press.

Kane, John and Haig Patapan. 2006. 'In Search of Prudence: The Hidden Problem of Managerial Reform, *Public Administration Review*, September-October: 711-724.

Kapur, Devesh and Pratap Bhanu Mehta. (Eds). 2005. *Public Institutions in India: Performance and Design,* New Delhi: Oxford University Press.

Kapur, Jagadish c. 2000. 'IT and Good Governance,' *Indian Journal of Public Administration*, July-August: 386-395.

Kar, Samit. 2006. 'Ideals Vs Realities: Limitations of Governance,' *Economic and Political Weekly*, October 14: 4322-4324.

Karwal, Anita. 2007. 'Effective Public Service Delivery and e-Governance: Who Drives Whom,' in Anil Aggarwall (Ed) *e-Governance: Case Studies*, Hyderabad, University Press.

Katakam, A. 1999. 'Towards E-Governance,' *Frontline*, 16(25):78-80.

Kaushik, P D and Singh, Nirvikar. 2004. 'Information Technology and Broad-Based Development: Preliminary Lessons from North India,' *World Development*, 32(4):591-607.

Kaviraj, Sudipto. 1997. 'The Modern State in India' In Martin Doornbos and Sudipto Kaviraj (Eds) *Dynamics of State Formation: India and Europe Compared,* New Delhi: Sage Publications.

Kenniston, Kenneth and Kumar, Deepak. (Eds.) 2004. *IT Experience in India: Bridging The Digital Divide*. New Delhi: Sage Publications.

Kenniston, Kenneth. 2002. 'Grass roots ICT Projects in India: Some Preliminary Hypotheses,' *ASCI Journal*,31(1&2)

Kernaghan, Kenneth and Justin Gunraj. 2004.'Integrating Information Technology in to Public Administration: Conceptual and Practical Consideration,' *Canadian Public Administration*, 47(4):525-546.

Kessinger, G. Tom. 1970. 'Historical Materials on Rural India,' *The Indian Economic and Social History Review*, 7(4), December: 489-510.

Kettl, Donald F. 2000. 'The Transformation of Governance: Globalisation, Devolution and the Role of Government', *Public Administration Review*, 60(6), November-December: 488-497.

———. 2000. *Global Public management Revolution: A Report on Transformation of Governance*, Washington,DC: Brooking Institution Press.

Khuntia, S C et al. 1997. 'Computerisation of Land Records in Karnataka: A Case Study of Gulbarga District' in Abdul Aziz and Sudhir Krishna (Eds) *Land Reforms in India*, Volume. IV, New Delhi: Sage Publications.

King, Anthony . 1975. 'Overload: Problems of Governing in the 1970s,' Political *Studies*, 23(2&3), p. 284-296.

Kleine, Dorothea and Tim Unwin. 2009. 'Technological Revolution, Evolution and New Dependencies: What is New ICT4D?', *Third World Quarterly*, 30(5):1045-1067.

Klijn, Eric Hans and Geet R Teisman. 2004. 'Managing Public-Private Partnerships: Influencing Processes and Institutional Context of Public-private Partnerships,' in Mark Bevir (Eds) *Public Governance*, Volume-3, London: Sage Publications.

Kohli, Atul and Rani D Mullen. 2004. 'Democracy, Growth, and Poverty in India', in Atul Kohli et al *States, Markets and Just Growth: Development in the Twenty First Century*, New Delhi: UN University Publications and Rawat Publications.

Kohli, Atul. 1987.The *State and Poverty in India: The Politics of Reform*, New Delhi: Cambridge University Press and Orient Longman.

———. 2006. 'Politics of Economic Growth in India, 1980-2005', *Economic and Political Weekly*, April 8:1361-1370.

Kraemer, Kenneth L. and Dedrick, Jason. 1997. 'Computing and Public Organisations, *Journal of Public Administration, Research and Theory*, 7(1):89-112.

Kraemer, Kenneth L. and John Leslie King. 1987. 'Computers and Constitution: A Helpful, Harmful or Harmless Relationship,?' *Public Administration Review*, 47(1): January-February: 93-105.

———. 2005. 'Information Technology and Administrative Reform: Will E-Government be Different'?, IJEGR-Finaldoc

(http://www.Jlking.people.si.umich.edu/IJEGR-Final.pdf (accessed March 30,2010)

Kraemer, Robert. 1999. 'Weaving the Public into Public Administration,' *Public Administration Review*, 59(1):89-92.

Krishna, S and Geoff Walsham. 2005. 'Implementing Public Information Systems in Developing Countries: Learning from a Success Story,' *Information Technology for Development*, 1192:123-140.

Kumar, Dharma. 1965. *Land and Caste in South India*, Cambridge University Press.

Kumar, Rajendra and Michael C. Best. 2006. 'Impact of Sustainability of E-Government Services in Developing Countries: Lessons Learned from Tamil Nadu,' *Information Society*, 22(1) :1-12.

Kumar, Rajesh and Murali Patibandla. 2009. *Institutional Dynamics and the Evolution of the Indian Economy*, New York, Palgrave Macmillan.

Kurian, Renee, Isha Ray and Kentaro Tayama. 2008. 'Information and Communication Technologies for Development: The Bottom of the Pyramid Model in Practice,' *The Information Society*, 24(2):93-104.

Lahiff, Edward, Saturnino M Borass, Jr and Christobal Kay. 2008. 'Market Led Agrarian Reform: Policies, Performance and Prospects' In Saturnino Borass, Jr, Christobal Kay and Edward Lahiff (Eds) *Market-Led Agrarian Reform: Critical Perspectives on Neo-Liberal Land Policies and the Rural Poor*, London: Routledge.

Landbergen, David Jr and George Wolken Jr. 2001. 'Realizing the Promise: Government Information System and the Fourth Generation of Information Technology,' *Public Administration Review*, March/April, 61(2): 206-218.

Langford, John and Yvonne Harrison. 2001. 'Partnering for e-Government: Challenges for Public Administrators,' *Canadian Journal of Public Administration*, 44(4), Winter, December: 393-416.

Laxminarayan, H. and S S Tyagi. 1977. 'Tenancy: Extent and Interstate Variations,' *Economic and Political Weekly*, 12(22), May 28. 872-885.

Learner, Wendy. 2000. 'Neoliberalism: Policy, Ideology and Governmentality,' *Studies in Political Economy*, 63, Autumn: 5-25.

Lemke, Thomas. 2002. 'Foucault, Governmentality, and Critique,' *Rethinking Marxism*,14(3), Fall:49-64.

Lijphart, A. 1997. 'Unequal Participation: Democracy's Unresolved Dilemma', *American Political Science Review*, 91(1):1-14.S

Lips, Miriam, John A Taylor and Frank Bannister. 2005. 'Public Administration in the Information Society: Essays on Risk and Trust,' *Information Polity*, 10:1-9.

Loader, Brian, D.(Ed). 1997. *The Governance of Cyberspace: Politics, Technology and Global Restructuring*, London: Routledge.

Lobo, Alberto and Suresh Balakrishnan. 2002. *Report Card on Service of Bhoomi Kiosks: An Assessment of Benefits by Users of the Computerised Land Records System in Karnataka*, Public Affairs Centre, Bengaluru, November.

Lowi, Theodore J. 1992. 'The Political Marriage of Information Technology and Bureaucracy,' in Larry B. Hill (Ed) *The State of Public Bureaucracy, London*: Me Sharpe, Inc.:203-208.

Lowndes, P. 1997. 'Varieties of New Institutionalism: A Critical Appraisal', *Public Administration*, 74 (2) :181-197.

Madon, Shirin. 2008. 'Evaluating the Developmental Impact of the E-Governance initiatives: AN Exploratory Framework,' in Aswani Saith, M Vijayabaskar and V Gayatri. 2008. *ICTs and Indian Social Change: Diffusion, Poverty and Governance*, New Delhi: Sage Publications.

Mahajan, Gurpreet, Sudha Pai and Niraja Gopal Jayal. 1994. 'State and Neo-liberal Agenda in India', *Economic and Political Weekly*, 29(19), May 7: 1112-1116.

Malhotra, Paven. 2005. 'Technology and Politics of Corruption: Andhra Pradesh's CARD Experience,' in R K Bagga et al (Eds) *The State, IT and Development*, New Delhi: Sage Publications.

Manoj Kumar, T. K. and A. P. Singh. 2006. 'Assessment of Computerisation of Land Records in Rajasthan: Serving to Some Extent,' *The Administrator*, Vol. XLIX, June: 11-40

Manor, James. 2009. 'Successful Governance Reforms in Two Indian States: Karnataka and Andhra Pradesh' in Mark Robinson (Ed) *The Politics of Successful Governance Reforms*, London: Routledge: 23-49.

———. 2010.'What do they Know of India who Only India Know? The Uses of Comparative Politics,' *Commonwealth and Comparative Studies*, 48(4): November: 505-516.

Mansell, Robin. 2002. 'From Digital divides to Digital Entitlements in knowledge Societies,' *Current Sociology*, 50(3), May: 407-426.

Margetts, Helen. 1995. 'The Automated State,' *Public Policy and Administration*, 10(2):88-123.

———. 2003. 'Electronic Government: A Revolution in Public Administration?' In Guy Peters and Jon Pierre (Eds.) *Handbook of Public Administration*, London: Sage Publications.

Mathur, Kuldeep. 2001. 'Strengthening Bureaucracy: State and Development in India' in Niraja Gopal Jayal and Sudha Pai (Eds) *Democratic Governance In India: Challenges of Poverty, Development and Identity*, New Delhi: Sage Publications.

———. 2004. 'Administrative Reform in India: Policy prescriptions and Outcomes,' In Surendra Munshi and Biju Paul Abraham (Eds) *Good Governance, Democratic Societies and Globalisation*, New Delhi: Sage Publications

———. 2008.'Administrative Reforms and Demand of Good Governance' In Bidyut Chakravarty and Mohit Bhattacharya (Eds) *The Governance Discourse: A Reader*, New Delhi.

——— . 2010. 'Governance as Networks: Emerging Relationships among the State, Business and NGOs in India,' *Indian Journal of Human Development*, 4(2):253-279.

May, Christopher. 2002. *The Information Society: A Sceptical View,* Blackwell Publishers, Malden, MA (USA).

Mayer-Schonberger, Viktor and David Lazer (Eds). 2007. *Governance and Information Technology: From Electronic Government to Information Government*, Cambridge: MIT Press.

Mazzarella, William. 2006. 'Internet X-Ray: E-Governance, Transparency and the Politics of Immediation in India,' *Public Culture*, 18 (3):473-506.

Mearns, Robins and Saurabh Sinha. 1999. *Social Exclusion and Land Administration in Orissa, India, Policy Research Working Paper no 2124*,The World Bank, South Asia Region, Rural Development Sector Unit,May, p. 38. http://www.worldbank.org.html/dec/Publications/Workpapers/home/html (accessed November, 29, 2008)

Mishra, B. K. 1962.*Land Tenure and Land Reforms in Orissa*, Government of Orissa. Board of Revenue, Orissa, Cuttack.

Mishra, Niraja. 2003. 'Computerisation of Land Records: A Pragmatic View,' *Economic and Political Weekly*, 28(20), May, 17:1921-1922.

Mitchell, Dean. 1999. *Governmentality: Power and Rule in Modern Society,* London: Sage Publications.

Mitchell, Timothy . 1991. 'The Limits of the State; Beyond Statist Approaches and Their Critics,' *The American Political Science Review*, 85(1): 77-96.

Mitra, Raja. 'Emerging State-level ICT Develop Strategies'. In Subash Bhatnagar and Robert Schware (Eds.). *Information and Communication Technology in Development: Cases from India*. New Delhi: Sage Publication, 2000.

Moon J . 1995. 'The Evolution of E-government among Municipalities: Rhetorics or Reality,' *Public Administration Review*, 62:424-434.

Moore, Nick. 1997. 'Neo-liberal or Dirigiste? Policies for an Information Society,' *Political Quarterly*, 68(3): 276-283.

Mosco, Vincent. 1998. 'Myth-ing Links: Power and Community on the Information Highway,' *The information Society*, 14: 57-62.

Muid, Colin. 1992. 'New Public Management and Informatisation: A Natural Combination?,' *Public Policy and Administration*,7 (3):75-79.

Munshi, Surendra and Biju Pal Abraham (Eds). 2004. *Good Governance, Democratic Societies and Globalisation*, New Delhi: Sage Publications.

Musso, Juliet et al. 2000 . 'Designing Web Technology for Local Governance Reform: Good Management or Good Governance Democracy,' *Political Communication*, 17:1-19.

Nada, Andrew et al. 2003. 'Reinventing the Democratic Governance Project through Information Technology, A Growing Agenda for Debate,' *Public Administration Review*, 63(1):January-February:44-60.

Narayan, Deepa. 2004. 'Field visits to Karnataka, Bengaluru: The Bhoomi Programme. http://www.info.worldbank.org.etools/docs/reducingpoverty/doc/117/file/india-Fv-Facilitator%20Report.pdf (accessed 20 March, 2010)

National Informatics Centre. 2005. *Good Governance Through ICT*, New Delhi.

Nettl, J.P. 1968. 'The State As a Conceptual Variable,' *World Politics*, 20(4):559-592.

Nilekani, Nandan. 2008. *Imagining India: Ideas for the New Century*, New Delhi: Penguin Publishers.

Norris, Donald F. and Moon, M. Jae. 2005. 'Advancing E-Government at the Grassroots: Tortoise or Hare?' *Public Administration Review*, 65(1). January-February: 64-75.

Norris, Donald F. 2003. 'Building the Virtual State… or Not? A Critical Appraisal,' *Social Science Computer Review*, 21(4), Winter: 417-424.

———. 2007. 'Electronic Government at the American Grassroots,' In Ari Veikko Anttiroika and Matti Malkia (Eds) *Encyclopedia of Digital Government*, Hershey: Idea Group Reference.

North, Douglas. 1981. *Structure and Change in Economic History*, New York, WW Norton & Company.

———. 1990. *Institutions, Institutional Change and Economic Performance,* Cambridge University Press.

———. 'Institutional Change: A Framework for Analysis' http://www.ecsocman.edu.ru/images/pubs/2003/02/05/0000051624/9412001.pdf (accessed July 3, 2010)

Northrop, Alana et al. 1990.'Payoffs From Computerisation,' *Public Administration Review*, September-October, 50(5):505-514.

Nye, J. 2002. 'Information Technology and Democratic Governance' In J Nye and E Kamarack (Eds) *Governance.com: Democracy in the Information Age*, Washington DC: Brookings Institution.

O'Toole, Laurence j Jr. 1997. 'Treating Networks Seriously: Practical and Research based Agendas in Public Administration,' *Public Administration Review*, 57(1):45-52.

Oldenburg, Philip. 2006. 'Face to Face with The Indian State: A Grass root View,' In Lloyd I Rudolph and John Kurt Jacobsen (Eds) *Experiencing the State*, New Delhi: Oxford University Press.

Olsen, Johan P. 2004. 'Citizens, Public Administration and the Search for Theoretical Foundations,' *PS: Political Science and Politics*, Vol. 37:69-79.

Orlikowski, Wanda J. and C. Suzanne Iacono. 2001. 'Research Commentary: Desperately Seeking 'IT' in IT Research-Call to Theorizing the IT Artifact', *Information Systems Research*, 12(2), June: pp. 121-134.

Osborne, David and Ted Gaebler. 1992. *Reinventing Government: How the Entrepreneurial Spirit is Transforming the Public Sector*, Reading, MA: Addition-Wesley Publishing Company.

Pai, Sudha. 2000 . *State Politics: New Dimensions*, New Delhi: Shipra Publications.

Pal, J. 2003. 'The Development Promise of Information and Communication Technology in India', *Contemporary South Asia*,12(1),March:103-119.

Pani, Narendra. 2006. 'Icons and Reform politics in India: The Case of S M Krishna,' *Asian Survey*,46(2):238-256.

Parayil, Govindan (Ed.), 2006. *Political Economy of Information Capitalism In India: Digital Divide, Development and Equity*, Houndsmills, Palgrave-Macmillan.

Parliament of India. 2003. *Forty-Seventh Report of the Standing Committee on Urban and Rural Development*, The Thirteenth Lok Sabha, 2003-2004, New Delhi: Lok Sabha Secretariat.

———. 2003. *Fifty-Sixth Report of Standing Committee on Information Technology*, Thirteenth Lok Sabha, New Delhi: Lok Sabha Secretariat.

———. 2005. *Twenty Second Report of Standing Committee on Information Technology (2005-2006), Ministry of Communication and Information Technology*, December, New Delhi: Lok Sabha Secretariat.

———. 2007. *Twenty Seventh Report of the Standing Committee on Rural Development, 2006-2007*,The Fourteenth Lok Sabha, New Delhi: Lok Sabha Secretariat.

———. 2008. *Forty Second Report of the Standing Committee on Rural Development*, The Fourteenth Lok Sabha, 2008-2009, New Delhi: Lok Sabha Secretariat.

———. 2011. Fifteenth Report of the Standing Committee on Rural Development, Lok Sabha Secretariat, New Delhi, August.

———. 2012. *Thirty Third Report of the Standing Committee on Rural Development, 2011-2012*, Fifteenth Lok Sabha, Ministry of Rural Development, New Delhi: Lok Sabha Secretariat.

Parthasarathy, Balaji and Janaki Srinivasan. 2008. 'How the Development of ICTs Affects ICTs for Development: Social Contestation in the Shaping of Standards for the Information Age,' *Science Technology and Society*, 13(2):279-301.

Patibandla, Murali and Amal Sanyal.(Eds) 2009. 'Corruption, Market Reform and Technology' In Kumar Rajesh and Murali Patibandla (Eds) *Institutional Dynamics and The Evolution of the and Indian Economy*, New Delhi: Palgrave Macmillan.

Paul, Samuel.et al. 2004. 'State of India's Public Services: Benchmark for the states,' Economic *and Political Weekly*, February 28: 920-933.

———. 2006. *Who Benefits from India's Public Services: A People's Audit of Five Basic Services*, New Delhi: Academic Foundation.

Pegnato, Joseph, A. 1997. 'Is Citizen A Customer', *Public Productivity and Management Review*, 20(4), June: 397-404.

Peled, Alon. 2000. 'The Politics of Outsourcing: Bureaucrats, Vendors and Public Information Technology (IT) Projects,' *Information Infrastructure and Policy*, 6: 209-225.

———. 2001. 'Do Computers Cut Red Tape?' *The American Review of Public Administration*, 31(4):414- 435.

———. 2001. 'Outsourcing and Political Power: Bureaucrats, Consultants, Vendors and Public Information Technology,' *Public Personnel Management*, 30(4): 495-523.

Perry, James L. 2007. 'Democracy and the New Public Service,' *The American Review of Public Administration*, 37(1) March: 3-16.

Peters, B. Guy. 2001. *The Future of Governing*, University of Kansas Press.

———. 2004. 'Governance and Public Bureaucracy: New Forms of Democracy or new Forms of Control?,' *The Asia Pacific Journal of Public Administration*,26(1): June:3-15.

Peterson, S. B. 1998. 'Saints, Demons and Wizards and Systems: Why Information Technology Reforms Fail or Underperform in Public Bureaucracies in Africa,' *Public Administration and Development*, 18(1): 37-60.

Phani Kumar, M. 2005. 'E-Seva: Transforming Service Delivery to citizens in Andhra Pradesh'. In R K Bagga et al (Eds) *The State, IT and Development*, New Delhi: Sage Publications.

Pierre, Jon. (Ed). 2000. *Debating Governance: Authority, Steering and Democracy*, Oxford University Press.

Pina, Vincent et al. 2007. 'Are ICTs Promoting Government Accountability? A Comparative Analysis of e-Governance Developments in 19 OECD Countries,' *Critical Perspectives on Accounting*, 18: 583-602.

Pitroda, Sam. 1993. 'Development, Democracy and the Village Telephone,' *Harvard Business Review*, November-December.

Planning Commission of India and UNDP. 2002. *Successful Governance Initiatives and Best Practices: Experience from Indian States*, New Delhi.

Prakash, Amit and Rahul De. 2007. 'Importance of Development Context in ICT4D projects: A Study of Computerisation of Land Records in India,' *Information Technology & People*, 20(3): 261-282.

Prasad, Rohit and Rupamanjari Sinha Ray. 2006. 'Critique of the Common Service Centre Scheme', *Economic and Political Weekly*, 11 February: 18-23.

Pratchett, L. and Wingfield, M. 1996. 'Petty Bureaucracy and Wooly Minded Liberalism? The Changing Ethos of Local Government Officers,' *Public Administration*, 74(4):656-669.

Pratchett, Lawrence. 1999. 'New Technologies and the Modernisation of the Local Government: An Analysis of Biases and Constraint,' *Public Administration*, 77(4): 730-750.

Provan, Keith G and H Brinton Milward. 2001. 'Do Networks Really Work ? A Frame work For Evaluating Public Sector Organisational Networks,' *Public Administration Review*, July-August, 61 (4):414-423.

Pushpendra and B. K. Sinha. 2009. 'Some Aspects of Tenancy Debate: Implications for Policy Reforms,' in D. Narasimha Reddy (Ed) *Agrarian Reforms, Land Markets and Rural Poor*, Mussoorie: Centre for Rural Studies, LBSNAA: 47-68.

Puri, Satish K. and Sandeep Sahay. 2007. 'Role of ICTs in Participatory Development: An Indian Experience,' *Information Technology for Development*, 13(20): 133-160.

Radhakrishnan, Smitha. 2007. 'Rethinking Knowledge for Development: Transnational Knowledge Professional and 'New India,' *Theory and Society*, 36:141-159.

Radice, Hugo. 2008. 'The Developmental State under Global Neoliberalism,' *Third World Quarterly*, 29(6):1153-1174.

Ramachandriah, C. 2003. 'Information Technology and Social Development,' *Economic and Political Weekly*, March 22-29:1192-1195.

Ramdhyani, R. K, ICS. 2001. *Report on Land Tenures and the Revenue System of the Orissa and Chhattisgarh States, Volume-I, General Report*, Cuttack: Reprinted by The Survey and Map Publication Department, Orissa.

Rawal, Vikash. 2008. 'Ownership Holding in Rural India: Putting the Record Straight,' *Economic and Political Weekly*, 8 March:43-47.

Reddick, Christopher G. 2005. 'Citizen Interaction with e-government: From Street to Servers,' *Government Information Quarterly*, 22:38-57.

Rethemeyer, Karl, R. 2007. 'The Empires Strike Back: Is the Internet Corporatising Rather than Democratising Policy Processes?,' *Public Administration Review*, March-April: 199-212.

———. 2006. 'Policy Networks Analysis', in Michael Moran et al. (Eds). 2006. *The Oxford Handbook of Public Policy*, Oxford University Press.

Riggs, Fred W. 1962, 'Trends in the Comparative Study of Public Administration,' Reprinted in *International Review of Administrative Sciences*,2010, 76(4): 750-760. Robinson M. C. and J. E. King. 2006. *The Neo-liberal Revolution: Forging the Market State*, Houndsmills: Palgrave Macmillan.

Robinson, Mark. (Ed) 2009. *The Politics of Successful Governance Reforms*, London: Rutledge.

Robinson, Scott E. 2006. 'A Decade of Treating Networks Seriously,' *The Policy Studies Journal*, 34(4):589-59

Rocheleau, Bruce. 2007. 'Whither E-Government?,' *Public Administration Review*,67(3):584-588.

Rodan, Garry. 2005. 'Neo-liberalism and Transparency: Political Versus Economic Liberalism' In Richard Robinson (Ed) *The Neo-liberal Revolution: Forging the Market State*, New York: Palgrave -Macmillan.

Rooney, David et al., 2005. *Handbook on the Knowledge Economy*, Cheltenham: Edward Elgar.

Rose, Nikolas and Peter Miller. 1992. 'Political Power Beyond the State: The Problematics of the Government,' *The British Journal of Sociology*, 43(2):173-205.

Rose, Nikolas, Pat O'Malley and Mariana Valverde. 2006. 'Governmentality,' *Annual Review of Law and Social Sciences*, 2:83-104.

Rose, Nikolas. 1999. *Powers of Freedom*, Cambridge University Press.

Rose, Richard . 2005. 'The Internet and Governance in a Global Context', *Journal of Public Policy*, 25(1):1-3.

Rosenbloom, David. H. 1993. 'Have An Administrative Rx? Don't Forget the Politics,' *Public Administration Review*, November–December,53(6): 503-507.

———. 2001. 'History Lessons for the Reinventors,' *Public Administration Review*, 61(2), March-April: 161-165.

Rothermund, Dietmar. 1969. 'Government, Landlord and the Tenant in India', 1875-1900,' *The Indian Economic and Social History Review*, 6(4): 351-367.

———. 1971. 'The Record of Rights in British India,' *The Indian Economic and Social History Review*, 8(3), September: 443-461.

Roy Burman, B. K. 1987. 'Historical Process in Respect of Communal Land and Poverty Alleviation among Tribals,' *Social Action*, Volume. 37, October-December, 1987.

Saith, Aswani, M. Vijayabaskar and V. Gayatri. 2008. *ICTs and Indian Social Change: Diffusion, Poverty and Governance*, New Delhi: Sage Publications.

Salskov-Iversen, Dorte et al. 2008. 'The Governmentality of Globalizing Managerial Discourse: The Case of New Public Management in Local Government Practices,' in

Bidyut Chakravorty and M Bhattacharya (Eds) *The Governance Discourse: A Reader*, New Delhi: Oxford University Press.

Saraswati, Jyoti. 2008. 'The Indian IT Industry and Neoliberalism: The Irony of Mythology,' *Third World Quarterly*, 29(6):1139-1152.

Sarma, E.A.S. 2005. 'ICT and Good Governance' In R K Bagga et al (Eds) *The State, IT and Development*, New Delhi: Sage Publications.

———. 2002. 'Towards Sociology of Information Society,' *Current Sociology*,50(3):365-388.

———. 2006. *Territory, Authority and Rights: From Medieval to Global Assemblages*, Princeton University Press.

Satpathy, C. 2000. 'Role of the State in E-World,' *Economic and Political Weekly*,35(39), 23 September: 3493-3497.

Saurabh Sinha. 2003. 'Computerisation of Land Records', *Economic and Political Weekly*, August 30-September 05:3739-40.

Saxena, K. B. 2011. 'Land Reforms: Unfinished Agenda or Reversal of Policy,' in *India: Social Development Report 2010; The Land Questions of the Marginalised*, Council for Social Development, New Delhi, pp. 183-185.

Saxena, Naresh C. 2005. 'Updating Land Records: Is Computerisation Sufficient?' *Economic and Political Weekly*, 40(4), January 22-28:313-321.

———. 2010. 'The IAS officer-Predator or Victim?', *The Administrator*, 51(10:96-109.

Scavo, Caramine and Yuhang Shi. 2000. 'Public Administration: The Role of Information Technology in Reinventing Government Paradigm-Normative Predicates and Practical Challenges,' *Social Science Computer Review*, 18(2), Summer: 166-178

Schneider, Anne L. and Helen Ingram. 2008. 'Policy Design' in *Encyclopedia of Public Administration & Public Policy*, New York: Taylor & Francis.

Scott, James C. 1998. *Seeing Like a State: How Certain Schemes to Improve the Human Condition Have Failed*, New Haven: Yale University Press.

Sein, Maung K and G Harindranath. 2004. 'Conceptualising the ICT Artifact: Toward Understanding the Role of ICT in National Development,' *The Information Society*,20(1): 15-24.

Self, Peter. 2000. *Rolling Back the Market: Economic Dogma and Political Choice*, New York: St Martin Press.

Sen, Amartya and Jean Dreze (Eds). 1997. *Indian Development: Selected Regional Perspectives*, United Nations University.

Sen, Amartya. 1999. *Development as Freedom*, Oxford University Press.

———. 2003. 'Development as Capability Expansion' In Sakkio Fukuda Parr and AK Shiv Kumar (Eds) *Readings in Human Development*, Oxford University Press

Sengupta, Arjun, K. P. Kanan and G. Raveendran. 2008. 'India's Common People : Who Are They, How Many Are they and How Do they Live,' *Economic and Political Weekly*, 43 (11)15,March :49-63.

Sengupta, Jati and Chiranjib Naogi. 2009. *India's New Economy: Industry, Efficiency and Growth*, Houndsmills: Palgrave-Macmillan.

Sharma, R. 1994. 'Distribution of Landholdings in Rural India, 1953-54 to 1982: Implications for Land Reforms,' *Economic and Political Weekly*, March 26: A12-A25.

Sikor, Thomas and Daniel Muller. 2009. 'The Limits of State–Led Agrarian Reform: An Introduction,' *World Development*, 37(8):1307-1316.

Simon, Herbert A. 1973. 'Applying Information Technology to Organisation Design,' *Public Administration Review*, 33(3):268-278.

Simons, Jon. 1995. *Foucault and the Political*, London: Routledge.

Singh, Nirvikar. 2002. 'Information Technology and India's Economic Development,' http://papers.ssrn.com/so13/papers.cfm?abstract_id=345940 (accessed on December 4, 2008)

Singhal, Arvind and Everett M Rogers. 2001. *India's Communication Revolution: From Bullock Carts to Cyber Marts*, Sage Publications, New Delhi.

Sinha, Aseema. 2003. 'Rethinking the Developmental State Model: Divided Leviathan and Sub-National Comparisons in India', *Comparative Politics*, 35(4), July: 459-476.

———. 2004. 'Idea, Interests and Institutions in Policy Change: A Comparison of West Bengal and Gujarat,' in Rob Jenkins (Ed) *Regional Reflections: Comparing Politics across India's States*. New Delhi: Oxford University Press.

Sinha, B. K . 2002.'Dynamic Land Records management System: A Pressing Need' in B K Sinha and Pushpendra (Eds) *Land Reforms in India; An Unfinished Agenda-Volume-V*, New Delhi: Sage Publications.

Sinha, Dipankar. 2000. 'Info-Age and Indian Intellectuals: An Unfashionable Pose,' *Economic and Political Weekly*, 25 November: 4188-4194.

Sinha, Rita. 2010. 'Modernising India's Land Records Management System,' *Administrator*, 51(1):58-64.

Sinha, Saurabh. 2003. 'Computerisation of Land Records,' *Economic and Political Weekly*, 38(35), August 30:3739-3740.

Smith, Richard Saumarez. 1985. 'Rule by Records and Rule-by-Reports: Contemporary Aspects of the British Imperial Rule of Law,' *Contributions to Indian Sociology,* (n.s.) 19(1):153-76.

Sood, Aditya Dev. 2001. 'How to Wire Rural India: Problems and Possibilities of Digital Development,' *Economic and Political Weekly*, October 27:4134-4141.

Sorensen, Eva and Jacob Turfing. 2005. 'The Democratic Anchorage of Governance Networks,' *Scandinavian Political Studies*, 28(3)195-218.

Sreekumar, T. T. and Milagros Riveria-Sanchez. 2008. 'ICTs and Development : Revisiting the Asian Experience,' *Science, Technology and Society*,13(2):159-174.

Sreekumar, T. T. 2007. 'Decrypting E-Governance: Narratives, Power play and Participation in the Gyanadoot Intranet,' *The Electronic Journal of Information Systems in Developing Countires*,32(4):1-24.

———. 2007. 'Cyber Laws and Dilemmas of Social Inclusion in Rural India,' *Media, Culture and Society*, 29 (6): 869-889.

Starr, Paul. 2010. 'The Liberal State in a Digital World', *Governance: An International Journal of Policy, Administration and Institutions*, 23(1):1-6.

Taylor, John A. and Howard Williams. 1991. 'Public Administration and Information Polity,' *Public Administation*,69, Summer:171-190.

Taylor, John A. 1992. 'Information Networking in Public Administration,' *International Review of Administrative Sciences*, 58:375-389.

Terry, Larry D. 1993. 'Why We Should Abandon the Misconceived Quest to Reconcile Public Entrepreneurship with Democracy,' *Public Administration Review*, 53(4), p. 393-395.

The Economist. 2002. *E-Trends: Making Sense of the Electronic Communication Revolution*, London.

———. 2008. 'The Electronic Bureaucrat,' February 16, 2008.

Thomas, Jayan Jose and Govindan Parayil. 2008. 'Bridging the digital Divides in Andhra Pradesh and Kerala: A Capability Approach' in *Development and Change*, May 39(3):409-435.

Thomas, Jayan Jose. 2006. 'Informational Development in Rural Areas: Some Evidence from Andhra Pradesh and Kerala,' in Govindan Parayil (Ed) *Political Economy of Informational Capitalism in India: Digital Divide, Development and Equity*, Houndsmills: Palgrave-Macmillan.

Thomas, John Clayton and Gregory Streib. 2003. 'The New Face of the Government: Citizen Initiated Contacts in the Era of E-Government,' *Journal of Public Administration Research and Theory*, 13(1):83-102.

Thompson, Frank. and M Riccuci. 1998. 'Reinventing Government,' *Annual Political Science Review*, Vol. 1:231-257.

Thompson, Mark. 2004. 'Discourse and Digital Divide: ICTs and the World Bank,' *Review of African Political Economy*, 31(99):103-123.

Thorner, Alice and Daniel. 1962. *Land and Labour in India*, New York: Bombay: *Asia Publishing House* (reprinted in 1974)

Tiwari, Meera. 2009. 'ICTs and Poverty Reduction: User Perspective Study of Rural Madhya Pradesh,' *The European Journal of Developmental Research*, 20(3):448-461.

Tripathy, A K. 1992. 'Revenue Laws and Land Administration in Orissa: A Critique', *The Administrator*, 37:115-33.

UNDP. 2001. 'Information Communications for Development,' September 2001:1-31. http://www.undp.org/eo/documents/essentials_... (accessed October 31, 2009)

UNDP and NASSCOM. 2004. *ICTs for Human Development in Asia: India*, New Delhi.

Upadhaya, Carol. 2005. 'Community Rights in Land in Jharkhand,' *Economic and Political Weekly*, October, 8: 4435-4438.

Vachhani, Ashish and N. K. Kumaresan Raja. 2008. *Computerisation of land Records in India: Achievements and Experiences*, Mussorie: Centre for Rural Studies, LBSNAA.

Vijayabaskar, M. and V Gayathri. 2003. 'ICT and Indian Development: Processes, Prognoses, Policies,' *Economic and Political Weekly*, 38(24),June: 2360-64.

Vittal, N. 2005. 'Role of ICTs in Minimizing Corruption in India,' R K Bagga et al (Eds) *The State, IT and Development*, New Delhi: Sage Publications.

Wade, Robert. 1985. 'The Market for Public Office: Why the Indian State is not Better at Development,' *World Development*, 13(4):467-494.

———. 2002. 'Bridging the Digital Divide: A New Route to Development or New Form of Dependency,' *Global Governance*, 8(4):53-85.

Wadhwa D. C. 1989. 'Guaranteeing Title to Land,' *Economic and Political Weekly*, 14 October: 2323-2334.

———. 2002. 'Guaranteeing Title to Land,' *Economic and Political Weekly*, 23 November: 4699-4722.

Waksberg-Guerrini, Ana and Eduard Aibar. 2007. 'Towards a Network Government? A Critical Analysis of Current Assessment Methods for E-Government,' in M A Wimmer, H J Scholl, A Gronlund (Eds) *EGOV2007, Lecture Notes in Computer Science 4656*, pp. 331-340.

Wallis, J. and B. Dollery. 1997. 'An Evaluation of Leadership as A Response to Agency Failure in Public Sector,' *Public Administration*, 75:247-265.

Walters, William. 2004. 'Some Critical Notes on Governance,' *Studies in Political Economy*, 73, Spring/Summer: 27-46.

Walsham, Geoff. 2010. 'ICTs for Broader Development of India: An Analysis of the Literature,' *EJISDC*, 41(4):1-20.

Weiner, Myron. (Ed). 1968. *State Politics in India*, Princeton University Press.

West, Darrell M. 2004. 'E-government and the Transformation of Service Delivery and Citizen Attitudes,' *Public Administration Review*, 64(1), January-February: 15-27.

———. 2005. *Digital Government: Technology and Public Sector Performance*, Princeton: Princeton University Press.

Wheeler, Mark. 1998. 'Democracy and the Information Super Highway,' *Democratisation*, 5(2):217-239.

Willocks, Lesile. 1994.'Managing Information System in UK Public Administration: Issues and Prospects,' *Public Administration*, 72, Spring: 13-32.

Wilson, James Q. 1994. 'Reinventing public Administration,' *PS political Science and Politics*,27 (4), December:667-673.

Wilson, Wong and Eric Welch. 2004. 'Does E-Government Promote Accountability? A Comparative Analysis of Website Openness and Government Accountability', *Governance: An International Journal of Policy, Administration and Institutions*, 17(2):275-297.

Witsoe, Jeffrey. 2012. 'Everyday Corruption and the Political Mediation of the Indian State: An Ethnographic Exploration of Brokers in Bihar,' *Economic and Political Weekly*, February 11, pp. 47-54.

Wolfered, Wendy. 2007. 'Land Reform in the Time of Neo-liberalism: A Many Splendored Thing,' *Antipode*, 39(3):550-570.

World Bank. 2000. *Reforming Public Institutions and Strengthening Governance: A World Bank Strategy*, November.

———. 2002. 'Using Information and Communication Technology to Reduce Poverty in Rural India,' PREM NETWORK Notes, Report no 24856, June.

———. 2004. *'Building Blocks of e-Government: Lessons from Developing Countries,'* August, Number-91, The World Bank PREM notes.

———. 2006. *World Development, 2006: Equity and Development*, Washington: A Co-production of World Bank and Oxford University Press.

———. 2006. *Reforming Public Services in India: Drawing Lessons from Success*, Report No. 35041-IN, 28, February, Poverty Reduction and Economic Management Sector Unit, South Asia

———. 2007. *India: Land Policies for Growth and Poverty Reduction*, Report No-38298-IN, 9 July. World Bank Institute.http://www.wds.Worldbank.org/external/default/main?menu (accessed February 10, 2010)

———. 2008. *World Development Report, 2008: Agriculture for Development*, The World Bank, Washington DC.

———. 2007. 'The Paradoxes of Administrative Reform' in Mark Bevir (Ed) *Public Governace-Volume.III*, London: Sage Publications: 96-102.

Yadav, Yogendra and Suhas Palsikar. 2008. 'Ten Theses on State Politics in India,' *Seminar*, 591.

http://www.India-seminar.com/2008/591/591_y_Yadav &_s_palsikar.htm. (accessed February 13,2011)

Yang, Kaifeng. 2003. 'NeoInstitutionalism and E-Government: Beyond Jane Fountain', *Social Science Computer Review*, 21(4) :432-442.

Zurmond, Arre. 2005. 'Organisational Transformation through the Internet,' *Journal of Public Policy*, 25(1):133-148.

Websites Accessed

http://bhoomi.kar.nic.in/bhoomi
http://darpg.nic.in
http://dolr.nic.in
http://indiagovernance.gov.in
http://itformasses.nic.in
http://nic.in
http://orissagov.nic.in
http://planningcommission.nic.in
www.unpan1.org
http://worldbank.org
http://itformasses.nic.in
http://www.mit.gov.in
http://parliamentofindia.nic.in
http://orissagov.nic.in
http://knowledgecommissionofindia.gov.in
http;//capam.org
http://www.nasscom.org

Index